JAN SMUTS

A BIOGRAPHY

Jan Smuts, field marshal.

F. S. CRAFFORD

JAN SMUTS

A BIOGRAPHY

DOUBLEDAY, DORAN & CO., INC.
Garden City, New York
1943

THIS BOOK IS
COMPLETE AND UNABRIDGED;
MANUFACTURED UNDER WARTIME
CONDITIONS IN CONFORMITY WITH
ALL GOVERNMENT REGULATIONS
CONTROLLING THE USE OF PAPER
AND OTHER MATERIALS.

TO PAT

ACKNOWLEDGMENTS

I AM DEEPLY INDEBTED to scores of friends and acquaintances (among them a large number of Members of Parliament and ex-Cabinet Ministers) for furnishing me with material, documentary and otherwise, advice, and encouragement. To mention names would be invidious. With one exception, General Smuts's friends and colleagues, private secretaries (past and present), and other persons intimately connected with the Prime Minister proved to be most helpful. Equally helpful, but, of course, in a different way, were the statesman's political opponents.

A full list of the books and newspapers consulted by me is given at the end of this volume, where due acknowledgment is made of my indebtedness to the authors and editors concerned.

F. S. C.

PREFACE

NEITHER the attacks of slanderers nor the empty praise of sycophants can do irreparable injury to the reputation of Field Marshal the Right Honorable Jan Christiaan Smuts, but both constitute a temporary menace to the good name of the South African Premier.

It is clearly the biographer's duty to be neither swayed by the former group nor influenced by the latter, but objectively to seek the truth and set it down without bias. This I have endeavoured to do; I trust that my efforts have succeeded in furnishing a balanced and comprehensive account and that from this book will emerge the picture of a great and powerful man who is a "human being and not a plaster saint."

To an artist who was about to paint his portrait, Oliver Cromwell said, "Paint me warts and all!" No craftsman, whatever his medium, can do justice to his subject, unless he gives heed to these words. "The biographer," says Mr. Hesketh Pearson, "who overlooks defects is not only dishonest to himself but a detractor of the man he is trying to whitewash; for the greatness of a man can only be measured by the quantity and quality of his defects which help to mould his character and act as a brake on his efforts." I have tried constantly to bear this advice in mind. Nevertheless, wherever I have "debunked," I have striven to do so with fairness and to avoid all traces of partisanship.

Here, then, is an unbiased picture of Smuts—soldier, statesman, scientist, and philosopher (the world's leading holist). Quite recently, General Sir Thomas Blamey described him as "the Empire's greatest asset." That he may be. It is a moot point. But it is not too much to say, in the light of past events, that the future happiness and prosperity of the peoples of this world and a lasting peace among the nations might be affected—to a not inconsiderable extent—by the thoughts that are burgeoning today in the dynamic mind of Jan Smuts, aged seventy-three, as he hikes youthfully across the veld or up a mountain slope, or flies north to give expert advice on military matters in the Middle East or hurries down to Cape Town, amid his multitudinous duties, to be present, in his capacity of godfather, at the christening of the baby Princess Irene of Greece.

F. S. C.

FOREWORD

To MR. F. S. CRAFFORD falls the honour of being the first Afrikaans-speaking South African writer who in a biographical work attempts to do justice to the greatest living South African. The task he has undertaken is likely to prove beyond the scope of the most eminent writers of the day. It is indeed to the historian and biographer of the future that we look for a full reflection, for the real perspective, in which the figure of General Smuts will be seen in its proper relation to all the aspects of his manifold activities. Such a complete presentation cannot now be given, for only the passage of years will reveal all the facets of a very composite pattern. But that does not preclude biographies written by contemporaries. On the contrary, historians of the future will have to base their conclusions upon the evidence contained in biographies such as this one, which forms an indispensable portion of the cumulative data on so worthy a subject.

As one whose good fortune it is to have been closely associated with General Smuts during a period of forty years, I can testify that Mr. Crafford's work casts a true reflection on events. His work has the additional merit of being right up to date, and he has performed his task with a conscientiousness which is greatly to his credit. He has made a valuable contribution to the knowledge of South Africa's great leader, who occupies a proud place among the politicians, philosophers, scientists, soldiers, and statesmen of the world.

When asked by me, some years ago, what he regarded as his most important service to his country and his people, General Smuts replied without hesitation: "The struggle for self-government in the Transvaal and the Free State. It was my privilege to persuade Campbell-Bannerman to grant self-government to the Transvaal and the Free State, and from that step the new South Africa was born."

Those of us who have followed him closely find it difficult to differentiate between the many valuable services he has rendered South Africa. His own choice, as stated above, may be regarded as a very modest one.

LOUIS ESSELEN

Pretoria
July 1943.

ILLUSTRATIONS AND MAPS

JAN SMUTS

A BIOGRAPHY

SECTION I

I

ONE FINE MORNING in the year 1652 three stately ships sailed into Table Bay and cast anchor a few yards from where Table Mountain sloped gently from the sea and then rose suddenly into the sky, a sheer three thousand feet of forbidding sandstone. The vessels were the *Dromedaris,* the *Reiger,* and the *Goede Hoop,* belonging to the Dutch East India Company and carrying a small band of Dutch settlers to the land of Good Hope, there to establish a halfway station between Holland and the Dutch East Indies. In charge of these people was a doctor, Jan van Riebeeck, who held the rank of commander and was the first of a long line of commanders and governors to rule the fair and sunny land which stretched northward from the once dreaded Cape of Storms.

In 1688, in consequence of religious persecution in their motherland—particularly after the repeal of the Edict of Nantes—one hundred and eighty French Huguenots fled from France and sought refuge in this new country.

They were outnumbered by the Dutch and, within a few generations, lost their language and their race identity through complete absorption. From that fusion of blood there sprang a new nation—a sturdy race of Afrikaners possessing the predominating characteristics of their Dutch and Huguenot forebears and regarding the Cape as their homeland and the sole object of their patriotism. The language they spoke was the High Dutch of the seventeenth century, which evolved along lines of its own in a country remote from Holland, was subjected to various external influences—principally those of slaves coming from the East—and in the course of time developed into the Afrikaans language, which is spoken by the majority of Europeans in South Africa today.

In and around Cape Town the colonists built their homes—large, white houses with spacious, airy rooms containing rafters and floors of yellow wood, enormously thick clay walls, fine gables in the old Dutch

style, wide stoeps, and thatched roofs. And round about their home-
steads they planted many oaks and great vineyards, and they cultivated
the fields and reared cattle. The pleasant Land of Good Hope fulfilled
the promise of its name and is today the most beautiful region in all
South Africa, noted for its ancient oaks, its great vineyards, its orchards,
its old Dutch houses, which still grace the countryside, and all the natural beauty with which it has been profusely endowed.

The colonists were a hard-working and thrifty people but at the same
time they were an independent, freedom-loving race of pioneers, inclined, on occasion, to be headstrong and intolerant of interference.

In 1806 the Cape, after a temporary occupation from 1795 to 1803,
fell permanently into the hands of the British. About 25,000 whites and
26,000 slaves lived there at the time, occupying approximately 150,000
square miles of territory.

The Dutch burghers could not at first complain of their treatment at
the hands of their new rulers, but there was a distinct change of front on
the part of the British authorities immediately after the Treaty of Vienna
of 1815 had finally confirmed Britain's claims to the conquered territory.

In quick succession the majority of their time-honoured rights and
privileges were taken from the burghers. No longer were they allowed to
serve on juries; the Burgher Senate was abolished; so were the *Landdrosts* and *Heemrade* (magistrates and local councils), who had formerly been chosen from the ranks of the burghers and had constituted
the judiciary in all the outlying districts. English became the sole official
language in spite of the fact that over 80 per cent of the people spoke
only Dutch.

The Boers, as the burghers came to be known ("Boer" means
farmer), had many other grievances: they complained about the weakness of the Administration's native policy on the frontiers where, despite
frequent murderous inroads made upon Boer territory by native thieves
and murderers, effective measures were never taken to check these dep-
redations; they were deeply incensed at the sudden emancipation of
slaves and particularly by the way in which the payment of compensation was effected; but nothing, probably, angered them more than did
the unhappy events at Slagtersnek in the years 1815 and 1816. These
constitute a tale both interesting and tragic.

Fourteen Hottentot soldiers in charge of a man Rousseau, a lieutenant,
went, at the end of 1815, to arrest a burgher, Frederik Bezuidenhout by
name, living in the Eastern Province of the Cape Colony. As the men
marched up, Bezuidenhout fled to a cave where he was shot by one of
the Hottentots, while resisting arrest. A tremendous uproar resulted.

Martial law was proclaimed, and a number of Boers were arrested. Seventeen of them were either fined heavily or sentenced to banishment, while five were condemned to death. A large gibbet was hastily erected at Andrew's Post, and the condemned men were taken there on March 9, 1816. They stood in a row beneath the gallows tree and were allowed to sing a last hymn. Surrounding them were three hundred soldiers on guard, and near by stood sixteen of their burgher comrades whom the authorities had ordered "to witness the execution." The hangman placed nooses round the necks of the doomed men and at a given signal knocked aside the "drop." Only one man stayed aloft. The rest fell to the ground with broken ropes around their necks and then rose uncertainly to their feet. The bystanders, deeply moved and with tears streaming down their cheeks, begged Cuyler and Stockenström, the government's representatives, to spare the lives of the survivors. But these agents had no authority but to carry out the executions. There were no spare ropes; so the defective ones were knotted together, and eventually the men were hanged. It was a gruesome spectacle and an event filled with future evil for South Africa. The Boers have never forgotten or forgiven Slagtersnek (Butcher's Neck), and to this day it throws its shadow across the South African scene.

At length, driven on by the urge for freedom which they had inherited from their fathers, large numbers of Boers rounded up their cattle, packed their most cherished possessions in their great, hooded wagons, inspanned their teams of oxen, and with their families trekked away from British rule into the vast hinterland of Southern Africa. The Great Trek—famous in South African history—had begun. It was a slow and arduous process, and one fraught with great danger. For many months the unwieldy wagons lumbered along, travelling where white man had never been before, crossing large rivers and great mountain ranges, and traversing many hundreds of miles of trackless country.

Scores of these Voortrekkers (pioneers) fell by the wayside: some died of hunger, thirst, and disease; wild animals accounted for others; and in the fearsome hours of the early dawn savage Bantu tribes slew many in their sleep with club and assagai, and dashed out the brains of infants against the wagon wheels. Sometimes entire families were wiped out.

The Zulu impis of Dingaan the Treacherous killed many of the Boers, including Piet Retief, one of their leaders. After grievous losses the Boers organized a punitive expedition. On the banks of a river they prepared to meet the enemy, drawing their wagons in a circle, end to end, to form the "laager" fortress famous in South African warfare. In a solemn invocation of Divine assistance before the battle the Boers vowed that if victory was vouchsafed to them they would in thanksgiving build a place of worship and commemorate the day in the Lord's name. Though greatly outnumbered by the fearless savages, they inflicted a shattering defeat, and the river ran red with the blood of Dingaan's warriors. They called it Blood River and their day of victory, December 16, is "Dingaan's Day" in South Africa, a public holiday observed by many as a day of worship. The church they built where the city Pietermaritzburg, capital of Natal, stands today.

The Voortrekkers founded the village of Weenen (the place of weeping) at the scene of one of the massacres. Several other hamlets sprang up, and naming the country Natalia, the Boers declared for themselves a republic. But the British came in from the sea and claimed the land, which then became a British colony. The Boers placed their goods and chattels in their wagons once again and trekked slowly back across the mighty Mountains of the Dragons, the highest in South Africa, and established two republics—one north of the Orange and the other north of the Vaal—which they called, respectively, the Orange Free State and the Transvaal.

Then came Sir Harry Smith in 1849 and annexed the Orange Free State on behalf of Great Britain and gave it a new name. But at the Sand River Convention of 1852 and the Bloemfontein Convention of 1854 the British Government formally recognized the independence of the two Boer republics.

In 1870, however, large deposits of diamonds were discovered in the Western Free State and, according to James Anthony Froude, "there was a notion that the finest diamond mine in the world should not be lost to the British Empire." So Great Britain annexed the diamond fields, and from every part of the empire men came to seek their fortunes. Within a few years the discovery of diamonds was to change substantially the economic and political life of South Africa, and the subsequent discovery of gold would revolutionize it completely.

It was a remarkable year—this year of 1870: the nations of Europe were getting ready for the "scramble for Africa"; the Americans were feeling the after effects of a bloody civil war; and the Prussian war machine, destined to become the scourge of Europe when finally it was perfected, was ruthlessly smashing and blasting its way through France. On May 24 of that year (the date on which Queen Victoria celebrated her birthday in the thirty-third year of her reign) the wife of Jacobus Abraham Smuts gave birth to a son on the farm Bovenplaats near the hamlet of Riebeek West in the Cape Colony.

2

The boy was named Jan Christiaan. A sickly, rickety child he was from early infancy, thin and pallid. Until his twelfth year he had no schooling, but remained at home on the farm, an unprepossessing lad showing no signs of promise. "He is a poor, unhealthy youngster," said his father, "a queer fellow without much intelligence. It is best that he remain at home." His parents felt sorry for Jannie and looked pityingly at him as he wandered about the farm or looked after the cattle and sheep, and tended the pigs and the poultry. His interests were the changing seasons and other natural phenomena. He lived close to the soil among the farm animals and the coloured workmen. And he loved the green fields in the spring and the golden-brown harvests in summer. He was as yet unable to read or write, but he would listen for hours to the wonderful tales told him by his friend, Old Adam, the wrinkled old Hottentot shepherd, as they sat by a fire in the open.

On Sundays Jacobus Smuts and his wife used to attend services in the church at Riebeek West. They were a devout couple. Frequently they took Jannie along. For the quiet boy these visits to the village were always a high adventure.

Riebeek West lay in the Swartland (the Black Country) several miles north of the larger town of Malmesbury, not very far from Cape Town. It was a pleasant hamlet, with streams of clear water and vineyards and orchards nestling against the lower slopes of an isolated mountain. North and west of it, as far as the eye could see, were fields of grain in season, for the Swartland was the granary of the Cape. The country was open towards the west with here and there a hill or a low mountain, the undulating plains sweeping right up to the Atlantic seaboard. Also to the east lay level land, stretching a score of miles to the foot of the high Drakenstein range with its great peaks and its forbidding buttresses, the first great barrier encountered by the traveller going up to the Free State and the Transvaal.

A few years after Jannie's birth the family left Bovenplaats and settled on the farm Klipfontein, about twelve miles from the village. The new farm had great cornfields but few fruit trees and no vineyards. The farmhouse was a thatched building with a stoep and neat red shutters. In the distance one could see the Berg River, a mere trickle of water in the hot and dusty summer but a swiftly flowing brown torrent when the heavy winter rains fell on the Drakenstein Mountains and in the Valley of the Huguenots. Frequently it overflowed its banks and carried away much soil from the surrounding fields as it wended its turbulent way to St. Helena Bay, which lies some miles north of the historic Bay of Saldanha, calling place of the early sea voyagers.

Jacobus Smuts was a heavily built, healthy, and hearty son of the soil whose forebears had come from Holland. An able, hard-working, honest farmer, he was respected by all who knew him, and his advice was frequently sought by relatives and friends from the surrounding farms, for he was a man of sound practical judgment. Interested in public affairs, he served on numerous public bodies and for many years represented Malmesbury in the old Cape Legislative Assembly. He belonged to the Afrikaner Bond party, the first political organization to voice the sentiments of the Dutch-speaking element of the Cape, but was never a politician of any distinction, noted in the House for his rustic geniality and long silences rather than for anything else.

His wife, known by all as Tante (Aunt) Cato, was a sister of the Reverend Bodewyn de Vries, the first Dutch Reformed minister to accept a call to Riebeek West, where he remained for twenty-one years. Tante Cato was a sharp-witted woman, surprisingly quick at repartee and apt observation. Outspoken by nature, she often added a farmyard flavour to her sharp wit. She was very emotional, had a particularly vivid imagination and a highly impressionable nature, being easily moved to tears or laughter and, in conversation, subject to alternate moods of hilarity and seriousness. She could easily create an imaginary world of her own and make other people live in it too. This gift she imparted in full measure to her son Jannie. She had been to school in Cape Town for a few years and had some knowledge of French and music. In her veins ran a mixture of French and Dutch blood.

When Jannie was twelve years old his elder brother, Michiel, fell ill with typhoid and died. The parents then decided to send their second boy to Riebeek West to be educated, so that, if possible, he might become a minister of the Dutch Reformed Church, a calling for which their eldest son had been destined. The prospect of going to school held no attractions for Jannie, but he had no voice in the matter.

Michiel had boarded and lodged with the Malan family who lived on the beautiful old farm Allesverloren which adjoined the village, but Jannie went to the school hostel, Die Ark, run by Mr. T. C. Stofberg, the schoolmaster. The lad was shy and reserved and obviously unhappy in his new surroundings. He longed intensely for the free life on the farm: the animals, the birds, the flowers in the fields, the growing grain, the coloured labourers, and Old Adam.

But when the first term had passed, he found his feet and began to develop a tremendous thirst for knowledge. He progressed by enormous leaps and bounds, and within record time he caught up with the other pupils of his own age, who had come to school several years before him. He read all the Dutch literature he could lay his hands on, and as soon as he had mastered the elements of English, he read as extensively as possible in that language. He refused to play games with the other boys but would walk to a secluded spot with his books and delve into them until the failing light warned him that the supper bell would soon be ringing.

The schoolmaster and the parson, the Reverend A. J. Louw, were the most influential men in the village in those days and the leaders of the community. They were bosom friends. Both were deeply religious men of high principles and stanch character. Both were men of strong personality and brought their influence to bear upon Smuts, who thought that there were no finer men in all the world.

He developed religious tendencies and became one of Mr. Louw's assistants in the local Sunday school. One of his pupils was a small boy from the farm Allesverloren, D. F. Malan by name, whose political views in the years to come were to differ vastly from those of Smuts. For many years now the schoolmaster's widow has written to Smuts from time to time to praise or reprimand him sternly—according to her judgment—as she did in the days of his early youth. She believes also that Providence has assigned to her the task of praying daily for Smuts and for Malan, the leaders of her people, and she never fails to do so.

Mr. Stofberg was very proud of his school and its record. Since his arrival at Riebeek West at the age of seventeen to become the local schoolmaster, he had had no failures in any of his classes. He used to say to his pupils: "No child may fail! I shall be bitterly disappointed if all of you don't secure first-class passes."

As soon as he realized that Jan Smuts was a boy of exceptional ability, he gave him all the attention and encouragement he could. It was not necessary to urge the lad on. His hunger for knowledge and ever more knowledge was insatiable. He worked early in the morning, throughout the day, and late at night. One day the senior class had been given a difficult mathematical problem which none succeeded in solving. In the early dawn of the next day the schoolmaster saw a light in Smuts's room and went there to investigate. Opening the door quietly, he asked: "Are you up already, Jannie?" "No sir," replied Smuts; "I have not been to bed yet. But the problem is solved."

During his holidays on the farm, his parents wondered at the change that had taken place in the lad. He was no longer interested in the farm but was constantly poring over books, and often at night they had to remind him to go to bed and put out the light. He would walk about on the farm with his hands behind his back and his pale blue eyes looking into space, immersed in his own thoughts. One day, on returning from the fields on horseback, Jacobus Smuts dismounted and handed the reins to his son, saying: "See to the horse, Jannie!" An hour later he found the animal standing in the stable still saddled and bridled. And on the stoep sat the boy reading a book. The old man shook his head in perplexity and walked off without saying a word. It was clear now that the boy was no farmer. Perhaps he would be successful as a minister of the Church.

Back at school again, Smuts was happier than on the farm. He progressed with astounding rapidity, taking in and digesting everything that his master could teach him, going his own way unsmiling and with an air of detachment. His schoolfellows disapproved of his ways. They did not like him. Indeed, they did not know him, for he avoided their company always and lived only with his books.

After spending four years at Riebeek West, he easily passed the examination which entitled him to enter a matriculation class at any college. He then proceeded to Victoria College, in the sleepy old Afrikaner town of Stellenbosch, near Cape Town.

3

Klipfontein,
June 12, 1886

Mr. C. Murray
Professor, Stellenbosch

Dear Sir,
    Allow me the pleasure of your reading and answering these few lines. I intend coming to Stellenbosch in July next, and, having heard that you take an exceptionally great interest in the youth, I trust you will favour me by keeping your eye upon me and helping me with your kindly advice. Moreover, as I shall be a perfect stranger there, and, as you know,

such a place, where a large puerile element exists, affords fair scope for moral, and, what is more important, religious temptation, which, if yielded to, will eclipse alike the expectations of my parents and the intentions of myself, a real friend will prove a lasting blessing for me. For of what use will a mind, enlarged and refined in all possible ways, be to me, if my religion be a deserted pilot, and morality a wreck?

To avoid temptation and to make the proper use of my precious time, I purposely refuse entering a public boarding department, as that of Mr. de Kock, but shall board privately (most likely at Mr. W. Ackermann's) which will, in addition, accord with my retired and reserved nature. . . .

This is part of a letter written by Smuts prior to his departure for Victoria College. The serious, youthful lines speak for themselves.

To Stellenbosch the young man came in due course, and he went to live with Mr. Ackermann in the oldest part of the town, in Dorp Street, where grew a great avenue of ancient oaks, many of which had been planted by the old Dutch governor, Simon van der Stel, at the end of the seventeenth century, when Cape Town had already become known as the Tavern of the Seas.

When Smuts came to Stellenbosch, it was a quiet Dutch town with spacious, white-walled, thatched houses, and shady streets with pleasant streams of cool, clear water running on either side to irrigate the profusion of vineyards, orchards, and flower gardens; there was an Old World atmosphere about the town, which it has retained in some measure to this day. It was surrounded on almost every side by hills and mountains: to the west lay Papegaaisberg (the Hill of the Parrots) where, in the days of Van der Stel, shooting contests were held on public holidays; there were mountains on the southern side—Stellenberg and Helderberg —and west of these a road wound sinuously down to the sea; Simonsberg with its great buttresses and its billowing foothills, containing shady dells, rose in the north; and in the east one saw the lofty peaks of Jonkershoek, below which, in the great catchment area between the mountains, the historic Eerste River had its source.

Smuts was somewhat bewildered at first by the large number of students in the town, but before long he settled down to work with a vengeance, and progressed rapidly. There was, however, some difficulty about securing tuition in Greek; and when he went home for a short holiday before the commencement of the last term, he had not as yet acquired any knowledge of the subject. The examinations were looming ahead, and in desperation he began to work at his Greek grammar as soon as he reached the farm. In six days he memorized the contents of the book. In December, when the class examinations were held, he came top of the list.

He took little interest in any of the branches of social life at the college. Occasionally he attended a meeting of the Union Debating Society, but as a rule he was to be found at home, working. He regarded sport as sheer waste of time. He was the same awkward, serious, hard-working youth who had gone his own way at Riebeek West. He deliberately avoided the company of other young men and they, in turn, avoided him, resented his aloofness, and sneered at his hermitlike, bookish ways. He was obviously, said they, a bookworm and little else; a conceited young cockerel, who would bump his head severely sooner or later. It was no use bothering about him. And they left him to his ways, and he was glad to be left alone.

For exercise he went for long walks into the veld and climbed the lower slopes of the mountains. Almost invariably he used to take a book or two along with him to do some work out in the open. Sometimes a fellow student, a girl, Sibella Margaretha (Isie) Krige, accompanied him.

She lived with her parents in a beautiful old Dutch house at the lower end of Dorp Street, on the banks of the Eerste River. She was slight in build and small in stature, with short, dark hair which clung close to her head. She was a pretty girl with finely moulded features and wide-awake, intelligent eyes in her oval face. Her parents were Afrikaners of Dutch-Huguenot ancestry. Smuts had met her some months after his arrival at Stellenbosch. They became close friends and in the course of time fell in love with each other. They had much in common: both were quiet and reserved and both were fond of botany, English, and German literature, and other intellectual pursuits. Smuts taught the girl what Greek he knew. He found her an attentive listener and an apt pupil. When they first met, she was sixteen and a half and he seventeen years of age.

On Sundays, in addition to attending services regularly in the old Dutch Reformed Church near the Theological College, he expounded the truths of the Bible to a class of coloured youths, always addressing them at length and with great solemnity. He also belonged to a Bible circle, which met on the Sabbath for prayers and discussions.

Goethe and Schiller, Milton and Shakespeare, Shelley and Keats, and Walt Whitman were his favourite poets. Ever since first reading Shelley's *Prometheus Unbound* he had loved poetry. Often, standing alone in the veld, he would recite immortal lines with emotional appreciation. He was greatly interested also in philosophy and devoted much time to this absorbing subject. He did a certain amount of writing in verse and prose:

General Smuts's parents in October 1893.

General Smuts and granddaughter.

he wrote *inter alia,* essays on subjects such as slavery, freedom, and politics. The future of South Africa as a growing organism expanding northward interested him exceedingly. At the same time it was also obsessing the mind of Cecil John Rhodes.

Rhodes visited Stellenbosch in 1888, and Smuts was asked by the college rector to respond to the great man's address, on behalf of the students. The youth was reserved and very shy, but he rose to the occasion and performed his task very creditably. He spoke on the topic dearest to the heart of the visitor: Pan-Africanism. Rhodes made a note of the young man's name for future reference. Next day in Cape Town he said to Jan Hendrik Hofmeyr, leader of the powerful Bond party, "Keep your eye on that young fellow Smuts." And John X. Merriman, towering figure in Cape politics, remarked to Jacobus Smuts, as together they sat listening to the boy: "Jannie will be the first man in South Africa." The words were prophetic ones.

4

IN 1891 Smuts took his degree in science as well as literature at Stellenbosch and received honours in both. Having won the Ebden Scholarship, he decided to go to Cambridge to study law. He had long since abandoned the idea of becoming a minister of the Dutch Reformed Church, to the intense disappointment of his parents, both of whom had desired ardently to see their son in the pulpit.

Since the scholarship at the time amounted to a mere £100 a year, Smuts borrowed money from a friend, Professor Marais of the Theological Seminary, and sailed for England. It was only with difficulty that he managed to pay his way in the beginning but, fortunately, in July 1894, "an additional grant of £100 a year was voted to Mr. J. C. Smuts, Ebden Scholar, in consideration of his distinguished success as a student at the University of Cambridge."

On his arrival at Cambridge, Smuts was registered as a student at Christ's College. He settled down to work almost immediately, and throughout his years at the university he did little else. As at Stellenbosch, so here he kept clear of his fellow undergraduates, whose lighthearted pranks he regarded with disdain and whose occasional drinking bouts he looked upon with undisguised disfavour. Student life at the university had no meaning for him. He had time for nothing but work. One who knew him in those days speaks of him as a young man with "a pale face and white hair, conspicuous in the university library on hot afternoons when all the undergraduate world was at play."

He would go for long walks along the quaint old streets of the ancient town and into the lovely countryside, but he never fell in love with Cambridge, as have for centuries the vast majority of her privileged alumni. But, then, he never was part of the university nor did its spirit ever enter into him, so that today he has no cherished memories of his life there.

His academic achievements were remarkable. In one of the issues of the *Cape Times* in 1894 a friend wrote: "Smuts's success is unprecedented in Cambridge annals. He took parts I and II of the Law Tripos both at the same time and was placed first in the first class of each, and has been awarded the George Long prize in Roman Law and Jurisprudence, a prize only awarded in cases of special merit. . . ." In the faculty of law the year 1894 became known as "Smuts's year." He was admitted to the Middle Temple after passing the necessary examinations with distinction. And, finally, in December 1894, South Africans read in their newspapers that "the Council of Legal Education awarded to Smuts, J. C., a special prize of £50 for the best examination in Constitutional Law (English and Colonial) and Legal History." It was an amazing series of successes.

Smuts could have had a distinguished career in England. He was asked to accept a professorship at Christ's College. He declined the honour, however, as he was longing to get back to South Africa.

He sailed for home in June 1895, and was glad in his quiet, undemonstrative way to get back to the land of his birth.

After brief visits to the farm at Riebeek West and to Isie Krige at Stellenbosch, he settled down in Cape Town, determined to carve out a legal career for himself. He was called to the Cape bar and began to practise as a junior barrister.

On his return from Cambridge, the South African press had been full of his splendid academic achievements and had predicted a brilliant career at the bar for an exceptionally gifted young man. And in the beginning a fair amount of work did come his way, but gradually the number of his clients diminished. Despite his sparkling intellect and his thorough knowledge of law, success was denied him, for he was lacking in qualities the possession of which brought dozens of briefs to his mental inferiors. His cold austerity repelled people; his unsociable habits provoked hostility in his colleagues; and his aloofness and tactlessness antagonized both judge and jury. Indeed, having never mixed with people, he failed to understand them and to appreciate their problems. His world up till then had been a world of books and dreams and unsubstantial things. And so, both constitutionally and by virtue of his having always been completely out of touch with life in the raw, he was incapable of applying his knowledge effectively to the realities of life.

Since there was little work for him to do in his profession, he began to write articles for the leading Cape newspapers in English and Dutch. He criticized severely the Transvaal Government's employment of Hollanders in preference to South Africans. Writing about Johannesburg, he made mention of its "colossal materialism which is destined to play a great part in South Africa." In the newspaper *Ons Land,* he attacked Dr. Muir, superintendent of education for the Cape Colony, for importing his departmental officials from England and Scotland instead of employing educated South Africans. He reviewed at length Dr. van Oordt's *Plato and His Times.* He completed a treatise—begun at Cambridge—on Walt Whitman, and sent it to England for publication, but it was rejected. He wrote articles on a variety of subjects, such as immigration, the native problem, the Hex River Valley, and the moral conception of existence. Sometimes he attended sessions of the Old Cape Parliament as a reporter. At first he was only mildly interested in the proceedings. But soon he became enthusiastic about politics, and steadily the conviction grew within him that his future lay not in the legal but in the political world.

And then, suddenly, one day he received a note from J. H. Hofmeyr (Onze Jan—"Our John"), leader of the provincial Bond party, requesting him to call at the party's headquarters. Smuts was thrilled. Perhaps, he thought, his chance had come. He rushed over to see Hofmeyr. He was received kindly and given a message from Cecil John Rhodes.

5

IT IS NECESSARY at this stage to turn back to the year 1877.

Seven years after the discovery of the diamond fields, Sir Theophilus Shepstone annexed the Transvaal on behalf of the Government of Great Britain. Mr. Joseph Chamberlain declared subsequently that this violation of the Sand River Convention, which recognized the Boer republics, had been committed "upon false information supplied to the British Government by the officials in South Africa." Be that as it may, the

Transvaal Boers rose up in their indignation and the First Anglo-Boer War (1880–81) ensued. At length, after the disaster at Majuba, where the British forces were soundly defeated, came peace and the restoration of the Transvaal to the Boers by William Ewart Gladstone. The terms of retrocession, embodied in the Pretoria Convention of 1881, substantially restricted the liberty of the Boers by conceding to Britain suzerainty over the republic, but this agreement was superseded in 1884 by the London Convention, which re-established the Transvaal as a completely independent republic.

While the defeat at Majuba rankled somewhat in the minds of the British people, they took little interest in the affairs of the Transvaal after 1881, for no one knew that underneath the Witwatersrand—"Reef of the White Waters"—on the barren Transvaal veld there lay hidden vast stores of gold, the like of which had never before been heard of.

Gold was discovered on the Rand in 1885 in almost unbelievable profusion, and South Africa's future was thereby changed completely.

When the old Boer general, Piet Joubert, was told of the wonderful discovery, he said to his informant, who believed himself to be the bearer of glad tidings: "You would do better to weep, for this gold will cause our country to be soaked in blood."

To the new Eldorado there streamed from the four corners of the earth men and women from almost every nation: Russians, Poles, Germans, Jews, Americans, Englishmen, and many others. There was, however, a distinct preponderance of Jews. Fortune hunters came, and gamblers, harlots, cardsharpers, jailbirds, and other criminals from every continent. Sir William Butler, commander in chief of Her Majesty's forces in South Africa and, for a while, governor of the Cape Colony and High Commissioner for South Africa, himself regarded the Uitlanders (aliens) as "probably the most corrupt, immoral, and untruthful assemblage of beings at present in the world."

On the bare and dusty veld hundreds of tents and tin shanties appeared and steadily increased in number. From these beginnings rose Johannesburg, the City of Gold—a "mushroom city," but the wealthiest for its size in all the world.

In the space of a few years one hundred thousand aliens swarmed into the republic and began to clamour for the franchise (while retaining their own nationality) and for "reforms" in a country to which they had come solely to get their pickings, and the population of which they outnumbered. But Uitlander demands became stridently vociferous and Uitlander agitation vehemently importunate only when vested Boer interests in the Transvaal began to clash with the interests of rapacious mine magnates, influenced and encouraged by the Empire ambitions of that crafty and powerful figure, Cecil John Rhodes, prime minister of the Cape Colony and multimillionaire.

On July 5, 1853, the wife of F. W. Rhodes, vicar of Bishop's Stortford, gave birth to a son—her fifth. The boy, a sickly child, was christened Cecil John.

"No franker materialist," it has been said, "ever issued from a country vicarage." He was sent to South Africa for his health. Soon after the discovery of diamonds at Kimberley he arrived there with his brother Herbert. "I am afraid," he wrote home afterwards, "that life on the diamond fields has not tended to strengthen my religious principles." This admission was an understatement: the fact of the matter was that Rhodes "was corrupted in early youth by the diamonds of Kimberley."

He accumulated a fortune without effort and, in doing so, became a man of influence and power. He took part in bigger and ever bigger business transactions. As his confidence grew so his appetite increased for ever-greater wealth and ever-greater power, and "big ideas" began to burgeon in his restless and acquisitive mind.

At the age of twenty-five, pointing to a map of South Africa, he said to Leander Starr Jameson, a medical practitioner and budding politician: "All this is to be painted red!" And then he cried fervently: *"All* this to be painted red!" And he remarked to General Gordon: "It is no use having big ideas if you have not the cash to carry them out." As he dipped his hands into a bucketful of gems placed before him by Barney Barnato, he was thrilled not by the beauty of the stones but by their cash value.

He set about amassing all the cash he could. Assisted by Alfred Beit, he outwitted Barney Barnato and his kindred spirit Woolf Joel and became the most important man on the diamond fields, as the chief shareholder and great Pooh-Bah of De Beers Consolidated Mines, Limited. He spoke of the Rand (the Witwatersrand gold fields) as "the biggest thing in gold the world has ever seen"; but he believed with Jameson that Matabeleland and Mashonaland, north of the Transvaal, "consist not of one but of fifty Randts." So, after establishing the gold fields of South Africa on the Reef, he turned his coldly calculating mind to the land of the Mashona and the Matabele, invaded it without compunction with a strong force well equipped with arms, and pitilessly shot down thousands of Lobengula's people. "He's death on niggers, is Rhodes!" said Trooper Peter Halkett of fiction fame. Subsequently Rhodes managed to secure a charter for the British South Africa Company in the land north of the Limpopo, and thereafter Matabele-Mashonaland became known as Rhodesia.

Contrary to expectation, Rhodes failed to reap a golden harvest in the new country, and the chartered company was landed with a debt of £10,000,000. And so the Colossus turned his greedy gaze upon the Transvaal with its vast supplies of gold—a modern Ahab, casting covetous eyes on Naboth's vineyard. For years he had been scheming to unite all the states of South Africa as part of an ultimate plan to establish in Africa a Pan-African federation of states, stretching from Cape Agulhas to the land of the Pharaohs—"a vast all-British dominion." He had already done much in the way of annexation to secure his ends. But to achieve his heart's desire, he required not only the wealth of the Rand but the conquest of the Transvaal, which lay athwart his chain of states stretching northward. In order to bring his plans to fruition, there was need of speedy action, for his days were numbered: he was suffering from heart disease. But there was a strong disruptive and obstructive element that seemed determined to baulk him: to keep from him the sheaves of gold and wreck his Cape-to-Cairo project. That element found its embodiment in the person of Stephanus Johannes Paulus Kruger, president of the Transvaal Republic.

The Colossus astride the southern part of Africa had swept ruthlessly from his path whatever and whoever resisted him. But in Paul Kruger he found "the only opponent worthy of his steel that he was destined to encounter." A great, square, bearded block of a man was Kruger, with heavy features, an unwieldy body, long arms that had once possessed tremendous power, and a voice that could bellow like the Bull of Bashan.

A boy at the time of the Great Trek, he had grown up in a school of hardship and tribulation, his early life being one continuous record of fortitude and stoicism. At the age of twenty, for example, he fired at a rhinoceros one day; the gun exploded and hurt his left hand very badly. Some time later, when the thumb became gangrenous, Kruger himself removed it neatly with a knife at the lower joint.

He was deeply religious in the narrow and bigoted fashion of his day and appeared to arrogate to himself and to his church a monopoly of Christianity. A man with but the merest smattering of education, he nevertheless possessed a generous fund of sound common sense and a keen and active brain. He loved his country with a great and abiding love, and in his unprepossessing features were deep lines of suffering, drawn there by his people's tragic history. He hated the British with an implacable hatred as the "traditional enemies of my people."

Foursquare he stood across Rhodes's predetermined path—a grim and resolute old hulk of a man with a flaming spirit—the unyielding champion of Transvaal republicanism and of Afrikanerdom.

During the last two decades of the nineteenth century the Rhodes-Kruger contest was, in a sense, the epitome of South African history.

6

IN STRANGE CONTRAST with Kruger, J. H. Hofmeyr, the Afrikaner leader in the Cape, was more than sympathetically inclined to many of Rhodes's ideas and had for some years been the Englishman's intimate friend and political ally. He had, in fact, been chiefly responsible for Rhodes's rapid success in politics, since the powerful backing of the Afrikaner Bond party had helped the millionaire to achieve the premiership in the Cape Parliament.

The ostensibly singular friendship between these two strikingly different men was promoted by an identity of interests, in respect of what they called Colonialism or Colonial Home Rule—a sort of Dominion status— their common goal being "the union of Dutch and British into one South African nation, with a common feeling of South African nationhood" and, to quote Rhodes, "the government of South Africa by the people of South Africa with the Imperial tie for defence."

Subscribing wholeheartedly to these tenets, Smuts had become a member of the Bond party. As his knowledge of South African politics grew and he began to identify himself with political life at the Cape, his ambition sprouted. He visualized a great future for himself in a united South Africa as conceived by Hofmeyr and Rhodes. He had few, if any, anti-British feelings, so that the "isolationism" of Kruger did not appeal to him, while the "big ideas" of Rhodes held for him a peculiar fascination.

He became more and more active as a member of the Bond party, and in numerous articles in the press he lauded the Hofmeyr-Rhodes combination, and he saw ever more clearly and with ever-increasing ardour glowing visions of vast expansion into the hinterland of Africa. Invariably in disputes he took up the cudgels for Rhodes. He also stepped into the breach for Britain. "The true explanation [of Britain's unpopularity in France and Germany]," he wrote, "is not British pharisaism but British success. It is the success with which Great Britain is pursuing the policy of colonial expansion, and the comparative failure of the attempts of other peoples in the same direction, which lies at the root of this international dislike of Great Britain."

The message which Hofmeyr had for Smuts, the day he summoned him to his party's headquarters, contained a request from Rhodes for assistance. The Cronwright-Schreiners (Olive Schreiner, the famous South African novelist, and her husband), said Hofmeyr, had been slandering the Cape Prime Minister in Kimberley and had hinted at collusion between him and the Rand Uitlanders for the purpose of overthrowing Kruger's government in the Transvaal. Rhodes, added Hofmeyr, was very much upset about the whole matter and wished to silence their calumnious tongues. Hofmeyr had suggested sending Smuts to Kimberley for that purpose, and Rhodes, falling in with the idea, had asked him to get into touch with Smuts. Would he go? Yes, replied Smuts, he would. He was not only willing—he was eager to undertake the task.

Here was his chance at last. It was a heaven-sent opportunity.

He left for Kimberley well "primed" as to what to say at a special meeting of the De Beers Consolidated Diamond Mines Political and Debating Society. The meeting was held in the Kimberley Town Hall on October 29, 1895. The mayor was in the chair. The hall was packed. The subject of Smuts's address was "The Political Situation." The speaker put up a spirited defence of Rhodes, attempting vigorously to rebut the Schreiners' accusations. He sought to justify the "dual position" held by Rhodes as Premier of the Cape Colony and mine magnate with great financial and, therefore, political interests in the Transvaal Republic. His eloquent refutation of charges against the Prime Minister of blatant dishonesty, corruption, ruthlessness, opportunism, and bribery, rang somewhat false in the ears of people not entirely ignorant of Rhodesian methods. But, on the whole, the effect of the speech was good and Smuts journeyed home highly pleased with his mission.

Hofmeyr's friendship with Rhodes dated from the time of the Englishman's renunciation of rabid imperialism with the words: "I was a rabid Jingo once. I am no longer. . . . The Imperial factor must be eliminated." It was a friendship resting on very insecure foundations, for Rhodes was an incorrigible opportunist and, despite his protestations, his ultimate ambitions in Africa and the imperial dreams of the powerful British coterie of Conservative leaders of the Chamberlain School were almost identical. In point of fact, at the very moment that Smuts was asked by Hofmeyr to go to Kimberley on the Premier's behalf, that gentleman was secretly scheming to bring about what the Schreiners had foreshadowed.

The Imperialist Conservative party's majority of one hundred and fifty-three at the general election in Britain, in 1895, induced Rhodes to strike at Kruger soon after Smuts's return from Kimberley. He imported arms secretly into the Transvaal to equip his fellow conspirators among the Uitlanders, and he despatched Dr. Jameson with a strong detachment of armed men to Pitsani near the border of the Transvaal. The troops were to invade the republic and, assisted by the Uitlanders rising in revolt, were to overthrow the Boer Government.

From the start there was gross mismanagement. The force at Pitsani, apparently with the approval of their leader, imbibed overfreely in anticipation of a glorious victory and "invaded" the Transvaal in a besotted condition. "It was," says Vulliamy, "apparently some time before anyone could be found who was sober enough to cut efficiently the telegraph wires, and in the meanwhile the news of the move had got through to Pretoria." After one or two skirmishes the raiders surrendered ingloriously to Piet Cronje at Doornkop. "Dr. Jameson, I have the honour to meet you," said the Boer general ironically.

Meanwhile the Uitlanders' efforts to effect a *coup d'état* in Johannesburg and Pretoria were easily frustrated by the Boers. "I shall wait for the tortoise to stick out its head," Paul Kruger had said. He waited, and at the opportune moment he acted.

In spite of the comic-opera atmosphere about the raid, its repercussions were both serious and far-reaching, particularly when it was definitely established that Sir Henry Loch, Her Majesty's High Commissioner at the Cape, Lord Rosebery (then Premier of Great Britain), Mr. Joseph Chamberlain, the British Colonial Secretary, and various of his Cabinet colleagues were "privy to the proposed violation of Transvaal territory." The whole of Europe was taken aback at what was termed "international brigandage" and Germany, ever jealous of her rival, became, for a time, openly hostile; the Afrikaner Bond party, thoroughly scandalized at Mr. Rhodes's complicity in the affair, renounced him with contumely. He was ousted from the premiership; and he presided no longer at meetings of either the Chartered Company or De Beers. There was an extraordinary revival of racialism and anti-British feeling in the Cape Colony as well as in the northern republics; a "defence alliance" was established between the Free State and the Transvaal, and both states began feverishly to import guns and ammunition from abroad. The Jameson Raid subsequently proved to be the chief "predisposing cause" of the Boer War of 1899–1902.

The news of the Raid came to Smuts like a bolt from the blue on New Year's Day, 1896. Never in his life had he suffered such a shock. He

was on holiday at the farm Klipfontein at the time. He found it hard to
believe the reports of Rhodes's complicity. The man whom he had idol-
ized and whose cause he had espoused had deceived him and, while
pretending to co-operate with Afrikanerdom in the interests of the commonweal, had grossly betrayed it. All his hopes were shattered. The
proud future he had visualized for himself could never now materialize.
He felt thoroughly miserable, deeply humiliated, and angry. Rhodes had
made a fool of him. His fellow Afrikaners would look scornfully at him
and ridicule him. They would never forgive him for singing Rhodes's
praises in Kimberley.

He retired into his shell again, avoided people, and took no part in
public life for many months.

He found it impossible to free his mind of Rhodes and the enormity
of his betrayal of the Afrikaner Bond and Jan Smuts. He could not forget
what he called the Englishman's "treacherous duplicity." The man became an obsession with him. Practically all his articles in the press dealt
with Rhodes and were couched invariably in terms at once derisive and
abusive.

Yet deep down in his heart there lived, with lustre almost undimin-
ished, the image of Rhodes, the man with great and inspiring ideas, the
image of the Colossus astride a continent. Little did he know that the
spirit of Rhodes would be with him for the rest of his days and that in
time he, Jan Smuts, would be called *Rhodes Redivivus*. Little did he
know that he and Rhodes were kindred spirits.

Deciding that there was no longer a future for him at the Cape, he
left for Johannesburg before the first rains of winter fell in 1896, after
having previously travelled north in March to have a look around. He
was duly accorded citizenship of the Transvaal Republic as a burgher of
the second class, of his own accord renounced his British nationality, and
became a member of the Transvaal bar in the spring.

7

BEFORE SMUTS'S DEPARTURE from Cape Town, the Afrikaner Bond's
organ, *Ons Land,* making mention of his plans to practise as an advocate
in the Transvaal, had said that "it would be cause for regret if the Cape
were to lose one of its cleverest and most promising sons." But Smuts

exhibited the same traits that had deprived him of briefs in Cape Town and, consequently, he was as unsuccessful as a barrister in Johannesburg as he had been at the Cape. He found it even more difficult to associate with the cosmopolitan money-making, race-going, gambling, flashy young men of the Reef than with his comparatively reserved acquaintances and colleagues in the Cape.

He had always loved the natural beauty of the Cape peninsula and had frequently gone for long and lonely but happy walks along the slopes of Table Mountain. But here in Johannesburg he could not get away from the unsightly mine dumps, the ugly, corrugated-iron shanties, and the barren Transvaal veld. And all around him he saw always the swarming thousands of men of all nations, feverishly bent upon one pursuit—the rapid acquisition of wealth. He was unhappy. The things that mattered to these people meant nothing to him. He neither smoked nor drank nor indulged in any of the other excesses which were common in the great mining town where the scum of the earth had gathered. He craved only success in life—the fulfilment of his ambitions.

In order to supplement his small income he lectured to students at night on jurisprudence and law and wrote articles for various newspapers. Gradually, however, as he slowly adapted himself to circumstances, his law practice grew and he began to make a comfortable living from legal work. His chambers were in Commissioner Street. An acquaintance who often saw him there describes him as being at the time "a pale-faced, tremendously serious-looking young man who appeared much taller than he really was owing to his thinness; given to holding converse with the pavement, always in thought, and seemingly taking no notice of what went on around him; with high cheekbones and a hungry look."

Slowly he regained confidence in himself and decided to try his hand at politics once again—this time as an active supporter of Paul Kruger and Afrikaner isolationism. Early in 1897 he visited his parents at Riebeek West and Isie Krige at Stellenbosch. Before returning to the Rand he addressed various meetings in villages and towns near Stellenbosch and in the Swartland wheat belt, the tenor of his speeches always being anti-Rhodes and anti-British.

At Kuilsriver he said: ". . . [the British] have set the veld on fire. We lift our voices in warning to England so that she may know that the Afrikaner Boer stands where he stood in 1881. If England sends Rhodes back to us, the responsibility will be hers. The blood be on England's own head."

In April, at Stellenbosch again, Smuts was married quietly to Isie

Krige one morning and immediately returned with his bride to Johannesburg, where the young couple took an unpretentious house in Twist Street. Here they lived quietly, being fully satisfied with each other's company, and making few friends and social contacts.

While Smuts was scouting around for political opportunity, he was suddenly briefed as counsel for the defence in one of the most sensational cases ever to be tried on the Rand.

One morning the news of the "dramatic shooting" of Mr. Woolf Joel —brother of the multimillionaire, Mr. Solly Joel—burst upon Johannesburg like a thunderclap. The crime was attributed to one Von Veltheim, alias Ludwig Kurtze, a German who, it was alleged, had visited Joel at the offices of the brothers Barnato and had suggested to him a plan to kidnap President Kruger. When his proposal was rejected, Von Veltheim, so the story goes, swiftly pulled a pistol from his hip pocket and shot Joel. The assailant was arrested and locked up in jail.

Mr. Harry Smith, a well-known Johannesburg attorney, was approached on behalf of the accused and, after due consideration, decided to brief Smuts for the defence.

But some weeks before the trial was scheduled to begin a serious crisis, involving President Kruger, the chief justice of the Republic, and various other people of importance, gave to Smuts the chance of a lifetime.

8

THE OLD Boer patriarch, Paul Kruger, ruled his people like a feudal lord. His autocratic habits had antagonized many of his colleagues in the *Volksraad* (People's Parliament) as well as numerous of his other associates, but he was so strongly entrenched in his presidential position— particularly after the Jameson Raid—by virtue of his many undeniably great qualities, that none had dared to question his authority or dispute his will.

Only when he began to interfere seriously in the affairs of the judiciary did he meet with hot and determined opposition. While disapproving strongly of the man's meddling with the findings of the courts of law and deprecating other kindred irregularities perpetrated by him, the judges were loath, in the beginning, to raise their voices against the powerful autocrat. But when, in contravention of the Constitution, the

President began to change the laws of the State by the simple expedient of passing "resolutions" to that effect in the Volksraad, the chief justice, Mr. Kotze, and his colleagues protested vigorously and angrily. "The Constitution," they averred, "must be protected against hasty alterations by resolutions. A written and fixed Constitution is the sheet anchor of the State and a protection of the minority in political hurricanes."

Subsequently the Supreme Court ignored laws passed by resolutions and thereupon incurred the thunderous wrath of the irascible old President. Before long the dispute assumed alarming proportions and the Supreme Court ceased to function temporarily. The chief justice of the Cape Colony went to the Transvaal to intercede. But the upshot of the matter was that Mr. Justice Kotze, an old rival of Kruger's for the presidency, was dismissed from his high office, much to the chagrin and consternation of his supporters. Lawyers, magistrates, and judges all over South Africa were scandalized, and in the Transvaal hardly a single legal man stood by Paul Kruger.

Then Smuts stepped in and upheld the President. Never in his wildest dreams had he thought that such an opportunity of commending himself to the old Boer leader would ever come his way. This was his great chance in life. In defence of Kruger's standpoint he issued a cleverly devised and nimbly evasive statement which was read with great interest throughout the Transvaal and was brought to the President's notice. It caused acute resentment among members of the legal profession in the Republic and was evocative of much criticism and hostility. But Smuts could well afford to ignore the gibes and sneers of those around him, as the event proved.

Meanwhile the state attorney, Dr. J. Coster, a Hollander, resigned his post after a series of differences of opinion between him and the President had culminated in an open breach. Speculation was rife in Johannesburg and Pretoria as to who his successor would be, particularly as Kruger seemed determined to get rid gradually of the Hollanders in the State Departments and in the Government itself and to appoint educated young Afrikaners in their stead. This change of policy had been prompted largely by public agitation. Emanating chiefly from the Young Akrikaner Movement, of which Smuts had been a leading member since its inception, much propaganda had been directed against the President's policy of employing Hollanders to fill most of the important positions.

Be that as it may, as a result, seemingly, of the publicity he had received from his participation in the Kotze crisis and his dramatic espousal of the President's cause at the time, various newspapers predicted that the vacancy caused by Coster's resignation would be filled in time by the appointment of Jan Smuts. The Johannesburg *Star* stated on May 25, 1898: "His [Smuts's] visit to Pretoria yesterday was made with the view of seeing how the land lay." And Kruger's own mouthpiece, *Die Volkstem,* regarded "Mr. Smuts as a suitable candidate for the post."

Smuts had not been idle in the meantime. Hans Malan, an acquaintance, had introduced him to Paul Kruger's favourite grandnephew, Piet Grobler, who had practically grown up in the President's home and was the old man's secretary. Grobler took Smuts along to the President one morning and, presenting him, suggested that he be appointed state attorney. Kruger was glad to meet the man who had stood by him in the crisis. But he was surprised at Smuts's youth.

"What!" he exclaimed, looking from Smuts to Grobler. "Do you want me to appoint this young boy?"

"Yes, Uncle," Grobler replied; "he's a well-qualified, clever young Afrikaner—as you know."

The more the President pondered on the matter the more attractive became the idea of having in his service, in spite of his youth, the Afrikaner from the Cape who had sided with him against all the lawyers and judges in the land and was reported to be a clever and serious young man.

Smuts duly became state attorney of the Transvaal, when he had just turned twenty-eight, although the law of the land had fixed the minimum age of persons eligible for the post at thirty. "He is able and conscientious," said the *Star* on June 2, "but though he may have all the precociousness of a Pitt, we still consider that twenty-eight is rather too young an age for the state attorney of the South African Republic."

After his appointment Smuts could not act as defending counsel in the Von Veltheim trial, and so he persuaded Mr. Harry Smith to transfer his brief to Dr. Coster, with whom he sympathized. As a result of the combined efforts of the Hollander and junior counsel for the defence, Mr. Foster, Von Veltheim was acquitted, "to the astonishment of all concerned," it was said.

9

IN THE MIDDLE OF 1898 the Smutses moved to Pretoria, the capital of the Republic. It was a quiet little place with neat gravel streets, flower gardens, and low, inconvenient single-storied houses with thatched roofs.

After his first visit to the capital, Smuts had said: "I was agreeably surprised by the aristocratic quiet pervading this handsome little town."

Here one met the tall, heavily built bearded farmers of the Transvaal and their buxom Boer women—all too frequently given to corpulence—with large white bonnets, neatly starched, and long, flowing gowns. Pretoria was essentially a Boer town, unlike Johannesburg, "where the Browns were outnumbered by the Cohens and where the Boer, supposed in some obscure way to be the proprietor of the country, was hardly seen."

For years Smuts had been straining at the leash which had bound him to a life of frustration and comparative stagnation. But now he was free to rush ahead and show what he could do, and he set to work with a will to prove his worth, to clean up his department, set his political house in order, and to extirpate whenever he could inefficiency, dishonesty, bribery, and corruption in an administration which, after the advent of the Golden Calf in the Transvaal, had lost its quondam probity. Wherever he probed he met with opposition and resentment from officials who disliked and feared the gaunt young man with the coldly staring, steely eyes, inexhaustible working power, and amazing efficiency.

One of his first tasks was to purge the Transvaal police force of corrupt officials and to reorganize the whole police system. For years men had spoken openly of the lucrative "illicit traffic in liquor and gold," which was steadily increasing; but neither Schutte, the head policeman, nor Bob Ferguson, the chief detective on the Reef, had been able to discover the leaders of the gangs. Smuts, suspecting connivance, dismissed both Schutte and Ferguson. He brought no accusation against the latter, but, staring menacingly into his eyes, told him to go, and he went. "I don't know how to explain my dismissal," Ferguson complained subsequently. "I am described by the state attorney, Mr. Smuts, in a communication to the Government as a 'particularly smart man, singularly unsuccessful in getting at criminals!' "

Smuts at that stage decided to assume control of the Criminal Investigation Department, which had, theretofore, been directed by the commissioner of police in Pretoria. "It is a big task," stated the *Standard and Diggers News,* "but that it is a wise movement we are convinced. No one doubts the integrity or ability of Mr. Smuts. . . . He has it in him to make the law respected." But before the state attorney could achieve his object, a bill making provision for the proposed change of control had to be passed by the Volksraad. In the teeth of tremendous opposition Smuts forced it through the House, and no sooner had he secured control than he set about cleaning up the Augean stables. He dismissed undesirable elements in the force, made new appointments, and, using every means at his disposal, set about hunting down criminals of every description with ruthless determination.

His whole being was immersed in his work. He was driven on by an ever-present urge to remedy faults in the fabric of the Kruger government and to forge ahead. His impatience, therefore, at meeting everywhere with inefficiency, inadequate documentation, insufficient interdepartmental cohesion and co-ordination, and a general lack of system, can well be imagined. It was impossible to modernize rapidly the obsolescent methods employed by the Transvaal Administration or to rectify within a few months the defects inherent in the Kruger regime. It is necessary to breathe the atmosphere of old Pretoria of the nineties to realize what Jan Smuts—young, energetic, forceful, and ambitious—had to cope with.

The President and his second wife, Gezina Wilhelmina du Plessis, whom he had married in 1846, lived in a very simple iron-roofed house in Church Street near the Dopper (strict Calvinist) Church, where they worshipped regularly. They had spent together a long life beset with many hardships and trials, which had greatly strengthened the bonds between them. Tante Siena[1] had borne Oom Paul seven daughters and nine sons, and almost always children and grandchildren were to be found in and about the house.

Paul Kruger lived as his forebears had lived—a quiet, unpretentious, religious life. It was his habit to rise in the early hours of the morning, take his Bible from a shelf and pore over it for a long time. Then came the family prayers; *"Zonder God vermag ik niets* [Without God I attempt nothing],"* he used to say. After devotions he would go to the front stoep, where he would sit down, a few yards from the street. Here he would consume numerous cups of strong coffee and puff for hours at his pipe, which rarely left his mouth during the day. As the people passed by he would hail them with a gruff "good morning," and then exchange a few words with them, for in Pretoria he knew them all.

In the course of the day many callers would turn up on business, official or otherwise, or merely to converse with the President. All were equally welcome. As soon as visitors came, coffee would be poured and handed round and then Oom Paul and his friends would discuss the weather, the crops, the Uitlander question, or anything else of interest. His people had great belief in the wisdom of Paul Kruger, and young and old, rich and poor, town dwellers and rustics from the backveld—all

[1]The old couple were known as Tante (Aunt) Siena and Oom (Uncle) Paul to all and sundry in the Republic and beyond its boundaries.

used to come, singly or in groups, to seek advice. And the President was always ready and even eager to receive them, no matter how pressing official business might be.

When deputations visited him, he would light his pipe and draw at it thoughtfully for a minute or two before saying: "Now Oom Paul is with you. Tell him what you will—or ask what you will—speak!" And then, regardless of time, he would converse with them until they were ready to take their leave.

One morning an excited burgher arrived from Johannesburg to consult Kruger. The proprietor of a hotel at which he had been staying had denied receiving from him a sum of one hundred pounds in gold, which, the burgher swore to Oom Paul, he had previously given to the man for safekeeping. "What am I to do, President?" he inquired anxiously. "My money has been stolen."

"Take another hundred pounds," came the reply, "and in the presence of two witnesses, ask him to put it in the safe. Go the next morning alone, and ask him for it. He will give it to you, because he knows you have witnesses. The next day go with your two witnesses, and ask him for the hundred pounds they saw you hand to him. He will then be bound to give you the money. You have him where he had you in the beginning, his word against yours!"

In a fairly large room in his house the President used to preside over meetings of his executive council. Here and in a couple of smaller rooms, used as offices, he conducted his official business, which, much to the annoyance of Smuts, was carried on in a casual, unsystematic way and was subject to frequent interruptions from children and visitors.

Once Smuts entered a room where the President, State Secretary Reitz, and a British journalist were conversing. Being in a hurry, as usual, and desiring to speak to Kruger, he touched Reitz's shoulder and said, without attempting to lower his voice: "Who is this fellow who wastes His Honour's time?" The President was much annoyed. He spoke sternly to Smuts afterwards.

"Smuts," he declared, "your whiplash cracks too sharply!"

The youthful state attorney with his hustling ways and his tactless behaviour frequently irritated Kruger, who objected to being prodded on by his impetuous junior when he wished to examine at his leisure, as was his wont, projects which had been suggested to him by the young man. But the wise old Boer realized only too well the worth of Smuts, whom he described as "one of the cleverest lawyers in South Africa and a man of versatile attainments besides. He is personally a very simple man and to meet him one would not suspect that he possesses so iron a will and so determined a character as he does. . . . Smuts will yet play a great part in the future of South Africa."

Smuts treated Kruger with respect, and the old man liked him, but he was far from popular with the majority of his associates and acquaintances, who regarded his grim and haughty ways with acute distaste. He sought no man's friendship and paid scant attention to his fellow citizens in the streets of Pretoria. His elders disapproved of him for not showing them the respect they regarded as their due. Not infrequently he clashed with fellow burghers.

He clashed also with the Uitlanders.

With the passage of time the Transvaal Uitlander question had become increasingly serious. The Rhodes cabal, having secured control of the majority of South African newspapers as well as several important overseas publications, contributed not a little to the ever-growing friction between the foreign element in the Republic and the Boers. "The South African press," wrote A. M. S. Methuen, the English author, "became a manufactory of outrages."

That the Uitlanders had certain legitimate grievances no one can deny: English was neglected in the schools; sanitary arrangements in Johannesburg left much to be desired; and the Government had farmed out to privileged persons certain monopolies which should not have existed, or might, at least, have been competed for in an open market. There were also other grievances, but on the whole they were unimportant. And there can be no doubt that they were added to and magnified out of all proportion by Mr. Rhodes and his clique to serve—as the Uitlander E. B. Rose himself said—as "part and parcel of the crusade of calumny upon the Boers, having for its object eventual British intervention and destruction of Boer independence."

From the start Smuts adopted a stern and uncompromising attitude towards the Uitlanders, who, he averred, were claiming peremptorily, as their due, benefits and prerogatives to which they had no legal right as aliens in a foreign land. Soon he clashed with them.

While demanding citizenship and all the privileges pertaining thereto, the Uitlanders—most of them were British subjects—refused point-blank to renounce their nationality in order to become Transvaal burghers. They went further: they declined to belong to the Republic's Defence Force or to make any payments whatsoever towards the upkeep thereof. They were there simply to make money, said Smuts, and refused to do their share in regard to shouldering the responsibilities and burdens of the State. He would compel them, he swore, to make their contribution either in service or in money. He prevailed on the Volksraad to pass a bill requiring all Uitlanders to subscribe to either of these alternatives.

From time to time he either fell foul of the foreign element or they fell foul of him.

Once he issued orders for the arrest of two Uitlander leaders, newspaper editors, Moneypenny of the *Star* and Pakeham of the *Transvaal Leader,* both of whom, it was alleged, had exceeded their rights as journalists by the publication of flagrant untruths in disparagement of the Boers and by an all-too-blatant denunciation of the Kruger government. Pakeham was imprisoned. Moneypenny, however, avoided arrest. The Uitlanders went mad with rage, and, in consequence of their impassioned demands, Pakeham was released. Smuts cleverly evaded responsibility.

Men began to say that he was wily as a fox, and they began to call him *Slim* (crafty) Jannie.

Developments arising from the death of an Englishman, Edgar by name, created along the Reef an even greater stir than did the Moneypenny-Pakeham fiasco. Quarrelling one night with an acquaintance, Edgar struck the man down. When they heard shouts and scuffling, the neighbours rushed up to see what was happening and found Edgar's victim (who died subsequently) lying unconscious on the ground. Believing the man to be dead, they summoned the police with shouts of "murder!"

As four policemen ran up, Edgar decamped to his house and bolted the door, defiantly refusing admittance to the constables. But the four men succeeded in breaking down the door and entered the house in single file. Edgar, using a heavy stick weighted with iron, fiercely attacked the leading policeman, an Afrikaner named Jones, who drew his pistol and killed his assailant with the first shot.

Jones was arrested soon after and charged with manslaughter. He was released on bail but was rearrested on Smuts's orders, and a charge of murder was brought against him. He was subsequently acquitted by a jury.

While the case was *sub judice* the South African League, a Uitlander organization, convoked a meeting of citizens to discuss the whole affair on the Johannesburg market square. Messrs. Dodd and Webb of the league were the principal speakers. According to a Uitlander who was present, "the meeting very nearly culminated in a serious riot, the town being in a state bordering on actual terror for the remainder of the day, and far into the night."

After Jones's acquittal the Uitlanders exploited the case to the full in order to prove to the world in general and Great Britain in particular how badly foreigners were being treated in Paul Kruger's land. Another meeting was called for January 14, 1899.

Smuts, expecting serious trouble this time, offered the leaders of the South African League adequate police protection against interference, but the men refused his offer. What he had feared, happened. An angry mob of anti-league Uitlanders and Boers stormed the amphitheatre in which the agitators had assembled, and a free fight ensued.

Arising out of the Edgar case, a petition was sent by the South African League to the British Government, begging it to come to the aid of the afflicted subjects of Her Majesty the Queen in the Transvaal. But Sir William Butler advised the British Government in a dispatch to ignore the petition, which they did.

For a time there was comparative peace on the Rand. But serious trouble was brewing, and behind it was the sinister figure of Sir Alfred Milner.

IO

MILNER WAS APPOINTED Governor General of the Cape Colony and High Commissioner for South Africa at the instance of Mr. Joseph Chamberlain when Lord Rosmead resigned in 1896. Born of an Irish mother and a German father, he received his early education on the Continent and thereafter became a distinguished scholar at Balliol College, Oxford. He is said to have obtained from the ancient university "her peculiar gift of dry and impervious arrogance."

His appointment to the high position in South Africa was a calamitous one. He was primarily responsible for the Boer War. He came to South Africa fully resolved to "crush Afrikanerdom." Nor did he scruple to say so. Long before Mr. Chamberlain fell a victim to the war psychosis, Milner had already made up his mind to "provoke a quarrel" with the Transvaal. His methods were essentially Prussian. Soon he was hand in glove with the Rhodes clique, plotting for the speedy overthrow of Kruger.

At the earnest solicitation of President Steyn of the Free State and others—both Englishmen and Afrikaners—desiring to evade war, and somewhat to the relief of Sir William Butler, the British commander in chief in South Africa, Kruger and Milner met at Bloemfontein, capital of the Orange Free State, ostensibly to attempt a settlement of the differences between the Transvaal Government and the Uitlanders. Sir William, while hoping against hope that the Bloemfontein Conference might be successful, was not oversanguine in his expectations, for he distrusted Milner as he distrusted Rhodes and his satellites on the Rand. "All political questions in South Africa," said Sir William, "and nearly all the information sent from Cape Town to England, are now being worked by . . . a colossal syndicate for the spread of systematic misrepresentation."

The Bloemfontein Conference was not a success. Starting on May 31, 1899, it ended on June 5. Milner came with a large retinue: Viscount Belgrave, A.D.C., Mr. M. S. O. Walrond, the High Commissioner's private secretary, Mr. G. V. Fiddes, the Imperial Secretary, Lieutenant Colonel J. Hanbury-Williams, the military secretary, and some others. Accompanying Kruger were Messrs. A. D. Wolmarans and Schalk Burger, members of the Executive Council, W. J. Fockers and D. N. R. van Hoytema, officials, and Jan Christiaan Smuts.

The conference opened on an inauspicious note. Sir Alfred Milner arrived a few minutes late at a reception given by President and Mrs. Steyn in honour of their distinguished guests. As he came up, President Kruger stepped forward to greet him, but he pretended not to see the old man's outstretched hand and walked on to pay his respects to their hostess. It is recorded that President Steyn's eyes held "a glance of pity and indignation" on witnessing the episode. Kruger withdrew his hand silently, and on his rugged old face there was not a sign of emotion.

The matter of the franchise—on which Milner had determined to concentrate—occupied most of the delegates' time. In this connection the High Commissioner made far-reaching demands right at the start, insisting on immediate concessions, the granting of which would have been almost suicidal to the Boers. "The number of the enfranchised burghers," replied the President, "is about thirty thousand; the number of the Uitlanders demanding the franchise is about sixty thousand—and if we give them the franchise . . . we may as well give up the Republic." However, in response to Smuts's urgent advice, the President began to make "concessions" to Sir Alfred, but the High Commissioner was not prepared to "bargain." He had stated what he wanted. Nothing else would satisfy him.

With Kruger's consent Smuts hurriedly drew up a "complete reform bill" in accordance with which Uitlanders were to be granted the franchise seven years after their arrival in the Transvaal. From the British point of view it was a tremendous step forward. But Milner, having perused the document, thrust it from him angrily and stuck to his original demands. He even threatened to "break off negotiations" unless the Boers agreed to do as they were told.

His haughty demeanour throughout the proceedings infuriated Smuts as he sat next to Kruger plying him with advice. And it was with difficulty that the young man managed to give all his attention to the work of the conference, for the High Commissioner's attitude was decidedly provocative. But Smuts pulled himself together. He was Kruger's mainstay. It was his duty to steer clear of personalities.

He was constantly in consultation with the President and, since there was nothing else to be done in the circumstances, gradually prevailed on him to make further concessions. They were made. But Milner was adamant. He refused to compromise. He would have what he had demanded in the beginning—or nothing.

Then tears came into Kruger's eyes. "It is my country that you want," he said. "It is our independence you are taking away." And he referred with feeling to the landing of British troops in Cape Town and elsewhere in South Africa. "The franchise," he added, "is merely a pretext to egg on people. . . ." And when, finally, he perceived that nothing could be gained from Milner, he said sternly: "I understand from His Excellency's arguments that if I do not give the whole management of my land and government to strangers there is nothing to be done. . . . I am not ready to hand over my country to strangers." And as he spoke these words, beside him sat Smuts, a pale and intense young man with unflinching light-blue eyes, staring coldly and ruthlessly at Milner in whom he had found more than his match in arrogance and whose attitude had aroused in him a burning resentment. He had required all his power of will to hold himself in check in the face of Milner's contemptuous treatment of him and his colleagues. He was to meet the man again.

Arriving back in Pretoria he said to Piet Grobler at the railway station: "It is absolutely clear to me that Milner is planning to make war." Lord Oliver subsequently attributed hostilities to "Milner's determination to round off the Empire before it was too late."

At the instance of Smuts and several other influential men, Oom Paul, on August 19, suggested giving the Uitlanders a "five years' residential franchise." This was practically what Milner had demanded at the Bloemfontein Conference. Prompted by his indefatigable state attorney, the President went further. In a note to the British Government he declared himself willing to do much more, provided that "(a) Her Majesty's Government will agree that the present intervention shall not form a precedent for future similar action, and that in future no interference in the affairs of the Republic will take place; (b) that Her Majesty's Government will not further insist on the assertion of the suzerainty (resuscitated by Chamberlain at the London Convention of 1884), the controversy on the subject being allowed tacitly to drop; (c) that arbitration (from which foreign element other than the Orange Free State is to be excluded) will be conceded as soon as the franchise scheme has become law."

Meanwhile Mr. Joseph Chamberlain had become Prime Minister of Great Britain in all but name. His usurpation of power in the British Government was remarkable. It was also extremely unfortunate, for he had been led gradually by Mr. Rhodes and Sir Alfred Milner to see eye to eye with them on all matters pertaining to the Transvaal. He rejected Kruger's peace offer as given in the Boer Note of August 19, made demands for additional concessions, and reiterated Britain's title to suzerainty over the Transvaal.

On his return from Bloemfontein Smuts had entered into negotiations with Mr. Conyngham Greene, the British agent in Pretoria, in a desperate personal effort to avoid war. On August 25 he wrote finally to Mr. Greene: "The terms of a settlement as contained in a formal note of this Government, dated 19th August, were very carefully considered, and I do not believe that there is the slightest chance that these terms will be altered or amplified. Your decision will therefore have to be arrived at on these terms as they stand."

But neither the Smuts-Greene discussions nor any further communications with the British Government had any effect on the growing menace of the situation.

Milner announced to Whitehall in a cable, dated August 31, "that British South Africa was prepared for extreme measures"—which, actually, was not the case.

Less than a month later the High Commissioner examined closely a dispatch sent him by M. T. Steyn, President of the Orange Free State, to be forwarded to the British Government. Before cabling its contents to Whitehall he struck out "all the passages containing powerful arguments for peace."

In England Mr. Rhodes remarked cynically to some friends: "Three years ago I made a raid and everybody said I was wrong. Now the Queen's Government are preparing another raid, and everybody says they are right." "The British flag," he added later, "is the greatest commercial asset. . . . We are not going to war for the amusement of Royal families as in the past, but we mean practical business."

Mr. Chamberlain severed diplomatic relations with the Kruger gov-

ernment on September 22. Large numbers of troops were landed soon
after in Natal and began to take up positions on the borders of that
colony. The Boers could wait no longer. Smuts drafted an ultimatum
which was dispatched to Great Britain on October 9. It requested "an
immediate withdrawal of Her Majesty's forces." "Kruger," declared
W. T. Stead of the *Review of Reviews,* "would have been a traitor to his
own people if he had not launched the ultimatum."

A fortnight previously, when matters had begun to be very critical,
the editor of one of New York's leading newspapers had cabled the
Transvaal Government to ask "if they would put up a fight if necessary."
Replying on behalf of Kruger, Smuts had said: "Yes. It will be a fight
that will stagger humanity."

On October 11 the war commenced. And the Free State, deciding to
stand by her treaty obligations, went to the assistance of the northern
republic.

Speaking in England of his "pride in the war," Mr. Chamberlain
added that, "if, as his opponents asserted, he was the author of the war,
such an exploit would be a feather in his cap."

A final telegram reached Paul Kruger from the business associates of
Cecil John Rhodes. This was its text: "For what you are about to receive, may the Lord make you truly thankful!"

II

SOME WEEKS BEFORE the war began there was published in England a
book called *A Century of Wrong,* being the translation by Mrs. Smuts
of *Een Eeuw van Onrecht,* a book written by Smuts in High Dutch, the
official language of the Transvaal Republic. Abounding in metaphor
and rich in classical allusions, it expatiated on the wrongs and injustices
perpetrated by the British on the Boers since the beginning of the century. "In this awful turning point in the history of South Africa, on the
eve of the conflict which threatens to exterminate our people, it behoves
us to speak the truth in what may be, perchance, our last message to the
world. . . .

"As the wounded antelope awaits the coming of the lion, the jackal,
and the vulture, so our people all over South Africa contemplate the
approach of the foe.

"Every sea in the world is being furrowed by the ships which are conveying British troops from every corner of the globe in order to smash this little handful of people. . . ."

Perhaps in his whole life there are few things that Smuts regrets more than he does the authorship of *A Century of Wrong*. As a piece of Boer propaganda before and during the war the purpose it served was negligible and afterwards it was invariably cast in his teeth by his countrymen. Ever since the first days of his transmutation from Afrikaner Nationalism to British imperialism men have taunted him with it, saying: "Behold, he who so eloquently censured the imperialistic freebooters has now become the chief champion of their cause." *A Century of Wrong* has been a disturbing factor in Smuts's life. He prefers never to speak about it.

The first shot of the war was fired at Kraaipan near Mafeking on the western border of the Transvaal.

Two great Boer commandos entered Natal simultaneously. One of them, under the leadership of Lukas Meyer, defeated General Penn-Symons' army at Talana Hill. Soon afterwards Piet Joubert's men routed the British under Generals White and French at Nicholson's Nek. This Boer victory led to the siege of Ladysmith. Repeated attempts on the part of General Buller to drive off the investing cordons ended in disaster for the British at Colenso and Spioenkop.

Meanwhile Lord Methuen was severely trounced in the Free State at Modder River by Cronje and Delarey, and General Gatacre, who had been hastily dispatched to Burghersdorp in the Cape Colony to check raiding Free State commandos, was heavily defeated by Grobler at Stormberg. A few hours later General Wauchope attacked Cronje and Delarey at Magersfontein. Within the first minute after the Boer leader had given the signal to fire, seven hundred Highlanders lay dead on the field of battle. Soon the Black Watch was practically annihilated and Wauchope himself was a bullet-riddled corpse. The panic-stricken remnants behind the famous regiment fled from the field before the terrible fusillade poured out by the best riflemen in the world. Scotland was plunged into mourning.

This rapid succession of disasters dismayed the British nation. Not since the eve of Trafalgar had it been so thoroughly alarmed and bewildered. According to the *Times* neither the Indian Mutiny nor the Crimean War had imperilled the Empire to a greater extent. In the east the Boers seemed to be on the point of overrunning Natal and sweeping the British into the sea. On the southern and western fronts the position was equally dangerous, and the Cape Colony lay exposed to any attacks the Boers might choose to make. Complete disaster, however, was staved off by Cronje's stubborn temporizing in the south and west and by Joubert's senile amiability in Natal. "It would be barbarous," said the latter, "to pursue and slaughter a beaten Christian foe."

It is a remarkable fact that both the Boers and the English were hampered in the beginning by the senility of their respective commanders in chief. Joubert, a veteran of Majuba and a great fighter in his youth, was on the verge of decrepitude, while Sir Redvers Buller, a V.C. of the Zulu war, was an irresolute old bungler.

Badly shaken by the calamitous events of the Black Week, the British Government immediately sent to South Africa Lord Roberts of Kandahar and Lord Kitchener of Khartoum, most famous of all the generals in the English-speaking world. And from every part of the British Empire men flocked in overwhelming numbers to the Cape "to avenge Majuba." And soon there was in South Africa a great British army, "the largest ever assembled in a foreign campaign." So ended the first phase of the war.

With forces outnumbering the Boers by at least six to one in the beginning and with the balance rapidly increasing in his favour, Lord Roberts soon turned the tables on the foe. Kimberley, Mafeking, and Ladysmith were relieved. Cronje was encircled at Paardeberg and capitulated with thirty-seven hundred men.

On March 13, 1900, the British commander in chief entered Bloemfontein and on the Queen's birthday he annexed the Orange Free State by proclamation. The fall of Johannesburg was imminent. Nor could Pretoria, Kruger's capital, withstand the invader.

Smuts was still in Pretoria. Hitherto he had taken no part in the actual fighting. He had visited the fronts and had strongly advised the President to appoint Louis Botha as Joubert's successor after the old commandant general's death on March 28. He was actively engaged in the work of his department, which had multiplied exceedingly since the outbreak of war. In regard to proclamations, dispatches, general correspondence, and the organization of war supplies he was of inestimable value to Kruger. He shouldered the brunt of the work in the Government offices. Relentlessly he drove himself along, labouring incessantly, since he was incapable of entrusting important tasks to others. He became more gaunt and grim than ever, aloof and taciturn, a harsh and callous taskmaster, intolerant of failure and inefficiency, riding roughshod over the feelings of others.

While the British juggernaut was advancing inexorably towards

Johannesburg, the Boer morale was at its lowest ebb. Scores of burghers deserted daily and returned to their farms. Large numbers surrendered. It seemed that the end was near.

The lack of discipline in the commandos filled Smuts with a cold fury. Despite the apparent hopelessness of the position he did not lose courage, being as grimly determined as ever to strain every nerve to avoid defeat. There burned within him fierce fires of resentment against the British, whom love of gold had set upon the path of war.

Paul Kruger and his government now moved hurriedly to Machado-dorp near the Portuguese border. But Smuts remained behind in Pretoria with Schalk Burger, the acting president. Soon, however, the latter departed with his family and Smuts was left alone to remove whatever money, munitions, and stores he could get away.

Commandeering every burgher within reach, he marched towards Irene with four hundred men in an attempt to check the advancing enemy while the military supplies were being removed. But soon he had to return posthaste to Pretoria, for the enemy were coming up by another route.

By now the capital was in a state of wild disorder. There was looting in all quarters. This Smuts encouraged to prevent any commodities from falling into the hands of the enemy.

On June 4 the British attacked the capital. For several hours Smuts's four hundred men defended the town while their leader hurriedly dispatched the last load of munitions from the fort and, accompanied by fifty policemen, forcibly removed the Government's money from a bank. This sum, amounting to over half a million pounds in gold, was rushed to the station and sent off in a special train just as the first British shells began to fall in the town. Proudly Smuts says today that this money enabled the Boers to go on fighting for another two years. And during that time the British Treasury spent over two hundred million pounds sterling on the war.

On June 5 the Union Jack was hoisted in Pretoria. All appeared to be lost. Calling a council of war at Hatherly in the office of Samuel Marks, a Russian Jew, Botha, after listening to the defeatist speeches of the Transvaal generals, counselled immediate surrender to the British. Then from the Free State, from President Steyn and General de Wet came impassioned protests against the very thought of surrender. However, nothing came of the peace proposals. For, before a final decision could be reached, a series of amazing successes achieved by Danie Theron (whom Botha had sent to the Free State) and afterwards by Christiaan de Wet, bolstered up the Boer morale and killed the germ of submission.

De Wet's brilliant victory at Sannaspos, after the fall of Bloemfontein, had revived the spirits of his countrymen in the nick of time. Now, at the second critical phase of his nation's struggle, he stepped into the breach once more. With his opportune revival and brilliant execution of guerrilla fighting (which, incidentally, was to prolong the war for two years) he harassed the enemy incessantly. He dynamited their railways, captured their convoys, launched sudden and devastating attacks at unexpected points, and wiped out isolated garrisons. In many places men caught fleeting glimpses of the intrepid guerrilla chief. He was ubiquitous. Lightly he passed from commando to commando bringing hope, advice, and inspiration, flitting here, flitting there, appearing and disappearing like a phantom. "His rapid, almost uncanny successes made him a name to conjure with among his own men and in the British Army. . . . Hunted by almost every British general all over South Africa, he was never caught, and every failure on the British side seemed to almost be condoned if he was supposed to have had a hand in it."[1]

Lord Roberts' rapid march into the very midst of the enemy's vast territory with a great army whose life depended on the retention of its lines of communication was a hazardous undertaking, the speed of which was accelerated by feverish injunctions from Whitehall to save the gold mines. His straggling lines were the answer to the guerrillas' prayer. His communications were attacked unceasingly. In the rear and on the flanks he was harassed mercilessly.

Indeed, at the end of 1900, when he returned to England to receive an earldom from the Queen at Osborne, the Order of the Black Eagle from his brother field marshal, the German Kaiser, and one hundred thousand pounds from the British Parliament, the state of affairs in South Africa was serious for Britain. But Lord Roberts believed that the war was over, apart from the requisite mopping up. He said so. And Lord Kitchener succeeded him as commander in chief.

The war continued.

I2

IT WAS an epic struggle. The nations of the world were interested spectators. The incongruity of the opposing forces was laughable. It was also

[1] *Times History of the War in South Africa.*

tragic. On one side there fought the greatest, wealthiest, and most powerful empire the eye of man had ever seen, commanding inexhaustible
resources; on the other, a mere handful of untrained farmers amounting
to—men, women, and children all told—less than Birmingham's population at the time.

Meanwhile a warship sent by the Queen of Holland had fetched the
aged Paul Kruger at Delagoa Bay and taken him to Europe, where, a
few years later, he died in exile, a broken old man apathetic even to the
thought of death since the day he had received the news of his wife's
demise in British Pretoria.

The position of the new commander in chief was far from enviable.
The elusive De Wet, egged on by his undaunted compatriot Steyn, was
carrying the "fiery cross of revolt" either personally or by proxy into
every district of the Orange Free State and the remotest corners of the
Transvaal, and pitilessly punishing the enemy with his swift, mobile columns. Delarey, Beyers, and Kemp, and, later, Jan Smuts, emulated his
will-o'-the-wisp tactics with feats hitherto unparalleled in guerrilla warfare. The British lost heavily.

With a view to crushing the Boer resistance Lord Kitchener ultimately
resorted to indiscriminate farm burning, wholesale devastation of property, and a general denudation of the land. At the same time, in imita-
tion of General Weyler's Cuban precedent, the women and children
evicted from towns and farms were placed in concentration camps,
where close on thirty thousand victims died and were buried in nameless
graves. On the field of battle there were fewer fatalities.

The British sent Mrs. Smuts to Maritzburg, where there was a concentration camp. She, however, lived in a house, a sad and lonely woman
separated by force of circumstances from her husband and still bewail-
ing the loss of her first three children, twin girls and a boy, who had died
in the Transvaal.

On May 24, 1901—her husband's birthday, the first they had spent
apart since their marriage—Sir Alfred Milner was being received by the
King in London; he became Baron Milner of St. James and Cape Town,
as well as a privy councillor and a G.C.B.

When the farm burning, general devastation, and the concentration
camps did not have the immediate success he had anticipated, Lord
Kitchener commenced his tremendous drives, aided by great rows of
blockhouses and barbed-wire entanglements. The famous night raids also
started. Their efficacy was due almost entirely to the spying and scouting
activities of renegade Boers and native auxiliaries. Before long the Transvaal leaders were clamouring for peace again.

Shortly after his enforced departure from Pretoria, Smuts had joined that fine old warrior, Delarey, an uninspiring figure on his Basuto pony, with flapping felt hat and dusty brown coat, but a great leader of men with a head like a pagan god. His chivalrous treatment of the wounded Lieutenant General Lord Methuen, second in command to Lord Kitchener, was to amaze and delight the world when he captured the Englishman at Tweebosch, treated him courteously, and sent him back to the British lines.

Smuts liked Delarey and admired him. He learned from him the tricks of guerrilla warfare, displaying from the start a decided aptitude for this mode of fighting. Smuts was obviously a leader. And a courageous one. He was a natural fighter. He enjoyed fighting. To this day he takes greater pride in Smuts the soldier than in Smuts the philosopher, or, for that matter, Smuts the statesman of world repute.

His dry-as-dust legal tomes belonged to another world. Now that he could no longer bury his nose in books and documents, he forgot about them. Instead, he revelled in the free life of the veld, the raids, the capturing of convoys, and the storming of towns. It was both a strenuous and an instructive apprenticeship, which, in the days to come, was to stand him in good stead.

He stormed and captured the Modderfontein ridge with the dash and finesse of a seasoned campaigner, thereafter defending it resolutely against the enemy. One day he charged at the head of a small commando into a mealie (corn) field where there was a company of British soldiers. A boy of seventeen fired at him but missed him, whereupon, terror-stricken, the lad threw down his gun, crying: "For God's sake, sir, think of my mother!" Smuts glanced at him and swept past.

On June 20 the two republican governments met for consultation at the farm Waterval, near Standerton in the Transvaal. Victories gained opportunely by Kemp and Muller, as well as Kruger's injunction to "hold out," had put new courage into the leaders of the Transvaal. It was decided to go on with the war. But what was to be done in the heart of the winter? There was no grass for the horses. Nothing was left but to advise complete dispersion for three months while a commando entered the Cape Colony to harass and embarrass the enemy, to foment rebellion among the Cape farmers, and to ease the pressure on the republics. Since the majority of farmers in the Cape were friendly and the country had not been denuded, a mobile column, it was believed, would exist there quite comfortably. The consensus of opinion was to the effect that it was incumbent on the Transvaal to supply the column. It agreed to do so.

Jan Smuts had proved his mettle as a disciple of Delarey. He knew the Cape. He was chosen to lead the commando on its bold adventure.

It was a gallant company of men comprising some of the finest and best of Kemp's and Delarey's fighters. Smuts had carefully selected them himself.

13

WITH the utmost confidence Smuts embarked upon his bold and arduous undertaking and with a quickening pulse, for the thrill of adventure had set his blood racing. Dangers lurked in every hollow; this was the spice of life. He had changed much since the outbreak of war. He was no longer the sallow youth of prewar days, with lean and hungry look. His muscles had developed, his shoulders broadened, and his complexion had become ruddy through constant exposure to the elements. A yellow beard made him look older than his thirty-one years. His outlook, too, had altered greatly during those months with Delarey. For the first time in his life he had really lived. For the first time he had experienced the joys of physical action which his repressed youth had never known, tasted willy-nilly the pleasures of companionship which, heretofore, he had eschewed. But he had not become a "mixer," and he sought, whenever possible, the solitude of his own company, reserved, aloof, aware always of his own superiority.

He was given the command of all the Boer commandos south of the Orange River, and the rank of general.

It thrilled him to the core to feel that he, Jan Smuts, held an independent command—the chief command in a vast theatre of war outside the republics. The realization that the members of a large commando looked to him for guidance and entrusted to his care their very lives, relying on his leadership, stimulated and warmed him and gave to him maturity.

In his saddlebag he carried Kant's *Critique of Pure Reason* and a Greek Testament. Ahead of him lay the happiest period of his life, as he himself says, and also the most strenuous and hazardous.

After accompanying his lieutenant, Commandant van Deventer (afterwards General Sir Jacobus van Deventer), with two hundred and fifty men into the Free State, he went back across the Vaal to a rendezvous, where a commando of one hundred men were waiting.

On his way there with a small bodyguard, he decided to spend the night near a native kraal. Wrapped in a khaki blanket, he soon fell asleep. He was rudely awakened in the dead of night by sounds of scuffling and gunfire. A detachment of British soldiers had attacked his camp, having been led there by a native. Smuts escaped into the undergrowth. More than half his party had been either killed or wounded and the remainder had disappeared. His horses were gone. His personal attendant, a trusty native, lay dead in the camp. He picked his way warily on bare feet through the bushes. In his sudden flight he had left his boots behind. Presently he was joined by three of his men, one of them his brother-in-law. Painfully he hobbled along over the rough veld. His companions bound up his feet with strips of a towel. But even then the sharp thorns and sticks and jagged stones played havoc with them. After some miles he could go no further, and only after the lapse of many days could he use his feet again.

His men found a few horses. They set him upon one. And on they went across the Vaal and joined the waiting commando—to be attacked soon after by a company of Australians. That night they rode south.

Unfortunately for Smuts and his band, they entered the Free State when Lord Kitchener had just started the greatest of all his mighty drives to date to clear up that territory. Consequently, throughout the month of August the ex-state attorney and his men were ever on the run, dodging in and out like hunted animals, dexterously evading innumerable patrols, often by the skin of their teeth. Everywhere there were soldiers, thousands of them, and all of them seemingly intent on wiping out the little band. And during those dreadful days the only Boer commando Smuts came across was a small one led by Judge J.B.M. Hertzog, his future archenemy. Towards the end of the month he linked up with Van Deventer on the border of the Cape.

The chief problem now was that of crossing the Orange River, the fords of which were closely guarded by order of General French, whom Kitchener had specially detailed to bar the way to Smuts. But Fortune favoured the Boer leader. Among the many crossings there was one that was unsecured. Silently he slipped across with his men in the early dawn near the border of Basutoland. At last they were in British territory. The raid could now begin. But of the original total of three hundred and sixty men, more than one hundred had been lost.

No sooner had they crossed the river than they were attacked by an organized band of Basutos who slew six of Smuts's men before they were driven off.

As the Boers hastened south, four British columns were on their trail,

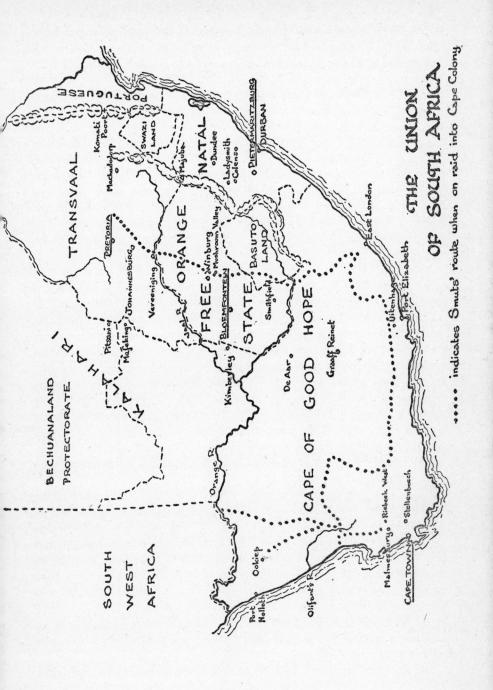

THE UNION OF SOUTH AFRICA

..... indicates Smuts' route when on raid into Cape Colony

TRANSVAAL

PORTUGUESE

Komati Poort
Machadodorp
Pretoria
Johannesburg
Vereeniging
Mafeking
Pitsanio
KALAHARI

SWAZI LAND

Majuba
Dundee
Ladysmith
Colenso
Pietermaritzburg
Durban

NATAL

ORANGE FREE STATE

Winburg
Mushroom Valley
Bloemfontein
Smithfield

BASUTO LAND

V. R.

BECHUANALAND PROTECTORATE

Kimberley
De Aar
Graaff Reinet

CAPE OF GOOD HOPE

East London
Uitenhage
Port Elizabeth

SOUTH WEST AFRICA

Orange R.

Ookiep

Olifant's R.

Port Nolloth

Malmesbury
Riebeck West
Stellenbosch
CAPE TOWN

43

and wherever they twisted and turned native spies and Europeans, chiefly Afrikaners, informed against them.

Then the rains came—torrents of driving, soaking rain—and biting wind that chilled them to the bone. There was no shelter and no rest for all around them were British patrols ready to pounce upon them. Once, for almost three days and three nights, they were constantly on the move. Some of their horses died under them from exhaustion and starvation.

There was no end to the rain. Soaked to the skin, they pushed on through mud and water; and at night, whenever it was safe, they lay down in the slush side by side, sharing their sodden blankets and deriving warmth from one another. In later years, when Smuts held important ministerial positions, men would come and ask him to do something for them, saying that they had slept under the same blanket with him in the Boer War. "And after a time," says Smuts, "I began to wonder if I really had shared blankets with so many different people."

Towards sunset one day they came to a place called the Murderer's Gap, and were told that there were British troops near by. Smuts decided to go reconnoitring himself. There was still in him that innate inability to delegate tasks to others. He imagined that nobody could do a thing as well as he. As a rule he accompanied his scouts. He now went off with three men to spy out the position.

When night had fallen a lonely figure came out of the shadows, on foot. It was Smuts. His horse had been shot under him. Of his companions, Captain Adendorff had been killed and the others, severely wounded, were in the hands of the enemy. He himself had escaped into a little kloof. "One Boer escaped," ran the official British account, "but he probably had so many bullets in him that he would be no further danger."

Hurriedly the Boers left this place, to be ever on the move again—hungry, cold, exhausted, and wet from the interminable rain.

Once, with the pangs of hunger gnawing at their vitals, some of them ate a poisonous fruit and became violently ill. They lay on the ground, retching and gasping, and for some time they were unable to proceed. Smuts was in a bad way. He was tied on to his horse. The commando had to move on. The enemy was on their heels, attacking them in the rear. In his agony the Boer leader directed their flight until they were free from danger again.

Their horses became weaker by the day—lean, wretched, pitiful creatures that had to be led most of the time. The men themselves were in a sorry state. Their clothes were in tatters. Their boots fell from their feet. Occasionally on a farm they would find a few sacks. In these they would cut holes for head and arms and then slip them on to serve as coats. They wound sacking round their tortured feet or old pieces of hide if they were fortunate enough to find any. They had hardly any ammunition left.

The British were everywhere. In an effort to elude them Smuts drove his tired band along inexorably for twenty-four hours until they reached the top of the Stormberge range. But the enemy was with them. From all sides they came to harass the exhausted commando with rifle and machine-gun fire. This, thought the Boers, must be the end.

But in the dusk a hunchback came up to Smuts from a near-by farmhouse. He could lead them to safety, he said. They placed him on a horse and he led the way across a bog, through the British lines. They were comparatively safe again and half dead with fatigue, but Smuts drove them along relentlessly, for almost twenty-four hours longer, through the rain and the mud. Occasionally they would be forced to stop for a short time at a fence or some other barrier. Then, invariably, scores of men would fall asleep on the ground in ridiculous postures. As last, however, after having marched continuously for three days and two nights, they were allowed to rest.

But the dawn of the following day had hardly broken when once again they were forced to flee before the foe along the soggy ground and through the ever-pelting rain, dispirited and dismayed. For days their stomachs had not felt the comforting warmth of hot food nor had their chilled and aching bodies thawed before a blessed fire. For what fuel there was, was sodden with rain water, as was everything else.

Many had been wounded. The worst cases had, perforce, to be abandoned.

The whole trek was a hideous nightmare. What was the point of it, asked the burghers, looking askance at their leader, who, sullen and uncommunicative, sought advice of no man and vouchsafed to none any information as to his plans. But although growls of resentment were heard, all the members of the commando quailed before the indomitable spirit behind the frosty, grey-blue, ruthless eyes of their undaunted leader.

He appeared to be tireless, driven forward by an irresistible urge. For all their grumbling his burghers had the utmost confidence in him. For his part he had freely and even lightly taken upon his shoulders the grave responsibilities inseparable from leadership. But he never spared himself, doing more than his share of work—ever watchful, always scheming. A leader of brave men, he proved to be fearless to the point of recklessness, often needlessly exposing himself to danger. Yet in all those perilous days he never received so much as a scratch.

Towards the middle of September, when their position was wholly desperate, the Boers were told that two hundred British soldiers, well equipped with guns, ammunition, horses, and stores, were lying in wait for them.

Addressing his men briefly and curtly, Smuts told them that unless they captured these things it was all up with them. They attacked fiercely, with a determination born of despair, firing with their customary accuracy from behind every bit of available shelter. The enemy surrendered. Their horses, ammunition, supplies, and uniforms were taken. They were allowed to return to their lines, leaving behind them a commando of jubilant burghers, revived and invigorated and imbued with a new enthusiasm for the fearless man who had led them to victory.

14

SMUTS had long since realized the futility of attempting to stir up rebellion in the Cape Colony. It is true that many rebels were joining his commando. Indeed on account of that Lord Kitchener proclaimed martial law in the Cape in the month of October. But a general rising was out of the question for various reasons, the chief one being the fact that practically all the horses in the province had been seized by the British military authorities. Only mounted commandos could operate in the Cape Colony successfully. Even if horses had been procurable, the absence of grass would have been a serious obstacle. "The question of horses and forage is thus the great stumbling block for our cause in the Cape," said Smuts.

At this stage the guerrilla leader decided to set out for the western Cape, where only scattered detachments of the enemy were posted, where the farmers were particularly sympathetic to the Boer cause, and fodder might be procured with comparative ease, where roads were bad, distances great, and railways non-existent, and where there were several raiding bands which he could organize and, when necessary, consolidate into a single formidable striking force or disperse into small but mobile raiding units.

By now the commando had crossed the Cape midlands and had penetrated beyond the Suurberge right down to the neighbourhood of Algoa Bay. In the distance the men could faintly discern the Indian Ocean and the lights of Port Elizabeth.

But they were forced to retreat to the Suurberge and, when halfway up the mountain, were pursued by a British column in charge of Gorringe. "They [the enemy] were immediately attacked," wrote Smuts, "and hurled down the dangerous incline with great loss. Men and horses trod one another to death, pursued by the embittered Boers. According to the verbal report of some of the members of this column who were captured afterwards their losses in dead and wounded and hurt were two hundred men and seven hundred horses."

Thereafter, dividing his force in two, Smuts ordered Van Deventer to hasten westward to a prearranged rendezvous. He himself, pursued by British columns, cut across the province by way of the Little Karoo in the direction of the Atlantic coast, and then swerved northwest towards Calvinia and the Olifants River, shaking off his pursuers and establishing his headquarters in the mountain fastnesses of that desolate region.

Of the two hundred men who had crossed the Orange River two months previously, forty-five had been lost by death or capture. In the course of traversing "almost every district" in the Cape Colony, Smuts and his commando had been surrounded many times only to escape again, had crossed several great mountain ranges in sight of the enemy, had been engaged in dozens of skirmishes and battles, and had accomplished the longest and most arduous trek of the whole war.

On the results of his expedition Smuts immediately issued a very favourable statement, which caused a stir in Europe, was published in pamphlet form by pro-Boers in Britain, and greatly cheered the hard-pressed burghers in the Free State and the Transvaal. The morale of his men, he wrote, was excellent. Nothing could daunt them; no suffering prevent them from prosecuting the struggle till Right triumphed over Might.

To President Kruger in Europe he sent a report on the war situation in January 1902. It was recently published verbatim in a book by General Kemp, implacable political enemy of Smuts, under the caption "Jan Smuts and John Bull," ostensibly to show what Smuts, today one of the Empire's foremost champions, thought of Britain in 1902. But besides unleashing a venomous attack on John Bull, Smuts's report contained a detailed and very optimistic account of conditions in the republics and the Cape. He wrote of the great danger which threatened British supremacy in the Cape Colony and took a very bright view of the situation in the Free State and the Transvaal, where twenty thousand disciplined veterans were fighting splendidly. Not only was her own tremendous army living on Britain's treasury, but the Boer commandos themselves were doing so. All their rifles, field guns, ammunition, horses, saddles, and bridles, and even, partly, their clothes and, largely, their food were taken from the inexhaustible supplies of Lord Kitchener. Almost invariably did the Boers emerge from battle with more ammunition than they had possessed before the fight. Often they captured such large quantities that whole wagonloads which they could not use were set alight by them. Thus the policy of extermination and attrition from which the enemy expected so much was obviously an idle dream. It was clear that the enemy had no right to assert, as they were doing, that the Boers were fighting a hopeless fight. When Smuts considered how tired and dejected were the British officers and men who fell into their hands and how cheerfully the Boers were fighting, he felt convinced that hope was on their side and hopelessness and despair with the enemy.

Smuts found seventeen commandos in the northwestern Cape. These he divided into three groups, to each of which he assigned a commanding officer promoted by him to the rank of general. One group under Maritz was to operate in the region stretching from the German southwest border along the Atlantic seaboard right down to the Western Province; the second, under Lategan, was to cover the remainder of the northwestern Cape; and the third, under Wynand Malan, was to harass the enemy in the Eastern Province and in the Midlands.

Maritz had only recently returned from a raid in the south, where he had taken much booty, disarmed hundreds of soldiers, and captured several villages. The citizens of Cape Town were greatly alarmed at the report of his approach. Field guns were drawn to the heights above the city in preparation for a determined defence. But Maritz and his band of seventy-five did not venture to launch an attack. On the outskirts of the metropolis they intercepted a post cart and learned from a dispatch in one of the bags that Smuts "had been appointed as assistant commandant general and had already arrived in Calvinia."

At Darling, a town near Smuts's birthplace, one Boonzaaier, an adjutant of Maritz, and five others rode towards the coast, where a British cruiser was lying peacefully at anchor, and fired a few rounds at the vessel. Indignantly the great guns of the ship hurled back defiance in the shape of whistling shells which struck an empty shore, for Boonzaaier and his men had hurriedly decamped. Soon they had joined Maritz again and were speeding north to meet Jan Smuts.

Smuts's work of organization—recruitment and co-ordination—took him on many a long journey over the bare and windswept wastes of the northwest, even right up to the Orange River. There were constant brushes with mounted patrols of the enemy and several battles. In one of these Van Deventer distinguished himself by severely trouncing and putting to flight General Smith-Dorrien and a large force, capturing one hundred and thirty wagons with supplies.

In one of the small commandos operating in the vicinity of Vanrhyns-dorp was a Boer named Lambert Colyn, who was a traitor. One night he slunk quietly into a Boer camp, leading a detachment of British soldiers. They killed and wounded seventeen of Smuts's men and hurried off. But within a week Smuts stormed a British camp successfully and, finding Colyn skulking there, took him prisoner.

Not far away was the farm Atties, belonging to the local Member of Parliament, Mr. van Zyl. Colyn was taken there to be court-martialled.

In a room where lay wounded Ben Bouwer, formerly a clerk under Smuts in Pretoria and now one of his most able commandants, the trial of Colyn was held. Smuts presided. At length he said curtly: "Take him away and shoot him!"

Colyn fell upon his knees, crying, "Have mercy! Have mercy! For the sake of my wife and children, have mercy!"

But Smuts glanced at him coldly, almost dispassionately.

"No, Colyn," he replied, "for you there can be no mercy. You have done the dirty work of the English." And he strode out to the breakfast room, asked one of the farmer's daughters for a cup of coffee, and sat down at a table staring into space.

Close by, a guard on either side of him, passed Colyn, creeping along the floor on his knees and shrieking, "Mercy! Mercy!" But Smuts did not look up.

Hysterically one of Van Zyl's daughters said to Krige, Smuts's brother-in-law: "O God, the man is begging for mercy, and he is to be shot!"

In an outhouse Pastor Kriel spoke to Colyn. "Kneel down and pray!" he said.

"I cannot," replied the doomed man.

"Say the Publican's Prayer."

"I don't know it."

Then the pastor himself knelt down and prayed.

Towards sunset the prisoner was taken out to be shot. A grave had been prepared. Colyn was blindfolded. He begged to see Smuts. But the firing party, knowing Smuts, knew that there was no hope for a reprieve, and the man was shot.

Early in January Smuts had planned to scatter throughout the Cape Colony the commandos operating at that time in their allotted areas under generals immediately subordinate to him.

At a conference held at the farm Soetwater, he gave his lieutenants his reasons for the intended dispersion. Small commandos, acting independently, he said, could commence an offensive in many parts of the Cape. This would compel the Birtish to spread their troops throughout the vast territory and fight in many places, so that they would require many more men and much more equipment. Thereby the prestige of the Boers would be enhanced, the British military authorities in South Africa seriously embarrassed, and British confidence in the war party in England badly shaken, since the latter had already claimed that the war was practically over. So argued Smuts.

But before his plans could be carried into effect the war suddenly ended. Indeed, shortly after the towns of Springbok and Concordia had fallen to his men, while in Namaqualand he was attacking O'okiep with its valuable copper mines, two British officers turned up carrying a white flag and a communication from the British commander in chief, informing Smuts that peace negotiations had been started between the belligerent governments and that his presence was required in Pretoria.

Before leaving for Port Nolloth, whence an English ship was to take him to Cape Town, Smuts addressed his men. "Burghers," he said, "don't worry about the peace during my absence. Don't consider your work to be over. Peace may be concluded, but, on the other hand, the war may be starting only now. An undesirable peace is out of the question. If I come back and there is no peace, we shall go south. Cape Town must be our goal."

Since an armistice had not been declared, fighting did not cease on any front. Maritz continued to hurl crudely fashioned dynamite bombs into O'okiep. But the town held out. Then Maritz became desperate. He recalled the terrible havoc wrought at Braamfontein at the beginning of the war, when two dynamite trains collided. Ruthlessly he decided to blow up O'okiep. His men filled a railway coach with seventeen thousand dynamite cartridges and set it going downhill towards the fort in the town. The fort itself contained a huge supply of dynamite. The burghers held their breath. The coach reached the fort. There was no explosion! The town was saved miraculously!

On board ship Smuts received every attention and was given that measure of respect and courtesy which British diplomacy is wont to accord to a distinguished guest, particularly a hostile one. Although he thawed slightly under the blandishments of the officers whose immediate task was to conciliate him, Smuts remained silent and aloof.

Travelling north by train from Cape Town, he was met at numerous railway stations by British guards of honour. At Matjesfontein General

French paid him a visit and referred admiringly to his amazing trek across the Cape. But Smuts was not to be cajoled, and the abruptness of his manner did not change.

When the train stopped at Kroonstad in the Free State Lord Kitchener himself was there to meet him, a magnificent figure seated on a black charger and surrounded by a bodyguard of Pathans with scimitars, resplendent in oriental dress. The great man entered Smuts's coach and sat down. He started chatting in a very friendly manner. A continuation of the war, he said, would serve no useful purpose. He had four hundred thousand soldiers in South Africa, while the Boers had barely eighteen thousand men. He would be magnanimous to the enemy if they submitted. Smuts remained strictly non-committal. Nor did he shed all his hostility, though he unbent slightly in the face of his visitor's geniality.

15

A PROPOSAL had been made a few months before by the Dutch Prime Minister, Baron Kuyper, that the "Netherlands Government should act as an intermediary between the Boers and Great Britain, as exceptional circumstances precluded the Boers still in the field from negotiating either with the British Government or with the deputation which had been sent by them to Europe." Lord Lansdowne, on behalf of the British Government, had refused to countenance "foreign intervention" but had suggested that the "Boer leaders negotiate directly with Lord Kitchener." Acting on this suggestion, Acting President Burger of the Transvaal had immediately seen fit to commence *pourparlers* with the British commander in chief. Under the circumstances the Free State Government had no option but to discuss the situation with the Transvaal leaders. The meeting was held at Klerksdorp with Lord Kitchener's permission.

When it became obvious that the British Government was determined to deprive the republics of their independence, it was decided that a mandate from the people was required before the executives could negotiate with the invader "on any basis other than independence." Kitchener agreed to provide facilities for the election of delegates in both republics "who would voice the will of the people." These representatives, thirty from each state, were to meet the governments at the village of Vereeniging on the Vaal, on May 15.

In the Free State the authority of Steyn and De Wet was paramount. They were determined to wreck the negotiations. They saw to it that their delegates were unrelenting die-hards, inflexibly opposed to the idea of surrender. They were decidedly optimistic as to the ultimate outcome of the war, since, so they said, the Tommies were "war-worn," while the morale of the burghers was definitely on the upgrade.

On the appointed day the delegates assembled at Vereeniging. It was a cold and cheerless morning, with the mist swirling thickly up from the river.

As a result mainly of De Wet's influence the greater part of the representatives from the Free State had been entrusted by their people with a mere "fixed and limited authority" which compelled them to regard the maintenance of independence as a *sine qua non*. The hands of Delarey's burghers from the Western Transvaal had been tied similarly. But the remaining delegates had been given *carte blanche* to act in the interests of their people. After discussing at some length the abstruse issue of "limited authority," Hertzog and Smuts, the legal experts, cleared up the matter by asserting that "a delegate must be a plenipotentiary with a right to use his vote as he deemed best." Thereupon the actual discussions commenced.

It soon transpired that the Transvaal had decided to surrender at any price. Botha's account of the situation in that territory was disheartening, while Smuts, notwithstanding the fact that the reports sent by him from the Cape had been most encouraging—indeed excessively optimistic—now spoke somewhat gloomily about the Boers' chances in that area. At length even old Delarey threw up the sponge. "Fight to the bitter end?" he cried. "Do you say that? But has the bitter end not come?"

In direct contrast to the defeatist attitude of their brethren from across the Vaal, the majority of the Free State delegates, with Steyn and De Wet in the lead, were uncompromising and defiant. At length, however, they were persuaded to yield a little; and in a tent where President Steyn lay gravely ill, a commission consisting of Botha, De Wet, Delarey, Hertzog, and Smuts was appointed to negotiate with Kitchener and Milner in Pretoria on a "revised basis"—failing which they were to have what was tantamount to blank power of attorney to do what they deemed best.

Kitchener had much sympathy with the Boers, but Milner was cold and somewhat disdainful. He demanded "complete surrender." Smuts tried to compromise. Milner was adamant. Smuts tried to enlist Kitchener's support against the proconsul. Milner tripped him up. Until late at night they argued. "He was impossible," said Smuts afterwards. They arrived at an impasse. Smuts was at his wits' end. Then someone gently touched his arm. It was Kitchener.

"Come out, come out for a little," he whispered. And they quietly left the conference chamber and walked up and down, side by side, in the dark.

"Look here, Smuts," said the great soldier, who was heartily sick of the war, "there is something on my mind that I want to tell you. I can only give it you as my opinion, but my opinion is that in two years' time a Liberal government will be in power: and if a Liberal government comes into power, it will grant you a constitution for South Africa."

"That is a very important pronouncement," said the Boer leader. "If one could be sure of the likes of that, it would make a great difference."

"As I say," came the reply, "it is only my opinion, but honestly I *do* believe that that will happen."

Kitchener's words turned the scale. The Boers with one or two exceptions became tractable. And soon they returned to Vereeniging with a draft agreement bearing Milner's *imprimatur*.

The commission's report was immediately submitted to the delegates. By some it was accepted without enthusiasm, by others it was denounced with scorn. Feeling ran high. Hertzog rushed into Steyn's tent to tell him that Botha and De Wet were having a serious altercation. The latter, speaking heatedly, had said: "Individual members of the deputation have not the moral right to hold private conversations with Lord Kitchener, as Louis Botha and Jan Smuts have done." Unless the President intervened, said Hertzog, anything might happen. Everyone knew that Steyn alone could control his hot-tempered colleague. He summoned De Wet to his tent and pacified him.

Meanwhile, it seems, Smuts had jettisoned the majority of his anti-British prejudices. His conversation with Lord Kitchener had opened up new vistas to his active mind: visions of a union of the Boer states within the British Empire with "a constitution for South Africa," as Kitchener had said; dreams consistent with his "holistic" philosophy of life as evidenced by his quondam enthusiastic recommendation of Rhodes' United South African and Pan-African aspirations and his subsequent espousing of the cause of Kruger in the spirit of the old man's famous utterance in the memorable year of Majuba: "Then shall it be from Zambesi to Simon's Bay, Africa, for the Afrikaner."

To the Reverend Mr. Kestell, chaplain to Steyn and De Wet, he said at Vereeniging: "The idea of the *imperium* grips me. It is something wonderful."

Thus with a few simple words Kitchener had sown a seed of Empire in the heart of Smuts, with what results the world knows.

Smuts was not a delegate himself. At the commencement of the deliberations he had been brought in by Botha in an advisory capacity. But he was asked to address the assembly. And with a greater eloquence than men had believed him capable of he spoke: "The nation calls out. . . . From the prison, from the camps, the graves, the veld, from the womb of the future the nation cries out to us to make a wise decision. . . . We fought for independence, but we must not sacrifice the nation on the altar of independence. . . . Let us bow before the will of God. No one shall ever convince me that this unparalleled sacrifice which the African nation has laid upon the altar of freedom will be in vain. It has been a war for freedom. Its results we leave in God's hands. Perhaps it is His will to lead our nation through defeat, through abasement, yea, and even through the Valley of the Shadow of Death, to the glory of a nobler future, to the light of a brighter day."

By the evening of Saturday, May 31, Kitchener and Milner required a final acceptance, or otherwise, of their terms. But on Saturday morning the Boers had failed as yet to come to an agreement.

There were two proposals before them. One by General Nieuwoudt of the Free State; the other by General Smuts of the Transvaal. The former called for "rejection of the British terms"; the latter urged that they be agreed to without delay. Only the influence of De Wet could move the die-hards. Delarey and Botha knew this.

In desperation they turned to the old guerrilla and begged him to agree to their proposals. And in the end he capitulated. Since Steyn's departure a week previously, he had been acting president of the Free State. He now summoned to him his fellow delegates. "How great was their emotion!" wrote Reverend Mr. Kestell. "I saw the lips quiver of men who had never trembled before a foe. I saw tears brimming in the eyes that had been dry when they had seen their dearest laid in the grave. . . . The men agreed to remain united."

At length the vote was taken on a final proposal drafted by Smuts. The count was: For—fifty-four; against—six. "Here we stand at the grave of two republics," said Acting President Burger. At eleven o'clock that night a treaty of peace was signed in Lord Kitchener's house in Pretoria. It was the Treaty of Vereeniging.

Silently the Boer plenipotentiaries left for their homes, having looked upon the wreckage of their proudest heritage.

Part of Rhodes's dream had been realized. From the Limpopo to the southernmost point of Africa the map was red. But the Colossus never saw the fulfilment of his desire. Several weeks before hostilities ceased, he had gone to his account, having died of heart disease in his tiny cottage at Muizenberg near Cape Town on March 26.

An acute attack of appendicitis on the part of King Edward synchronized with the conclusion of peace. Never in the memory of our fathers has an unhappy event been so opportune. It seemed to soften overnight the hearts of the Continental detractors of the British race. It had an extraordinarily favourable effect on what was at best a delicate situation, "and there was a happy revival of benevolence among the nations."

SECTION II

16

THE COUNTRY which for three years had been ravaged by the dogs of war was now at peace. Back to their commandos went the Boer leaders to bring to their men the tidings and to face their anger and their scorn.

At Soetwater, near Calvinia, in the northwestern Cape, Smuts met his burghers. In the evening of June 14 he addressed them. "Officers, burghers, countrymen," he said, "my task here tonight is a sadder one than has ever hitherto fallen to my lot." He told them of Vereeniging and the conditions of surrender. He beheld in their faces bewilderment, unbelief, and agony. He saw many strong men sobbing like children, while several fell down in a faint. He heard Japie Neser shout out hysterically, "Jan Smuts, you have betrayed us!" His heart was sick, for he knew what they had suffered. But he said no more, and, though his face was pale and drawn, he gave no further sign of emotion.

He went back to Pretoria to start life anew. He returned to the bar where, as formerly, he was not an outstanding pleader, and few important briefs came his way. But he made a good living.

His defence of Stefanus Johannes Paulus Smit, grandson of Paul Kruger, was sensational. Smit was arraigned on a charge of having murdered a man called Davis, a moneylender, near Swartspruit. Smuts saved him from the gallows on a flimsy plea of insanity—one without precedent in the Transvaal and based on a single fact: the man's mother had been an epileptic. The accused was duly sent to an asylum for the insane. A year or two later he was released. In 1914 he joined the rebels and fought against Smuts!

His legal work gave Smuts little satisfaction. Normally it would have acted as a very inadequate outlet for his ebullient energies. But engulfed as he was in a sea of despair—as is evidenced by excessively pessimistic letters to his friend, Miss Emily Hobhouse—he had little inclination for

56

work. The reaction following upon the war had set in, and it weighed heavily on him. The drab existence of a moderately successful barrister held no attraction for an ambitious man who before his thirtieth year had been Paul Kruger's lieutenant and a "national leader"; who in the course of an adventurous and romantic, if tragic, war had felt the stimulus of leadership and tasted the joys of power; and who in the wild phantasmagoria of his dreams had seen himself elevated to the very pinnacle of fame. And now there was this dull stagnation, and nothing else. He fretted and fumed. He yearned for the free life in the veld, the joy of tired muscles relaxing under the stars, pulsating adventure, and the spur of achievement. He longed for power. But he was helpless and hopeless. "I see no ray of light in the future," he wrote to Miss Hobhouse.

Meanwhile Jameson, a few years after his release from Holloway Prison whither his Raid activities had taken him, was about to become Prime Minister of the Cape; and Lord Milner, in addition to being High Commissioner of the Cape, had also become governor of the newly conquered crown colonies. He was engrossed in reconstruction work. His headquarters were at Johannesburg.

Aided by his famous "Balliol Kindergarten"—a galaxy of university graduates whom he had specially selected in Britain—Milner had taken over the administration of the former republics at the end of the war. Among the proconsul's talented assistants were John Buchan and Patrick Duncan (later governors general of Canada and South Africa respectively), Lionel Curtis, Geoffrey Dawson, and Philip Kerr (who became Lord Lothian).

It was the avowed object of the new regime to bring about "a federated British South Africa in a federated British Empire" with an Imperial Parliament in Britain directing its destinies from afar. They reckoned, however, without the growing momentum of that rampant Colonial Nationalism which was soon to change radically the character of the old imperialism. In an ill-conceived attempt to anglicize the Boers in record time, they all but banished Dutch from the schools. But all their attempts to denationalize these people were doomed from the outset, for they failed to take into consideration the unyielding firmness of the Boer character. Their efforts served but to stir up extreme resentment and to precipitate a fresh outbreak of Afrikaner nationalism.

Of the foremost opponents of Milner and Milnerism were J. C. Smuts and J. B. M. Hertzog; the former in the Transvaal, the latter in the Orange River Colony, as the Free State was now called.

Racked by envy and galled by frustration, Smuts beheld the haughty Milner and his "kindergarten" occupying those selfsame seats of government from which he and his Boer colleagues had been forcibly ejected. An almost unreasonable bitterness, begotten of his thwarted ambition, tortured him. And Milner epitomized those forces of oppression which shackled him—Milner the satrap, whose hauteur invariably infuriated him and whose arrival in Africa had spelled ruin to Afrikanerdom in general and Jan Smuts in particular. Milner was his archenemy. He and what he stood for must be destroyed.

But it was only when Botha moved to Pretoria that Smuts's ideas about accomplishing the undoing of Milner crystallized into a definite plan of action. During their talks on the stoep of Botha's house at Sunnyside the two friends agreed that the future of South Africa lay within the British Empire. Botha had been to Europe with De Wet and Delarey to collect money for reconstruction purposes and had spoken to leading British politicians. He assured Smuts that the self-government which Kitchener had all but promised the ex-republics must inevitably come. Botha had a soothing influence on his friend, who gradually became revitalized and began to dream once again dreams of the future and to evolve schemes wherewith to expedite the advent of self-government by bringing to pass the speedy downfall of Milner.

The acquiring of responsible government for the conquered states did not constitute the ultimate goal of Smuts's ambitions. At heart he was still the disciple of Rhodes, and no sooner had he shaken off the fetters of his dark despair under the influence of Botha than the idea of empire which had gripped him at Vereeniging revived within him, and he saw visions of a united South Africa stretching from Cape Agulhas to the Limpopo and beyond—a nation in its own right, but within the Empire.

The sooner to achieve his end, he attacked the Milner administration and the governor himself whenever and wherever possible, with Botha and the other Boer leaders backing him up strongly. Milner promptly riposted with an invitation to Smuts, Botha, and Delarey to serve on the Legislative Council of the Transvaal. But this they declined to do, and a Rand capitalist newspaper launched a scathing attack on Smuts. "Who is Mr. Smuts?" it asked. "He is one of the five men chiefly responsible for the war, a man of intensely bitter feelings, a type of Afrikaner who . . . used every effort to keep the races apart. . . ."

Smuts took little notice of personal attacks. He pursued unswervingly his chosen way. To assist him and his friends in their campaign against Milner there came a great drought; and after it, violent storms, severe frosts, and a locust plague destroying what crops remained. There was suffering throughout the land and much dissatisfaction with the new regime. The position was aggravated by the temporary failure of the gold mines, which, affected adversely by a shortage of native labour, were giving unsatisfactory returns.

The decline in the gold output was a serious blow to Milner who, having envisaged a great postwar expansion of the gold-mining industry, had laid his reconstruction plans accordingly. Seeking to remedy matters, he forthwith imported very cheap Chinese labour, and thereby brought about his ears a hornets' nest. From the Liberals in England there came the cry of "Chinese Slavery," while from the throat of Afrikanerdom there rose a mighty roar of protest against the wilful importation, so it was said, of another colour problem.

The clamouring tongues found their foremost champion in the person of Jan Smuts. He was the spearhead of all the violent attacks made on Milner, his kindergarten, and his whole administration on platform and in private, in letters and in the press. He accused the governor of seeking to benefit his friends with an administration which was a "carnival of extravagance" in a country "which seems to be verging on public bankruptcy," and charged him with plotting to extirpate the very soul of the Afrikaner race.

In an open letter signed by Botha but written by Smuts, the Repatriation Department was dubbed "a complete and dismal failure," the veracity of Milner's dispatches questioned, his policy of denationalization severely censured, sharp judgment passed on the Chinese labour question, and the mine magnates, alleged associates of the governor, fiercely taken to task. "The Transvaal Government is almost completely dictated to by the magnates. The whole policy of the Government is inspired by fear and distrust." Elsewhere he called the gold mines "a sham industry . . . a bogus industry, with its reputation kept going for the purpose of still further swindling the investing public of Europe."

Much of his criticism was based on incontrovertible facts, but a great deal of it was wanton misrepresentation. Nevertheless, in the course of time, it had the desired effect. Not only did it bring Lord Milner into disrepute, but, combined with Hertzog's efforts against imperialism in the Orange River Colony, it accelerated the growing revival of Afrikaner sentiment, stimulated the awakening "Spirit of South African Nationalism," and gave impetus to the increasing demands for responsible government.

Soon the Transvaal and the Free State were beehives of political activity. In the former colony many British South Africans allied themselves to the solid phalanx of Afrikaners clamouring for self-government with ever-growing urgency. The speedy fulfilment of their demands seemed more than likely. From England came encouraging reports predicting an overwhelming victory for the Liberals at the coming elections. The war cry of "Chinese slavery in the South African gold mines" was being exploited to the full, and there was much evidence of its potency. Obviously there would soon be a Liberal government at Westminster.

Smuts and Botha, excited to action by these reports and by the increasing vehemence of the people's nationalist aspirations, united the Afrikaners in the Transvaal—Hands-uppers as well as Die-hards—in one political party which they named *Het Volk* (The People). Among its avowed aims were self-government and conciliation of the races. In the Free State a similar organization came into being. It was sponsored by Steyn and Hertzog. It was called the *Orangia Unie*. At the same time in the Cape Colony the Afrikaner Bond was reorganized "on a broader basis" and renamed the South African party in order to make it more palatable to would-be British supporters. "The leaven of South Africanism was commencing to work powerfully."

At this time Smuts's father still represented Malmesbury in the Cape Parliament. Often, after the war, he had listened quietly to scurrilous attacks on his son made by men like Francis Oates and John Laing of the so-called Suspensionist movement. They had stated with emphasis that Jan would end his life on the gallows. But John X. Merriman's prediction of "a great future in a great unified South African Parliament for Jan Smuts" had more than compensated the old man for the unfriendly words of the Suspensionists.

With the establishment of Het Volk Smuts had become an active politician again. It was the first rung upon the ladder which was to lead to the fulfilment of Merriman's prophecy.

Jan Smuts had once more found his métier.

17

OF THE TWO LEADERS of Het Volk, Botha was by far the more popular. A great, massive, almost grossly moulded, swarthy Afrikaner, with large eyes under arched eyebrows and full lips in keeping with his heavy face, he was warm-hearted, gentle, and courteous, entertaining lavishly and benevolently on his farm in the hospitable old Boer fashion—a genial host. Tact and patience he had in abundance, and that valuable and indefinable quality of personal magnetism which is not the prerogative of the

great. With trusting hearts men came to him with their troubles great
and small. Always he had the time and the patience to hear them out, and
greatly encouraged they would take their leave, firmly believing that
Louis Botha was their personal friend and that they—each and every
one, individually—meant a great deal to him.

Much slighter in build and very fair in contrast with his colleague's
swarthiness was Jan Smuts, spare, and lively in his movements. He was
almost entirely wanting in tact. His uncommunicative nature, cold inaccessibility, and all-too-obvious lack of interest in people and their problems beyond the immediate difficulty on which they had come to consult
him as clients, repelled and antagonized his fellows, and many members
of Het Volk looked askance at him while their hearts warmed to Botha.

But Smuts's brain directed the organization of Het Volk, and behind
the rapid growth of that organization lay, in the main, his extraordinary
capacity for hard work and clear thinking.

The Lyttleton Letters Patent, making sweeping concessions in respect
of a new legislature for the Transvaal, were rejected by the Boer leaders
prompted by Smuts. They reiterated their demand for full self-government.

It was with great relief that they witnessed Lord Milner's departure
in the winter of 1905, when his term of office was over. His administration, Smuts said afterwards, was "the darkest period in the history of the
Transvaal."

This haughty Colonial Governor was succeeded by Lord Selborne, a
tactful and courteous gentleman and a diplomat whose first speeches
particularly were triumphs of diplomacy. He played up to both Botha
and Smuts, and was soon in their good graces.

Meanwhile, in Great Britain, matters were swiftly approaching a
climax. The Conservatives were in bad odour. They had been so for
some time. The people of Great Britain had had a surfeit of the maffick-
ing Jingoes who for nearly twenty years had ruled the country. The
Liberals began to win almost every bye-election. They found that their
most potent battle cries were those relating to "Chinese slavery in the
South African gold mines." They promptly coined a large number of
them, and, armed with these and with bloodthirsty tales luridly depicting
this "Slavery under the Union Jack," they dealt heavy blows. And finally,
in December of 1905, Balfour's ministry fell and the Liberals were
returned to power with a tremendous majority, the like of which had not
been seen since the days of the Reform Act in the first half of the nineteenth century. Mr. Henry Campbell-Bannerman became Prime Minister.
His Cabinet included Mr. Winston Churchill, Mr. Lloyd George, Mr.
H. Asquith, and Lord Morley.

No sooner had the Conservatives been defeated than Smuts was hurriedly dispatched to England by Het Volk to sound Campbell-Bannerman
about responsible government.

He went to interview all the great men among the Liberals. Of these
he knew only Winston Churchill, whom he had met near Ladysmith
during the Boer War, soon after the Englishman had been taken prisoner. Churchill and Morley were none too optimistic about the ultimate
success of Smuts's mission; indeed the former was not in favour of self-
government for the Transvaal. Lloyd George, however, was hopeful and
promised his assistance.

Last of all Smuts visited Campbell-Bannerman, with whom he had a
heart-to-heart talk. "I explained our position to him," he stated afterwards, "and said we were anxious to co-operate with the English. . . .
I could see Campbell-Bannerman was listening sympathetically." At
length the Prime Minister said, "Smuts, you have convinced me." "That
talk," in the words of Smuts, "settled the future of South Africa."

Next day a Cabinet meeting was held. Addressing his ministers,
Campbell-Bannerman said: "I have made up my mind that we must scrap
the Lyttleton constitution and start afresh and make partners of the Boers.
. . ." He spoke for ten minutes, but so convincingly that when he
stopped his whole Cabinet was with him. "The speech," said Lloyd
George afterwards, "moved at least one member of the Cabinet to tears.
It was the most impressive thing I ever saw."

Proudly Smuts returned to South Africa. And he had reason to be
satisfied with himself, for it is to be doubted whether any other man in
the Transvaal could so effortlessly have achieved what he had done.
Self-government for the Transvaal would not be long delayed. The
leaders of Het Volk, the strongest party by far in the northern colony,
would undoubtedly take over the administration. In Smuts's heart there
was joy and a feeling of great thankfulness towards Campbell-
Bannerman. The Boers would rule the Transvaal again, and to Smuts
would come once more those things which to him were the essence of
life and which had so long been denied him: political opportunity, scope
for ambition and power. A great future for himself within the vast British
Empire.

As these thoughts crowded into his mind and the world seemed bright
again, the disciple of Rhodes, looking beyond the immediate future,
visualized afresh, and with a greater clarity than before because of the
greater certainty of fulfilment, a united South Africa, of Afrikaners and
Englishmen, having towards the north unlimited opportunities for expan-

sion—a great and growing whole, but always within the greater whole of the Empire.

Inspired by his ultimate vision, he toured the country to spread the gospel of race conciliation. And since there was so much at stake he curbed his impatience with his slow-thinking fellows, schooled himself to forbearance and a show of friendliness, and pleaded eloquently for conciliation, co-operation, and "a blending of races." "Let us work," said he, "to attain . . . a united South Africa."

Botha admired the keen insight of this man of thirty-five, eight years younger than himself, and was stirred by the Smutsian vision. Others, too, responded favourably. But more often than not Smuts ran up against a stone wall of hostility: for to the majority of men of both races he had become known as "slim" (crafty) Jannie, and they wondered what ulterior motives lay behind his pleading; moreover, they were torn by a strong racial antipathy that could not be uprooted in a day.

Even in Mrs. Smuts he found no willing disciple but a hostile critic whose feeling of bitterness towards the English had not abated. She remained at heart an Afrikaner woman and a republican, so much so that of her six surviving children all—with the exception of the youngest, a girl, who first saw the light of day during the rebellion of 1914 and bears the name of Louis Delarey Smuts, after old General Delarey—were born literally under the republican flag which she caused to be unfurled over her bed whenever the birth of a child was imminent. For many years she shunned public life, giving politics a wide berth and always staying at home when her husband went overseas—as he frequently did. "My husband," she says, "warned me that I would probably be punished for my bitterness by our children marrying Englishmen." And, indeed, the husbands of two of the three married daughters are Englishmen.

In December 1906 full responsible government was granted to the Transvaal, and a few months later the Orange River Colony received similar constitutional rights. Absolute majorities were gained at the elections by Het Volk in the northern and the Orangia Unie in the southern colony. Of the latter Abraham Fischer became Prime Minister, Generals de Wet and Hertzog becoming members of his cabinet.

It was rumoured that Smuts would be called upon to become the first Prime Minister of the Transvaal. His claims were indisputable: he had served under Kruger as a member of the patriarch's government; the acquiring of self-rule had been due primarily to his efforts; and intellectually he towered over all his colleagues. But he supported Botha's title to the premiership and afterwards wrote to John X. Merriman: "I considered it would be a mistake to take precedence over Botha, who is really one of the finest men South Africa has ever produced." Standing down for Botha, as was proved by the event, was one of Smuts's wisest acts throughout the course of his long and changeful political career. Botha, then, became Prime Minister with Smuts as his Colonial Secretary and Minister of Education.

Thus, less than six years after Vereeniging, the ex-republics were ruled again by Boers—Boer generals of the Boer War. And although South African Nationalism was in the ascendant, as was Canadian and Australian Nationalism, yet the "magnificent venture of faith" of Campbell-Bannerman was destined not only to preserve South Africa for the British Empire but to maintain in times of great stress the solidarity of that empire taken as a whole—through the person of Jan Smuts.

Campbell-Bannerman's treatment of the Boers was, according to Smuts, "one of the wisest political settlements ever made in the history of the English nation." It undoubtedly was—mainly because Smuts's conversion to British imperialism became complete when the Liberals gave responsible government to the Transvaal, and Smuts was fated to become the leading champion of the Empire in the days of her direst need.

Campbell-Bannerman was once known as "the Apostle of Imperial Disintegration." It was indubitably a misnomer. He was, in point of fact, the originator of that new and saner imperialism which kept the Empire intact.

SECTION III

18

EAGERLY, indeed, almost too eagerly, the new regime took over the Milner administration and rapidly brought about changes in it. Smuts was the brain of the Ministry. "It was a Botha government," wrote a sagacious commentator, "but Smuts pulled the strings." He was regarded by all as the "Power behind the Throne." A cartoon by A. W. Lloyd, in an English paper, depicting a meeting of Botha's Cabinet gave to each of the Ministers the face of Smuts. Underneath was this explanation of the picture: "The controlling interest of General Smuts in the Cabinet is so apparent that the Government may be said to be concentrated in him alone." And this was not an overstatement. For Smuts was, in truth, the whole Government.

Whenever it was possible, however, he sought to avoid the limelight, always pushing Botha into the foreground while he himself worked silently behind the scenes.

When the Prime Minister addressed the House, Smuts would sit by, prompting him whenever he was at a loss for a word, and aiding him in every possible way. But, as a rule, Smuts himself was the Government's mouthpiece in the House, announcing its policy on important questions, submitting schemes for the members' approval, introducing bills which he had drafted himself, and taking them through all the stages, replying to questions (not necessarily concerning his own particular departments), and invariably evincing an encyclopaedic knowledge of all the affairs of the Government.

He laboured almost without cessation, gladly giving vent to that great store of bottled-up energy which, throughout the years of enforced idleness and frustration, had eaten the very life out of him. He worked much more than was necessary, for he was, as he had been in the days of

Kruger, incapable of entrusting tasks to his underlings, having absolute confidence only in his own powers. He would take over the portfolios of any Minister who, through ill-health or otherwise, might be absent on leave. It was said that he worked so hard that he was often forced to soothe his jaded nerves with a wet towel twisted round his head. Lane, his private secretary, was a great help to him. It was this man's chief task to keep everybody away from Smuts when he was busy.

With the great prospect of a united South Africa always impinging on his thoughts, Smuts made tremendous efforts, particularly in the beginning, by effecting compromises and with every other means at his disposal, to smooth out those differences between the races which had been responsible for so much strife and misery.

It is more than possible that matters developed along lines different in many essentials from what had been anticipated by the members of his own race, who had been led to expect developments with a definite pro-Afrikaner bias, such as Hertzog was bringing about in the Free State to offset the anglicizing influence of the old regime. However that may be, Smuts managed in a great measure, with a display of patience highly commendable in a man so impatient by nature, temporarily to uproot active racialism from the body politic.

Before long, however, he became again imperious in his ways, and he began to apply the bludgeon where formerly he had made use of honeyed words. He "tasted the delight of having his own way and found it good." At heart he was a dictator.

The strain of his unceasing labours affected his nerves. He was high strung and easily provoked. Often he would flare up unnecessarily.

Driven on by a fury of energy and impatient of the long-winded discussions of his mental inferiors and of those dreary delays which are inseparable from the slow-working machinery of parliamentary procedure, he told Botha to instruct party members to speak their minds in the party caucus but to say as little as possible in the House. Already men said that he regarded Parliament as an unnecessary institution to be tolerated only because the law of the land demanded its survival. His restless impatience was understandable. For, in the end, despite all the discussions and palaver of Parliament, the will of Smuts prevailed. Thus did he become increasingly dictatorial in his manner, having absolute confidence only in himself and fast becoming intolerant of all opposition.

The development of the "masterful side" of his nature soon brought him into bitter conflict with Hertzog and Afrikanerdom, with the capitalists and with organized labour and with Mahatma Gandhi.

Both in the Free State and in the Transvaal the Boers, in a desperate effort to preserve their own cultural identity by opposing Milner's policy of "Anglicization through Education," had in the years immediately after the war established their own Christian national schools. It was the spearhead of that powerful cultural reaction which, together with the political reaction led by Botha and Smuts in the Transvaal, and Fischer and Hertzog in the Orange Free State, constituted Afrikanerdom's natural resistance to what the Boers regarded as "the scourge of Milnerism."

With the advent of responsible government Hertzog was determined to obtain "absolute equality of treatment" for the two races in the Free State. In his capacity as Minister of Education he insisted on that equality for children and teachers of both races and on the enforcement of equal language rights in the schools. In the course of pressing home his policy, he saw fit to dismiss three English inspectors who promptly took legal proceedings against him, thereby entrenching him the more firmly in the hearts of all Anglophobes. The Director of Education, an Englishman, resigned. For his pains Hertzog was showered with abuse by the British minority in the colony and denounced throughout the subcontinent as an anti-British agitator and a die-hard racialist.

While both cultural and political movements were very powerful in the Free State, the former had but little strength in the Transvaal where Botha and Smuts were willing to sacrifice cultural privileges for political supremacy. It was part of their calculated policy of conciliation both to condemn the continued existence of Christian national schools and to introduce into the Transvaal a system of education devised by Smuts which undoubtedly pandered to British sentiment to the detriment of Afrikaner interests in the Transvaal, in that English was made a compulsory subject in the schools while Dutch was merely optional.

Smuts's educational policy antagonized Hertzog, who, as the coming champion of Afrikanerdom, began to regard the doings of Smuts and Botha with ever-increasing distrust. These leaders, he believed, were consenting to "a position of inferiority for the Dutch." Here began his quarrel with them. It was destined to break up the first government of a United South Africa, to cleave Afrikanerdom asunder, and to influence for more than two decades the course of South African history.

19

WHEN SMUTS BEGAN to repatriate the Chinese, the mine magnates were up in arms. Their representatives took the matter to Parliament. The millionaires had great wealth, great influence, and much power. But they were up against Smuts who was, in effect, the supreme ruler of the Transvaal. He scorned to fence with them. He bludgeoned them into silence. The Government had decided to repatriate the Chinese. Nothing would stop it. He would show the magnates *who* ruled the Transvaal. If they were not careful the Government itself would work the mines. . . . The Chinese went home. The capitalist newspapers one by one began to call Smuts "General."

Having ended his skirmish with the bosses, Smuts had his first brush with the miners themselves. It was not a serious affair in itself, but it set in motion a train of events which was to hurl Smuts from office when he was in the fullness of his powers. Six thousand miners came out on strike. With two English regiments Smuts drove them back to their tasks. It was his thirty-seventh birthday. An evil day for him—this day on which he first antagonized organized labour by brandishing the mailed fist.

Of all the problems Smuts was called upon to face, the Indian question irritated and puzzled him most, mainly because, in tackling it, he had to pit himself against the exasperating passive resistance and baffling Soul Force (*Satyagraha*) of Mohandas Karamchand Gandhi.

This man had arrived in Durban several years before the close of the nineteenth century—a cultured British Indian gentleman, a barrister come to act as counsel for a countryman in a court case.

It was soon made clear to him that in South Africa he was nothing more than a common or garden coolie. Travelling by train to Pretoria with a first-class ticket, he refused to remove himself to the van when a fellow passenger objected to his presence. At a wayside station a policeman was summoned and forthwith Gandhi was seized by the collar of his coat and flung out onto the dark platform. Later, in the Transvaal, he was brutally assaulted by a train conductor for refusing to sit on a piece of sacking on the footboard of a coach when, as usual, he was travelling with a first-class ticket. Then, again, he was arrested one evening and told that "niggers" ought not to venture abroad without a pass after the nine-o'clock curfew. Slowly it dawned on Gandhi that there was work for him to do in Africa—work relating to "colour prejudice."

Soon after his assumption of office Smuts, as Colonial Secretary, passed legislation making provision for compulsory registration of all Indians and other Asiatics in the Transvaal and effectively limiting immigration by demanding, *inter alia,* that all would-be immigrants be subjected to an "education test." Then from all sides there came howls of resentment and formal statements of disapproval—from the Transvaal Indians, from Natal, from the Cape, and from Mother India with her teeming millions.

The champion of the Indians was Gandhi, a quiet, unassuming, dark little figure of a man with "indomitable spiritual qualities" that had been nourished on the oppression of the Transvaal of Kruger and of Milner, and were now becoming strong in the Transvaal of Smuts.

There resulted a struggle which soon resolved itself into a duel between Smuts and Gandhi and was watched with interest by almost the whole of the English-speaking world outside America.

Only when finally the Imperial Government itself endorsed Smuts's legislation did it become apparent that the Boer had drawn first blood.

But Gandhi was not to be daunted. Again and again he appealed strongly to Smuts to remove the "stigma of discrimination" against his countrymen. But impatiently and not without anger Smuts brushed his protests aside. And then Gandhi lunged back with the "weapon of passive resistance," which he had forged in Africa and the power of which in days to come the British Empire and the world would learn.

Smuts understood force. He could deal with it. He *had* dealt with it. But passive resistance baffled him. It was so perplexingly resilient. He threatened Gandhi. But Gandhi remained calm and unruffled. He sent some Indians to prison. Gandhi led them into prison himself. Smuts then decided to compromise. He made certain promises about concessions—so, at least, Gandhi alleged. When, afterwards, Smuts denied having made them, Gandhi quietly returned to civil disobedience.

In this dingdong battle Gandhi would beg "for an improvement in the position" of Indians in South Africa, and Smuts would occasionally propitiate with small concessions, particularly after "earnest representations" had been made by Whitehall. But, on the whole, he was adamant. Sometimes Gandhi would lead unregistered Indians across the Transvaal border from Natal, thus setting at nought the law of the land. And then gladly he would go to prison. About his imprisonment in Bloemfontein he said: "The prospect of uninterrupted study for a year filled me with joy."

With the birth of the Union of South Africa the duel between Gandhi and Smuts was carried on on a wider stage, with Smuts seeking by legislation to prevent any further immigration of Asiatics and Gandhi insistently demanding "free entry and the grant of full citizen rights to Indians in South Africa on a basis of equality with Europeans." For many reasons the setting open of the gates of the Union to a great brown flood of Untouchables would from every point of view have been catastrophic for the white population. Nevertheless, such had become the Indian barrister's demands.

Throughout the great struggle he practised assiduously his doctrine of self-abnegation and his vows of chastity (bramacharia), and gradually he tempered and burnished those spiritual weapons until they were bright and flawless like Toledo blades and far more dangerous.

In 1913, flouting the authority of Smuts, he led twenty-seven hundred of his followers into the Transvaal and was thrown into jail. There were serious repercussions, and then a settlement of sorts. But Smuts's Immigration Act became law—not, however, before the word "Asiatic" had been deleted from the bill in deference to Gandhi's feelings.

Then, acquiescing in the Indian Relief Act and expressing satisfaction with various promises given by Smuts anent "vested rights," Mohandas Karamchand Gandhi returned at last to India with a "profound distrust of Western civilization" and a feeling that it represented nothing but "a triumph of gross materialism and brute force." For services rendered to India he received the Kaisar-i-Hind gold medal.

Thus ended the struggle between the powerful blond European, backed up by the material forces of the West, and the weak little dark Oriental, strengthened by the mysterious spiritual forces of the East—the former destined to become the most potent cohesive influence in the fabric of the British Empire; the latter, as the deified leader of three hundred and fifty million Indians clamouring at his instigation for Swaraj, fated to be the most powerful disruptive force in that selfsame organism.

20

ALWAYS a restraining influence on Smuts, Botha was very necessary to his young colleague. There was all the world of difference between the two men. Not only in physical appearance were they wholly dissimilar, but in almost every other respect. Each had his own peculiar distinctive qualities, but, as Lord Buxton says, "they were essentially complementary the one to the other."

Smuts, a voracious reader all his life and an indefatigable worker, took no interest whatsoever in games, much to the surprise of Botha, whose interests were normal. For relaxation the latter loved a game of bridge, conversation, and company, while the former, as a rule, sought recreation amid his dry documents and papers and his books.

It has been said that Botha regarded the world with the eye of a cattle farmer, while Smuts's outlook has been described as that of a physicist.

In contrast with Smuts's erudition Botha had little education, his knowledge of English, for example, being rudimentary. With amazing intellectual power and a ready gift of epigram, his friend could, when necessary, turn platitudes into paradoxes and lead his audiences up the garden path, but Botha himself was incapable of imitating such subtle ingenuity.

While Botha demanded less of people than Smuts and was tactful, long-suffering, and kind, the younger man was maladroit in dealing with people, intolerant, and, often, high-handed. He frequently antagonized members of his own party, either by his abrupt ways and moodiness or by failing to notice people when he was deeply engrossed in a problem. Botha, however, was a practical politician and an excellent "mixer" who would, in his pleasant way, offer his tobacco pouch to an opponent, have a heart-to-heart talk with him over a cup of coffee, and frequently turn him into a supporter—not by the weight of his arguments but by sheer friendliness and personal magnetism.

For all his sparkling intellect, energy, and general ability, Smuts was sadly lacking in the great gift of human sympathy and understanding with which Botha was generously endowed—a quality which is indispensable in public life. Botha managed all persons with consummate ease. Not so Smuts. Instinctively men turned to the older man and were repelled by the younger, so that often Botha had to come to the rescue of his brilliant junior, and with quiet, soothing words calm wrathful men in whom Smuts had evoked hostility.

Smuts, phenomenally energetic and overeager to forge ahead without losing time, was frequently too hasty in his conclusions and inclined rather "to decide a question himself than discuss it," while Botha, with calm endurance, would inquire into a matter at length and consider arguments put forward by advisers and others before taking action. But often Botha perceived instinctively with an intuition transcending reason what his colleague achieved by cold, logical reasoning.

Smuts could never have ruled the Transvaal without Botha. It was mainly the realization of this that induced him to stand down in favour of the older man in the matter of the premiership.

21

SMUTS'S ELOQUENT PLEADING with Campbell-Bannerman had been inspired largely by his ultimate goal of a united South Africa. Now, firmly entrenched in his new position of influence and power, he began to strain every nerve towards the attainment of his heart's desire. Various great men, in their time, had entertained this idea of a federation of the states of southern Africa. Among them there had been the British Colonial Secretary, Lord Carnarvon, J. H. Hofmeyr, Paul Kruger, and Cecil John Rhodes. But it had been left to Smuts to consummate the great notion conceived by them all and to bring into actual existence the Union of South Africa.

The time was opportune. It was being gradually realized that a union of the colonies must ultimately come. It was natural. It was urgent. That South Africa should be partitioned into four sections independent of one another was both artificial and unsound. It had given rise to numerous tariff difficulties which Lord Milner had sought to clear away by establishing a temporary Customs and Tariff Convention, and it had brought into being a multitude of other problems the solution of which obviously lay in union. The abolition of tariff barriers was essential. The establishment of one railway system, one educational system and, in short, one common centralized system in respect of almost everything, under the direction of one government, would, while involving less expenditure of public money, be far more effective than a plurality of such bodies. Moreover, the native, coloured, and Indian questions and, for that matter, every other problem which the four colonies had in common could be dealt with suitably only by a central authority representing a concert of the states in a union.

Numerous conferences held by delegates sincerely desirous of effecting some solution of many of the problems arising out of the artificial partitioning of the subcontinent had invariably proved to be abortive.

Inspired by Oliver's *Alexander Hamilton,* the former members of Milner's kindergarten—who in Smuts had found a master as brilliant as

Lord Milner and more exacting—began actively to discuss the practical aspects of that union which their new chief so ardently desired. Smuts and Botha discussed with the chief justice of the Cape Colony the practicability of establishing a federal Court of Appeal.

Soon in every part of South Africa men began to agitate for "closer union." In the Cape, Merriman (the new Prime Minister), Hofmeyr, F. S. Malan, and Jameson strongly supported the idea; so did many influential men in Natal. The Free State appeared to be indifferent, but in time Hertzog and ex-President Steyn began to display some enthusiasm; and in the Transvaal, Botha and other leaders were obviously inspired by the ardour of Smuts. A memorandum issued by Lord Selborne emphasized the immediate desirability of bringing the matter to a head. Before long the idea of some sort of federation of the four states was foremost in the minds of all South Africans, for it was powerfully propagandized in the street, in the press, and on the public platforms throughout the land. The parliaments of the four colonies discussed it at great length and duly declared themselves in favor of it. In every city and in the large towns closer union societies came into being. Finally, at an intercolonial conference held at Pretoria in May 1908, ostensibly to adjust customs difficulties and clear up railway problems, Smuts proposed six resolutions—which Merriman seconded—demanding "a national convention to discuss the closer political and economic union of the South African colonies." These formal proposals were subsequently confirmed by the parliaments of the four states.

All, it seemed, was set fair for union.

But there remained for Smuts a great deal of spadework in the Transvaal itself before he could get down to the actual task of achieving a final union of the states, for the project met with a good deal of opposition from those who felt that its accomplishment would be detrimental to their own personal interests. In contrast with the other states, which were poor, the Transvaal possessed fabulous wealth in its gold mines. The prospect of a division of these riches could hardly be contemplated with equanimity by the people living on the Reef itself, and even by those who gained only indirectly by the profits of the mines. Then there were racial malcontents: Englishmen who distrusted the scheme, believing that it connoted the setting up of an Afrikaner bloc, and Afrikaners who had a rooted aversion to uniting with the English of Natal.

Smuts was not to be baulked at this stage of developments. Where it was possible, he curtly brushed aside any objections that were raised with his customary impatience. But where tact and patience alone could effect his purpose he rose to the occasion in a manner that even Botha could not have excelled and pleaded and reasoned with recalcitrant Transvaalers with an eloquence and a finesse born of his great idealism. He was prepared to sacrifice much—even to the extent of temporarily divesting himself of his imperious manner—in the interests of the speedy consummation of his goal, which meant to him not merely a "closer political and economic union" of the colonies but the birth of a nation.

Probably nowhere is to be found a clearer exposition of his attitude to a united South Africa than in a letter to Chief Justice de Villiers of the Cape. He wrote:

. . . from a purely selfish point of view the Transvaal has little to gain from Union. Economically the strongest factor in the South African situation, it is also largely independent of any particular colony, and can, therefore, view the situation with complete equanimity. Hence the chief danger and opposition will always come from the Transvaal. . . . But I do not despair. We who love South Africa as a whole, who have our ideal of her, who wish to substitute the idea of a United South Africa for the lost independence, who see in breadth of horizon and in a wider and more embracing statesmanship the cure for many of our ills and the only escape from the dreary pettiness and bickerings of the past, we are prepared to sacrifice much; not to Natal or to the Cape, but to South Africa.

In order to wean the Transvaal from a selfish attitude of isolation, he toured the country with tireless energy, addressing dozens of meetings and inspiring the people with that eloquence which has never failed him when in pursuit of a great vision.

"We must have Union," he said. "Two such peoples as the Dutch and the English must unite or try to exterminate each other. There is only one road to salvation . . . the road to union . . . to a South African Nation."

And then again: "The Boer has fought for his independence; the Englishman has fought for his Empire; all have fought for what they consider highest. . . . Now the highest is Union. . . . Let us have Union, not of top dog and under dog, but of brothers." And he added, speaking with the voice of Rhodes: "Let us make one big South Africa and do our best as wise and prudent sons of South Africa to start a Union here and to rule the country from Table Bay to the Congo and even beyond that. Let us be the inventors of a great South Africa."

As the result mainly of his exertions, it was decided to hold a convention of the states at Durban. No sooner had this decision been reached than Smuts began feverishly to prepare his brief for the assembly. Making a thorough study of all the federal and union constitutions obtainable, he perfected his plans to the smallest detail with the assistance of a large body of expert advisers, not the least important of whom were the members of the former Milner kindergarten. Sparing neither himself nor his collaborators, he devised in record time a scheme which, he hoped, would be acceptable to the members of the convention. Then he submitted it to the political leaders of the four colonies and, having considered their criticisms and suggestions, drew up a final memorandum, with which he left for Durban.

22

COMING from all parts of South Africa, the delegates to the convention assembled in Durban, the beautiful seaport of the province of Natal with its wide streets, its magnificent sea front, its languorous November air, and its flamboyant trees and other subtropical vegetation.

The chief justice of the Cape Colony was elected to the chair and the conference opened for many in an atmosphere of hope and expectation. It was thought that everything would run smoothly towards the great goal of their desires. Soon, however, it became known that most of the delegates were not clear in their minds as to what they desired and had little knowledge of constitution-making. Indeed of all those present Smuts alone knew his mind, and he had resolved to carry into effect his own particular scheme. He towered above all his compatriots at the convention and called the tune. He alone had his thoughts systematically pigeonholed, his ideas catalogued, his facts carefully marshalled, and all his plans worked out to perfection. The work of the convention, therefore, ultimately amounted to little more than a gradual toning down of Smuts's original thesis, to satisfy preconceived notions, whims, and sometimes fears of some of the delegates.

One or two of the Natal delegation seemed to favour a federation after the Australian model, but Smuts had long since determined to bring about unification with an all-powerful central government to direct the destinies of the country. He wanted power. He became the "Alexander Hamilton of the convention." As he had ruled the Transvaal, so now it was his firm purpose to rule with almost absolute power a union of South Africa.

He had great ideas, the "big thing" being always in the forefront of his mind. Much in evidence to the discerning onlooker in the days of the Union Convention was the greatness of his ambition, the scope thereof being comparable only with the range of his vision.

It is possible that he would have established there and then "a United States of South Africa of Empire size," if he had been allowed to do exactly as he pleased. Indeed there is a marked similarity between some notes of Rhodes's—visualizing a great league comprising the states of South Africa and Rhodesia together with Portuguese territory on the Zambesi—and the Botha-Smuts memorandum arising out of Lord Selborne's minute recommending a federation of the South African Colonies. In spite of his almost fanatical denunciation of imperialism in *A Century of Wrong*, he has always been an imperialist at heart, craving for ever-greater wholes, exhibiting invariably the traits of Cecil John Rhodes. Indeed, even while fighting against the British Empire during the Boer War, he expressed a desire to see "a great South African republic filling the subcontinent."

Vision, ambition, a craving for power—these were the driving forces in Smuts's life at the end of the first decade of this century; and, marching with them, a sincere desire to do what he deemed best for his country by substituting, as he had written to De Villiers, "a united South Africa for the lost independence." He was both an idealist and a materialist—a peculiar mixture indeed, and possible only in a character with as many facets as Smuts's.

Because so much was at stake and because so much depended on his powers of persuasion, Smuts curbed his dictatorial manner and employed tact and infinite patience where he would have preferred ruthlessly to crush opposition. For him it was a slow and trying process because of his congenital impatience with his—relatively speaking—dull-witted and unimaginative fellows. Nevertheless, adapting himself admirably to the role which necessity dictated, he was obliging and considerate to all, persuasive and always willing to compromise—within strict limits. Assisted by an extremely competent staff of nineteen secretaries and skilled advisers—a retinue of counsellors larger by 50 per cent than the sum total of experts from all the other states—Smuts was able easily to handle any difficult situation that cropped up in the conference hall and convincingly, if tactfully, to rout those opposed to his scheme by bringing to light opposite precedents, necessary facts, parallel situations, and incontrovertible arguments at a moment's notice.

While ruffling the tempers of the majority of the delegates and impairing their physical and mental powers, the sultry atmosphere of Durban's summer had no effect, seemingly, on Smuts. He remained calm and efficient, working unceasingly and tirelessly throughout the long and tedious days, shepherding the delegates cleverly and tactfully in whatever direction he would have them go, placating troublesome colleagues, solving knotty' problems, dexterously avoiding a state of stalemate on essential matters, and generally dominating the proceedings.

The end always justifying the means to him, he sometimes made promises which, he knew, could not be fulfilled. The prospective provincial councils were a case in point. They were to supplant the provincial parliaments in the future Union. He promised the die-hards that the powers of these councils would approximate those of the existing parliaments, knowing full well that, with a strongly centralized government, that would be out of the question. Other refractory colleagues were cleverly hoodwinked by subtle draughtsmanship, but in a few cases he was caught out. One such instance related to an agreement he had reached with Merriman and J. W. Sauer, the Cape leaders. They had compromised on a certain matter and Smuts had undertaken to amend a minute he was preparing in accordance with their agreement. But when he read out the document in question in the convention, it became apparent to Sauer and Merriman that, although everything seemed to be in order, Smuts had actually juggled so skilfully with words as to reproduce in the minute what was, in effect, his original standpoint. Merriman had long since nicknamed Smuts the Grey Cardinal. Seething inwardly, he now heaved his great length slowly and deliberately from his seat, stuck his hands into his front trouser pockets, and strolled over to the offender. "Smuts," he murmured gently but audibly, "you slippery little b——r." And afterwards he added: "Jannie must be careful or Jannie will end in smuts."

All too frequently for Smuts's peace of mind there were serious deadlocks, such as on the question of a capital for the future union, on the matter of the native problem, and in connection with language rights. But almost invariably he produced a solution. In regard to a capital (the states all had their own particular claims) he compromised by suggesting that there be two, one in each of the larger provinces, Pretoria and Cape Town to be respectively the executive and legislative capitals. After much trouble the delegates were prevailed upon to vote for equal-language rights. The solution of the native problem was left—at Smuts's suggestion—to the Parliament of the future Union of South Africa. As a rule Smuts managed to steer clear of deadlocks by heading his colleagues away from details. It was the convention's task, he said, not to discuss the details of problems but to create a united South African Parliament.

"Give us," said he, "a national Parliament, a national executive, and trust to them for a solution of those questions that have troubled us in the past."

Hertzog was the chief advocate of language and race equality. Luckily his quarrel with the British in the Free State was still in its infancy. If the convention had been held a mere nine months later, the Free State delegates, led by Hertzog, would probably have caused it to break down. As it was, few of them were very enthusiastic about union at the time of the convention. In fact, Hertzog proved occasionally to be rather difficult.

Smuts, however, proceeded along his appointed path with that dogged persistence which has always characterized him, and gradually managed to persuade the delegates that the welfare of South Africa lay in unity and that union was preferable to any form of federation.

In the end his project was accepted by the convention, and after this body had assembled again in Cape Town and lastly in Bloemfontein to round off discussions on the constitution and to attend to amendments, it was finally dissolved.

Before long the proposed constitution was passed by the parliaments of the four colonies. A deputation consisting of nine of South Africa's foremost politicians, led by Smuts and Botha, took the draft to England, where it passed through both Houses of Parliament as an imperial bill, which, before the year was out, became law, bearing the signature of King Edward VII.

23

BEFORE RETURNING to South Africa five of the delegates—Smuts, Botha, ex-President Steyn, Hertzog, and Jameson—lunched with the King. Queen Alexandra wore the great Cullinan diamond, which had been presented to her by Botha and Smuts on behalf of the people of the Transvaal—despite the undisguised disapproval of the majority of them —as a token of their appreciation for the gift of responsible government.

The act had been regarded as despotic and had been attributed almost entirely to Smuts. Even the mineowners had disapproved, pointing out that the Transvaal could not afford to give presents worth hundreds of thousands of pounds even to the Queen. In reply to their protests Smuts had merely said: "When I see the Knight Commanders and D.S.O.'s rise and unblushingly oppose the motion, it shows me that although there may be great financial power among them, there is little political insight."

However much indignation the episode of the Cullinan diamond may have aroused, two high-handed actions by Smuts—immediately after he had returned to South Africa—probably overshadowed that event.

He prevailed upon the retiring members of the moribund Transvaal Parliament to vote themselves a parting gift of approximately two hundred and fifty pounds each. Nothing loath, they passed a resolution to that effect.

The parliaments of the other states were scandalized by what they imagined to be a wanton waste of public money belonging to all the colonies jointly. A storm of protest was raised by the Transvaal senators. They resolved to defeat the resolution. Hearing of this, Smuts decided completely to ignore the Upper House in the matter and to apply directly to the deputy governor for written authorization to receive the money required. Thus were the members of Parliament of the only wealthy colony about to receive as compensation at the sudden termination of their political careers their moral, if not their legal, due.

The senators were furious. Some of them, as taxpayers, took the matter to the Supreme Court, which duly decided that the disbursements were illegal but that it could do nothing in the matter. It suggested, however, that the Crown might. But the Colonial Office, on being approached, advised the deputy governor to carry out the wishes of the ministry—in effect, of Smuts. And so the members of Parliament each received their present and the Treasury was the poorer by over twenty thousand pounds.

At Westminster His Majesty's Opposition proposed the severest condemnation on the Colonial Office for having authorized the deputy governor, the representative of the King, to become a partner in a definitely declared breach of the law. That was all. Smuts had his way, and, once again, he found it good. There was no need any longer to play up to others as at the convention. The old Smuts was there again, the absolute autocrat.

The other action of which many disapproved at the time concerned Pretoria. It was to be the administrative capital of the Union. If Smuts had had his way, it would have been the sole capital. Failing that, he decided to give it the finest block of administrative buildings the brain of Rhodes's architect could devise. At a cost of one and a half million pounds—the remainder of the Transvaal's surplus—Sir Herbert Baker erected the majestic Union Buildings on Meintjies Kop. Smuts was severely criticized for his arbitrary appropriation of so huge a sum, but he had no regrets. Today the Union Buildings are the pride of Pretoria.

24

THE ACT OF UNION was scheduled to take effect as from May 31, 1910. Lord Gladstone had been appointed Governor General of the Union on the recommendation of Botha and Smuts. He arrived in the country in the beginning of May and was entrusted with the task of appointing a Prime Minister to form a government. It was not an easy matter. In the end the choice lay between Botha and John X. Merriman.

It would have been the natural thing to offer the premiership to Merriman, "the Premier of the Mother State of South Africa and the Grand Old Man of South African Politics," who had been a member of Parliament of the Cape Colony since 1869. He was a great and skilful debater, a gifted scholar, and the wittiest of all South African parliamentarians, both past and present. His pertinent, if somewhat caustic, reference to Rudyard Kipling during the Boer War as "a rowdy Tyrtaeus" was much appreciated in pro-Boer quarters in Britain at the time. He was very thin and very tall and he possessed enormous feet—a caricature of a man, the subject of many an amusing cartoon. His transparent honesty was proverbial. After spending fifty-five years in Parliament, he died in 1926, two years after his retirement, revered alike by Briton and Boer. In the British Empire no man has had a longer or more honourable parliamentary career.

The honour of becoming the first Premier of the Union of South Africa was not granted him. It was given to Botha. Merriman ascribed the fact of his being overlooked to King Edward's dislike of him, and to his having antagonized Lord Selborne by declining emphatically to attend the National Convention if Selborne presided.

Probably, however, his defeat was due to Smuts's powerful backing of Louis Botha more than to anything else. Had Merriman become Prime Minister the history of South Africa would have developed along lines vastly different from those it actually followed, for Smuts could never have dominated Merriman. The history of the first ten years of the Union is largely the result of his commanding influence over Botha.

Equally significant in this connection is the fact that Hertzog and Steyn backed Merriman.

Botha's chief difficulty in forming a ministry lay with Hertzog. He was the Free State's first choice as its representative in the Union Cabinet. But far from being *persona grata* with the British voters, he was regarded by them as an incorrigible anti-British agitator in consequence of the leading part he had played in the Free State's language quarrel. The British press in the Union could not stomach the thought of his inclusion in the Ministry. It said so with great emphasis. Moreover, Botha and Smuts, as the high priests of conciliation, saw disaster for their policy in the person of Hertzog. But they could not ignore him. So Smuts invited him to breakfast at the Mount Nelson Hotel in Cape Town and suggested that he accept a seat on the Court of Appeal in lieu of a portfolio in the Cabinet. This Hertzog refused with contumely.

It was no use trying to persuade him. He was inexorable. On a second occasion he visited the Mount Nelson by invitation—this time from Botha. "There," he wrote afterwards, "I was taken by General Smuts to his room, where I was informed that I should be included in the Cabinet with the portfolio of Justice. Afterwards I met General Botha, who did not speak a single word to me personally on the subject. . . . There was no mistaking the reluctance with which the Prime Minister accepted me as a colleague."

Of nine portfolios Smuts was given three—Mines, Defence, and Interior—all important ones.

One day, a month or two later, the Prime Minister met a prominent young Free Stater who was afterwards elected to the Legislative Assembly.

"What do the people of the Free State say about our new Ministry?" asked Botha.

"As far as I could make out," was the reply, "they are satisfied with it except, perhaps, for the inclusion of General Smuts."

The Prime Minister was silent for a while. Then he said: "Old son, you people don't know Jan Smuts yet. Our country is still too young to play about with brains."

SECTION IV

25

STRIDING on to the greater stage of a united South Africa as virtual masters of a subcontinent, Botha and Smuts realized that more would be demanded of them than in the past, but they little knew how strenuous were to be the days that lay ahead.

They founded the South African party—in which the Afrikaner element preponderated—comprising the old Cape Bond party, the Orangia Unie, Het Volk, and a fair number of English-speaking supporters from Natal.

For a time the "convention spirit" of friendship and trust between the races showed promise of living on and ultimately finding its consummation in an identity of interests and wholesale fusion into one South African nation. In this atmosphere, then, pregnant with hope and expectation, Botha and Smuts set to work to co-ordinate and establish the machinery of government.

As in the past, everything revolved around Smuts. And, as in the past, he had mastered the intricacies of Kruger's administration and afterwards that of the Transvaal under responsible government, so now, working night and day, he acquired with amazing rapidity a complete knowledge of all the departmental details of the four provinces. Then, bringing all the parts into their proper relation to the Central Government and adding, where necessary, to the governmental machinery, he soon had everything in working order.

It would be unfair not to give credit to the efforts of the other Ministers, each in his own particular sphere. But there is no doubt that, as far as the general organization of government went, Smuts had the lion's share of the work. He wanted it. Always he was busy thinking and scheming—sometimes sitting quietly in his chair or pacing restlessly up and down his room, oblivious to everything but the ideas growing in his mind. As a rule he would hastily gulp down his tea and proceed immediately to work again, but frequently he would rise, cup in hand, and, engrossed in his thoughts, start walking up and down, sometimes completely forgetting the cup. He was a glutton for work. He revelled in it. For a time he appeared to thrive on it. The robust constitution which the Boer War had given him seemed to be able to endure any amount of wear and tear, as it has—since those first days of a united South Africa —for more than thirty years.

Soon Botha was summoned to London to a conference, and Smuts took over his friend's work in addition to retaining his own.

In spite of his great ability and his tremendous capacity for work, he was not very well liked by his colleagues. Practically all of them disapproved strongly of his aloofness and his autocratic ways. He also made numerous enemies among the heads of departments and their subordinates and was distinctly unpopular with many of the ordinary members of the Legislative Assembly, as well as with persons not in public life.

Impatient as ever of opposition, particularly the opposition of slow-thinking members who wasted his time and theirs with what he considered to be unimportant details, he frequently, with an Olympian arrogance, ignored their demands for a debate on matters which he had long since settled to his own satisfaction, if not to theirs, and thus incurred their wrath. At other times, again, he would refuse point-blank to give information which he alone could supply, and then neither threats nor abuse could drag it from him. Even his own party members began to speak disapprovingly of his overbearing ways and to say with the Opposition that Smuts found Parliament an unnecessary encumbrance and would rather do without it.

With the civil servants in his departments he was often unpopular for driving them on as pitilessly as he drove himself and even then finding fault with their work, accusing them of slowness and lack of discernment. But they never ceased to admire the concentration and energy with which he himself worked from early morning till late at night whether Parliament was in session or not.

His departmental heads, while wondering at his intellectual brilliance, were frequently puzzled by his stubbornness. As he increased in mental and political stature his imperiousness, too, was augmented, and where, formerly, he might gracefully have yielded to the superior knowledge of a departmental chief, he seemed now constitutionally incapable of doing so. He must have his own way. And, to be sure, more often than not it was the quickest and most effective one. But occasionally it was not; then he would clash with senior officials, and of course the latter would have to give way.

Once he came into conflict with Warrington-Smythe, the highly efficient Secretary of Mines, over a bill which the latter did not approve of, as there was very little to be said for it from a departmental point of view. They argued for hours. Then, suddenly, Smuts cupped his chin in his hands and sat glowering at the floor, saying nothing. . . . At last Warrington-Smythe, his patience thoroughly exhausted, began to rant and rave. Still Smuts said nothing. Because of his angry tirade, Smythe fully expected to encounter an irate Minister of Mines when next he met him, a day or two later, but Smuts was cool and suave—yet wholly determined to proceed with the bill.

To private persons, whether he met them as individuals or as members of a deputation, he could be very courteous—when he chose. Generally he was cold and impersonal and often brusque, not scrupling to convey the impression that his time was being wasted. Deputations on several occasions left his rooms fuming and indignant at being treated in an off-hand manner, only to be shepherded by tactful secretaries into Louis Botha's office, where oil was skilfully poured on troubled waters.

26

THE PERIOD OF PEACE, good will, and hope ushered in by the Act of Union was, for a variety of reasons, unfortunately short-lived. Nor could it have been otherwise, in the nature of things.

The main reason is not far to seek. It lay in the speed with which the accomplishment of union was effected. After a century of internecine racial antagonism culminating in the tragic Anglo-Boer War, there was brought about—a mere eight years after the cessation of hostilities—what many people fondly imagined to be a "complete national union." The healing hand of time had not as yet been able to expunge soreness from the heart and bitterness from the soul. And, therefore, it was manifestly absurd to claim that true race unity had been arrived at. It was out of the question from the nature of the case. Sentiment is an infinitely more powerful factor in human affairs than political exigency. This Hertzog realized—as will be seen—but Botha and Smuts, in their urgency, either overlooked or failed to appreciate it.

As the political leaders of the Afrikaner race and of the union they had successfully negotiated their first hurdle by forming a ministry without too obviously evoking hostility in the English, while keeping intact the ranks of Afrikanerdom.

The second obstacle to be cleared was the first general election to be held in the Union. Smuts and Botha, desirous of catching all the British votes available, found it expedient to quench, as far as possible, the ominously smouldering fires of anti-Hertzogism which the Opposition press was constantly fanning into vicious flame. Hence they decided to conciliate Hertzog's enemies by watering down his language and education policy for the Free State, which, with its distinctly pro-Afrikaner bias, had initially stirred up the anger of the British element. It was a decision prompted by political necessity. Unfortunately it took no account of certain forces stirring strongly in the womb of Afrikanerdom.

Concentrating as they did on the Afrikaner political revival, Smuts and Botha failed to perceive the potency of the cultural reaction which, while wholly unobtrusive, was nevertheless a more deeply rooted and a more enduring product of Afrikaner national sentiment. It contained the spiritual force common to all such causes particularly when there is present a "consciousness of cultural inferiority."

While Smuts and Botha were patently unaware of the latent power of this movement, Hertzog had become one of its leading protagonists by virtue of his efforts on behalf of Afrikaner language and education rights. Therein lay his strength and their weakness.

Hertzog was violently angry when he realized that it was Botha's and Smuts's intention to appease British sentiment by curtailing the language rights of Afrikaners in the schools of the Free State. Then ensued the first quarrel in the Cabinet, and Hertzog had his way. The Opposition demanded in vain that he be forced out of the Ministry and that the Free State School Acts be invalidated.

Then, at the election, Botha, to the surprise of almost everybody and the delight of not a few, was defeated by Sir Percy Fitzpatrick in his constituency of Pretoria East. A safe seat, it is true, was immediately found for him at Losberg, a Transvaal rural constituency, but he felt his downfall very keenly and blamed Hertzog for it.

On November 24, 1910, Sir C. P. Crewe moved in Parliament "That in the opinion of the House the provisions of the Orange Free State Education Acts are in conflict with the principles of freedom and equality of opportunity embodied in the South African Act, 1909. . . ." Hertzog was in fighting fettle. He replied vigorously and with great effect, scoring repeatedly off Crewe and, in one instance, even off Smuts and Botha and carrying the majority of Afrikaners in the House with him.

He had entered the lists as the "champion of the Free State Dutch." Gradually now he began to be looked upon as the champion of Afrikanerdom in general. His political views became a creed. Men called it Hertzogism. Its general purport was summarized in the words: "South Africa first" and "South Africa for the South Africans." Both phrases in time became slogans, appealing alike to Afrikaners and others imbued with the spirit of Colonial Nationalism. Friendship and co-operation between the two white races in the interests primarily of South Africa was what Hertzog advocated.

Even some of his colleagues seemed to prefer Hertzogism to the more liberal policy of Botha and Smuts, and before long Ministers were giving expression to widely divergent views on political questions.

It was with relief that Botha and Smuts witnessed the end of the first session in April 1911. Almost immediately the former went to London to attend a colonial conference which, for the first time, was being called an "Imperial Conference."

He was made much of, wore full court dress, with knee breeches and silk stockings—although he took measures to prevent any photos of himself in this garb from being published in South Africa lest he suffer political injury. He suggested state-aided immigration in a speech at the Eighty Club, stressed the desirability of making a contribution to the British Navy, and afterwards was made a privy councillor and an honorary general in the British Army—the latter being a distinction which, as a rule, is bestowed only on royal personages. Later, at the unveiling of a memorial to Rhodes at Groote Schuur, he eulogized the Colossus.

All these things, taking place less than a decade after the Boer War, were as gall and wormwood in the mouth of Hertzog. A contribution to the Navy he dubbed "a folly"; state-aided immigration, "a crime." He strongly suspected Botha of being much too susceptible to the blandishments of empire builders and imperialists, although he was careful not to say so—yet. But he spoke openly of certain British South Africans as "foreign fortune hunters" and "cosmopolitan capitalists." As far as South Africa was concerned, imperialism was largely a snare and a delusion and "only important to him when it was useful to South Africa. Wherever it was at variance with the interests of South Africa, he was strongly opposed to it. He was ready to stake his future as a politician on this doctrine."

It was with a feeling of amazement and unrest that the citizens of the

Union listened to the members of the Government speaking "with two voices."

Addressing a congress of the South African party at Bloemfontein, Smuts said: "I do not know how long this Government is going to last; it sometimes happens that governments disappear sooner than people expect." His words were prophetic, as the event proved a little more than twelve months later. He was referring to trouble with Hertzog. But the Free State firebrand was not implicated in the first Cabinet crisis.

Side by side in the Government there sat republicans from the Free State and British imperialists from Natal, as well as Transvaalers with a strong anti-colour prejudice, and men from the Cape who favoured franchise for the coloureds. For that matter there was lack of agreement on almost every fundamental question. Nor did the all-too-evident "personal prejudices and inter-provincial jealousies" augur well for the future. Trouble was to be expected. But the sudden resignation from the Cabinet of H. C. Hull, after a serious clash with J. W. Sauer, a fellow Minister, on the question of railway finance, came like a bolt from the blue even to ordinarily well-informed circles.

Smuts, "the handyman of the Government," temporarily took over Hull's portfolio of Finance, which, in the subsequent reshuffle, he held on to together with Defence, relinquishing Mines and Interior.

The crisis affected the Government seriously and, incidentally, strengthened Hertzog's position, since, in addition to Justice, he now, too, received Native Affairs, obviously as a sop.

But he refused to be appeased. Having mapped out his course, he was determined to follow it. Soon he was on the warpath again. The English newspapers took particular umbrage at speeches made by him at Nylstroom and De Wildt in the Transvaal which had a markedly secessionist flavour, and they demanded more loudly than ever that "Hertzog must go."

Once, when taunted at a meeting about his militant colleague's offensive allusions to "caked dung hanging on the wall" and "bastard sheep," Smuts calmly asked the audience to regard these references as "veld similes." Nevertheless, he knew that matters were moving towards a grave crisis.

Resultant upon Jameson's retirement from active politics a bye-election was held at Albany in the Eastern Province of the Cape where the British element preponderated. In spite of the intervention of the Prime Minister himself, the Government candidate was badly beaten on the Hertzog issue.

Soon after a Natal representative in the Cabinet, Sir George Leuchars, handed in his resignation. The De Wildt speech had enraged him and had "come as a last straw." He told Botha that he was leaving the Cabinet "because he could not endure the anti-imperial and anti-British sentiments and speeches of General Hertzog."

Abraham Fischer, the other Free State member of the Cabinet, asked Hertzog to sign a letter in which he apologized for what he had said at De Wildt and promised not to give offence in future. But, on finding that the letter had been drafted by Smuts, Hertzog pushed it away from him in disgust, and said bitterly: "The man in whose head it could have come to write such a thing must either have taken me for a lunatic or the place where he belongs is the lunatic asylum."

He refused to resign.

Then Botha himself resigned and formed a new Cabinet containing neither Leuchars nor Hertzog.

27

HERTZOG WALKED OUT ALONE into the political wilderness, deserted even by his friend and former colleague, Abraham Fischer. Of the one hundred and twenty-one members of the House, only five Free State men stood by him. A blank and dreary future appeared to await him. His political career was, seemingly, over. The power of the press was levelled against him. His situation was indeed unenviable.

But he was a man of great courage, with all the persistence of a fanatic and the obstinacy of a mule. As the High Priest of the new faith of Hertzogism, of Afrikaner nationalism, he gathered around him disciples with whom he wandered for many years in the wilderness before he came again into the Promised Land—to drive Smuts out.

Immediately after his ejection from the Cabinet he set out for the Free State, where he travelled from town to town addressing meetings and spreading the gospel of Hertzogism. In large numbers the people flocked to hear him and were converted in thousands; everywhere Hertzog vigilance committees sprang up like mushrooms. "The alliance of Botha and Smuts with British imperialism," wrote P. T. Moon, "from now on encountered important elements of opposition."

In November 1913 the final break came at the annual Congress of the South African party held in the Hofmeyr Hall in Cape Town. After much argument and recrimination the Hertzogites, led by Christiaan de Wet, marched out of the hall. At the door the old guerrilla chief turned to face the Bothaites and, waving his hand, cried, "Adieu!"

Not many weeks passed before the Nationalist party came into existence with Tielman Roos and D. F. Malan as leaders respectively of the Transvaal and Cape branches, and Hertzog as the head of the party in the Orange Free State and the supreme chief.

To the Afrikaner cultural movement, wherein from the beginning his strength had lain, he had given a "political bias," and, in doing so, had sounded the knell of Smuts and Botha as the accepted leaders of Dutch South Africa. Some believe that his timely action saved the Afrikaner race from losing its identity through absorption by the British.

The fight was on. It was to resolve itself into a long and bitter duel between Hertzog and Smuts, lasting for twenty years and more, thereafter to be carried on by Smuts and D. F. Malan, both of Riebeek West. It was a fight which was to epitomize the political history of South Africa over a period of thirty years.

It has been said that between Smuts and Hertzog there always was the "temperamental antagonism" that existed between Alexander Hamilton and Thomas Jefferson. Probably much of their difference in outlook was due to the dissimilarity of their environment in the formative years of their lives, Smuts having been educated at Cambridge and Hertzog in Amsterdam. Intellectually Smuts was head and shoulders above Hertzog and could always have accomplished greater things. The latter had a one-track mind. In the circumstances, however, it served him well, since it enabled him to achieve much along the straight and narrow path of limited nationalism which Smuts could not have trodden half so well, endowed as he was with a facile opportunism, a superior and expanding intellect, and a political outlook definitely antagonistic to narrow chauvinism and wholly consonant with his philosophic tenets. If Smuts had been in Hertzog's position in 1912, he would have compromised—temporarily, and, in time, he would have persuaded his colleagues to adopt his standpoint.

Urged strongly thereto by Smuts, the Prime Minister, in order to stem the flowing tide of Hertzogism, changed his tune considerably, giving to his utterances a definite pro-Afrikaner bias, avoiding too obvious contact with Jameson's Unionists, all but renouncing state-aided immigration, rejecting the idea of an imperial federal parliament with paramountcy over the colonial legislatures, recanting in respect of the proposed annual contribution to the British Navy, and generally striving to cut away the soil from under Hertzog's feet.

Before these tactics could have any effect, however, the essential nature as well as the course of South African politics was altered radically by serious industrial upheavals, rebellion, and war and their attendant circumstances.

28

FATEFUL TO THE WORLD was the year 1913, with its social disturbances, sabotage, spiritual unrest, and anarchy—the forerunners of an impending cataclysm. Nor was South Africa without her afflictions.

On July 4, 1913, trouble started on the mines of the Witwatersrand. Not since Smuts had forced the miners back in 1907 had there been a strike. Now an unimportant dispute between the manager of the New Kleinfontein Mine and some of his men acted as a spark to start a conflagration. The trade-unions took up the matter, stood by the men, and a general strike of miners on the Rand was declared. The mineowners rushed to interview Smuts, who refused to intervene.

When it became known that a great mass meeting of workers was to be held on the Johannesburg Market Square on July 4, he forbade it. Nevertheless, on the appointed afternoon, thousands of excited miners streamed towards the square and soon filled it. Then all heads were lifted towards a trolley on which stood the strike leaders, Bain, Morgan, and Matthews together with Colonel Truter, chief of police.

The speakers conveyed Smuts's decision to the multitude and begged the people to go home. But shouts of derision drowned their voices. Then Bain, who had as yet said nothing, rose. "We are here for the rights of free speech," he said. And then the police rushed towards the trolley, and the fighting began.

As the police charged up with their batons, showers of stones were hurled at them and some were beaten down. Reminiscent of Madame Defarge, a woman bearing a red flag mounted a barrel and harangued the mob, who then followed her to the trams in the streets where conductors and drivers were roughly dragged from their posts.

Towards evening the Johannesburg Railway Station was set on fire and the building which housed the capitalist newspaper, the *Star,* was burned down, and in the light of the leaping flames the strikers danced around the carcases of horses.

There was a great deal of looting.

Enraged bands hunted high and low for the mineowners, but these gentlemen were nowhere to be found.

During the night a body of imperial troops was rushed to Johannesburg to assist the police.

Next afternoon the strikers stormed the Rand Club and were held back with difficulty by the combined forces of police and soldiers. Suddenly into the middle of Loveday Street strode one Labuschagne, a striker, in his shirt sleeves. Theatrically he tore open the front of his shirt and with arms flung wide defiantly shouted to the soldiers: "Shoot! Shoot!" The order was given to fire, and Labuschagne sank to the ground. Twenty others were killed and forty-seven wounded, a large number of them being innocent bystanders.

The situation was critical. Smuts decided to put in a personal appearance and to deal with it himself. He called for Botha, and in an open car they sped to Johannesburg, arriving there shortly after sunrise. They drove slowly through hostile crowds to the Carlton Hotel, where they went into conference with the strike committee members, all of whom were armed.

Smuts and Botha carried no weapons. A temporary truce had been arranged, but throughout the negotiations the leaders of the Government were covered with revolvers and they were told that they would be shot if the soldiers opened fire again. Their peril was great. They realized this, but remained quite calm. They also realized that they were in no position to make demands. Smuts said afterwards: "We made peace because the imperial forces informed us that the mob was beyond their control. . . . Anything could happen to Johannesburg that night: the town might be sacked, the mines permanently ruined. . . ." They agreed to terms dictated to them. They signed a document to that effect. "One of the hardest things I have ever had to do," Smuts said subsequently in the House. The strike leaders gloated over him whom they had hated since their ignominious defeat in 1907. They rejoiced in his humiliation.

Botha and Smuts left the Carlton Hotel without an escort, driving through great crowds of undisciplined people mad with hatred and thirsting for blood. At any moment they might have been killed. Frequently revolvers were thrust into the car and menacing faces leered at them. "Shoot! You can shoot!" shouted Botha. "We are unarmed, but you know this: that we are here to make peace for you people, and if we are shot, that is all finished." But Smuts said never a word, contemptuous of the mob and planning retribution.

In the period of uncertainty that followed, it was clear that the struggle between Smuts and the workers was by no means over. Proposed retrenchment on the railways caused keen resentment among the working classes and brought about a fresh crisis towards the end of the year. There was by that time strong co-operation between the trade-unions, and it was feared that the impending strike might involve practically all branches of industry. In January 1914 matters came to a head. A general strike was proclaimed, over twenty thousand men participating.

But Smuts was not caught napping a second time. He had prepared everything carefully in anticipation of trouble, having utilized to the full his powers under the Defence Act. He struck without delay, calling out the burgher commandos as well as the Active Citizen Force and proclaiming martial law on the Rand. He sent this telegram to the officer commanding the Rand Light Infantry: "Exercise greatest severity. Keep all strikers off the railway line or railway premises. Don't hesitate to shoot if any attempt to enter after warning, or if on apparently malicious intent." Everything went like clockwork. The strikers were frightened into submission. To the Trades Hall, the strike leaders' headquarters, Smuts dispatched General Delarey with a commando and field guns and instructions to blow up the building if necessary. The leaders surrendered. The strike was over.

Thereupon, without consulting Parliament or even seeking the opinion of the Cabinet as a whole, Smuts hurriedly sent nine of the strike leaders —none of them South African by birth—by special train to Durban whence they were deported to England on the steamship *Umgeni*. Accommodation had been reserved on board for ten men, but one of them, on hearing that all the strike leaders were to be court-martialled and shot, had managed to escape to Durban, disguised as a parson. Thence he went to England via Australia.

On the day after the *Umgeni* had steamed out to sea, there was a great hullabaloo about the deportations. Prominent Labour leaders applied to the Supreme Court of the Transvaal for a writ of *habeas corpus*. The judges were scandalized by Smuts's illegal act. A tug, chartered by Colonel Cresswell, the Labour leader, and some others, was sent in pursuit of the *Umgeni* but failed to find her.

A bill to indemnify the Government was subsequently carried in the House after a long discussion during which Smuts was attacked with great violence by the four Labour members and by others. Indeed so virulent did the Labourites become in their denunciation of the Minister that they were all suspended in turn by Mr. Speaker in the course of the debate. Smuts spoke for a total of almost six hours in his own defence. While admitting the illegality of his conduct, he stated with emphasis that he had had no option in the matter. He had resorted to the "illegal deportations because he knew that Parliament would never give him authority in cold blood to expel the men in question."

"The only crime," he said, "which fits this state of affairs is high treason, but you attempt to indict these people for high treason and see what will be the result. Our law of high treason comes from the Middle Ages. Our treason law does not fit these new and extraordinary conditions which have arisen in the present case, and if you were to indict these people for a crime they have really committed, you will never obtain a conviction."

It was, nevertheless, a heinous act to deport men from a free country without trial. The whole of the English-speaking world thought so, and said so. The matter was broached in the Commons. The Secretary of State for the Colonies, Mr. Harcourt, reminded a critical House that South Africa was a self-governing country and that it could settle its own affairs. In connection with the Governor General's "acquiescence," the Colonial Secretary intimated that Lord Gladstone had "properly assented to the only method which his responsible advisers recommended . . . on the assurance that his Ministers would immediately endeavour to obtain from their Parliament the ratification of, and an indemnity for, the action they proposed to take." Indeed "his consent and concurrence," so it seemed, had neither been "sought nor obtained." Smuts had taken full responsibility. Mr. Harcourt attempted to smooth over matters by referring to the Dominions as "our constant pride and only our occasional embarrassment." But, for all the Minister's attempts to dispel their apprehensions, Members felt that a precedent had been established by Smuts's illegal act, particularly dangerous to the cohesiveness of an Empire evolving along lines both free and untried. They recalled the fact that the Union's Indian policy had already created oversensitiveness between at least two of the important component parts of the Empire. They could hardly look on with composure while it was "flouting the liberty of white British subjects."

The fact that Smuts could deliberately disregard the law when it suited his purpose struck fear into the hearts of many of his countrymen. Even members of the South African party became apprehensive. Merriman spoke of "that ruthless philosopher."

The anxiety of the workers was exceeded only by their hatred. In this connection Smuts tells this story against himself: "The strikers said that Old Nick went on leave and the Almighty allowed Jan Smuts to act for him. When Satan returned the Lord would not let Smuts go, as he had given proof of understanding the work of Hell better than his predecessor."

The deportees returned to the Union in due course. Their later history is interesting. One became a South African party organizer under Smuts; another was given an important post in the Chamber of Mines and retained it for many years; another joined the Government service, becoming attached to the Public Works Department; and a fourth became a member of the Union Parliament.

The industrial upheavals had a profound effect on the political situation in the Union. Giving pride of place to industrial and economic questions, racialism took a back seat, while Labour tore itself away from Botha and Smuts, whom it had supported against the Progressives (the Capitalist party) in the Transvaal since 1907, and became the friend of Hertzog. Taking place shortly after the deportations, when feeling ran high, the Transvaal Provincial Council's general election resulted in an overwhelming victory for Labour.

There was no denying the fact that the Government was becoming unpopular: twice it was defeated in the House on financial schemes devised by Smuts, but it decided to carry on; there was a large deficit in the national budget; the people were becoming uneasy and were freely criticizing the Government.

But amid all these disturbances in the political fabric of the Union there came suddenly the sound of the Trumpet of War. The whole of Europe became convulsed. It was the beginning of the Great Struggle. Nowhere in the British Empire were its effects to be as far-reaching as in the Union of South Africa, where a great part of the people either wished to remain neutral or were definitely anti-British, where the old aspirations and inclinations were to be revived and the old wounds reopened, and the body politic parted asunder into two hostile camps, and where the blood of brothers engaged in civil strife was to drench the red African earth.

29

No SOONER had hostilities begun in Europe than the South African Government suggested taking over *in toto* the defence of the Union on land and setting free for service elsewhere the imperial garrison still in the country. Falling in gladly with the suggestion, the British Government at the same time requested that a South African force be dispatched immediately to German South West Africa to destroy the important wireless stations at Lüderitzbucht and Swakopmund. Forthwith, without consulting either Parliament or people—indeed there was little time to do so—the Union Cabinet decided to invade South West Africa with Smuts's Defence Force and to commandeer men where necessary. It was a grave decision.

Before presenting Parliament with a *fait accompli,* Smuts and Botha hastily summoned the commandants of the Transvaal districts as well as the staff officers and colonels of the Permanent Citizen Force and told them that defence measures had to be taken and a force of at least twenty thousand men raised, but did not, as yet, apprise them of the pending invasion of South West Africa, knowing that they were opposed to it almost to a man. Hoping, as was said afterwards, "to evoke a discussion," an officer, Jan Kemp by name, Smuts's colleague of Boer War days, asked the Minister what he intended doing with so large a force. Glancing angrily at the offender, Smuts pulled him up sharply, and the matter was not pursued.

On September 4 a special session of the Union Parliament commenced. It lasted ten days. Botha moved an address to the King in which he made mention of "whole-hearted determination to take all measures necessary for defending the interests of the Union and co-operating with His Majesty's Imperial Government to maintain the security and integrity of the Empire." Smuts seconded the resolution. Exactly twenty-five years later (September 4, 1939) he was, in even more dramatic circumstances, to play the leading role in a similar declaration of war on Germany.

The subsequent debate manifested an almost unbelievable recrudescence of race hatred since the outbreak of the war and a complete fading out of the "convention spirit." Hertzog and his followers attacked Smuts and Botha furiously in speeches which were all rabidly anti-British. They both denounced the proposed invasion of South West Africa and gave expression to strong doubts in respect of "the justice of the Allied cause in the war." Even among the members of the South African party there were many who shared the Nationalists' standpoint. It took all Smuts's and Botha's powers of persuasion to prevail on their party caucus to support them. Nevertheless, in the end their resolution was carried by ninety-two votes to twelve. And then the fat was in the fire.

Throughout the country, but particularly in the Transvaal and the Free State, there was an outcry not only against the projected invasion of South West Africa but against any participation at all in the war. There was also wild talk of rebellion in certain quarters.

On September 15, the day after Parliament had been prorogued, General Christiaan Beyers, commandant general of the Union forces, resigned his position. He had been expected to assume the supreme command in the South West Africa campaign. Some two years previously Smuts had been pleased to place at the head of a defence force of his creation so handsome and fine a figure of a man as Beyers. It was with mixed feelings of regret, therefore, and with intense annoyance that he read the commandant general's bitter letter of resignation, in which England was pilloried in a style strangely reminiscent of the more pungent passages of *A Century of Wrong*.

For Beyers the fifteenth was a fateful day. So, too, it was for Old General Delarey, one of the senators of the Union Parliament. He was killed on that day by a stray bullet. He was the victim of a chain of unfortunate events and, in a sense, also of decrepitude. It is a sad story.

At Vereeniging Botha had induced him to agree to the treaty by telling him that a favourable opportunity for regaining the Boer independence would come later on, when Britain was in trouble. At heart he had always remained a republican, waiting patiently for the dawn of that day which Botha had foreshadowed, the day on which he fully expected Smuts and Botha to lead the Boers into rebellion. With the outbreak of hostilities in Europe he believed that the time had come, and he began to plot for the establishment of a republic in South Africa. To those who asked him what Smuts and Botha would do, should they discover his plans, he replied that the Government was "all right" and that he had himself "acquainted General Smuts with every detail of his plans."

Now, Delarey was the uncrowned King of the Western Transvaal, and his influence in that great region was enormous. Lest he become estranged from them and they lose his indispensable support in those critical days, the Government had humoured the old man, given non-committal and ambiguous replies to his inquiries, and somehow managed to convey to him the impression that they shared his republican sentiments. But suddenly, on August 13, he was summoned to Pretoria and Smuts disillusioned him. While attaching no blame to Botha for taking him in, he appears, for a reason unknown, to have fixed the responsibility on Smuts.

Although firm with him, Smuts and Botha were also gentle with Delarey, for whom they cherished both respect and affection. Throughout one whole long night they argued fervently with him in an effort to persuade him that he held mistaken views. They had a measure of success. But there were stronger influences in the old man's life. One was an almost fanatical belief that God willed that the Boers should sever the British connection; the other, a man known as the "Prophet" van Rensburg, reputedly a seer, in whose prognostications Delarey had implicit faith. In a vision this man had beheld a fight among bulls from which the grey bull, Germany, had come forth the victor. He had seen Botha returning to the bosom of his people, but Smuts had vanished from the scene. He had seen Delarey and a carriage and flowers and a black cloud with blood gushing from it and the number fifteen on it. And he seemed to think that it was Delarey's destiny to move along with the grey bull. Whether Delarey finally made up his mind to do so will remain forever a mystery.

On September 15, the day on which the Union forces left for Lüderitzbucht, Generals Beyers and Delarey were on their way by car to Lichtenburg, where a meeting of protest against participation in the war was to be held. It so happened that a band of reputed criminals, known as the "Foster Gang," was terrorizing certain areas on the Rand. A cordon of police had been thrown round Johannesburg with orders to fire on any car refusing to stop when challenged. Towards evening Delarey and Beyers entered the encircled zone and were challenged by a constable, who shouted, "Halt!" "Shall we stop?" asked Beyers. "No!" said the old man. "We go on." And on they drove through the suburbs past a number of challenging policemen, one of whom fired at a tire of the car as it sped past. The bullet ricocheted from the road. It struck Delarey and killed him.

There had been the number fifteen on the black cloud of the seer's prophecy. Obviously the carriage and flowers referred to the funeral which was held at Lichtenburg.

Smuts and Botha attended without an escort. It was a venturesome undertaking, for the temper of the great crowd that had arrived by special train was dangerous. It had been freely stated that Delarey had been murdered and that Smuts and Botha were responsible for the crime. Both Ministers spoke at the graveside and could feel about them the chill menace of the hostile multitude. A suggestion "to capture them and take them secretly to the Free State as the first step in a brilliant *coup d'état*" was scouted by General de Wet and turned down.

After the funeral Beyers, Christiaan de Wet, and several other leaders organized meetings in various towns and villages of the Free State and the Transvaal to protest against the Government's war policy and to demand that the South African forces be moved away from the German border. As yet no trouble impended—so it seemed. But suddenly, on October 9, Manie Maritz, officer commanding the Union troops on the South West border, rebelled against the Government and went over to the Germans, taking with him the great majority of his men.

Smuts immediately proclaimed martial law and began to commandeer Transvaal burghers to proceed against Maritz.

Meanwhile Beyers' life had been threatened on the Rand and his watchdogs had been stabbed to death in his front garden. He, therefore, retired to a farm where he was joined in time by hundreds of men who had mutinied after being commandeered.

Larger numbers were flocking to De Wet, who had been holding meetings in the Northern Free State. Smuts had not yet dared to commandeer men in that "stronghold" of the Nationalist party, and so comparative calmness prevailed here, but many wondered whether it could last, for De Wet was on commando. Before long he had occupied a couple of villages, was interfering with the recruitment of volunteers, and was obviously planning to link up with Maritz.

As soon as the internal trouble began, Botha took the field himself with Afrikaner commandos loyal to the Government, while Smuts remained in Pretoria to superintend the tremendous work of organization connected with maintaining on active service a large army in South West Africa and several commandos in the ex-republics.

Smuts spent many hours at his desk every day of the week during those trying months. He was tireless and coldly efficient, driving both himself and his assistants along remorselessly. On several occasions he joined Botha on commando to see for himself how things were going, and then he would hurry back again to his office in the Union Buildings. "Nobody," said Botha after the rebellion had been quashed, "nobody can ever appreciate sufficiently the great work General Smuts has done—greater than that of any other man throughout this unhappy period. . . ." His duties were many and varied.

Once there was almost a mutiny among the troops because the regulars were being fed on dry bread and coffee without either milk or sugar, while the commandos were all too obviously receiving butter, cheese, and other luxuries. A young officer was sent to Smuts to point out the danger of this unfair discrimination. The Minister listened patiently to the report and then said quietly: "Do you realize that it is a matter of policy to keep the Boer commandos satisfied? So many of them would just as well be on the other side." And with these words he dismissed the officer.

On another occasion, after actual fighting had started, a senior officer high up in the Defence Force was reported to be causing a great deal of trouble. His sympathies were wholly with the rebels, and he had already assisted several rebel officers to escape. An action in the Bushveld of the Transvaal had recently been lost on account of him, and the loyal officers who had been jointly in charge of operations with him and had been blamed for their failure were demanding to be tried by court-martial. But Smuts refused their petition for an inquiry on grounds similar to those he had advanced in the former instance. "I have heard more than enough of the whole business," he said angrily. "I refuse to create political difficulties in order to exonerate certain officers." The scapegoats were furious. They had been left in the lurch wantonly. But the act was typical of Smuts, who was always willing to sacrifice even his friends when an important issue was at stake.

30

BOTHA AND SMUTS gave the commandos strict injunctions in the beginning not to fire on the malcontents. It was hoped to prevail on them to disband and return home. There were very influential men among them. A peaceful settlement of the unhappy affair was earnestly desired. Englishmen were counselled to "stand aside" from what was "purely an Afrikaner quarrel." In the beginning it was little more than a serious political squabble, but it did not long remain so. It could not, under the circumstances. For armed anti- and pro-Government commandos trekking about the former republics were bound sooner or later to clash, however keen they might be to avoid one another.

One morning Botha attacked Beyers near Rustenburg and routed him easily, as the rebels were in the minority and poorly armed. The defeated leader attempted to escape on horseback over the Vaal, which happened to be in full flood. A bullet killed his horse under him. His bootlaces became entangled in the stirrup straps and he was drowned.

Frequent brushes between De Wet's burghers and the Government troops took place in the Free State. In one of these the old guerrilla's youngest son was killed. Bitterly vengeful after this event, De Wet decided to fight to a finish although the majority of his men were unarmed.

By now Botha was much too powerful for him, having forty thousand men in the field, most of whom were Afrikaners. British "town regiments" took little part in the actual fighting since the Prime Minister wished to avoid a "war of races."

After a brilliant display of his old tactics of dispersal and evasion De Wet was defeated in Mushroom Valley by a superior force led by Botha himself. He was finally captured together with a small commando by troops in Ford motorcars on the border of the Kalahari Desert, while on his way to join Maritz. Of the insurgent leaders Kemp was the only one to reach Maritz. After De Wet's defeat the rebellion was practically over. All that remained was the mopping up of isolated groups.

Botha had aged greatly during those unhappy days. At Mushroom Valley and after other engagements he had looked upon the upturned faces of dead rebels who, in other days, had been his comrades. Tears had sprung to his eyes, and he had wept unashamedly. He became old and weary, and his health suffered greatly.

But Smuts was as energetic as ever, and as healthy. But for the rings of tiredness around his eyes, he showed no sign of strain. As for emotion —he kept himself firmly in hand always and appeared to be callous and insensible of the misery around him, when actually the tragedy of civil war weighed heavily upon him. Only once, when caught unawares, did he weaken in the presence of others. He was holding a consultation with staff officers when the news of Beyers' death reached him. For a moment he appeared to be stunned. Then he shaded his eyes with his left hand and, taking a piece of notepaper, he started writing to Mrs. Beyers. "I cannot let her hear this officially," he said. "A friend must tell her." And while the officers waited, he wrote. Nor did he remove his hand from his eyes. Unlike Botha, he was too proud to let men see his tears.

The rebel leaders got off lightly on the whole, but Captain Jopie Fourie, a former officer in the Defence Force, was condemned to death for high treason. His was the only death sentence to be carried out after the rebellion.

Great efforts were made by the Nationalist party to save Fourie. Delegation after delegation came to plead with Smuts in Pretoria, on his farm at Irene, and in Cape Town. He received anonymous letters threatening him with death should the condemned man die. But he was inexorable. Fourie was guilty. Fourie must die. Of course others were as guilty. But Smuts, people said, did not dare to shoot them. An example must, therefore, be made of Fourie.

He was to be executed on a Sunday morning. On Saturday a deputation headed by Dr. D. F. Malan went to interview Smuts at the Union Buildings on behalf of the condemned man, taking along several petitions. But the Minister, they were told, was not in Pretoria. He had left for his farm at Irene. The deputation followed him but failed to find him at home. He had gone for a walk into the veld, a maidservant told them. They decided to await his return. Half an hour passed. A motorcar drove up and left again. Then the waiting men were told that the Minister had suddenly been summoned to the capital by his department.

Arriving back in Pretoria, the party failed to secure an interview with Smuts, and so they handed the petitions to Lieutenant Louis Esselen for transference to the Minister.

But, in spite of all these efforts, Fourie was led from his cell early on Sunday morning and taken to a yard where he was blindfolded and placed on a chair. Then he sang the old Dutch hymn, "When we enter the Valley of Death, we leave our friends behind us." As the last words left his lips, the bullets pierced his heart.

Smuts had the legal right to have Fourie executed, but it was an unwise act. It was not policy in the circumstances, and his race have not yet forgiven him the deed.

An analysis of the motives that actuated the rebels to rise against the Government is interesting. With some the rebellion was merely an "armed protest," after the old Boer style, against the invasion of a neighbour's territory—"Cursed be he," quoted old General de Wet, "who removeth his neighbour's landmark"; others again desired ardently to get rid of Botha and Smuts and what they stood for; many were moved by the personal influence of famous leaders like De Wet, Delarey, and Beyers; but the great majority, nursing their Boer War grievances against Britain, were undoubtedly impelled by a spirit of vengeance, not surprising in the circumstances, and inspired by an all-too-evident desire to sever for all time the British connection.

Most of the rebels were Nationalists. They became Afrikaner martyrs, and the Nationalist party grew apace because of the rebellion. Indeed, the Great War was to be the "determining factor" in the advancement of Hertzogism; the South West and East African campaigns in time brought grist to its mill. Botha and Smuts, depicted as the champions of Britain at any price, even against the interests of South Africa, lost the majority of their Afrikaner supporters. Finally, in 1917, matters came to such a pass that republicanism as a political programme was proclaimed throughout the land.

Even before the rebellion had been finally quashed the Union Government intimated to the British Cabinet that an expeditionary force would soon embark for Walfish Bay in South West Africa. A week or two after the dispatch of the troops Botha followed them. Smuts was eager to accompany the Prime Minister, but it was required of him first to attend to his numerous parliamentary and other duties and to pilot an indemnity bill through both Houses. For the second time within twelve months he had to be secured against legal responsibility for acting under martial law.

31

IN SOUTH WEST AFRICA there were two principal war zones: the northern and the southern parts of that vast territory.

Arriving at Swakopmund on February 11, 1915, Botha assumed command in the former sector while Smuts landed at Lüderitzbucht two months later to take charge of operations in the latter area.

Making Walfish Bay his base, Botha attacked the enemy at Jakalswater, marched rapidly right up to Otjimbingwe, seized Karabib, Friedrichsfelde, Wilhelmsthal, and Okahandja in turn, entered Windhuk, the capital, on May 12, after isolating the enemy's forces from the southern part of the territory, and then proclaimed martial law. He now prepared to conquer all the northern districts. He divided his forces into four sections. One of these, under his favourite commander, Coen Brits, he sent northward through the territory west of the railway up to Otjivarongo and thence to the Etosha Pan via Outjo, thus severing completely the German line of retreat towards the Cunene and the Kaokoveld. A second column, under Lukin, went along the railway line, while the remaining two led by Manie Botha and Myburgh worked along east of the railway and reached Tsumeb and the Otavi junction respectively. All means of retreat being cut off by these swift manœuvres, the Germans were well and truly cornered, and Governor Seitz and the commandant, Colonel Francke, had no alternative but to capitulate. Close on four thousand officers and men surrendered.

Meanwhile Smuts was pushing on rapidly in the south and, by the beginning of May, Keetmanshoop and Gibeon had fallen to him. He was delighted to be out in the open again on commando, living the life he loved, away from the desk at which for eight years he had been labouring unceasingly. But, as always, he was impatient, impelled by an unreasoning urge to get to his goal. Officers and men as well as himself he drove on mercilessly through the dry and dusty desert land, sometimes outstripping his men in his precipitancy and getting lost in the arid wastes. Once, so the story goes, a detachment of his own troops took him prisoner when he had strayed too far, and brought him back to camp. Nevertheless, despite his undue haste, he obtained results, and in the space of a few weeks the Germans were driven up against Botha's lines in the north, and surrendered.

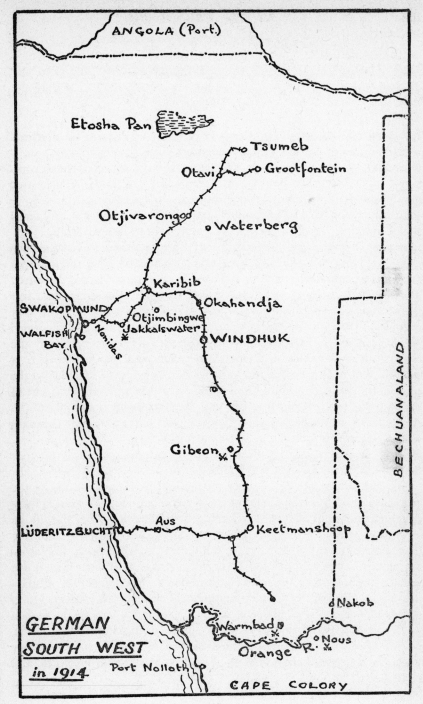

ANGOLA (Port.)

Etosha Pan

Tsumeb

Otavi
Grootfontein

Otjivarongo

Waterberg

Karibib

SWAKOPMUND
Okahandja

Otjimbingwe
Jakkalswater

WALFISH
BAY
Nonidas
WINDHUK

BECHUANALAND

Gibeon

Aus

LÜDERITZBUCHT
Keetmanshoop

Nakob

GERMAN
SOUTH WEST
in 1914
Warmbad
Nous

Orange R.

Port Nolloth

CAPE COLONY

The campaign was over. Its issue was completely favourable. Admitting the tremendous disparity between the opposing forces—eight thousand Germans as against fifty thousand South Africans—the campaign, nevertheless, had been remarkable both for the speed of its accomplishment and the complete efficiency with which it was carried out.

Both leaders had given fresh proof of their mettle. But the success of the campaign was due mostly to Botha's thorough knowledge of the art of war. Like Smuts, he had been delighted to be away from the cares of office and away from the slanderous tongues of his own people who were forever maligning him. He had been glad to be up and doing, overjoyed at being able to get to grips with a foreign enemy this time instead of with men of his own race. With singing heart he would heave his bulk into the saddle or rush across the great open stretches in a motorcar. He had seemed to be enjoying himself even while the bullets were whistling about his ears. At such times he would, if necessary, pass rapidly from post to post, oblivious to danger and regardless of the protests of the officer commanding his bodyguard. Like Smuts, he never appeared to consider his own personal safety.

Both men had set up records for desert marching. Once Botha's infantry covered one hundred and twenty miles in a week over difficult, sandy, waterless terrain. Addressing the victorious troops, Smuts said proudly: "If you go through the history of wars you will perhaps only find in the Boer War records like these. . . . If you tell them of the march from Nonadas to Karabib, they will not believe you; if you tell them how little water you drank and how few biscuits you ate, they will not believe you."

South African casualties (killed and wounded) in the South West African campaign amounted to a mere five hundred and thirty. The rebellion had claimed twice that number. The conquered territory was as large as France, although most of it was semi-desert land. It was the first campaign to be brought to a successful conclusion by the Allies during the war. As such its psychological effect was incalculable.

32

Smuts and botha returned to the Union in triumph in July 1915. In Cape Town, Johannesburg, and the other cities where the British element predominated they received tremendous ovations as the conquerors of South West Africa, but there was a distinct lack of enthusiasm and even an unmistakable feeling of hostility in the country districts, where men believed that Smuts and Botha were "subordinating the interests of the Union to those of an Empire . . . entangled at Gallipoli, threatened at the heart by the first submarine campaign, and helpless to aid its Russian ally staggering under the hammer strokes of Hindenburg."

If somewhat disconcerted by the attitude of the growing body of disciples of Hertzogism, Smuts attempted boldly to minimize the less-attractive aspects of the war in Europe by pointing to the northern hinterland and painting a glowing picture of South African expansion towards the north in his most alluring Pan-African colours. "There is now the prospect," he said, "of the Union becoming almost double its present area. If we continue on the road to union, our northern boundaries will not be where they now are, and we shall leave to our children a huge country in which to develop a type for themselves, and to form a people who will be a true civilizing agency in this dark continent. That is the large view." And in their fury and their hatred of Smuts the disciples of Hertzog shouted: "The large view! It makes one think of the World's View, where Rhodes is buried. What had Rhodes's imperialism not cost South Africa! What Smuts's imperialism has cost South Africa we also know! Our nation is torn asunder. The blood of brothers has been shed. There are thousands of broken hearts. What it will cost us in the future we do not know."

The five-year period of the first Union Parliament was about to expire when the troops returned home from South West Africa. The South African party's prospects for the coming election were uncertain. But Smuts and Botha hoped to bolster up the party's tottering position with the aid of the British party, the Unionists, who were standing by them on the war issue and had been highly gratified, if somewhat surprised, by "their loyal adherence to the British cause." They felt, moreover, that a substantial measure of support would be forthcoming from that section of Labour which consisted of British workers who had undertaken "to see the war through." Nevertheless, the two leaders were none too sure of the security of their position, for the country was torn by bitterness and hatred during those war years as no other country within the Empire, with the possible exception of southern Ireland. Indeed, even the South African party press, far from condemning Hertzogism lock, stock, and barrel, showed a disturbing tendency to approve sometimes of its more moderate tenets and not infrequently appeared to be mildly pleased about German successes.

The general election was scheduled to take place in October. The election campaign was the bitterest ever held in South Africa, and Smuts was the butt of the most vicious attacks ever made on any individual in South African political history.

The Afrikaner newspaper, *Die Burger,* edited by his boyhood acquaintance, Dr. Malan, and various other Hertzogite newspapers, assailed Smuts day after day, drawing particular attention to his undoubted ineptitude as Minister of Finance, his pro-British proclivities and what they termed his "shameful role" during the rebellion, and accusing him of a host of transgressions some of which were based on fact but the majority of which were fictitious. A clever cartoonist, Boonzaaier, for many years the bane of Smuts's life, drew ingenious cartoons for the Nationalist press depicting Smuts as the Tool of the Capitalists, Britain's Cat's-paw, and the Handyman of the Empire, and in the background, as a reproach, there would frequently be a book bearing the title *A Century of Wrong.*

Smuts's meetings were wild affairs, as a rule, and often broke up in disorder. Even in his own constituency of Pretoria West he could never be sure of a fair hearing, since crowds would come from far and wide to taunt him with shouts of "renegade," "murderer," and "shedder of brothers' blood." At almost every meeting men shouted: "Where is Christiaan Beyers?" "Who killed Delarey?" "Who murdered Jopie Fourie?" And the widows of Fourie and Delarey were used to whip up the feelings of the mob and to stimulate their hatred of Smuts.

The locality of Fourie's grave had not been disclosed to his relatives after his execution. Now it was bruited abroad that the body had been thrown into a hole behind the Pretoria jail—instead of being given a proper burial—and had been covered with unslacked lime so that all traces of it might disappear. The widow was brought into the limelight, and she told indignant audiences that she had thrice made representations to Botha and Smuts about her husband's body and thrice they had refused to give her satisfaction. Thus were the emotions of the populace stimulated. And Smuts's life was frequently in danger. A particularly bloodthirsty crowd received him in a public hall at Newlands in Johannesburg a few weeks before polling day.

The hall was decorated with bunting, flowers, and flags, and above the platform hung a great shield bearing the words: "Welcome to General Smuts." The meeting was advertised as a "social."

Smuts had been warned that there might be "trouble," but had replied laughingly: "We'll go and have a look at them; we'll face them." A friend said: "Jannie, you'll get killed." But Smuts repeated: "We're going to face them."

When he arrived with Ewald Esselen, the leader of the Transvaal bar, the hall was already packed with a hostile mob of Afrikaners singing lustily the old Transvaal anthem, some of them bearing enlarged photographs of Jopie Fourie and Beyers and a large placard reading: "The martyrs of the 4th of July."

As Smuts and his party mounted the platform they were received with loud catcalls and a fusillade of tomatoes, rotten eggs, and stones. Then some roughs began to chant: "Who drowned Beyers? Where is the body of Jopie Fourie? Who fired at us in the streets?"

A man mounted the platform and a woman handed a baby up to him shouting to Smuts: "That is Labuschagne's baby, the child of the man you shot!"

"Do take the child away!" said Smuts. "It may be killed."

A ruffian began to harangue the mob. He said that he was carrying dynamite in his pocket for Smuts and Botha.

Meanwhile Smuts sat staring contemptuously at the tumultuous crowd, and his obvious scorn seemed further to incense them, for a tremendous shower of stones and rotten eggs was hurled again at the platform.

"Esselen," said Smuts, "this is too much. It will only lead to very serious things; we had better not try any further to hold a meeting." But the words had hardly left his mouth when five roughs hurled themselves at him, and he went mad with rage. "Will you?" he shouted. "Now we'll wait!" And while Esselen, a tremendously powerful giant of a man, was shouting to the mob to be careful lest they kill the Minister, and at the same time was holding him back, Smuts almost went berserk in his efforts to get at his would-be assailants, shouting: "I'll show them!" Suddenly he recollected himself, and he and his friends began to fight their way out of the hall. Once he was knocked down but managed to rise again. When the party reached the street Smuts's chauffeur had started the engine of his car. A hooligan, however, switched it off. The chauffeur turned the crank again, but before his efforts finally met with success he was knocked down twice. As Smuts reached the car he was fired at three times, without effect. "Those poor fools can't shoot," he said subsequently. "A miserable mob. I felt sorry for them." A miner standing next to him was struck down with a pick handle and was carried off unconscious. The blow had been intended for Smuts.

On their way home in the car Smuts said to Esselen: "So you call this a social?"

The rigours of the election left their mark on Smuts. He became increasingly despondent and his face became drawn and pinched. To an unfriendly audience he said bitterly: "I would like nothing better than to be out of this hell into which I have wandered, and in which I have lived for the last two years. . . ."

The election results were significant. The Labour party lost heavily since the violent anti-German feeling engendered by the sinking of the *Lusitania* off the Irish coast had impelled almost all Britishers to vote for the Unionist party. The South African party, however, went down badly. It secured not a single seat in the Free State, where Hertzog was almost completely victorious, winning all the seats but one, which was taken by the Unionist party. Indeed, fully 50 per cent of the rural constituencies fell to the Hertzogites. It was a great victory for Hertzogism.

The Nationalists in Parliament were hereafter to constitute the official Opposition. Smuts's and Botha's position was insecure. Three of their Ministers had been defeated at the elections. They had lost their majority in the House and needed the support of the Unionists and the Independents to carry on. This assistance was guaranteed them for the duration of the war. But what was to happen when the war was over? Botha and Smuts were being deserted gradually by the members of their own race. They were in power again, but only by permission of the British electorate. They were there on sufferance.

33

DESPERATELY DESIROUS of being out of the hell into which he had wandered and in which he had lived for two years, Smuts eagerly accepted, in February 1916, the post of commander in chief of the imperial forces in East Africa with the rank of lieutenant general in the British Army. Thus fourteen years after he had harassed the King's soldiers in South Africa he became the second youngest general in His Majesty's Army. Soon he was to be known in England as "the general in whom the whole Empire has most confidence," but in the Union his enemies called curses down upon his head and cried loudly: "He has left for German East to escape his difficulties here."

Since the outbreak of war British and German contingents had been skirmishing incessantly on the frontiers of their colonies in East Africa. But only in the second half of 1915 had the British Cabinet decided to send sufficiently large forces to those parts to hurl the Teutons from British soil and seize the Kaiser's East African possessions. General Smith-Dorrien had been placed in command of His Majesty's forces but had unfortunately fallen desperately ill; hence the appointment of Smuts.

After landing at Mombasa with reinforcements on February 19, he drove straight up to Nairobi, where he remained for twenty-four hours to confer with certain military heads. The settlers organized banquets and other receptions for his entertainment, but he curtly refused all invitations and hurried on to the front through the thick bush to examine the situation.

It was bad. Ever since the beginning of hostilities the enemy had held the whip hand in East Africa, and, according to Smuts, had "been superior . . both in strategy and effective striking force" Nobody had been able to prevent him from making incursions into Nyassaland and the Belgian Congo and from crossing the British border and attacking the Uganda Railway. He had even dug himself in on British territory and had proved to be a constant threat to British lines of communication. In order to get at him from the sea, British forces had attacked his port at Tanga but had been hurled back ferociously and had suffered many casualties. Large numbers of native troops had been effectively trained by German officers in anticipation of events to come. Where, ordinarily, it would have been most vulnerable on account of the proximity of British bases, the enemy's frontier was protected along its entire length by the mighty bulk of Kilimanjaro and the great fastnesses of the Pare and Usambara mountain ranges stretching down towards the sea. In this huge barrier there was only one gap, about five miles in width, lying between the foothills of Kilimanjaro and the northwestern spurs of the Pare Mountains. It was the gateway to German East Africa, which, as Smuts said, was "the jewel of the German Colonial Empire." In this breach lay the British town of Taveta, whence His Majesty's forces had been dislodged eighteen months previously and where the enemy had entrenched himself strongly. Here lay his main forces, guarding the all-important gateway, a constant reminder of German superiority, at least in those regions, and, in view of the ever-growing native army, a deadly menace to the safety of British East Africa. Eight miles in front of the gap stood Salaita hill, which Major General Tighe, Smuts's predecessor, had attempted to storm, with disastrous results, a week or two before the arrival of the new commander in chief.

The situation was serious, as Smuts quickly recognized. He set to work immediately and launched a campaign which was unique in the history of the British Empire in that the conditions under which it was conducted were entirely without precedent. Within the space of ten months he all but drove a powerful enemy from an immense territory, three hundred and sixty-four thousand square miles in extent, and occupied the greater part of it despite a multitude of "natural obstacles and climatic difficulties," such as no general had ever before coped with successfully.

His army was an amazingly polyglot one. It was said by one of his generals that "it could not be possible to bring together a greater hotch-potch of units and mixture of races." There were men from the Gold Coast, Nigeria, and the West Indies, troops from Kashmir, Kaparthalu, Bhurtpur, and Jhind, Royal Fusiliers, South Africans, Rhodesians, Boer settlers in East Africa, Arabs, men from Uganda, natives of the King's East African Rifles, and others. Throughout the campaign these Allied forces varied between fifty-five thousand and one hundred and fourteen thousand men—outnumbering the enemy by far—but the vast majority of them were foreign to the terrain and subject to all the virulent diseases of the insect-infested jungles and germ-laden marshlands of tropical East Africa.

The German Army, on the other hand, consisted of a mere twenty thousand men, the majority of whom were Askaris, practically only the officers being Germans. But it was a well-trained, formidable fighting machine, immune to almost all the tropical diseases which took a heavy toll of Smuts's forces, and commanded by a resolute and skilful leader, Colonel von Lettow-Vorbeck.

He was known as Lettow the One-eyed. A brave and indomitable fighter, he was an inspiring leader, feared by his Askaris but nevertheless regarded by them with veneration. He was always with his men, encouraging and animating them. On three occasions he was wounded, and once he was on the verge of succumbing to blackwater fever. But he remained with his forces although he had to be carried about on a *machela*. He was ubiquitous, putting in unexpected appearances here and there and everywhere to infuse new life into disheartened companies. He was reputed to have sworn an oath on no account ever "to surrender to that damned Dutchman, Jan Smuts." Nor did he. He was a hard taskmaster who refused to tolerate failure. A certain major, Fischer by name, blundered at Moschi, and Smuts's lieutenant, Van Deventer, took the village. In a fury Von Lettow-Vorbeck summoned the culprit and handed him a pistol with the words: "Let me hear some interesting news about you in a day or two." The condemned man walked off with the weapon, but it took him two days to pluck up sufficient courage to shoot himself—in the stomach. Three days later he died. Only towards the close of 1929 did Smuts and Von Lettow-Vorbeck meet face to face.

The occasion was the annual East African dinner in London at which Smuts presided and the German soldier and his wife were the guests of honour.

While Smuts did not underestimate the strength of the enemy he was soon to realize that topographical, climatic, and other natural difficulties peculiar to German East Africa were to prove much graver obstacles to overcome than the enemy himself. Indeed, for the most part, Smuts battled against the country rather than against Von Lettow-Vorbeck.

Twice the size of Germany, the greater part of the colony lay on a vast plateau four to six thousand feet above the sea and stretched from the Indian Ocean in the east to the great lakes in the west. The Central Railway ran across the whole territory from Dar es Salaam to Ujiji on Lake Tanganyika. This had been the romantic meeting place of Livingstone and Stanley in 1871. Another railway, a very much shorter one, linked up the port of Tanga in the north with Moschi at the foot of Kilimanjaro. There were also a few fairly good roads. But on the whole it was a wild and almost trackless country with many thousands of square miles of dense scrub, treacherous marshlands, impenetrable jungle, vast primeval forests, unbridged rivers, grassy steppes, and sandy deserts. In the rainy season, which lasted for half the year, a great part of the terrain became an impassable swamp, making it impossible for soldiers to move about.

Smuts found it to be the loveliest land that he had ever seen and the most difficult to fight in. There were the lofty Uluguru, Nguru, Usambara, and Pare mountains, the volcanoes in the Rift Valley, the great lakes—Kivu, Tanganyika, Nyassa, and Victoria Nyanza—and, most majestic of all, the tremendous bulk of the extinct volcano, Kilimanjaro, heaving its mighty peak nineteen thousand three hundred and twenty-one feet into the air—the highest mountain in all Africa. While its summit was sheathed in snow and ice eternally and in the deep, narrow gorges in its sides were glaciers which fed great rivers, it stood, almost unbelievably, in the tropics. Below the snow line were dense forests, and, much lower down, plantations of maize, bananas, and coffee.

The fauna and flora of the country also added to its fascination and not a little to its danger. Lions and leopards roamed the forests. Poisonous snakes infested the undergrowth. The rhinoceros, the zebra, the antelope, and the giraffe were frequently encountered. Hippopotami and crocodiles sometimes attempted to bar the way through rivers. Near Dakwa crocodiles left the rivers and tore limbs from some native carriers on the tracks through the bush, and killed others.

Beautiful birds with the dazzling plumage peculiar to the tropics, nes-

tling in baobab, tamarisk, and sycamore; multi-coloured butterflies
flitting about the dense foliage; strange beetles and gorgeous dragonflies
in the tall grasses—all these and many more kindred creatures lent colour to the lovely land. They were everywhere. But everywhere, too, was
the malaria mosquito, which poisoned the blood of the troops; the tsetse
fly, which killed off the transport animals by the hundred; and the hateful jigger fly, which burrowed its way at night into the feet of the soldiers, laid its eggs under toenails, and had to be cut out painfully—
thousands of pestilential parasites bringing sickness and death to those
who had not been immunized.

"The real history of the war," wrote a military doctor at the time,
"begins with Smuts; for, before his coming we were merely at war; but
when he came we began to fight." Indeed, no sooner had Smuts arrived
at the front and studied the position than he decided to strike immediately. First the enemy must be dislodged from the supremely important
Taveta gap.

After thorough reconnaissance work lasting almost a week Smuts suddenly launched an attack on Salaita hill, outflanking the enemy on
March 8, driving him back, and taking from him important positions in
the foothills of Kilimanjaro. On the ninth, he hurled him from Taveta.
But the Germans retreated in an orderly manner and entrenched themselves on the hills, Latema and Reata, on either side of the pass. Here
Smuts had to risk a frontal attack, although, like all Afrikaners, he
always favoured the outflanking tactics which Chaka, the Zulu chief,
had taught the Boers. His army was raw and inexperienced, but he sent
them into the pass without hesitation. All night long, while the battle
raged, he paced nervously up and down. "It was his first great battle,"
wrote a friend. "His fate hung in the balance." With the first light of
dawn there came a laconic dispatch from one of the officers in command
of the operations. "I have Reata," it said. Soon after another officer
sent a second dispatch, stating, "I am in possession of Latema." Without
delay Smuts rushed back two messages in reply. They were: "You have
the D.S.O.," and "You have the Military Cross."

Meanwhile General van Deventer had been dispatched by a long
route round Kilimanjaro to take the enemy in the rear but failed to reach
in time the position assigned to him, so that the enemy's retreat was not
cut off. Nevertheless, there followed a quick succession of engagements,
all successful, at Euphorbia hill, Rasthaus, Massai Kraal, and on the
Ruwu and Soko-Nassai rivers, as a result of which the whole Moschi-
Aruscha area, the most fertile region in German East Africa, fell into the
hands of Smuts.

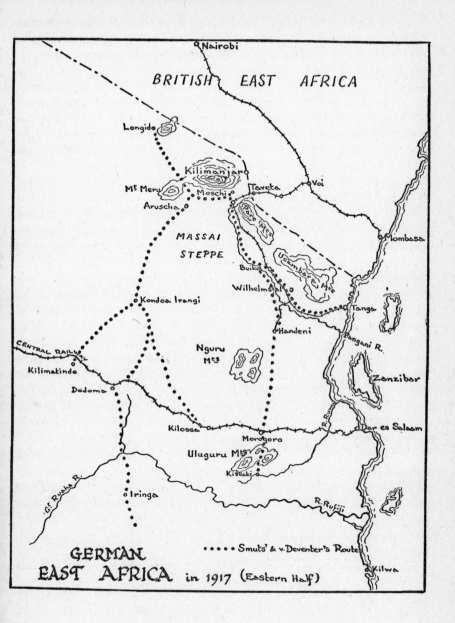

Nairobi

BRITISH EAST AFRICA

Longido

Kilimanjaro

Mᵗ Meru   Moschi   Voi

Aruscha   Taveta

Mombasa

MASSAI STEPPE

Usambara Mᵗˢ

Buiko

Wilhelmstal

Kondoa Irangi   Tanga

Handeni   Pangani R.

CENTRAL RAILW   Nguru Mᵗˢ   Zanzibar

Kilimatinde

Dodoma

Kilossa   Dar es Salaam

Morogoro

Uluguru Mᵗˢ

Kissaki

Iringa

R. Rufiji

GERMAN   ····· Smuts' & v. Deventer's Route

EAST AFRICA in 1917 (Eastern Half)   Kilwa

113

At upper Moschi, high up against the slopes of Kilimanjaro, the commander in chief now established his temporary headquarters, and here in the shade of giant banana trees he planned out his campaign.

The rainy season set in with a vengeance, and before long climatic conditions, transport difficulties, and disease effectively slowed down Smuts's war machine. But he pushed on inexorably. He decided to attack the enemy in his vast territory from every side and thus gradually to pin him down with an ever-contracting cordon of steel. From Lake Nyassa General Northey moved eastward; from the Uganda border Belgian soldiers from the Congo and a detachment of British swept through the bush towards the south, while a second Belgian force advanced eastward from Lake Kivu. From Portuguese East Africa came a Portuguese column heading north across the Rovuma River. Van Deventer was sent inland from Moschi with the second division to seize Kondoa Irangi— regarded by Smuts as "the most important strategic point on the interior plateau"—whence, after some weeks, he hastened by forced marches to Kilimatinde on the Central Railway. Smuts himself followed the main German forces, hastily withdrawing across the Ruwu River and along the Tanga Railway and the great Pangani River past the Pare range in the direction of the Usambara Mountains through Wilhelmstad. From here he cut south through Handeni to Morogoro on the Central Railway, while Van Deventer advanced eastward along the line to Kilossa, whence he swerved south to the great Ruaha River and Iringa. Although the enemy hotly disputed every inch of the way he was pushed south relentlessly, with Van Deventer and Smuts on either flank and in the rear of his main columns.

In the beginning of September, in consequence of all these strategical moves, the entire Central Railway, from Lake Tanganyika to Dar es Salaam, passing through the enemy's chief settlements and military supply depots fell into Smuts's hands, as well as all the territory north of this line, including the seaports and comprising two thirds of German East Africa.

The Germans were now pinned south of the railway. But even here Generals Northey and Van Deventer were systematically clearing the country, and by October Kilwa, in the south, was being prepared as a sea base from which to launch attacks on enemy forces south of the Rufiji River. Early in January 1917 a concerted effort was made by Smuts, General Beves, and others to settle accounts finally with the enemy on the great Rufiji, General Hoskins having been detailed to move up to the northwest from Kilwa to cut off the enemy's retreat. But

Von Lettow-Vorbeck eluded his pursuers as he had done often before in the thick African bush.

All these movements in the tropical East African jungle were accompanied by a tremendous amount of suffering, disease, and death. At one time almost one quarter of Van Deventer's forces was down with fever. With horses and mules dying off by the thousand and other transport difficulties in that marshy, pestilential country, supplies frequently could not be brought up for days and even weeks on end, and then men would suffer the pangs of hunger and some of them would die. Held up by torrential rains, the troops would stew in the steaming jungle, and sometimes they would freeze at night, often with only a blanket and a ground sheet to protect them. Bridges and roads would disappear in the floods, and the size of swamps would be increased a hundredfold and new lakes be formed.

Held up by continuous rains during the month of May, Smuts traversed thereafter in four weeks a distance of two hundred and fifty miles, although more than half of the Europeans with him were ill with malaria and many of the others were gaunt and grey with hunger and suffering.

The casualty list grew alarmingly large, and there was much dissatisfaction in South Africa. In October it became necessary to send back to the Union between twelve and fifteen thousand sick South African troops, and later almost all the Europeans were gradually repatriated and the fighting was done by native soldiers.

It has been said that the commander in chief made his men suffer unnecessarily by driving them too hard in the terrible conditions obtaining in German East Africa. But according to Smuts "timid Fabian strategy would, of all, have been the most fatal in this country and against this enemy." Frequently he drove his troops along at speed to negotiate fever belts with a minimum of casualties. At other times forced marches, ostensibly cruel in the circumstances, brought great rewards. An ordinary commander would have rested his tired troops and jaded animals at Buiko, where already hunger was gnawing at the vitals of both beast and men, but Smuts drove them on inexorably against the advice of "experts" further and further away from their supply bases to take Handeni and to occupy without opposition the eastern end of the all-important Central Railway, with such essential bases as Dar es Salaam and Morogoro. The speed factor enabled Van Deventer to capture Kondoa Irangi "almost bloodlessly"—after he had completed a great march from Aruscha, on Smuts's instructions—and made it possible for him to obtain success after success all along his line of march of close on eight hundred miles to the great Ruaha River. It also made it possible for Smuts to seize Wilhelmstad, without encountering resistance, after a forced march of one hundred and thirty miles.

Weariness, thirst, suffering, and even sickness—these things could not be considered, according to Smuts, "when the success of a big operation trembles in the balance." And he practiced what he preached, for with his men he endured hunger and thirst. He ate the same food. He went without sleep. And frequently he was sick with malaria. But he dosed himself with quinine and iron pills and with arsenic and refused to give in. Tired and pale and washed out, he remained upon his feet, working and planning, as he remains today when bouts of malaria assail him and he goes about his duties in the ordinary way with drawn face and fevered brow.

He was always on the alert, always moving about and doing things for himself, and, as in the Boer War days, he constantly went out to reconnoitre, taking unnecessary risks and being a source of continuous anxiety to his staff officers, who remonstrated with him in vain.

Once in the Pare foothills he went on ahead of his forces with a handful of men to spy out the land. As he was surveying the surroundings from the summit of a kopje, he saw a detachment of enemy soldiers coming up through the thick brush at the foot of the kopje. He shouted to his men, and hurriedly the small party beat a retreat down the hillside, and after a narrow escape reached their columns with clothes badly torn.

Once, in April, he was lost in the bush. Together with three staff officers he was driven by his chauffeur, Sergeant Hodson, from Moschi to Aruscha to confer with Van Deventer. On the way back he took a short cut along one side of the Meru Mountain and lost his way completely. When, finally, he reached his headquarters on the slopes of Kilimanjaro, he had been lost for twenty-four hours and had been driving about endlessly in enemy-occupied territory. But experiences of that kind never taught him a lesson. He appeared to be without fear.

A friend of his once saw him calmly reading a book on philosophy in East Africa during a lull between periods of very severe fighting. He walked up to him.

"Has anything ever really worried you?" he asked.

"Yes!" replied Smuts. "Yes! I once had a sleepless night about political affairs when we were forming the first Cabinet after the Union."

Thousands who were with him in East Africa bear witness to the fact that in the darkest days he alone brought light into their lives. The sight of "the big Vauxhall car in which Smuts daily risked his life" appeared to revitalize them. "The more I think of it," wrote Mr. Brett Young, "the more I realize how the personality of that one man dominated the course of the whole war in East Africa." His men believed in him.

Although still somewhat detached and unapproachable, he was much more human in the field, in most respects, than he had been at home, and by many a kind act he stole the hearts of his men. Early in the morning he would take cups of coffee to soldiers on guard near his tent. Then, again, he would see a wounded man struggling along and would jump from his horse, lift the poor fellow into the saddle, and take him in to camp.

Men and officers alike respected and admired him because he was willing to live as they lived and to face danger, sickness, and death, even as they did. Once, it is said, an irate non-commissioned officer came to interview him to complain about the state of his clothes and to ask whether he could not be supplied with a new uniform and accessories. Smuts appeared at the door of his tent, clad only in riding breeches and a vest, and said with a smile: "Excuse me for appearing like this. Unfortunately I have only one shirt, and it's being washed."

For all his acts of kindness Smuts was capable of excessive ruthlessness on occasion, particularly when he believed that military necessity justified such action. One day he led his men into an ambuscade and fifteen hundred were mowed down. After the battle Indians, native troops, Europeans—officers and all—were buried in two long trenches. There was great despondency among the soldiers, and many of them broke down and wept bitterly. Somebody in desperation ordered the band to strike up, and apparently the first tune that occurred to the bandmaster was "My Little Grey Home in the West." When it was played the tears flowed even more copiously than before. A short distance away stood Smuts, apparently wholly unmoved. Before the engagement he had promised to supply his famished troops with food after the attack, although he knew that it would be impossible to do so. It was a case of military necessity.

In the middle of January, 1917, while operations were still proceeding on the Rufiji River, Smuts was recalled to Cape Town, and asked by Botha to proceed immediately to England as the Union's representative at the forthcoming Imperial Conference. General Hoskins succeeded him as commander in chief in East Africa. Von Lettow-Vorbeck was still at large, and was never captured; until after the armistice he and his guerrilla bands roamed the country. But Smuts had taken the sting out of them, and they were no longer a menace.

SECTION V

34

HAVING brought about the resignation of Mr. Asquith from the premier-ship of Great Britain, the more vigorous and practical Lloyd George, the fiery Celt of the flowing mane, had formed a ministry himself and, soon after his accession to power, had called an imperial war conference.

Circumstances at home had made it imperative for Botha not to leave South Africa's shores; hence the invitation to Smuts to represent the Union at the conference. It was a heaven-sent opportunity for him to leave East Africa: the campaign no longer interested him as its big and spectacular phases were over and the process of mopping up here and there and the problematical cornering of the ubiquitous Von Lettow-Vorbeck could safely be left to others. Such details held little interest for Smuts.

Back in the Union he spoke in glowing terms of the conquest of East Africa. "Through our own efforts," he said, "and our own sacrifices, we have secured a voice in the ultimate disposal of this subcontinent. . . . We have followed in the steps of the Voortrekkers and pioneers, and I trust that the future pioneers will continue in these steps, and that South Africa, instead of being a small, cramped, puny country, gnawing at its own entrails, will have a larger freedom and a better life, and will become the great country which is its destiny. . . ."

His words resounded across the Union, but his countrymen, far from echoing his sentiments, inveighed against him with ferocity. Who was this man Smuts to identify himself with the Voortrekkers, whose ideas and ideals had differed so radically from his British imperialism? Rather was he the reincarnation of Rhodes, for, like the ruthless multimillion-aire, he had not scrupled to subordinate justice, national pride, the sacred spirit of Nationalism, and the honour of his race to dreams of imperial expansion. Let him go to England, his spiritual home, there to

118

become a privy councillor like Botha. South Africa was obviously too small for him and his great ideas. Let him get out and stay out.

It was with a feeling of profound relief that Smuts embarked for England.

In peculiar contrast to his reception by his own people on his return from East Africa, Smuts was hailed in England as the hero of the hour and the harbinger of hope to a sorely tried Britain.

The propaganda value of the "Conqueror of East Africa," the former Boer general now fighting for the Empire, was fully realized by the Government and thoroughly exploited.

On public platforms, in pamphlets, and in the newspapers Smuts was lauded as the first successful general of the Allies in the war; as "the general in whom the whole Empire has most confidence"; as "the destroyer of the German power in Africa"; as "the most conspicuous figure in greater Britain"; and as "a remarkable combination of talents not usually found in the same person, unless, indeed, that person belongs to the small and select class of which the Caesars, the Cromwells, and the Napoleons are the outstanding types." His character was described as "too spacious and complex to be read offhand." In an article in the press Mr. Winston Churchill wrote: "At this moment there arrives in England from the outer marches of the Empire a new and altogether extraordinary man. . . . The stormy and hazardous roads he has travelled by would fill all the acts and scenes of a drama. He has warred against us —well we know it. He has quelled rebellion against our own flag with unswerving loyalty and unfailing shrewdness. He has led raids at desperate odds and conquered provinces by scientific strategy. . . . His astonishing career and his versatile achievements are only the index of a profound sagacity and a cool, far-reaching comprehension. . . ." And while introducing him to the Imperial War Cabinet, Mr. Lloyd George referred to him as "one of the most brilliant generals in this war."

Much of this fulsome praise was deliberately planned propaganda, but much was inspired by genuine admiration for Smuts's great qualities and deep gratitude for his indispensable assistance.

Smuts arrived in England in the darkest days of the war and he became a "beacon in the gloom." The cataclysmic revolution in Russia had almost reached its zenith, the Tsar and his family had been murdered in cold blood, and the Russian Army which had sought to stem the flood of Teutons from the west was rapidly deserting the Allies; the German submarine menace had reached the peak of its devastating effectiveness and was threatening to bring about starvation in England; a serious mutiny had enervated the French Army and there had been resultant changes in the High Command and in the Cabinet; the mighty German armies, seemingly irresistible, were battering to pieces the fabric of France and the minds and bodies of hundreds of thousands of Allied soldiers; many thought that the French and British forces were on the verge of collapse; and effective assistance from the United States was as yet non-existent.

Into this atmosphere of disaster and desperation came Jan Smuts. Soon he stood revealed in the full glare of publicity, as an exceptional man; the eyes of millions were turned towards him. He did not fail them. He brought hope to the downhearted and courage to the weak. In a series of inspired addresses he lifted up the nation, and his name became a household word. His words were invariably full of hope and his tone was invariably cheerful. To those who looked aghast at Russia and the prostration of her great armies, he spoke with great calmness and great confidence, saying that "the spirit of freedom was on the wing and the Great Creative Spirit was once more moving among the nations in their unspeakable anguish. . . ."

Large crowds flocked to his meetings and listened intently to his speeches. Many of the things he said their own leaders had uttered frequently, but when Smuts spoke, in some way or other the old phrases acquired a new significance. He revived their faith in the Empire whose "permanence and strength" as a bulwark of civilization were indestructible. In their anxiety and fear many had begun to doubt the justice of their cause and the righteousness of their imperial zeal in the past. But here was a former enemy who had fought against them and their Empire, and he now assured them that empire was not "founded on might or force but on moral principles—on principles of freedom, equality, and equity. . . ." And he also said: "Fifteen years ago I was fighting against the British Empire. There is no change in me. The cause I fought for fifteen years ago is the cause for which I am fighting today. I fought for liberty and freedom then and I am fighting for them today. . . ." And the crowds would cheer Smuts with a religious fervor and leave his meetings revitalized and reassured as to the justice of their cause and the sacredness of their Empire. They would shoulder their burdens with new strength and fresh determination.

Smuts became known as the "Orator for the Empire." The great influence he wielded as such lay primarily in the fact of his having been a Boer general and a past enemy.

Writing in the *Daily News,* A. G. Gardiner declared: "It is not too much to say that the speeches he [Smuts] has delivered in this country since his arrival have done more than any utterances of the time to clear the issue and moralize our cause. . . ."

Everywhere in Britain he received the freedom of great cities, public receptions, university degrees, and whatever other honours could be lavished upon him. Receiving the degree of LL.D. at Cambridge he was referred to as "like the younger Scipio, our Second Africanus."

In May dozens of Britain's greatest men attended a banquet held in his honour in the Royal Gallery of the House of Lords. Among those present were Milner, Asquith, Bonar Law, Northcliffe, and Winston Churchill. Lord French presided and referred to Smuts's Great Trek across the Cape Colony in the Anglo-Boer War. "Day after day," he said, "week after week, month after month, our distinguished guest, with every disadvantage in the way of numbers, arms, transport equipment, and supplies, evaded all my attempts to bring him to decisive action." It was on this occasion that Smuts first used the phrase, "the British Commonwealth of Nations," and with eloquence and rare insight referred to "future constitutional relations and readjustments in the British Empire. . . ." In Britain his speech received great publicity and was eulogized throughout the land, but in South Africa the Afrikaner press spoke derisively of "Smuts, the bearer of imperialism . . . among the Lords in London." And even a friend, so the Nationalists said, cabled him: "Heartiest congratulations, but, I beg you, Jannie, come back before they find you out."

Once, shortly after he had joined the British War Cabinet, Smuts was asked to act as host at a dinner party—one of a number given by John Evelyn Wrensch in honour of visiting American editors. He took the chair willingly and spoke about the Commonwealth of Nations and its "war effort." In the course of the evening Wrensch received a note from General Seeley (later Lord Mottistone) who begged to be allowed "to propose the chairman's health." "As the only man present," he wrote, "who has actually had a shot at him (I admit a reflection on my marksmanship) and then sat in council with him, I should like the job." The toast, however, had already been assigned to Edward Bok of the *Ladies' Home Journal,* but Seeley was asked to second it. This he did very successfully, relating with gusto the story of his unsuccessful attempt on Smuts's life during the Boer War. "Our American guests were spellbound," wrote Wrensch afterwards. "This was unrehearsed propaganda with a vengeance! Here was a Dutch patriot who had fought Great Britain sixteen years before and now was one of the supreme directors of the destiny of the mighty British Empire exchanging chaff with a British general who had tried to shoot him among the boulders of a

South African kopje." How, thought they, could one reconcile this scene with the historical notion of Britain as the "oppressor of small nations"—an idea which had been assiduously fostered by many Irish-Americans and had been disseminated among the youth of various American schools?

At the meetings of the Imperial War Cabinet Smuts gave ample evidence of wisdom and farsightedness. He spoke rarely, but whenever he rose to address the council he was listened to with attention and respect. He brought to the meetings acute discernment and freshness of outlook which none of the other members could approximate. Suggesting to Lord Riddell that Lloyd George would be wise to make him a member of the War Cabinet, Winston Churchill spoke of him as "the only unwounded statesman of outstanding ability in the Empire." "By 'unwounded,' " wrote Lord Riddell in his diary, "he meant the only one who is fresh and bright, unwounded mentally and physically."

After his first fortnight in the Imperial War Cabinet Smuts had made so profound an impression on his associates that various generals, admirals, and statesmen with grievances—and there were surprisingly many of them with grievances—brought their troubles to him and found him both sympathetic and helpful. He was in his element here in London, the hub of the universe, giving advice to important men, solving problems, and settling difficulties.

Soon Lloyd George sent him to Belgium and France on an important mission. He was to examine the situation on the Western Front, to interview Painlevé, the French President, and to visit King Albert of the Belgians, whose dejection at the time was causing anxiety.

Not far from the Belgian front he met the King, who was utterly downcast. The prolongation of hostilities and the unspeakable suffering of his people had unnerved him. He despaired of the ultimate outcome of the war and the eventual fate of Belgium. But he was comforted somewhat by Smuts's positive declaration that the main purpose of the British Government's war effort was to look after Belgium's interests.

Smuts's talks with the French President were confined to a close examination of the Allies' ultimate war aims.

On the Western Front he was the recipient of Belgian and French decorations. He held discussions with Haig, and made a thorough examination of the military position. Then he hastened back to England to report to Lloyd George.

His memorandum dated April 17, 1917, was laid before the War Cabinet. In his report of the situation in France, he stated, *inter alia,* that "the most serious result of all is that our whole army (with the exception of the forces conducting campaigns elsewhere) has been locked up on the Western Front. . . . We have gradually shouldered more and more of the burden of defending France, and so both the French and English armies have become pinned down along the Western Front. . . ." It was his considered opinion that some of the British forces should be released, and that offensives on other fronts might have a beneficent effect on the eventual outcome of the war.

Neither the chief of the Imperial General Staff, Sir William Robertson, nor Sir Douglas Haig, nor, for that matter, the majority of British military experts, believed that the troop concentrations on the Western Front should be weakened in the interests of the establishment of "minor fronts," since they all believed that a conclusive victory could be achieved nowhere else than on the Western Front. But Lloyd George supported Smuts's idea. Indeed for many months the British Prime Minister had been a stanch advocate of minor fronts.

There were many points of resemblance between the two men: both were ruthless; to both the end frequently justified the means; both were exceedingly clever; both had great courage; neither could brook opposition; neither could bear delay; both were despotic; both loved power; and neither could tolerate the obstructive red tape of officialdom or the dull orthodoxy of trained soldiers. Lloyd George gave expression to the sentiments of both of them when he said. "There is no profession in which experience and training count less, while judgment and flair . . . imagination, resource, initiative, and flexibility are more essential to success in the vocation of the soldier than in any other."

Not satisfied with General Murray's progress against the Turks in the Near East, Lloyd George asked Smuts to take over the Palestine command.

The thought of driving unbelievers out of the Holy Land and of entering "Jerusalem the Blessed" at the head of a victorious army was one which appealed greatly to the romantic side of Smuts's nature. He was tempted to accept the command, but Sir William Robertson and others at the War Office did their best to dissuade him, assuring him that it would be impossible to furnish him with sufficient supplies and men to conduct an active offensive and achieve sensational results. But Lloyd George was insistent.

"Come direct to us and we will see you through," he said to Smuts.

"No, I don't believe you could," was the reply.

In his diary Field Marshal Sir Henry Wilson recorded the following at the time: "Long talks with Smuts and Leo Amery. Smuts sent over

by Lloyd George to ask my opinion on the following matter: would it
be a good plan to appoint Smuts as commander in chief and High Commissioner to Palestine, Mesopotamia, Armenia, Caucasus, and eastern
Mediterranean? He is to be outside and not under the War Cabinet, and
as such to deal direct with Government departments, the Sirdar, the
Viceroy of India, etc. At the same time he is to conduct operations and
issue orders to the admiral in the Mediterranean, to Allenby, to Mar-
shall, and so on. Whew! Whew! Whew! After a tremendous wrangle I
think I got it into their heads that such an appointment is quite out of
the question."

In the end Smuts declined the Premier's offer. Perhaps he was afraid
of being landed in the wings when he wished to play an important part
in the centre of the stage.

Lloyd George's disappointment was keen. "Smuts made a great mistake in not accepting the command in Palestine," he said afterwards.
"The conquest of Palestine would have been an historic feat of arms."

But Smuts knew what he was about. His decision was a wise one—
for Smuts. And for Britain. He did, subsequently, visit the Near East at
the instance of the War Cabinet. It was an important mission. He had
four advisers with him. At Versailles he consulted with Sir Henry Wilson, and in Rome he had conversation with the Director General of
Military Transport and the First Lord of the Admiralty. At Alexandria
and in Cairo he held various consultations and finally he devised plans
for a Palestine campaign with Allenby, who had been appointed to the
command in the Near East when Smuts had refused it. After numerous
hitches Allenby got going and, without the "great amphibious operation" of Smuts's dreams, triumphed over the Turks in Syria and entered
the city of Jerusalem.

35

THE SESSIONS of the Imperial War Cabinet having ended, it was time
for Smuts, in the normal course of events, to return to South Africa. But
Lloyd George was loath to lose his services. To the amazement of all and
the vexation of not a few, the Welshman asked him to become a member
of the British War Cabinet, the Premier's "innermost Cabinet," which
virtually ran the war for Britain. Smuts accepted. His status was tanta-

mount to that of a Minister without Portfolio. He was requested later to become a British M.P., in order to "regularize his position," but refused to take this step lest his political position in South Africa be jeopardized. The other principal members of the War Cabinet were Lloyd George, Lord Curzon, Bonar Law, Lord Carson, Barnes, and Lord Milner.

Smuts's inclusion in this Cabinet has been called "one of the great paradoxes of imperial history." And so it was. There was the Boer general of fifteen years before sitting in a British War Cabinet with Carson and Curzon and, strangest of all, with Milner—a body of seven men, all told, in whom had been vested more power than in any other similar body since the dawn of time.

In a letter to his brother, F. S. Oliver wrote: "I regard the taking in of Smuts to the War Cabinet as a most important step. So far as pure intellect goes he is the superior of any member at present on it; and by intellect I don't mean merely the power of understanding what is written . . . but that curious and most rare quality of seeing into the very heart of a subject, coupled with the further and still rarer quality, in combination with the foregoing, of being able to state clearly what he has seen. . . ."

Smuts was not particularly impressed by the majority of his colleagues. But he thought much of Milner and Lloyd George. "Lloyd George," he said, "is more than fascinating. He has genius. His mind is brilliant, energetic, resourceful, and courageous without limit. . . . History will show him the biggest Englishman of them all." With his former arch-enemy, Milner, he struck up a quick friendship, and the joint efforts of their incisive minds proved of inestimable value to the War Cabinet.

It has been suggested that Kruger's former lieutenant was taken into the War Cabinet not only because of his indispensable qualities as counsellor and plenipotentiary and the confidence he inspired, but largely also because the man in the street regarded him "as a counterpoise to elements it distrusted wholly." There is much in this suggestion. There is no denying the fact that in the dark days of 1917 and 1918 the War Cabinet on several occasions took "shelter behind the prestige of his name."

Speaking to Colonel Repington shortly after his appointment, Smuts said: "I am going to advise on military affairs, and will steer clear of politics."

"You are the only man in the War Cabinet with military experience," was the reply, "and we look to you to keep the politicians straight, and also to safeguard the interests of generals, some of whom, like Murray, have been scurvily treated. The War Cabinet has been twice condemned by the only commissions which have investigated their proceedings, and if other inquiries were made into Salonika, Palestine, and Home Defence, similar condemnations would result."

The Right Honorable Christopher Addison bears witness to the fact that Smuts "was at all times very scrupulous lest he should become involved in any differences of opinion or controversies that were of a strictly domestic character."

As a rule he said little during the meetings of the War Cabinet. In fact, on one or two occasions he said nothing at all. But his rare utterances were notable for their sagacity.

Here in England, far removed from the rancour and harassment of South African politics, he was happy. He loved to be busy all day with important work—doing big things, playing a very important part in directing the destinies of a great Empire at the time of her greatest need, and doing it all without the embarrassment of responsibility, for his services were gratuitous and his status only quasi-ministerial. He was happy, more tolerant than of yore, and much more human. Although his old reserve still clung to him like a garment, he was more accessible than he had been in South Africa. A colleague spoke of him as "a wise and sagacious counsellor and a good friend." Amid the turmoil and strife of a world gone mad, he was cool, calm, and collected—a steadfast rock and safe anchorage. "Nearly everyone I have met has asked me to be certain to meet Smuts," wrote President Wilson's special envoy, Colonel House, in his journal on November 13, 1917. "He has grown to be the lion of the hour. . . . He is one of the few men I have met in the Government who do not feel tired. He's alert, energetic, and forceful."

It was at this time that Lord Northcliffe earnestly exhorted the British Government to send Smuts on a special mission to America to clear up doubts in that country about the effectiveness of the British war effort. Reports extolling the deeds of the French and Canadians had been constantly getting through to the United States, but little had been heard in that country of British endeavour and achievement. The majority of Americans apparently believed that the forces of Britain were being kept at home while her allies were bearing the brunt of the war. Clearly an influential man must be sent from England to put matters right. "As to big men," said Northcliffe, "the only big military man who could help here [in America] is Smuts." Moreover, praise of the British war effort would be more palatable coming from him, an outsider, than from an Englishman. And then, to clinch the matter, Colonel House had recently stated that Smuts was looked upon in America as among the few great ones in the world.

In the end, however, Sir F. E. Smith (who became Lord Birkenhead) was sent because the War Cabinet felt that Smuts was indispensable in England.

Smuts was housed in the Savoy Hotel in a luxurious suite of rooms. Never before had he known such luxury. But his ascetic tastes would have been satisfied equally well in much humbler surroundings. However, he did not spend much time at the Savoy, for he was constantly working. "I had no time for anything but work," he remarked afterwards. "There was no end to the work they wanted me to do. I have never worked so hard in my life. My hair became white. My brother, at sixty, has hardly a white hair. My hair was nearly white at fifty."

He avoided social functions like the plague. Occasionally he would visit the Gillets at Oxford or some other friends but, as a rule, he remained in London and worked. He became a member of a club or two but rarely went to them. Even at the Savoy he lived very simply. The choicest dishes had little attraction for him. Frugal meals would have suited him better. Sometimes he longed for the simple but strengthening Afrikaner food. Sometimes he would receive biltong (strips of dried flesh) from home, and then he would tear at the brittle Afrikaner delicacy with his teeth, almost ravenously, and enjoy every bit of it.

Often amid the rain and sleet and the murkiness of the London fog he would pine for the undulating African veld under clear African skies. But he had little time to think of home because of his unceasing labours.

In spite of the severe strain imposed by his work he remained well because of his ascetic habits and his love of exercise. He rarely drank alcoholic beverages. He never smoked. He took long walks across Richmond Park. On Sundays he would motor into the country and walk briskly for hours on end. Once, while he was out on a tramp in Buckinghamshire, a sudden crisis demanded his immediate return to London, but only after searchers had combed the countryside for several hours was he found.

36

SMUTS'S VERSATILITY was such that the War Cabinet used him for a great variety of purposes.

He was offered the leadership of a secret expedition to Russia, but he turned down the proposal after due consideration, believing that a Russia in the throes of a revolution could no longer be of any assistance to the cause of the Allies. It was he who planned the Alexandretta campaign long before going to advise and assist Allenby in the Near East. When it seemed that Holland's neutrality might be violated by the Germans, he was given the task of elaborating a scheme to protect that country. He became a member of the Middle East Committee, which was presided over by Lord Curzon and which kept a watchful eye on the war in the East. He was a member also of the Northern Neutral Committee, of which Lord Carson was chairman and which concerned itself entirely with the campaign in northwestern Europe; over various committees he presided himself. Constantly he flitted from front to front and returned to report on the war situation, the state of the armies, and the problems of the navies. He was invited to preside over a convention on Ireland where loyalists and rebels were to meet, but he declined the invitation on the advice of Sir James Craig (later Lord Craigavon). Meanwhile also he was looking into the future and devoting much of his time to postwar problems and to the elaboration of a scheme for a league of nations; he continued making speeches of encouragement all over Great Britain, and by means of them continued to bring stimulation and hope to many an anxious heart and to rouse from languor many a weary body. He was sent on an important mission to Geneva to sound an Austrian envoy on the question of a separate peace. He was used to settle strikes. He co-ordinated and placed on an efficient basis the air defences of Great Britain, and established the Royal Air Force. He also brought into being the War Priorities Committee.

Working on numerous war committees, Smuts realized soon after his arrival in England that lack of co-ordination between the various departments of the great British war machine was the cause of much disharmony and dissipation of energy. As time went on, larger and larger quantities of war materials of every description and more men were required for the successful prosecution of the war. But, instead of working harmoniously together in the interest of the common cause, each of the various departments was selfishly concerned solely with its own welfare, its prestige, and its productive capacity, regarding the others as rivals and taking unfair advantage of them at every turn. Winston Churchill, for instance —who, with the backing of Carson and Smuts, had been made Minister of Munitions—complained that the output of munitions was being seriously curtailed by the fact that the War Office was recruiting large numbers of both skilled and unskilled munition workers. To be sure the War Cabinet was the "final court of appeal" in such matters as in all others, but it was overloaded with work and could hardly do justice to the difficult matter of priorities.

In the autumn of 1917 Smuts suggested that a priorities committee be established with the Secretary of State for Air, the Minister of National Service, the Minister of Munitions, the First Lord of the Admiralty, and the Secretary of State for War serving on it and with a member of the War Cabinet in the chair. His suggestion was immediately adopted. And Lloyd George asked him to act as chairman.

The committee was an outstanding success. But Smuts's task was not an easy one. "Never, I suspect," wrote Churchill, "in all the vicissitudes of his career has General Smuts stood more in need of . . . tact and adroitness."

From time to time severe damage was done to the nation's war effort by strikers. In their desperation the Government turned to Smuts. In South Africa it had been his custom to deal with industrial upheavals with the mailed fist, but in England he handled matters differently. He interceded in an unofficial capacity in labour disputes and other disturbances with remarkable success.

A police strike in London he settled without difficulty.

A strike by fifty thousand munition workers at Coventry was more serious. He left London with his colleague, George N. Barnes, to investigate matters and to persuade the men to return to work, and soon he was back in London again, having accomplished his purpose.

Meanwhile, however, very serious trouble was brewing in Wales, where the coal miners were in an ugly mood on account of pacifist agitation. Thousands of men were leaving the mines at a very critical time. "A paralyzing blow," said Smuts, "was being struck at us when we were being told by our navy that they only had reserves of coal for a week, and if the strike went on for another week, we should be paralyzed and finished."

Smuts left hurriedly for Wales. As he was going off the Prime Minister said to him: "Remember my fellow countrymen are great singers!"

At Cardiff he was honoured by the university with a doctorate. In the afternoon he set out for the coal fields, encountering strikers everywhere and frequently leaving his car to make a short speech. Towards nightfall he arrived at Tonypandy, which was the chief centre of the strike. Here tens of thousands of wrathful Welshmen had gathered to hear the man from Africa.

"Gentlemen," Smuts began, "I come from far away, as you know. I do not belong to this country. I have come a very long way to do my bit in this war, and I am going to talk to you tonight about this trouble. But I have heard in my country that the Welsh are among the greatest singers in the world, and before I start, I want you first of all to sing me some of the songs of your people."

There was silence. Then a man in the crowd started singing "Land of My Fathers." Immediately all the rest followed and with intense fervour they went through all the soul-stirring lines. The effect of the anthem was amazing. Deeply moved by its strains, the great mass of people stood silent. Then Smuts spoke. "Well, gentlemen, it is not necessary for me to say much more tonight. You know what has happened on the Western Front. You know your comrades in their tens of thousands are risking their lives. You know that the front is just as much here as anywhere else. The trenches are in Tonypandy, and I am sure you are actuated by the same spirit as your comrades in France. It is not necessary for me to add anything. You know it as well as I do, and I am sure you are going to defend the Land of your Fathers, of which you have sung here tonight, and that no trouble you may have with the Government about pay or anything else will ever stand in the way of your defence of the Land of your Fathers."

The same night Smuts addressed various other meetings on the coal fields in the same way.

Arriving back in London on the following afternoon, he attended a Cabinet meeting. His colleagues asked him: "What happened? All the men are at work. How did you settle it?" "Well," replied Smuts, "it is news to me that the men are at work." And afterwards he said, "The 'Land of My Fathers' saved us."

On a clear morning in July 1917 a big squadron of German airplanes suddenly appeared over London, dropped a great load of bombs in thickly populated areas, wrought much damage to buildings, took severe toll of human life—killing, among others, a number of children in the East End of the city—and flew off again unscathed.

Now, although there had been air raids before, they had never taken place on so great a scale nor had children been slain in the streets. Public indignation was surpassed only by public anxiety. If a thing like that could happen once, it could happen again. What protection was there for the citizens of London and for the inhabitants of the other cities and towns of Britain? The danger from the air was a very real one. What was the Government going to do about it? How was it that the air forces had allowed the German planes to appear over London and then to get away scot-free after doing their work of destruction? Was there anything the matter with Britain's air organization?

There undoubtedly was. The trouble lay mainly in the traditional jealousy between the Army and the Navy and the consequent lack of co-ordination between their air services, and in the multiplicity of air chiefs independent of one another and directly responsible to no central authority.

The efforts of Lords Derby, Curzon, and Cowdray to establish co-operation between the air arms of the Army and the Navy had resulted in nothing, and the creation of an air board had not prevented the "senior services" from taking matters into their own hands and from queering each other's pitch instead of promoting cohesion and collaboration in the interests of a common victory.

Now suddenly a successful German raid brought home to all Britons the realization of London's vulnerability from the air and the inefficiency of the separate British air forces in a protective capacity.

The Government was severely assailed from all sides and the whole thing threshed out in a secret session of the House of Commons. The Cabinet met, and, after lengthy discussions, decided to leave the solution of air-defence problems, the reorganization of the air forces, and all matters pertaining to the effective expansion of the nation's air arm as an offensive weapon to the Prime Minister and Smuts, who were to discuss all details with representatives from the Army and the Navy and the field marshal in command of the home forces. Lloyd George, however, backed out, and it was left to Smuts to get on with the great task.

He set about it with a vengeance, brushing aside ruthlessly any attempts to hamper him on the part of navy or army officers who were loath to part with the established order of things. With lightning rapidity he acquainted himself with all matters of detail, assimilating all that was necessary and casting aside irrelevant facts. Soon he had before him everything he wanted, and immediately he started breaking down and rebuilding.

For London he devised an effective defence plan, placing all air units in and around the city under one command, establishing anti-aircraft batteries at important strategic points, and making provision for the adequate training of fighter pilots whose work it would be to drive off or shoot down the enemy, long before he arrived at the outskirts of London.

Similar air-defence schemes were contrived for the other great cities of Britain.

But, besides making arrangements to protect the cities from air attacks, Smuts had planned to blend the air forces into one fighting service apart from the Navy and the Army, and to create an air ministry to look after its interests and control its destinies. All these projects were duly approved by the Cabinet, embodied in a Parliamentary Bill and accepted by both Houses. Thus did the Royal Air Force come into its being at the instance of Smuts.

With such amazing speed had he worked that in the space of three months he had completely reorganized the air defences of Britain, created a new fighting service and a new Ministry, and made it possible shortly to carry out his own wish of defending "this island effectively against air attacks by offensive measures, by attacking the enemy in his air bases on the Continent, and in that way destroying his power of attacking us across the Channel"—a Gargantuan task, the fulfilment of which had seemed impossible even within a couple of years.

In their enthusiasm newspapers demanded that Smuts be given "sole command of the United Air Services. Give him control. Let him have, without question, without delay, the things he asks for—supplies, men, money—and it will be the greatest day's work that any Prime Minister will ever have performed."

In England Smuts had long since become known as the Handyman of the Empire. Also in South Africa; but there it was a term of obloquy.

In his own country he was without honour among his own people.

37

In june 1917 Admiral Jellicoe, Sir Douglas Haig, and Sir William Robertson suggested to the War Cabinet a scheme for a tremendous offensive in Flanders, the object of which was to drive the Germans from their submarine bases at Zeebrugge and Ostend and thereby (according to Jellicoe) to enable the British Fleet to keep open the vitally important lines of communication between Britain and her army in France. There was a second and more compelling reason (according to Smuts) which made a Flanders offensive imperative. The French lines were gradually crumbling beneath the weight of the Germans, the latest disaster being the unexpected rout of large forces under Joffre's successor, Nivelle, in the Compiègne; a large number of Pétain's men had mutinied; the fall of Paris was more than possible; as yet only small numbers of reinforcements had arrived from America—too few by far to bolster up the tottering

French. "It seemed likely," says Smuts, "that if we did not draw the Germans away from the French, not only would Pétain fail to hold his line, but Paris might be taken and the war lost before even the weight of the American Army could be felt."

Lloyd George, scornful as ever of Haig and Robertson and professional soldiers in general, and still hankering after offensives on the minor fronts, was strongly opposed to the Flanders project. The victories at Vimy and Massines had resulted in nothing. They had been "brilliant preliminary successes," said he, "followed by weeks of desperate and sanguinary struggle, leading to nothing except perhaps the driving of the enemy back a few barren miles—beyond that nothing to show except a ghastly casualty list. I earnestly entreat our military advisers as well as the Cabinet to think again before they finally commit the British Army to an attack."

Bonar Law and Milner also opposed the venture. Curzon was lukewarm. But Smuts felt that Haig and Robertson "had made out their case for at least having a good try" and considered "the chances highly favourable." He felt that, if necessary, the sacrifice of half a million men would be justified by a successful attack. Balfour followed the lead he gave, and so, eventually, did the rest of the Cabinet. And despite the protestations of Foch—who, like Smuts, desired a British offensive in order to give the French relief, but who, unlike Smuts, knew the dangers inherent in a great offensive in the Passchendaele area—the attack was launched.

Before long the big guns tore up the drainage system of the flat country and the rain came down in torrents and the whole area became a great sticky swamp. The attackers floundered about helplessly in the omnipresent mud, making no appreciable progress and being mown down in their tens of thousands by the withering fire of the enemy. The carnage was appalling. Thousands of wounded men sank helplessly beneath the surface of the mud and were smothered to death. There were close on half a million casualties in that awful battle.

It was a dire calamity—this Passchendaele offensive. Lloyd George shifted the blame onto Haig's shoulders. Smuts continued to be his trusted adviser and plenipotentiary.

"As it happened," says Smuts, "the Channel ports were not freed by the offensive, and we lost four hundred thousand men. What there is to put against this terrible cost is that it probably saved the war." That, however, is a moot point.

On July 3, 1917, Sir Henry Wilson wrote these words in his diary: "I explained the situation in France and finished by saying that, although not desperate, it undoubtedly was serious. I was struck by the tone of the committee, except Smuts, who seemed rather to revel in the idea that the situation was desperate and impossible. Of course, this is nonsense."

The situation in France was grave to be sure. Everyone knew that. Feverishly the Cabinet groped round for allies.

In order to consolidate behind them the great power of World Jewry (and American Jewry in particular) the Government of Great Britain undertook to establish in Palestine, in the event of an Allied victory, a national home for the Jews. Smuts says that the undertaking was given "to rally Jewish sympathy for the Allied cause at the darkest hour of the war." The promise was duly embodied in a document signed by Balfour, as Foreign Secretary, on behalf of the British Government. It has been known since as the Balfour Declaration.

According to Lloyd George, the suggestion which gave rise to it emanated originally from Dr. Chaim Weizmann, at the time Professor of Chemistry at the University of Manchester, who, having made an exceedingly important discovery in regard to explosives, declined, on presenting it to the Government, to accept a personal reward, but begged that Palestine might become the national home of the Jews.

Now, exactly fifteen months after the commencement of the war, when the Allied forces were reeling under shattering blows, the British Government in its desperate need had promised Palestine, among other things, to Hussein in exchange for the assistance of the Arabs in the Near East.

The Balfour Declaration, therefore, was made in violation of a solemn undertaking given to the Arabs, as was the Sykes-Picot agreement of May 1916, whereby rights and territories previously promised to Hussein were assigned to the French.

Smuts was a party to the declaration. But he had nothing to do with the promises made to the Arabs, nor was he concerned in the Sykes-Picot agreement.

For a decade he had counted the Jews in South Africa among his stanchest supporters. He had been friendly to them since the early post-Boer War years because their support meant much to him.

For many years now he has co-operated with them. Perhaps, above all other world statesmen, he has been the most consistent champion of their cause. Nor have they been forgetful of his services: their efforts have added greatly to his stature in world affairs.

And in the ancient Valley of Zebulun, in the shadow of Mount Carmel, they purchased a piece of land some years ago. They called it Ramat Jochanan Smuts in honour of the man who in his own country has been called "King of the Jews." While Jewry controls that part of Palestine where stands Mount Carmel, the name of Smuts will never be forgotten in the Holy Land.

Meanwhile the Government was looking for assistance and relief in other quarters also.

It was rumoured that Austria, exhausted by the interminable struggle, torn by internal dissension and verging on starvation, was both anxious and ready to desert Germany and sue for a separate peace. The new Emperor Karl and his Bourbon queen were, it was stated, particularly desirous of putting an end to hostilities.

With characteristic obstinacy in the face of vehement protests from the Foreign Office, Lloyd George decided to get into touch with Austria. It was a most inopportune moment: a great calamity had just taken place at Caporetto; the Italian front lay open; there was a strong possibility of the Germans opening up a new front in the vicinity of Lyons after sweeping across northern Italy; on the whole the position in which the Central Powers found themselves was particularly sound. Nor was it conceivable that Germany, whose iron grip encircled Austria, would allow that country to leave her in the lurch. It should have been patent to every member of the British Government that Austrian peace overtures at such a time and under such circumstances must be spurious and must of necessity contain a dangerous ulterior motive.

But Lloyd George was determined to negotiate and, in carrying out his resolve, made the final blunder of dispatching to Geneva—which teemed with spies of every nation—General J. C. Smuts whose fame had spread throughout Europe; for thus he divulged to the enemy how earnestly desirous he was of enticing Austria away from her Allies and how great his need was.

Before Smuts was approached in connection with the mission to Switzerland, Lord Reading had been asked to undertake it but had refused to do so. "It would not do for me to go," he said, "because everyone would wonder what the Chief Justice of England was doing in Switzerland."

Smuts left for Geneva under the assumed name of Mr. Ashworth. Outside the War Cabinet only a few men knew of his departure, but soon after he had reached his destination the news leaked out.

He immediately opened negotiations with Count Albert Mensdorff, Austro-Hungarian Ambassador to London before the war and a kinsman of Queen Victoria. Their conversations lasted two days. Smuts accomplished exactly nothing. Mensdorff sent detailed reports of the meetings to the German Government.

"Lloyd George is a fool," said Clemenceau to Henry Wilson, "and an extra fool for sending Smuts, who doesn't even know where Austria is."

Soon after Smuts's return Henry Wickham Steed went to interview him.

"Well, General," he said, "here you are back again."

"Yes," replied Smuts, "I could not stand being cooped up in London any longer. I am used to a life in the open air, so I rushed off to Devonshire for a week and now feel a new man. Those Devonshire lanes are really wonderful."

"Devonshire!" cried Steed. "I thought you had been in Switzerland."

"Switzerland!" exclaimed Smuts. "What put that idea into your head? I have never been near Switzerland."

Towards the end of March 1918 the German armies, having forced their way forward in a spectacular manner, were closing in on Amiens. Paris was their objective; and nothing, so it appeared, could prevent them from reaching it.

Returning from a tour of inspection in France, Smuts informed the War Cabinet that only a miracle could save the British lines from caving in under pressure. In March and again in April they gave way in two places. The position was desperate.

But American troops arrived to fill some of the gaps; youths of eighteen filled others; seasoned troops were hastily rushed up from the minor fronts, and all kinds of extreme measures were adopted to stem the relentless Teutonic tide. And in the nick of time Marshal Foch was given supreme command of all the forces of the Allies on the Western Front. These comprised the British, French, American, Belgian, and Italian armies.

On July 15 the enemy commenced a tremendous onslaught, but they were beaten back miraculously. By August 8 it was clear even to the Kaiser "that the war could no longer be won." "August 8," said Ludendorff, "was the black day of the German Army in the history of the war." Then came the sudden collapse of the Central Powers: while the soldiers of the German Army demanded to go on fighting, their brothers in the Navy mutinied; Austria, Turkey, and Bulgaria surrendered; revolution broke out in Hungary and in the Reich; and the Kaiser and the Crown Prince, fleeing in panic, sought sanctuary in Holland. The Germans invoked the aid of the President of the United States, begging him "to take a hand in the restoration of peace."

This appeal was embodied in a formal diplomatic communication addressed to President Wilson by Prince Max of Baden, the German Chancellor. "As a basis for peace negotiations" it agreed to the American

President's Fourteen Points as elaborated in a special memorandum to Congress in January 1918, and "in his later pronouncements, especially his speech of September 27," and asked for "the immediate conclusion of an armistice on land and water and in the air."

On these terms an armistice was signed in the Forest of Compiègne in Marshal Foch's railway carriage on November 11 at 5 A.M.—a process which was to be repeated in the same carriage in the same forest but under vastly different circumstances just over two decades later.

The war had ended.

38

THE RINGING OF BELLS and the explosion of fireworks on the morning of November 11, 1918, told the people of England that an armistice had been proclaimed. Wild with excitement and delirious with joy, they swept along the streets of cities and towns giving vent to their pent-up emotions. In thousands of homes tears of joy were shed but also tears of sorrow, for millions of young men lay rotting in unknown graves all over the face of Europe, some cut off in the morning of life, and others in the pride of their manhood. Into the hearts of the living crept the spirit of vengeance and loudly they demanded retribution.

Mr. Lloyd George accused the German Emperor of "murder." In West Birmingham Mr. Austen Chamberlain said: "No indemnity which we can get is too high to ask for." Certain sections of the press, more than anything else, stirred up the emotions of the people. "Hang the Kaiser!" became both a slogan and a demand. On November 30 Mr. Barnes, a member of the War Cabinet, shouted hoarsely from a public platform, "I am for hanging the Kaiser!"

It was the ever-present fear of his own eclipse, in the event of the overthrow of the political bloc on which his position had been dependent for a long time, that impelled Mr. Lloyd George to pander to the revengeful feelings of the British masses, who quite naturally insisted that "we . . . squeeze the orange till the pips squeak." He went to the country at the psychological moment. His final manifesto was a "direct infringement of Britain's engagements under the Fourteen Points." He was returned to power, a "British Liberal . . . at the mercy of a jingo Commons and a jingo press."[1]

[1]*Peacemaking 1919*, Harold Nicholson.

A strange assortment of persons were elected to Parliament. "They are a lot of hard-faced men who look as if they have done very well out of the war," said a Conservative member at the time.

Thus Lloyd George set out for Paris with a mandate from the people of Britain which committed him to a line of action wholly incompatible with his pre-armistice pledges. "He had pledged himself and his Government to make of a helpless enemy demands inconsistent with solemn engagements on our part, on the faith of which this enemy had laid down his arms. There are few episodes in history which posterity will have less reason to condone—a war, ostensibly waged in defence of the sanctity of international engagements, ending in a definite breach of one of the most sacred possible of such engagements on the part of the victorious champions of these ideals."[2]

Smuts, detached, calm, and coldly rational, looking to horizons beyond the ken of ordinary mortals, could not associate himself with the cries for vengeance which rose around him. Realizing with the few who were capable of coherent thought, and who were in a position to think "beyond the emotions of the moment," that greater issues than mere retribution were at stake, he said, soon after the armistice: "It is not merely that thrones and empires are falling, and ancient institutions suddenly collapsing. A world order is visibly passing before our eyes, and the danger is that things may go too far and a setback be given to Europe from which she does not recover for generations. . . .

"What a doom has come over Germany! What a price she has paid for her ambitions and her crimes. . . .

"Now as we organized the world for victory let us organize it against hunger and unemployment. Not only the liberated territories of our Allies, not only our small neutral neighbours, but the enemy countries themselves, require our helping hand. Let us extend it in all generosity and magnanimity."

The Allies had won the war. Smuts was determined that the peace should be won too.

He resigned from the War Cabinet and from various committees, giving up also the presidency of the Committee for Demobilization to which he had been appointed soon after the armistice. He needed all his time to prepare for the struggle that lay ahead, for he was only too well aware of the fact that powerful forces were gathering their strength to operate against the accomplishment of a sane peace, forces of destruction whose challenge had to be accepted. Smuts was one of the very few to perceive that the establishment of a new order was a supreme necessity, and that

[2]*The Economic Consequences of the Peace*, J. M. Keynes.

beside it the national aspirations of individual European powers paled into insignificance. His standpoint was entirely objective, unlike that of Clemenceau, Lloyd George, Orlando, and others into whose hearts perhaps the war had bitten too deeply and whose outlook, in consequence, was dominated by a chauvinistic subjectivity.

Smuts came from a country remote from the melting pot of Europe and virtually untouched by the war. Hence his attitude towards the affairs of Europe was dispassionate and sane—indeed, vastly more so than that of the majority of his compeers. And he was determined to advocate a treaty which would act as a remedial balm for a sorely stricken continent.

He knew that a Carthaginian peace would, like a two-edged sword, cut both ways; that a magnanimous peace was not a matter of mere idealism, of sacerdotal nonsense, but of practical politics; and that those who desired to squeeze the Central European countries "until the pips squeaked" could, for the most part, not visualize the disastrous results of such a policy. The *status quo ante* 1870 argument, which many were already advancing, was untenable. Smuts felt that the restoration of the *status quo* would eventually "distort the structure of Europe, strain it beyond endurance, and set loose such revolutionary forces and active powers of destruction as would result in unprecedented social upheavals. The old shibboleths were gone and with them the old stability. Unless anarchy were to supervene and chaos rule enthroned in Europe, a new system, a new order must come into being, woven into the woof of the European fabric and the world structure."

A league of nations appeared to him to be the only solution. It was a "sheer practical necessity." "This league," he wrote, "will have to occupy the great position which has been rendered vacant by the destruction of many of the old European empires and the passing away of the old European order." He felt that "the primary and fundamental task of the impending Peace Conference must be the creation of a real league of nations—that league towards which all civilization had consciously and subconsciously been working."

For eighteen months amid all his other activities he had been giving the matter of a league of nations a great deal of thought. Others, too, had been contemplating similar projects. In 1916 Lord Robert Cecil had worked out a fairly comprehensive plan, and in the following year it had been adopted by the Phillimore Commission to serve as the basis of a draft plan for a league of nations. The French philosopher, Leon Bourgeois, and the American President had also been brooding on the subject.

But the idea of a league of nations had a special significance for Smuts.

It had very much in common with his philosophy of life as subsequently developed and embodied in his *Holism and Evolution*. Small units must needs develop into bigger wholes, and they in their turn again must grow into larger and ever-larger structures without cessation. Advancement lay along that path. Thus the unification of the four provinces in the Union of South Africa, the idea of the British Commonwealth of Nations, and, finally, the great whole resulting from the combination of the peoples of the earth in a great league of nations were but a logical progression consistent with his philosophical tenets.

On December 16 Smuts published his plan for a league of nations in pamphlet form. It was called "The League of Nations: A Practical Suggestion." It was given wide publicity and became famous overnight.

" 'The Practical Suggestion' of General Smuts was the first draft covenant at all deeply tinged with the idealism for which the postwar world was waiting."[3] Lloyd George told Lord Riddell that he thought it "the ablest state paper he had seen during the war."[4] Referring to the sentence, "The tents have been struck, the great caravan of humanity is once more on the march," Lloyd George said: "That is very fine."

Riddell: "An analogy drawn from Smuts' environment in South Africa. He has been accustomed to see men trekking away, perhaps with no definite objective."

Lloyd George: "That is just what occurred to me when I read the sentence."

In point of fact numerous splendidly phrased passages in Smuts's memorandum appealed tremendously to the President, who was particularly struck by this sentence: "Europe is being liquidated, and the League of Nations must be the heir to the great estate." According to a member of the British delegation, it "crystallized" for Wilson what in his own mind had been vague and formless. It cut to the very heart of things.

So to Lloyd George had appealed Smuts's concept of a Commonwealth of Nations, "at once naming and defining," in a few well-chosen words, a novel political idea, a new creed which might revolutionize the spirit of Empire and transmute what was intrinsically an obsolescent, predatory, and tyrannical system into something visionary and idealistic, something essentially fine, something more than palatable to the truly democratic mind as well as to the hard-boiled jingo. Smuts has few equals in the English-speaking world in the matter of apposite phrasing. His greatest thoughts have always been clothed in inspiring language, often biblical in its simplicity and sonorousness.

[3]*The Great Society of Nations,* Morley
[4]*Lord Riddell's Intimate Diary of the Peace Conference and After.*

39

EVER SINCE the outbreak of the Great War, in various countries of the world the minds of men had been seeking to evolve plans for the creation of some sort of confederacy of nations, the combined efforts of which might put an end for all time to war. Nevertheless, but for the insistent efforts of President Wilson, Viscount Cecil, and Jan Smuts, this idealistic concept might never have been translated into practical politics.

With the conclusion of hostilities, to be sure, several plans for a union of nations were put forward, but they aimed at little more than the creation of a league whose sole object would be "the prevention of war." It was only when Smuts published his great memorandum wherein he visualized "the League as the centre of diplomacy and an organization of international co-operation," that the scope of the new instrument of peace was extended tremendously. Smuts declared emphatically that "an international body to co-ordinate the activities of states was now a necessity."

It was clear, therefore, that the League, in Smuts's opinion, should fulfil a much greater purpose than the mere "negative action of preventing war." It was, in fact, to be "the chief organ for the rebuilding of Europe and the Middle East and for establishing and securing the harmony of a new world which was to arise from the ashes of the old."

The League could best serve the interests of those "inexperienced national units" which were soon to come into being. For them Smuts had planned an ingenious mandatory system. It was, in a sense, unique. Smuts was "the first statesman among the Allies to connect the territorial adjustment resultant upon the war with the League." His solution of what was at best an awkward question caught Wilson's fancy to the extent of his revising completely his original plans for a covenant, and adopting in his final draft both the ideas and the style of the South African statesman.

In short, "Smuts and his advisers had," as one writer puts it, "carried the conception of the League onto another plane. It had become an active instrument in international co-operation."

Furthermore, acting in his capacity as a South African delegate, Smuts was "the first to attempt to harmonize the rights of Great and Small Powers."

"General Smuts's proposals differed from previous suggestions of re-

sponsible statesmen in taking a much more ambitious view of the
League."[1] In more than one respect, for that matter, the General's ideas
were actually much too advanced to be agreed to *in toto*.

"But his general conceptions of the constitution of the League and of
its functions in preserving world peace were largely incorporated in the
Covenant as finally drafted."[2]

"This great paper, expressed in cogent and moving language, immediately had a profound effect. It crystallized ideas and aspirations which
had been held in many quarters and made a deep impression on both
Lord Cecil and President Wilson."[2]

"After Wilson had read Smuts' memorandum," said Lloyd George,
"he swallowed it whole." Not many months later he admitted to his
senate that he had rewritten his own draft of the covenant of the League
of Nations, "in the light of a paper by General Smuts, who seemed to
have done some very clear thinking in regard to what was to be done to
the pieces of the dismembered empires."

It was decided that the British Empire should be represented at the
Paris Conference by dominion representatives as well as by delegates
from England. The idea had not appealed to Lloyd George. The Foreign
Office disapproved of it. So did Winston Churchill. But the dominions
insisted that they had given ample proof of their nationhood during the
war and practically demanded representation. Smuts argued that it was a
matter of "status" and that their representation at the Peace Conference
and their signing of the Treaty would once and for all establish the
dominions in the eyes of the world as equal partners with Mother England in the British Commonwealth of Nations.

40

BOTHA JOINED SMUTS in London. He was a changed man. His Fal-
staffian girth had shrunken somewhat. For him the lush pastures of his
country had lost their beauty, and the boundless stretches of the Bushveld
and the lone Karoo held no appeal, for sick at heart and weighed down

[1] *A History of the Peace Conference of Paris*, Vol. VI, issued under the auspices of
the Institute of International Affairs.

[2] *The League of Nations in Theory and Practice*, C. K. Webster and Sydney Herbert.

with disease, he felt that his days were numbered. He was glad to be in England and with Smuts. Ever since his friend had left him, life had been unbearable to him. It had been a burden too heavy to carry, for Smuts had been his mainstay and his prop. Smuts, the glutton for work, had done almost everything for him, had protected him, and had taken punishment unflinchingly on his behalf. So that on Smuts's departure for East Africa and Europe, he had been almost lost in the maelstrom of venomous South African politics. The deeply rooted hatred of his enemies had been a source of constant torture to him. With strident voices they had fulminated against him. They had blamed him for increased taxation and the rise in the cost of living, and had said that he was ruining their country. They had called him "Murderer!" "Traitor!" "Judas!" He had received mortal injury.

When Smuts and Botha left for Paris, Viscount Esher wrote to a friend: "I am glad Smuts is one of the delegates. His contribution to the question [of a league of nations] is the only one that grapples with principles and details."

Together with the majority of the British Delegation, Smuts was housed in the Hotel Majestic in Paris. He became immersed in work almost immediately, taking little exercise except for an occasional brisk walk, and enjoying little relaxation apart from visiting a few museums and picture galleries. The gay life of Paris seemed to hold no attraction for him.

In fact, he was discontented and miserable. He regarded this period "as the unhappiest time" of his life.

The supreme body at the conference was the Committee of the Big Four, consisting of Lloyd George for Britain, Clemenceau for France, Wilson for America, and Orlando for Italy. Clemenceau was elected president of the conference on the recommendation of President Wilson, who said that "it was a special tribute to the sufferings and sacrifices of France." "And that," says Mr. Wells, "unhappily sounded the keynote of the conference, whose sole business should have been with the future of mankind."

Georges Eugène Benjamin Clemenceau, then Premier of France, was the main barrier on which Wilson's ship foundered. On hearing that Germany was asking for an armistice, he wept for joy with his head in his hands. He had seen the fires in Paris in the hateful year of 1871. He hated Germany, the traditional enemy of France, with a relentless and implacable fury. To him France was the universe.

He bore the nickname of "Tiger." He had been a skilful and fearless duellist in his time. Now a wizened old man, his parchmentlike features registering little beyond interrogation, he entered the council chamber determined to do battle for France. And he dominated the proceedings, having estimated the worth of his colleagues at the outset.

Of the "Big Four," the would-be reconstructors of a stricken world, to whose hands had been entrusted the destiny of mankind, he alone was conversant with both French and English. This was a significant fact; its effect upon history should not be minimized. He wore a square-tailed coat, clumsy black boots, and grey gloves, which, because of eczema, he never removed. A living mummy he seemed, and in years well past the allotted span, but behind that unprepossessing and ancient exterior there was a mind cool and calculating, keen as a rapier blade and ever on the alert, and a flaming spirit, dauntless and determined yet withal gamin-like. A "cynical and almost impish" wit occasionally gave vent to cruel and biting sarcasm, which respected neither God nor man. "President Wilson with his Fourteen Points," he said, "is worse than God Almighty. *Le Bon Dieu* only had ten. . . ."

From the outset Clemenceau was determined to dictate a peace of his own making or precipitate a bloody anabasis. What Germany had done since 1870 must be undone. The destruction of this country was a fitting end to what had been a veritable jihad. Believing implicitly that wars were inevitable in Europe, that the old order did not change, and that a magnanimous peace would be extreme folly, he was determined to break Germany. It would be wise ostensibly to pander to Wilson's wretched "ideals" while surreptitiously circumventing his Fourteen Points and all that they connoted, and thereby rearranging the balance of power in the interests of France. Indeed he made no secret of his aversion for the so-called New Order, nor did he pretend to be bound by the Fourteen Points, but left to his minions the perplexing task of constantly plotting to devise means whereby to salve Wilson's conscience and to outwit him.

When on Flanders' fields and elsewhere the tumult of battle had been silenced, the piteous cries could be heard of millions of starving men, women, and children turning their faces to the west, to Woodrow Wilson and to America, where lay their salvation.

The President's power in Europe and America and his prestige throughout the world were tremendous when he embarked for Europe on the *George Washington*. He had become the Prophet of a new age, the Saviour of a stricken world. The apotheosis conferred upon him was duly appreciated. Indeed it was said that in his own eyes he had acquired what was tantamount to the attributes of a Messiah. Nor was he being unduly generous to himself in this estimate, for Europe "lay at his feet," and, for that matter, so did the remaining four continents.

Wilson's conception of "international relationships" set out in his Fourteen Points and in speeches delivered immediately prior to his departure for Europe had come like a gospel of peace, a doctrine of salvation to a sorely afflicted and disintegrating Europe, utterly helpless and stricken with palsy. Each nation was to be the captain of its soul, the master of its fate; there was to be no more aggression; the dawn of a veritable millennium was presaged.

Wilson was armed with all the power in the world to carry his project into effect. According to Keynes, the American forces had reached the zenith of their power, while Europe was "at the mercy of the United States whom she already owed more than she could pay," and on whom she was utterly dependent for her very existence since bankruptcy and starvation were staring her in the face. "Never had a philosopher held such weapons wherewith to bind the princes of this world."[1]

President Wilson made a grave error when he decided to go to the Peace Conference himself. Familiarity has ever bred contempt. Had he remained in the United States, he could, like the sibylline oracle, have avoided that touch which contaminates, and have given voice across the waters as if to the sentiments of a nation; he could have remained the spirit incarnate of idealistic America, bringing balm to the wounds of a diseased and decadent Europe. But, disregarding the counsel of prudent advisers, he decided to cross the Atlantic. The results were disastrous.

Intellectually the President was no match for the "dangerous spell-binders" whom he met in the council chamber. He lacked the mental finesse, the cunning strategy, and artful sophistry which are the *sine qua non* of the war of chicane. Far from being a prophet or a philosopher, he was an ingenuous idealist with a flair for flamboyant utterances. But that was all. He was the "predestined victim" of men like Lloyd George and Clemenceau.

One would have thought, suggests J. M. Keynes, that the President, prior to leaving America's shores, would have evolved, with the aid of a multiplicity of advisers, an extensive scheme for a league of nations and for the requisite embodiment of his Fourteen Points in the Peace Treaty. "But," says Keynes, "he had no plan, no scheme, no constructive ideas whatever for clothing with the flesh of life the commandments which he had thundered from the White House." His knowledge of European conditions was astonishingly defective. This, it has been pointed out, was

[1]*The Economic Consequences of the Peace,* J. M. Keynes.

also the case with Lloyd George. But unlike the nimble-witted British Prime Minister, the President had a mind "slow and unadaptable."

There was about the President a spiritual arrogance which has been attributed by Mr. Lansing, American Secretary of State at the time, to an upsetting of the balance of his mind resultant upon his virtual deification subsequent to his landing in Europe. However that may be, he seemed to take a particular delight in thundering from Olympus, regarding himself "as an ambassador accredited to righteousness by all the world."[2]

His rigid inaccessibility was still tenable in the Council of Ten, but when this august body made way for the Council of Four, his fate was sealed. He was toyed with and hopelessly outwitted. He was inveigled into making concession after concession. These, indeed, he made with a bad grace, a show of reluctance, and only after he had brought them into alignment with his "Presbyterian conscience" by some strange manipulation of his religious tenets.

The Covenant of the League of Nations was his *idée fixe* and, lest the Ark of the Covenant should suffer, his Fourteen Points were surrendered one after another in propitiation to his colleagues to be torn to pieces, for it had been bruited abroad that Clemenceau "would swallow the League at a price."

41

WHILE POURING out the vials of their wrath upon him for the part he is alleged to have played in connection with the drawing up of the Versailles Treaty, Smuts's political enemies have not scrupled to exaggerate beyond all measure his unfortunate role in the creation of the mandatory system. It is necessary, therefore, to give as clear an exposition as possible of the facts of the matter. While these do not redound entirely to Smuts's credit, they nevertheless bring home to the reader the extent to which the South African was a dominating personality at the conference. Moreover, there are in his favour irrefutable extenuating circumstances which have been deliberately withheld by his detractors.

At the outset, therefore, it must be pointed out that whatever his personal motives may have been in respect of the virtual annexation of

[2]*Peacemaking 1919,* Harold Nicholson.

South West Africa to the Union, his mandatory scheme was prompted largely by expediency: it was a compromise between certain pre-armistice undertakings on the part of the Allied chiefs in respect of non-annexation of enemy territory and the Allied nations' very natural and just desire to annex such territory and extort from the Central Powers full payment for their sufferings. Had he realized at the start what the ultimate implications of his mandatory system would be, it is doubtful whether Smuts would have lent himself with any enthusiasm to the policy of mandates as it was finally developed. The tremendous breadth of his vision at the conference as evidenced by his prognostications and their eventual fulfilment; his constant pleas for magnanimous treatment of the Central Powers; his unceasing attacks upon the Treaty as it was being formulated; his letters of protest to Mr. Lloyd George and various other Allied leaders against the dismemberment of the enemy nations; his general behaviour at the conference—all these are wholly incompatible with the final elaboration of the mandatory system.

Here are the facts of the matter.

From Smuts's scheme for a league of nations President Wilson adopted a great deal of material. This included the whole of the comprehensive subsection dealing with the mandatory project. "It was first put forward by General Smuts, one of the rare original brains of the Peace Conference."[1] In his plan Smuts suggested the taking over of the mandated territories by the League as the "heir of the Empires." "This clever and attractive phrase," wrote Wilson's Secretary of State, "caught the fancy of the President as was evident from his frequent repetition and approval of it in discussing mandates under the League. Just as Smuts had adopted the President's 'self-determination,' so Mr. Wilson seized upon the Smuts idea with avidity and incorporated it in his plans. It unquestionably had a decided influence upon his conception of the right way to dispose of the colonial possessions of Germany and of the proper relation of the newly created European states to the League of Nations."[2] The word "mandatory" had a special appeal for Wilson, who, like Smuts, delighted in and realized the value of significant and apposite phrasing. According to Mr. K. F. Nowak, "it had just the ethical flavour which he was looking for."[3] However that may be, it is a well-known fact that the language of the mandates section in Wilson's revised Covenant "was taken almost verbatim from Smuts."[4]

[1]*Europe and Europeans,* Count Carlo Sforza.
[2]*The Peace Negotiations,* Robert Lansing.
[3]*Versailles,* K. F. Nowak.
[4]*The Intimate Papers of Colonel House,* Charles Seymour.

Apart from suggesting to the President an ingenious solution of the vexed question of the disposal of conquered territory, by pointing to the League as the "heir of the Empires," the mandatory project had a special significance in that it was the logical outcome of ideas that had been fermenting in the New World for years. The American people had been impregnated with idealistic concepts. In regard to "colonial obligations" they were to be the "trustees of weaker peoples." And they were to go further. It was their duty, as President Taft put it, "to arouse a national spirit, and not, as under older colonial theory, to suppress such a spirit." It was a conception which President Wilson did not fail subsequently to impress upon the American people, so that America's withdrawal from Cuba, an action "which was the greatest surprise the world ever had, politically speaking,"[5] and her treatment of the Philippines were but the natural result of a new ideology.

Along these lines then of unselfish "service to the world" American idealism had been developing. But Wilson, the High Priest of the new doctrine at the time of the armistice, never thought of applying it to his scheme for a league of nations.

It was Smuts's "Practical Suggestion" making provision for the establishment of "a mandatory system to deal with territories belonging to the old empires of Russia, Austro-Hungary, and Turkey" that crystallized into practical politics the plethora of the President's great dreams.

But much to the chagrin of some of the Empire's leading statesmen, who had intended the mandate system to be "a compromise between the imperialist secret treaties (and secret agreements the governments of the Allied Powers had arranged, in anticipation of victory, for the division of colonial spoils) and liberal anti-imperialist ideas," Wilson included all conquered territory in the mandatory system.

To his imperialist friends the President's decision was a severe blow. Smuts, who had set his heart on annexing German South West Africa to the Union, felt it keenly. So also did the majority of the other Allied statesmen. They pleaded earnestly with the President to change his mind. Smuts played a prominent part in their discussions. At first Wilson was inexorable. He contended that he was bound by the Fourteen Points. But gradually he allowed himself to be persuaded to compromise.

The new agreement, which was drawn up by Smuts and Mr. Philip Kerr (later Lord Lothian) and eventually embodied in Article XXII of the Treaty of Versailles, was a masterpiece of verbal strategy which altered Wilson's draft fundamentally.

The part the League was to play in regard to the appointment of

[5]*Woodrow Wilson and World Settlement*, R. S. Baker, Vol. I.

mandatories was purposely left undefined. Thus by usurping this office, which the President had originally intended to assign to the League, the Entente Powers "might appoint themselves as mandatories and enjoy almost the powers that could have been secured by annexation."

The President had stipulated that "the mandatory power should be nominated or at least approved by the people concerned." By considering only the peoples of Palestine, Syria, and Mesopotamia in this connection, Smuts and Kerr practically nullified Wilson's ruling.

"Resources" and "experience" had previously given the leading Entente Powers the right to become mandatories. "Geographical position" was now recognized as an adequate requirement in this connection so that the "inexperienced dominions" might acquire certain territory. And so on *ad infinitum.*

By dividing the mandates into three classes, A, B, and C, Smuts brought about what proved to be the most significant and far-reaching alteration in the mandatory scheme as contemplated by the President. In consequence of it Australasia and the Union of South Africa received certain South Pacific islands and German South West Africa respectively, as mandates subject to their control. They were called Class C mandates. These, according to the Smuts-Kerr draft, could "best be administered under the laws of the mandatory as integral portions of its territory." It was virtual annexation.[6]

With his Class B mandates, Smuts gave heed to British and French colonial interests, as the territories in the B group were not to be regarded "as adolescent nations preparing for independence but may be administered virtually as ordinary colonies."

So Class A mandates alone subscribed to Wilson's original stipulation which laid down that all mandates should be "subject to a provisional tutelage that would end in independence." In fact, the original mandate system was to operate nowhere else but in such territory as none of the Entente Powers would have taken as a gift. This, at all events, is what a critical analysis of Article XXII reveals.

"If the advocates of the system intended to avoid through its operations the appearance of taking enemy territory as the spoils of war, it was a subterfuge which deceived no one."[7] President Wilson may have realized that a very essential part of the Covenant was being nullified by the subtle draftsmanship of Smuts and Kerr; that is a moot point. At all events, he was no longer in a position to assert himself. His peculiarly adaptable conscience, the fact of his having become rather unpopular in

[6]See *What Really Happened in Paris,* Manley O. Hudson.
[7]*The Peace Negotiations,* Robert Lansing.

many parts of America, and his determination to save what he could of
the League were imponderable factors, preventing him from giving vent
to an effective counterblast.

42

SMUTS'S SHARE in the reparations discussions and conclusions was even
more unfortunate than the part he played in respect of mandates. Few
writers, however, have attempted to do him justice in connection with
this matter, and his political opponents have made much capital out of
it, wresting from their context certain facts detrimental to him, and, with
malice aforethought, intentionally withholding others which are to his
credit.

When the question of reparations came under discussion at the conference, it was determined to include as "part indemnity" the costs for
separation allowances and pensions which the Allied countries had undertaken to pay their fighting forces.

But it was found impossible to persuade the President that these pensions and allowances might legitimately be regarded as falling under the
heading of "damage done to the civil population." And according to one
of the Fourteen Points, reparation could be demanded only for such
damage.

Lord Sumner and Mr. Hughes, Premier of Australia, maintained that
damage to the civilian population meant "the actual costs of the war." A
fortnight was passed in argument. The Allies finally abandoned their
claims after President Wilson's vigorous rejoinder to the effect that the
view that war costs should be included in reparation "is clearly inconsistent with what we deliberately led the enemy to expect and cannot
now honourably alter simply because we have the power."[1]

But certain important Allied leaders were not to be baulked. If "damage done to the civilian population" could be made to include "separation allowances made to civilian dependents of soldiers as well as military
pensions," the enemy could be forced to pay almost any sum to the grati-
fication of all and sundry. But how were they to prove their case? For
men like J. M. Keynes, the British economist, and all Wilson's advisers

[1]See *The Making of the Reparation and Economic Sections of the Treaty*, Bernard
Baruch.

on finance insisted that they had none. In spite of numerous spurious arguments on the part of sophists the President would not yield to them. The dreadful controversy raged for months. But then, suddenly, the wrangling ceased. Smuts was called in to "establish a compromise between Lloyd George's election pledge to the British people to demand the entire costs of the war and the assurance to the contrary given to the enemy by the Allies at the time of the armistice." Smuts rose to the occasion. Wilson held him in great esteem, particularly on account of his enthusiasm for the League. He prepared a memo, which, according to the American delegates, "was the final argument which overbore the last scruples of the President."[2]

When told that all his legal advisers were strongly opposed to the pension project and that "all logic was against it," Wilson cried out: "Logic! Logic! I don't care a damn for logic. I am going to include pensions."[3]

Smuts's conduct was actuated largely by a strong conviction that, if allowances and pensions were not included, the continent, which had suffered invasion, would get the lion's share of reparation, while England, on whom the financial brunt of the war had fallen, would receive very little. In his Fourteen Points Wilson had made provision in regard to compensation for wrecked countries but not for ruined exchequers. Hence Smuts, who felt that Germany would pay only a fixed amount, argued that England could receive her just share of that sum only if pensions were included in reparation demands.

Nevertheless, it was subsequently found that pensions and separation allowances comprised two thirds of the Allies' claims against Germany. "The French," said Smuts in 1935, "used it [his opinion on pensions and separation allowances] to swell the reparation amount to fantastic proportions, and it became a vehicle of injustice to Germany—one of those things that are responsible for the Germany of today. . . ."

When this alarming fact became known, Smuts regretted intensely the part he had played in effecting the inclusion of pensions and separation allowances in the reparations scheme as finally drafted. And with all that thoroughness and persistence which he has always given to big causes, he now gave himself wholly to the task of undoing the mischief that had been wrought. In a desperate effort to make amends he now devoted all his time and energy to one cause: that of securing a just peace, in so far as it was humanly possible.

But the great majority of the Allied leaders had not a fraction of

[2] *A Revision of the Treaty,* Keynes.
[3] See also *What Really Happened at Paris,* Thomas W. Lamont.

Smuts's vision: either a very natural spirit of vengeance impelled them to demand that the enemy pay in full for the evil he had done or they had to satisfy their constituents by attempting to secure such payment. And when Smuts protested vigorously against the Treaty and begged them to "save the peace," they did not hesitate to cast in his teeth his mandatory project and the part he had played in connection with pensions and separation allowances; they applied to him Tiger Clemenceau's profane and bitter indictment of President Wilson: "He talked like Jesus Christ and acted like Lloyd George"; and they referred him to a memorandum issued by him and laid before the British Cabinet immediately prior to the Peace Conference. The memorandum contained this sentence: ". . . the British Empire should not pursue justice at the expense of its own legitimate future. . . ." "This," says R. S. Baker, "sounded 'a little cynical' even to Mr. Lloyd George, who points out, in quoting it, that Smuts no doubt had in mind the advice of Ecclesiastes: 'Be not righteous overmuch . . . why shouldst thou destroy thyself?' "[4]

The British Treasury's chief representative in Paris was Mr. J. M. Keynes. He and Smuts were close friends. In fact, he was the general's most ardent disciple, full of enthusiasm for his leader's sane outlook on European affairs, and equally drastic in his condemnation of the perilous treaty that was being drawn up in Paris, and of the men who, while ostensibly giving their support to the project of a league of nations, were in reality strangling it at birth and were furtively seeking to escape their obligations under the Fourteen Points. In his disgust and anguish Keynes resigned his post and left for London.

Not long after he wrote to Smuts saying that he felt that the sad events at Paris should be exposed and condemned. It was for Smuts to tell him what to do in that connection.

In a desperate attempt to save what he could of the treaty, Smuts replied: ". . . I think it would be very advisable for you as soon as possible to set about writing a clear, connected account of what the financial and economic clauses of the treaty really are and mean and what their probable results will be. . . ."

The result was the publication of *The Economic Consequences of the Peace*. It became famous within a week. It had far-reaching effects. It showed up the Treaty very effectively; but it also destroyed Wilson, for it lampooned the President and made him look ridiculous in the eyes of the world but chiefly in the eyes of his own people with whom he had already become unpopular. "In their hearts," says Smuts, "the Americans wanted him to go down; they wanted to evade the duties he im-

[4]*Woodrow Wilson: Life and Letters*, R. S. Baker.

posed on them. The book was absolutely to their purpose: it helped to finish Wilson, and it strengthened the Americans against the League."

43

In spite of the recriminations of his opponents and the serious setbacks suffered by the League project, Smuts's enthusiasm for the Covenant never showed any signs of abatement, nor did he spare himself in his efforts to save the peace. He never ceased to struggle against the ineluctable end. He "more than any other man typified British Liberal opinion at Paris."[1]

As at the opening of the Peace Conference, when, employing simple but forceful language, he had requested earnestly that the enemy be treated with "pity and restraint," reminding the delegates that "civilization is one body and we are all members of one another," so, in spite of his strange and incomprehensible lapses from grace, in the beginning he continued to press for the "generous treatment of Germany as a vital factor in the restoration of human civilization." And he demanded that "the final sanction of this great instrument [the Treaty] must be the approval of mankind."

"His piercing intelligence," wrote E. T. Raymond in 1919, "was the first to recognize the immense difference brought about by President Wilson's decision to enter the war. Today he, above all other statesmen, realizes that this is no dynastic struggle to be patched up by another Berlin or Vienna conference." On many occasions he protested vigorously to Mr. Lloyd George, to Mr. Balfour, and others against the Treaty as it was being formulated. It was an impossible peace. His was a lonely voice crying in the wilderness. "What has become," he asked, "of Wilson's Fourteen Points?"

"We cannot destroy Germany without destroying Europe. . . . We cannot save Europe without the co-operation of Germany. . . . My fear is that the Paris Conference may prove one of the historic failures of the world." It was a momentous prophecy. But then Smuts was in a position to prophesy, for he, above all men, exercised foresight at the conference and foreshadowed coming events with an uncanny prescience. His prophecy was contained in a memorandum: "You may strip Germany

[1]*Woodrow Wilson and World Settlement,* Vol. I, R. S. Baker.

of her colonies, reduce her armaments to a mere police force and her navy to that of a fifth-rate power; all the same, in the end, if she feels that she has been unjustly treated in the peace of 1919 she will find means of exacting retribution from her conquerors."

In one of his letters of protest to Lloyd George he wrote: "Whatever view one holds of these [Wilson's] formulas, I should say that our proposed disposal of the Saar Basin, of Danzig, and of Memel violates them. They are indisputably German territories with German populations, which we have no right under these formulas to tear off Germany. . . . And it is not necessary for the future Poland that there should be a free Danzig under Polish suzerainty, any more than it is necessary to have a free Hamburg as an outlet for the future Czechoslovakia."

In another attack on the Treaty he demanded the "removal of those provisions of the Treaty that were not covered by the Wilson formulas," and added in regard to Poland: "Poland is an historic failure and will always be a failure, and in this Treaty we are trying to reverse the verdict of history. . . . As the document stands at present [he concluded] I cannot vote for it and I doubt if I can sign it."

Botha gave Smuts vigorous support. No other delegates at the conference were half so sympathetic towards the Germans as they. Recalling Vereeniging and its aftermath, they spoke feelingly of "the value and healing power of mercy." Botha said, "I know what defeat means. My soul has felt the harrow."

Smuts's influence with Lloyd George was tremendous. The British Prime Minister, according to his biographer, E. T. Raymond, "was peculiarly susceptible to the influence of the last speaker [Smuts], and from a talk with General Smuts he would go to a meeting of the 'Big Four' with proposals which made M. Clemenceau wonder (sometimes aloud) whether the Allies were to ask Germany's pardon for having taken the liberty of beating her."

But Smuts's never-ending protests sometimes annoyed the fiery Celt to such an extent that Botha had to intervene. Smuts said some years later: "I never realized how near I came to breaking with Lloyd George." On one occasion the Welshman, mindful of Smuts's "mandates" and "pensions" contributions to the Treaty, asked him, "Are you prepared to forego the claims for pensions and so confine compensation to material damage? . . . Are you prepared to allow German South West Africa and German East Africa to be returned to Germany as a concession which might induce them to sign the peace?"

When invited by Mr. Lloyd George to become a member of a commission on Austrian reparations, he declined the honour politely. He had

had a surfeit of reparations. He would never forget the "pensions and separation allowances" lesson. "While I am willing," he wrote in reply to the British Prime Minister's invitation, "and indeed anxious to help with the work, I do not think . . . that my going on the commission will serve any useful purpose, and my opposition to what seems to be your policy will only waste time where speed is right. For the imposition of reparation on a broken, bankrupt, economically impossible state like Austria, or a new, friendly, allied state like Czechoslovakia . . . seems to be a hopeless policy which could only lead to the most mischievous results. I am against payment of all reparation of these countries for damage done by the dead and dismembered Austro-Hungarian Empire. And if it is (as it appears) your policy to exact reparation in these cases . . . I hope you will excuse me from serving on the commission. . . ."

Obstinately and persistently Smuts continued his lone attack on the Treaty. Through the alembic of his dynamic mind had passed the awful consequences of a bad peace. He felt that he was dealing with insensate fools. Where he had hoped to find his colleagues reasonable, he found them difficult and intransigent.

While the vast majority of the delegates were worn out physically and mentally even before they arrived in Paris for the conference, Smuts was fit and vigorous. His mind was as fresh and clear as it had been at the end of 1917 when Colonel House noticed that "Smuts was the only one among the governing statesmen who did not seem tired." "What a man!" wrote a colleague in April 1919. "His sense of values takes one away from Paris and this greedy turmoil."

While others were hard and uncompromising, Wilson was capable of listening to reason. Smuts wrestled hopefully with him. Unfortunately, however, Wilson's wings had already been clipped. He was like a rudderless ship in a storm. Smuts became desperate and exceedingly miserable; but a welcome interlude was about to present itself to him.

44

HUNGARY was in the clutches of Red revolutionaries under the leadership of one Béla Kun, who had deposed Count Michael Károlyi and established himself in power. This diffusion of bolshevism was the cause of much concern in Paris for a variety of reasons. The Big Four were of opinion that it "jeopardized all their plans for the reconstruction of the boundaries of Europe"; it decidedly appeared to menace the establishment of a workable league of nations; and it threatened the very accomplishment of the Treaty, since countries like Germany, Austria, Italy, and Bulgaria, if bolshevized, would—it was thought—refuse point-blank to countenance the Treaty of Versailles.

The Supreme Council thus decided to send General Mangin to restore order in Hungary. Then, suddenly, they rescinded that resolution, and Smuts was hastily dispatched to Budapest at the head of a "peaceful mission" to negotiate with Béla Kun.

One of the members of the party was Nicolson of the Foreign Office. "The ostensible purpose of our mission," he wrote, "is to fix an armistice line between the Hungarians and Rumanians, yet the real idea at the back is to see whether Béla Kun is worth using as a vehicle for getting into touch with Moscow."

Through Austria the train travelled very slowly. Smuts noticed that everybody looked starved and weary and yellow about the face.

In Vienna the streets were littered with rubbish, and the windows of houses and public buildings more often than not were broken and boarded up, and the people in tatters, gazing at Smuts and his entourage in open amazement. "And indeed," wrote Harold Nicolson, "we are a funny sight when viewed in a bunch like that. Smuts in his general's uniform, the French and Italian aides-de-camp, Heywood and Lane, in their red tabs, the neat English clothes of the civilians. I feel that my plump pink face is an insult to these wretched people. . . ."

At the British Embassy Smuts met Sir Thomas Cunninghame, head of the British military mission, and Mr. Philpotts of the Consular Service. It was immediately obvious that he had taken a great liking to the latter and a violent aversion to the former. Presently Sir Thomas took them to Sachers for luncheon. "We are followed by a staring, shambling crowd. The police walk with us. Smuts is silent, dignified, and reserved. A huge luncheon at Sachers which costs 1,200 kronen. Smuts is furious. He ticks Cunninghame off sharply. He calls it a 'gross error in taste.' He decrees that from now on we shall feed only upon our own army rations and not take anything from these starving countries. His eyes when angry are like steel rods" (Nicolson).

Back at the Embassy, Smuts regained his composure and the armistice line and the frontiers were explained to him, but not until he had further punished Cunninghame by evicting him from his own room and causing him to wander aimlessly "about the Chancery, nervous and apprehensive."

Meanwhile the local Bolshevik Commissar, Bolgar by name, had telephoned through to Béla Kun that Smuts was on his way to Budapest on a special mission from the Supreme Council at Paris. Béla Kun replied that "he would be delighted to see the general" and gave the party "every assurance of a courteous reception and full safe-conduct." Bolgar now asked to be allowed to go along with Smuts as an interpreter. His request was granted. When, however, he begged to be permitted to take his secretary, he was told that "he might, but that they would have to share a compartment," Bolgar raised no objections. His secretary turned out to be "a pretty little woman with flaming hair."

Meanwhile Hungary had been a looter's paradise.

The plundering of the great Hungaria Hotel was about to begin when the news of Smuts's imminent arrival came through. This preserved the hotel and saved its guests, for the Soviet Government could not risk incurring General Smuts's displeasure at such a critical time. On the eve, therefore, of Smuts's arrival the inmates of the Hungaria breathed freely, after weeks of terror, and crept furtively one by one into the room of Mr. E. Ashmead-Bartlett, who had acted as their repository, to recover from him their jewels—baronesses and counts and other aristocrats of every description. Before morning the huge sparkling heap of priceless gems—rubies, diamonds, emeralds, pearls, and other precious stones—had dwindled very considerably.

Hitherto Béla Kun's position had been far from secure. Indeed, his government had been on the point of collapsing. But his position was considerably strengthened by the arrival of Smuts, for the people of Hungary could now be told that "no less a person than General Smuts, the favoured delegate of the Supreme Council of the Entente, had come all the way from Paris, in a special train, accompanied by a large staff, to negotiate with him [Kun], thus, in fact, tacitly recognizing the *de facto* government now in power."

On being aroused from sleep on the morning of April 4, the Smuts mission found that the train had already reached Budapest and that Red guards had been posted on the platform. Large numbers of people stood about, "gaping across at our long brown train in astonishment."

Colonel Domorny was the first man to call on the general. He was to serve Smuts as liaison officer. "He stands to attention when addressing Smuts as if he were still in uniform. He looks bewildered and unhappy. He is evidently terrified of telling us anything about the situation. Realizing this, Smuts ceases asking him questions" (Nicolson).

More helpful visitors were Ashmead-Bartlett, Macartney, and Lieutenant Commander Freeman-Williams, courageous men who had taken their lives in their hands when they decided to stay on in Budapest when rapine and murder became common, daily events. They found Smuts "one of the most patient of listeners. . . . He takes in every detail and never interrupts—except to elucidate some point—and never expresses an opinion. . . ." They found the lunch "somewhat disappointing," for "Smuts is an apostle of austere living and refused to allow any luxuries aboard his train through a delicacy of feeling that they would form a painful contrast to the conditions of life in the countries which he was to visit. . . ." (Ashmead-Bartlett). These guests gave Smuts valuable information.

Before them, however, had arrived Béla Kun in new frock coat and top hat—an insignificant little figure of a man. He was conducted to Smuts's carriage whence he emerged again at twelve forty-five, obviously pleased with the world.

In their courtship of the general and in an effort to bring home to the people of Hungary the extent to which the representatives of the Supreme Council were on friendly terms with them, the Bolshevik leaders had reserved suites of rooms in the Hungaria for General Smuts and his staff. A Tricolour and a Union Jack had been hoisted over the entrance in honour of the visitors. But Smuts declined to leave the train and forbade his associates to enter the city. They had to be content with "army rations—beans and cheese."

The monastic regime of the train must have been somewhat irksome to those who had not grown up in the hard school of Smuts, but they respected the general for acting as he did. "Smuts," wrote Nicolson, in his diary, "presides at our trench meals as if giving us a banquet at the Savoy."

To a greater extent even than Vienna, Budapest was a city of misery and starvation. Lean and hungry yellow faces, tattered clothes, shabbiness, wretchedness, ineffable tragedy.

Béla Kun had several interviews with Smuts. "Smuts talks to him as if he were talking to the Duke of Abercorn: friendly, courteous, but not a touch of any surrender of his own tremendous dignity" (Nicolson).

The Bolshevik leaders made arrangements for a sumptuous banquet to be held at the Ritz Hotel in honour of Smuts and his colleagues. The South African, however, declined the invitation politely but firmly on behalf of himself and his staff.

Now the Bolsheviks were in a quandary. They had invited numerous guests to meet General Smuts. An elaborate banquet had been prepared. What were they to do? They were faced with a seemingly insoluble problem, but they found a solution—of sorts. It was noised abroad that the banquet was being given in honour of Macartney and Ashmead-Bartlett, representatives of the "foreign press."

"Will it be advisable for us to attend?" these two Britishers inquired of Smuts.

"There is no reason," he replied, "why you should not go; you are not in an official position like myself. It is possible you may learn many matters of great interest and importance."

They went.

On arriving at the Ritz the two Englishmen were given an overwhelming reception, and copious libations were poured in their honour even before they sat down at the festive board. The Comrades proved to be good trenchermen and seasoned topers. They drank frequently and deeply.

Regarding Smuts's absence as a personal affront, Béla Kun stayed at home. The majority of his henchmen, however, turned up. Among others there were Pogány, the People's Commissar for War, Árgosten, Deputy Minister for Foreign Affairs, and Boehm, the People's Commissary for Propaganda.

These gentlemen poured gallons of liquor down their thirsty throats, Boehm distinguishing himself as the outstanding bacchanal. In their besotted state the Comrades "revealed all the plans for the propaganda of bolshevism throughout the whole of Europe." The drunken revel continued until 3 A.M., when all the liquor in the dining room was finally disposed of. Then the "survivors" of the orgy truculently demanded fresh supplies.

Having caroused until 4 A.M., the merry tipplers swore "eternal friendship" and staggered home.

The following afternoon Smuts was given a full account of the Bolshevik plans, as divulged to Ashmead-Bartlett.

At 7 P.M. on Saturday, April 5, Béla Kun and several members of his clique paid what proved to be a final visit to Smuts. In his dimly lit dining car the latter read the note which the Bolsheviks had brought and then said: "No, gentlemen, this is not a note which I can accept. There must be no reservations." Smuts declined to negotiate any longer with Béla Kun, since he felt convinced that the Bolshevik leader had little power and less influence in the land.

"Well, gentlemen," said he finally to the sullen Comrades, "I must bid you good-bye." And he stepped onto the platform with his guests and shook hands with them all. And, as the train drew slowly out of the station, he saluted the dumbfounded revolutionaries.

"We then dine. Smuts is delightful, telling us stories of the veld with a ring of deep homesickness in his voice. A lovely man . . ." (Nicolson).

Arriving at Prague on Monday, April 7, Smuts drove to the palace to visit Masaryk, with whom he remained for an hour.

Not far from Innsbruck a coach bearing the Archduke Maximilian was hooked on to Smuts's train. This man, fearing the Bolsheviks, had sought safety in flight.

On reaching Paris, General Smuts and his party found that the newspapers were describing their mission as a "fiasco." And so it was. But if unprofitable, it had been a not-unpleasant interlude. It had, indeed, been remarkably anodynous. And it was with reluctance that Smuts returned to the mad and bitter wrangling in Paris.

45

MEANWHILE to Paris had come a delegation from South Africa headed by General Hertzog, who thought that the opportune moment had come for demanding that a republican constitution be granted the Union. There had been much talk of South Africa's being an equal partner with Britain within the Commonwealth and of the sacred rights of small nations. The Allies, it had been stated repeatedly, had waged war to protect such rights and to make the world safe for democracy. German aggression had been censured; German imperialism denounced. All this talk, thought Hertzog, was so much claptrap, inept fabrications to hoodwink the gullible plebs. The British and French imperialists were consulting their own interests. But one could exploit the position with an eye to the future. Even if his mission were to be a failure, he confided to his intimates, it would gain votes for him in South Africa and show up the sanctimonious British aggressors and imperialists for what they were.

When the deputation was about to embark for England in a Union Castle liner, the sailors refused to man the vessel. The propaganda value of this unprecedented step on the part of British seamen was duly appreciated. Thousands of Afrikaners were deeply incensed. The British admiral in command at Simonstown placed the *Minerva*, a British warship, at the deputation's disposal. But his offer was rejected, and the party set sail in a Dutch ship, which was going to Europe via New York.

Arriving in the French capital, they were amazed to find that an enormous polyglot assemblage had foregathered there. Besides Koreans, Chinamen, Circassians, Japanese, Negroes, Malays, Kirghizes, and Hindus, and men of scores of other nationalities, there were Armenians, Tartars, Persians, and bearded giants from Hedjaz and Bokhara, from Kurdistan and Samarkand, wearing fezzes and turbans and Eastern robes, the majority of them intent on missions somewhat similar to that of Hertzog and his retinue.

Lloyd George received Hertzog kindly, but stated bluntly that Smuts and Botha were representing the people of South Africa at the conference and that he (Hertzog) had no standing whatsoever.

Hertzog went away quietly. He had fulfilled his mission. He was undaunted, and his mind was full of crafty ideas. He would be able to tell the people of South Africa that Smuts and Botha were concerning themselves with matters that did not affect the welfare of South Africa. And he succeeded, to a large extent, in bringing the South African party leaders into disrepute in their own country.

In the meantime Smuts, on his return from Hungary, became immersed in his work once more. Wherever possible he criticized the Treaty, as he felt that the settlement as it stood "was based less on justice than on broken pledges, and that the League Covenant was the only part of it which might redeem the rest."

The South African statesman was happiest when working on the League. The commission which the conference had appointed in the beginning to present a plan for a league of nations comprised President Wilson, Colonel House, Viscount Cecil, and General Smuts. It was, according to Charles Seymour, "the most distinguished of the Peace Conference."[1] Here, away from vulgar wrangling, Smuts's mind could become engrossed in the splendid idealism of the Covenant, his soul know peace.

Not until June 23, when Foch made drastic threats about reopening the war, did the Germans agree to sign the peace.

Meanwhile President Wilson toured America pleading for the Treaty, making a last desperate effort to save the pieces. But the tempo of the times was too feverish for the American people, remote from the hurly-burly of Europe, and the President could no longer move them. Verbal pyrotechnics had no effect upon them. Badly broken in health and suffering from insomnia, Wilson would weep in public from sheer weakness, moving unsteadily towards the inescapable end, the ignominy of defeat, and a stroke that paralyzed his body.

[1] *Colonel House,* Charles Seymour.

America refused to sign the Treaty, and abjured the Covenant. According to Smuts, she left it "on Europe's doorstep."

46

ON JUNE 28, 1919, the historic Treaty of Versailles was signed between the Allies and Germany.

Smuts, who had been threatening for long not to put his name to the Treaty, told Botha a few days before the date of signing that he had decided to leave Paris. Impaled upon the horns of a nasty dilemma, Botha cabled to the Governor General of South Africa: "Smuts refuses to sign Treaty and will publish statement giving grounds for action. While I substantially share his difficulties against Treaty, I have decided to sign because my position as Prime Minister is different from his, and my signature is necessary to make Union a member of the League of Nations and secure for her the new status in the world."

At first it was hoped that Botha by signing and Smuts by refusing to do so would satisfy respectively the English and Afrikaner sections in South Africa, since the extreme harshness of the Treaty would make it repugnant to the latter, while the former would follow Britannia's lead. But it soon became apparent to Botha that Smuts's action would make his own position untenable as Prime Minister of the Union, since his friend might be made to shine in the light of righteousness while he himself might be cast out into the lonely darkness.

After much debating of the question, the Boer generals visited Lloyd George. The British Prime Minister advised Smuts to sign under protest. He could criticize the Treaty to his heart's content afterwards.

Smuts came to a decision rapidly. "I have decided to sign," he said. But he immediately sat down to draft his critical statement of the Treaty.

On June 28 the representatives of the nations foregathered at Versailles in the long Hall of Mirrors of the historic palace, and the erect, soldierly figure of Smuts was among them. Here Germany had once dictated a peace to France. Here the great German Empire had been born. On tables covered with golden cloths the representatives signed the treaty, Foch, Botha, and Smuts being the only ones who had fought against the enemy on the field of battle. At 4.15 P.M., when the last signature had been written, Clemenceau stated that peace once more reigned over Europe. But in a letter Smuts wrote: "This treaty is not the peace; it is the last echo of the war. It closes the war and armistice stage. The real peace must still come, and must be made by the peoples."

And so it happened that almost simultaneously with the ringing of the bells and the booming of the guns proclaiming the glad tidings to a weary world, there was published in the great newspapers of London Smuts's protest against the peace.

It was regarded as "one of the most striking events of that day." The other was the point-blank refusal of the Chinese to sign at all.

No formal declaration of protest in human memory has been more significant than was the Smuts document. Its chief value lay in the hope, the glowing promise with which, despite the Treaty, it furnished mankind: " 'Not in this Mountain, nor in Jerusalem, but in spirit and in truth,' as the Great Master said, must the foundations of the new order be laid. . . .

"And this new spirit among the people will be the solvent for the problems which the statesmen have found too hard at the conference. There are territorial settlements which will need revision. . . . There are indemnities stipulated, which cannot be enacted without grave injury to the industrial revival of Europe. . . . The real peace of the peoples ought to follow, complete, and amend the peace of the statesmen.

". . . I am confident that the League of Nations will yet prove the path of escape for Europe out of the ruin brought by this war."

Here indeed was envisaged the "function of the League," as Wilson visualized it when he saw all else crumbling to dust before his eyes. It was to be an organization founded upon good will with peace as its lodestar. It was also "to amend in calmer mood such settlements at Paris as might appear to be unjust, inacceptable, or unworkable."

Although every fibre of his being revolted against the Treaty of Versailles as finally drafted, Smuts signed it because he realized the necessity for the war's being "liquidated" and because, as he said, the foundations of the League would be laid by the Treaty and an end would be put to Prussian militarism. Subsequently in his philosophic treatise, *Holism and Evolution,* he described the League as "the chief constructive outcome of the war" and the "expression of the deeply felt aspiration towards a more stable holistic human society." It, or something very much like it, may still prove to be the panacea for which mankind is yearning.

While pleading earnestly for a more stable holistic human society and condemning the "national system," he cried passionately: "What is the good of all the wealth and comfort and glamour of the Victorian age, when the next two decades bring us to the graves of ten million young men slain because of the base passions of greed and domination which lurked below the smiling surface of the age?"

Although he believed in the League of Nations as "practically the only instrument wherewith to establish collective security," and although his efforts were largely responsible—as well as those of Nansen, Bourgeois, Branting, Beneš, Cecil, Politis, and Hymans—for the League's surviving its infancy, Smuts never attended any of its sessions, nor, on that account, have its activities detracted from or added greatly to the lustre of his name, whereas Hymans, Politis, Titulescu, Beneš, Briand, Stresemann, and Sir Austen Chamberlain became famous because of it and, in a few instances, lost prestige on account of it.

SECTION VI

47

IMMEDIATELY after the conclusion of the peace Botha hurried back to South Africa to face in his own country and amid his own people the sudden twilight of his days. In the cities where English preponderated he was acclaimed, but in the country districts his name had become an obloquy, and bitter and calumnious were the tongues that maligned him.

Meanwhile Smuts's position had become the subject of much surmise. He had forsaken the small South African stage for the great world stage, and on it he had become a famous player. He had rubbed shoulders with the great ones of this earth, with princes and presidents, potentates and kings. He had made history: important missions had been entrusted to him; he had played with the boundaries of empires and the destinies of nations. He had been called "one of the very few great world leaders developed by the Peace Conference." His name was on the lips of millions. Speculation was rife in regard to his future. He admits that he was called upon at that time to make the "hardest decision" of his life.

His English friends bade him remain with them, stressing the "crucial necessity" of his continued presence in England. He was begged "to stand for election and remain in the Cabinet." It was whispered that Lloyd George wished him to become British Ambassador at Washington. Leadership, power, and fame in regard to world issues were held out to him.

But there was more. "The world was beginning again," says Smuts, "and I had been present at its rebirth. There was the League—my thoughts were in it. To leave Europe in 1919 meant to give up any intimate share in working for these things—the new order and the League. It meant coming to a land where too often my countrymen hated my ideals and despised my larger hopes. . . ."

But he longed for the fauna and flora of Africa, for the sunshine and the mountains, for the dusty kopjes and the boundless veld. "I am not really happy," he says, "except on the veld." He longed also for his home and his family. ("I am a man that loves home. I do not care for social life.") He had been away for four years and had become estranged from his children. Even before his departure for East Africa, ever since Union, parliamentary sessions had taken him away from home for six months in the year. And now family considerations weighed heavily with him.

However, "in the end," says Smuts, "I came back because of Botha." His decision to return to South Africa was a momentous one. It preserved his reputation. It enabled him to become the African oracle, remote, inviolate, and unimpeachable.

Landing in Cape Town early in August, he found that his younger children, having been out of touch with him for so long, had almost forgotten him, while the elder ones strongly disapproved of his having signed the Versailles Treaty. And in less than a month Botha died, in his fifty-eighth year.

For Smuts it was a sad home-coming. He grieved sorely for his friend. They had co-operated for over twenty-one years, and a very intimate friendship had developed with the passage of time.

While the quidnuncs were wondering whether F. S. Malan, a senior Minister, would become Prime Minister, the Governor General called upon Smuts to form a Cabinet. Thus Botha's winsome and tactful personality made way for the unsympathetic, unapproachable, and impatient Smuts, who "lacked Botha's imaginative sympathy and his magnetic influence over all sorts and conditions of men."[1] It happened that at his first meeting with the South African party caucus the new Prime Minister told his followers that he, unlike Botha, "had neither tact nor patience, and that they must take him for what he was worth." They had no option. A born autocrat, Smuts ruled his Ministers with a rod of iron. They were mentally dragooned. There was no disputing his will. A veritable martinet was the Prime Minister. "The new Smuts," it has been justly remarked, "was more than the head of the Government. He was the Government. He was the Cabinet—all the departments of state—the party caucus—the civil service—the Army—Parliament." He was unable to consider anybody's viewpoint but his own. His despotism was the source of his strength. Unfortunately, however, it also contained the germs of political decline.

An almost fanatical revival of bellicosity on the part of his political opponents heralded Smuts's elevation to the premiership of the Union. His qualifications for the premiership were undoubted. But no sooner did

[1] *South Africa*, Jan H. Hofmeyr.

he assume leadership than an avalanche of caustic criticism descended upon his greying head.

His historic pronouncements in Europe were ridiculed. Why had he not stayed in England where so obviously he had been at home? South Africa was clearly too small a field for the scope of his mighty brain. Had he not become as sounding brass and a tinkling cymbal, a mere babbler of words? Had not his acts and his utterances at Versailles been diametrically opposed one to the other? Who had supported Wilson, and let him down? Who, while clamouring for a just peace, had invented the mandatory system—which, in fact, was tantamount to annexation—in direct contravention of the Fourteen Points? Who had signed the Treaty under protest because of its unfairness, while being actually responsible for two thirds of the burden of reparations laid upon the enemy? "Jannie Smuts," said the Nationalist, "who says without meaning, and means without saying." If that constituted greatness, they prayed that they might be preserved from the great. He was great, said they, in the sense that Rhodes and Machiavelli had been great, but he could never be great with Washington and Lincoln and Kruger and De Wet.

"His hide is thick," came the cry, "and he had no principle but opportunism."

But before many months had passed it was patent—and, indeed, it was admitted by the Premier's enemies—that "the personality of Jan Smuts in some way or other directed the politics and controlled the destiny of South Africa."

48

On returning to South Africa as a world statesman, Smuts had entertained great ideas for his country as an equal partner with Great Britain in the British Commonwealth of Nations, as a member of the League and as the country whose destiny it was to civilize Africa "from the South." He had long visualized a Union of South Africa embracing all the African territory south of the equator. Ever since the early days of self-government in the Transvaal, it will be remembered, "the big thing" had held a tremendous fascination for him. He had virtually annexed South West Africa. He cast covetous eyes on the Belgian Congo and Mozambique: as a result there were strongly worded protests from the governments of

Belgium and Portugal. He had plans for the incorporation of Rhodesia in the Union. It was a revival of the Rhodes policy.

But in South Africa there were few who held views such as his and dreamed dreams. South Africans, on the whole, were by no means anxious to become members of a great nation. Their own insignificant domestic problems concerned them deeply, to the exclusion of all else. The Afrikaner element particularly were swallowing thirstily Hertzog's "gospel of isolation." Smuts's overseas reputation served but to augment their distrust. Nor did their leaders hesitate to add fuel to the fire of their suspicion.

Smuts's reference to the British Empire as "a grouping of free states held together with a common allegiance" was openly scoffed at by Hertzog, who said: "It is the sole object of General Smuts to form a great British Empire. South Africa is too small for him. He wants to stand on a mountain instead of an ant heap, and to have his feet in two continents."

Once, while making an appeal to the Union "to live in the present and the future," Smuts said, "It is dangerous; it paralyzes a people to live in the past." He added that people who lived in the past were like cattle who ate old rotten bones on the veld and contracted *gallam* sickness. Whereat Tielman Roos, one of Hertzog's lieutenants and a clever opportunist, rose, and with a voice shaking with apparent fury and indignation, said that Smuts had referred to the bones of the sacred dead of the Boer War.

In the country towns and on the farms men shook their heads and clenched their fists and turned away from Smuts.

Soon after his accession to the premiership he took up residence at Groote Schuur, the beautiful estate on the wooded slopes of Table Mountain bequeathed by Rhodes to the prime ministers of a United South Africa as their official home.

During Botha's tenure of office the spacious homestead had always been crowded with people, for Botha was generous to a fault and his hospitality had become a byword. At his house in Pretoria, on his farm, Rusthof, and at Groote Schuur visitors were always welcome. Botha loved to have people round him. He enjoyed having guests at his table. And so, in his time, the great reception rooms at Groote Schuur were constantly in use and the house resounded with laughter and conversation.

But all this entertainment came to a sudden stop when Smuts arrived at Groote Schuur. He disapproved of extravagant living and discouraged lavish hospitality, as he found little pleasure in the company of people, preferring infinitely to be left alone with his books, his hobbies, and the grandeur of the countryside. The great majority of the thirty bedrooms at Groote Schuur were never occupied in those days. Smuts lived frugally and very plainly in the great house, eschewing its luxury and treasures and often longing for the simplicity of his wood-and-iron dwelling at Irene, some miles from Pretoria. Frequently he lived alone at Groote Schuur. Some of his children were at school in Pretoria: to bring them down to Cape Town whenever Parliament was in session would have been out of the question. Mrs. Smuts found it convenient to live on the farm with the younger ones.

While Smuts was not fond of living at Groote Schuur, the fact that it lay in magnificent surroundings in the shadow of Table Mountain meant much to him, for Smuts loved the mountain as passionately as Rhodes had. And, like Rhodes, he chose a bedroom facing it. He regarded it as "my cathedral." "I come here," he said, "for rest, relaxation, happiness, and meditation." Rhodes also used to think of the mountain as his church. "I find," he had said on one occasion, "that up in the mountains one gets thoughts, what you might term religious thoughts, because they are thoughts for the benefit of humanity."

In May 1923, speaking at Maclear's Beacon, on Table Mountain, at the unveiling of the South African Mountain Club's War Memorial, Smuts dealt with the Spirit of the Mountain. It was a magnificent and stirring speech that moved the large audience profoundly. Many regard it as Smuts's greatest speech. Referring to the mountaineers who had sacrificed their lives in the Great War, he said: "To them the true church where they worshipped was Table Mountain. . . . Table Mountain was their cathedral where they heard a subtler music and saw wider visions and were inspired with a loftier spirit. . . The mountain is not merely something externally sublime. . . . It is the great ladder of the soul, and in a curious way the source of religion. From it came the Law, from it came the Gospel of the Sermon on the Mount. We may truly say that the highest religion is the religion of the mountain."

So, while at Groote Schuur, Smuts often sought the solitude of the mountain. On Sundays one could frequently see him in his khaki slacks with alpenstock in hand, striding briskly along towards its lower slopes whence he would climb swiftly to the summit. At other times he would spend the day quietly in a shady glen or near a mountain stream with a few companions. And when the evening shadows fell he would swing homeward, covered with dust and perspiration, untired, happy as a lark, and looking very much more like a tramp than a world statesman.

Retiring after supper to the library, his favourite room at Groote Schuur, he would become immersed in some newly acquired book on philosophy or science and so beguile the hours. On the whole he would go to bed at a reasonable hour, unlike Botha, whose card parties and general entertainment had often lasted until late at night. Of the three Boer premiers, Hertzog retired earliest. When he was in residence the household was often asleep at ten o'clock.

Of the three—the only men who have held the premiership of a united South Africa—Botha alone used to have a valet, an Englishman who had been in the field against him during the Boer War. Smuts would shudder at the very thought of possessing a personal servant. He used to polish his own boots even when visiting his very wealthy friends, the Gillets, in England while he was a member of the War Cabinet.

Botha and Hertzog and their wives were never completely at home at Groote Schuur. Nor, to be sure, have Smuts and Mrs. Smuts been. To this day Groote Schuur remains Cecil Rhodes's home—with its Gobelin tapestries, its heavy furniture, its Eastern porcelain, and the books that Rhodes cherished. His spirit dwells there. The Prime Minister pays for the food and drink his household consumes. But everything else, including the servants' wages, is paid for with Rhodes's money. To add strength to the impression that the Colossus still dwells at Groote Schuur, nothing in his bedroom has been changed since the day, forty years ago, when he was taken to his seaside cottage at Muizenberg to die. Never since that day has his bedroom been used.

When Smuts became Prime Minister the political situation in the Union was in a state of confusion. It was obvious that the parliament which had been elected on the war issue in 1915 no longer enjoyed the confidence of the electorate. The Nationalist party had grown amazingly in the country districts, while the economic malaise resultant upon the war had given an impetus to Labour in the urban divisions. Only the active support of the Unionists had enabled Botha's government to remain in power. And when the war ended this support was still forthcoming, as the British party, dead set as it was against Hertzog's republican notions, was determined to prevent the downfall of the South African party and Smuts, who alone held South Africa to the British Empire. But it was an unnatural state of affairs since the Unionists, having no Cabinet representation, had no share in governing the country and could not under the circumstances be expected to bolster up Smuts's government indefinitely.

Coalition had been frequently suggested as a solution to the perplexing situation. But, as large numbers of Afrikaners belonging to the South African party held views very much like those of their Nationalist brethren, Smuts hesitated to adopt the expedient. He could depend on their loyalty to a party in which the Afrikaner element preponderated, but he was afraid of their reaction to a powerful British admixture. Precipitate action had to be avoided. A general election was imminent. Smuts hoped that it would indicate to him a course of action.

The election was held on March 10, 1920. The results were startling. The Nationalists emerged from the fray at the head of the poll, having taken eleven rural seats from Smuts, while Labour was phenomenally successful in the urban divisions, taking twelve seats from the Unionists.

Smuts, supported by the Unionists and the Independents, had a precarious majority of four over the combined forces of the Nationalists and Labour. For Smuts the situation was distinctly humiliating. It was also perilous. There was an air of uncertainty and an atmosphere of tense watchfulness about the House. The Nationalists were ever on the lookout for a chance to defeat the Government, and the Government constantly on the alert to avoid such a catastrophe. Suddenly one day only two votes saved Smuts from defeat. A close call indeed. It was a nerve-racking life, but Smuts clung desperately to the premiership. Day after day he sat in the House, hardly ever leaving its precincts until the final adjournment. He adjusted differences between members of his own party and the Unionists; he pleaded with and conciliated the Labourites; he forestalled dangerous moves on the part of the Nationalists; he laboured prodigiously. And every night he slept soundly, always having had the ability to "switch off" completely. Not once throughout that long session did he allow a decisive division to take place. "It was a triumph of parliamentary leadership."

At the conclusion of the session in July 1920 there still hung above his head the Nationalist majority, ever threatening to defeat him, ever menacing his political future. It was an impasse from which there seemed to be no escape. But Smuts was not to be baulked.

49

SOON AFTER the March election, desiring to form a Coalition government, Smuts made overtures to Hertzog and the other party leaders. But as Labour would not countenance the idea, and Hertzog was obstinate, negotiations soon broke down completely.

A few months later, however, a movement to reunite Afrikanerdom
was set afoot, and a determined effort was made to bring together again
the Afrikaner masses that had split asunder when Hertzog was ejected
from Botha's cabinet. It was a movement which evoked no response in
the heart of Smuts. Both he and his friends, the Unionists, were opposed
to it, since they feared a united Afrikaner front.

Apart from being sustained by the British faction in Parliament, the
South African party was entirely dependent on the active support of this
party in many electoral divisions. Smuts owed his position of power to
this factor plus division in the ranks of Afrikanerdom. None realized as
well as he that Reunion (*Hereeniging*) would break that power, as, in
the event of its materializing, the support of the Unionists would fall
away and the Nationalist section would preponderate in a United Afrikaner party.

Smuts, therefore, desired to wreck Hereeniging. But he had to step
warily, as many of his supporters favoured the movement.

A large number of delegates from both the Nationalist and the South
African parties met at the Reunion Congress at Bloemfontein in September 1920. There was tremendous enthusiasm. On many matters of
principle the parties were in complete agreement. But finally a deadlock
was reached on the basic question of "status." Hertzog's followers demanded that the congress accept as fundamentals the "theoretical right"
of secession from the British Empire and complete independence as well
as "the present right to work for such an objective."

When, at length, the secession issue dealt a deathblow to Hereeniging,
Smuts was much relieved. But the Nationalist majority in the House was
a bogy which still haunted his dreams and his waking hours.

Then, suddenly, he saw a way out of his dilemma. The key to his
deliverance was the corollary to the national status formula; viz., the
independence or secession issue.

For many years it has been truly said that, "the question of South
Africa's relationship to the Empire had been the determinative factor in
South African politics." It still is. The recrudescence of extreme National-
ism during and after the Great War stressed this factor at the time when
Smuts was battling to retain the premiership.

At a special session of Parliament held in September 1919, for the
purpose of passing an act to provide for the ratification of the Peace
Treaty and the acceptance of the South West African Mandate Smuts
declared that the Union had "achieved a new status of absolute equality
with all nations," in consequence of her being a signatory to the Treaty

and a member of the League of Nations. It was, therefore, not necessary to receive permission from Great Britain to pass the act.

Hertzog immediately questioned the veracity of Smuts's declarations. The Union's status, he averred, had not been altered one iota by any of the events that had taken place overseas. All the Premier's "fine-sounding phrases were meaningless." In the House Smuts was asked: "Has South Africa the right to secede from the Empire?"

He said: "My reply is absolutely and decisively 'No.' " It was an answer that hardly seemed to be logical. And many argued that Smuts had negatived his higher status claim by arguing that sovereign independence for the Union did not imply the right of secession. Others, again, regarded dominion status as a piece of sheer bluff, invented primarily by Smuts to offset the dangerous Nationalism which was fast gaining ground in the Union.

On many occasions the status claims were openly scouted, the question being asked as to why the signing of the Peace Treaty on the part of South Africa and the fact of her becoming a member of the League should confer on her a higher status, whereas India, which had enjoyed the selfsame privileges both as signatory and in regard to League membership, had not yet been invested with the elementary right of mere self-government. It was a pertinent question. It remained unanswered. Smuts avoided all troublesome questions with a studied vagueness of utterance.

It was said that he was the sworn enemy of the republican ideal, he who had pleaded so eloquently for the rights of small nations in his *Century of Wrong* and had so effectively reiterated that plea during the Great War and afterwards. "He has changed," said his opponents, "the grey jacket of the Boer fighter for the khaki uniform of the British general, and today he is embracing what he used to fight against and fighting what he used to embrace." Members of the Opposition called him the greatest imperialist of all time. It was an overstatement. But there was, perhaps, truth in it, for the most interesting and amazing feature of Smuts's premiership was the tenacity with which he fought for the preservation of the wholeness of the British Empire which once he would have destroyed.

In the period known as the centralization period (the beginning of which synchronized with his accession to power), when a common foreign policy for the component parts of the great Commonwealth of Nations was mooted, as well as the establishment of the imperial Cabinet on a permanent basis, and in the subsequent decentralization period when these efforts to establish closer Empire unity between the far-flung members of the Commonwealth failed completely and the British Empire appeared to be disintegrating, Smuts, the Boer general, excelled all others in the effectiveness of his labours and the earnestness of his pleas for the integrity and solidarity of the Empire, where—he seemed convinced— could be found the whole cornucopia of the blessings. Not without reason has he been called "the Boer prop of the British Empire."

His imperial zeal was, perhaps, nowhere illustrated more clearly than in his spirited denial of South Africa's right of secession under the new status in the face of statements to the contrary made by Lloyd George; Bonar Law, leader of the British Conservative party and the most influential Minister in the British Cabinet next to Lloyd George; Lord Milner; leading members of the government of Canada; and the Prime Minister of Australia, the arch-imperialist, Mr. Hughes.

Of all the points in dispute between the Nationalist party and Smuts, their differences on the secession issue were greatest: they were, in fact, irreconcilable. It was the barrier which wrecked Hereeniging. It was also the weapon which Smuts, in an inspired moment, decided to use against the Nationalist members in Parliament.

When the Nationalists, as a party, refused to jettison their republican ideals, and declared themselves irrevocably bound to the republican doctrine, Smuts utilized their battle cry to further his own ends. He said that the Nationalist motto was "South Africa a Republic," while that of the South African party was "South Africa a Nation." And he issued a call for the formation of a new "moderate" party to further the interests of South Africa as a nation.

"Now that the Nationalist party," he said, "is firmly resolved to continue the propaganda of fanning the fires of secession and of driving the European races apart from each other, the moderate elements of our population have no other alternative than to draw closer to one another in order to fight that policy. A new appeal must, therefore, be made to all right-minded South Africans, irrespective of party or race, to join the new party which will be strong enough to safeguard the permanent interests of the Union against the disruptive and destructive policy of the Nationalists."

It was a clarion call that roused the Unionists. Nor was it without its effect on the Afrikaner element of his party. To many of them fusion, even with the Unionists, in the interests of "South Africa, a Nation," seemed advisable, if they wished to combat successfully the "Nationalist hotheads" with their "disruptive and destructive" republican ideas. In the end, however, the only "moderate elements" who proved willing to throw in their lot with Smuts were the Unionists. In determining to join forces with them Smuts realized that the step would antagonize a substantial percentage of the Afrikaner element in his party. But he had no option.

After secret negotiations extending over a period of many months, the Unionist party was suddenly merged in the South African party. This, at all events, is what the public was given to believe. But, to all intents and purposes, the Unionist element lost neither its identity nor its influence. Nor did its power ever wane. The new party retained the name of Smuts's South African party. This was a sop to Afrikaner sentiment and a blind which deceived only the excessively stupid.

No sooner had the merger taken place than Smuts decided to go to the country to test the opinion of the electorate on the new division of parties. It was a wise move. The time was opportune. Sinister tales of Bolshevik atrocities in Russia were reaching the Union from abroad. Labour suffered a setback, for conservative people began to look askance at a party which was reputed to contain a large number of Bolsheviks. The reaction was further stimulated by public indignation at certain menacing trade-union demands.

Against the Nationalists Smuts used the secession bogey. "Secession," he cried, "means the blasting of all the great hopes which have sustained our people in the past!" South Africa's status had been changed and it was now "a free, equal, and independent state in the British Commonwealth of Nations."

Hertzog countered by saying that since South Africa was on an equal footing with Great Britain "it follows that we are fit to obtain and enjoy sovereign independence. It is absurd to state in one and the same breath that we enjoy equality with England but that we are unfit and unqualified for sovereign independence." His counterstroke contained the essence of logic but could hardly avail against Smuts's subtle enlistment of racial sentiment.

Realizing this, the Labourites as well as the Nationalists essayed to focus the attention of the electorate on economic matters by protesting vigorously against the high cost of living and loudly denouncing the alleged exorbitant profit-taking of the men whom the Labour leader called the "old Unionist profiteering crowd."

In England speculation was rife as to the outcome of the election, and a tremendous interest was taken in the contest. Smuts had become the demigod of the British imperialists and had reached the zenith of his fame in Britain. Almost every newspaper hailed him as the hero of imperial enthusiasm, "the enlightened fusionist of two white races, the champion of South African loyalty."

At the election the Nationalists gained one seat, but Labour went down very badly. Smuts was returned to power with an absolute majority of six.

There was a state of relief throughout the Empire, as the result of the election had been awaited with the greatest suspense. Imperialists throughout the Commonwealth had seen in the contest precisely what the Nationalists had seen; viz., a struggle between Imperialism and Nationalism and they had witnessed a victory for Imperialism. General Smuts's triumph was, to use the words of Lord Curzon in the British House of Lords, "a triumph for the whole Empire." In far-away New Zealand Mr. Massey, Prime Minister of that dominion, stated joyfully that the South African election had been fought on the issue of a "United Empire" and that the result proved "that we are all part of one great empire with one king, one flag, and one constitution." And in the space of one week responsible statements were made in respect of plans for closer co-operation between the nations of the Commonwealth by the British ministers, Lloyd George, Winston Churchill, and Lord Curzon.

Nor was anyone surprised when Smuts proved to be the most ardent advocate of imperial tariff preference and imperial economic solidarity at an imperial conference held subsequently.

From the political struggle Smuts had emerged the victor. But he had won a Pyrrhic victory. The factors that contributed to it were also responsible for his decline and ultimate eclipse.

Greatly to the delight of the Opposition and much to the vexation of his own followers, the Premier was established in office by the favour of his former opponents. But more. Smuts's fusion with the Unionists was scornfully stigmatized and skilfully employed to stir up feeling against the Prime Minister among the Afrikaner members of his party: it was recalled that his new colleagues had been the bosom friends of Rhodes and Jameson; they were the "erstwhile associates of Milner and the champions of the creed of jingo imperialism."

At the same time a drumfire of invective against the so-called "unholy alliance" emanated also from the ranks of Labour, for the Unionist party had been the party of the mineowners and other capitalists. In the circumstances, it was felt, it would not be difficult to stir up the proletariat effectively against its traditional enemies and their new leader, Smuts, from whose stinging blows, dealt at intervals over a period of many years, it was still smarting. Presently was to come grave trouble in the industrial areas. It was to be crushed ruthlessly by Smuts. In the resultant cataclysm he was to be engulfed.

As in his early years he had sought to insinuate himself into the orbit of Rhodes, the Colossus, who spelt power, so now he had thrown in his lot with the party which would enable him to retain that power which is to him the quintessence of life, and which would enable him to carry out his great holistic plans.

With amazing candour he admitted at Kimberley that the spirit of Rhodes was still alive, that he was working in that spirit, and that the great man's dream would be realized. He was promptly referred to this passage from his book, *A Century of Wrong:* "The spirit of South African capitalism found its incarnation in C. J. Rhodes."

His enemies assured Smuts that his liaison with capitalism would remain to his lasting discredit, but they felt that his bedfellows suited him well since they also subscribed to the dual allegiance which he advocated.

In spite of Hertzog's notorious bias, his accusation to the effect that Smuts had his feet in two continents seemed only too true. His thoughts were divided between Europe and South Africa, and in his heart there was a constant and natural longing for the footlights of the great European stage and the attention of the millions. His "dual allegiance" revealed a dual personality: the revered statesman of Europe full of sage advice and grand ideals, and the hard and practical South African politician to whom politics was "the science of exigencies," as remote from idealism as are the poles one from the other. "His ideas might soar to the clouds, but in his politics he came down to earth," wrote one who knew him well.

At a meeting held in Beaufort West on the Great Karoo, an elderly man speaking in a high falsetto constantly interrupted Smuts.

"Who are you?" asked the Prime Minister.

"Don't you remember me?" said the man.

"No."

"I am Commandant Negrini. General, do you remember the day you shot Colyn?"

"Yes."

"Do you remember how Colyn implored you to spare his life?"

No reply.

"General, do you remember what you said to him? You said: 'Colyn, you are one of those rotten Afrikaners who allow themselves to be used by the British to do their dirty work.' General, are you not perhaps one of those Afrikaners?"

Thus from every side was Smuts assailed and taunted for having linked up with the Unionists. But having made his choice, he drove steadily on towards his holistic goal. Neither threats nor abusive epithets could make him turn aside from his predetermined path. Even gross libel left him cold. It always has.

Smuts has never been revengeful. Almost unique in this respect among South African politicians, he has not a trace of vindictiveness in his make-up. Personalities are beneath him. He has frequently stayed his hand where he has been able to do grievous injury to a vulnerable political foe. This is a facet of Smuts's complex character that is not generally known.

50

IN THE new Ministry Sir Thomas Smartt, an eloquent Irishman, ranked as second in command to Smuts. He had been Rhodes's chief lieutenant during the siege of Kimberley, and had afterwards served in a similar capacity to Jameson in the political sphere; he had been an active participant in the abortive attempt to suspend the constitution of the Cape Colony in the early days of the century, and had in 1911 become leader of the Unionist party.

Deneys Reitz, aged thirty-nine, was perhaps the most romantic character in the new Ministry. He was a protégé of Smuts. The third son of ex-President Reitz of the Orange Free State, he joined the commandos at the outbreak of hostilities in 1899. He was then seventeen years old. Many months later he joined Smuts's famous guerrilla band shortly after it had embarked on its daring raid into the Cape Colony. Accompanying his chief to the Vereeniging peace negotiations, he refused to take the oath of allegiance to Great Britain and sailed for Madagascar. In the swampy, fever-stricken stretches of that tropical island he eked out an existence as a transport driver. He became exceedingly homesick, but it was a long time before Smuts and others by means of tactful letters managed to prevail on him to return to his native country. He arrived back in the Union broken in health and on the verge of prostration. Smuts took him home, and Mrs. Smuts put him to bed and nursed him devotedly until his strength returned. No wonder that he became his host's ardent disciple and his hostess's faithful friend.

After giving Smuts valuable assistance against the rebels in 1914, he left for South West Africa, where the campaign against the Germans was in full swing. Thereafter he led a regiment in German East Africa

The Union Cabinet in 1921, after the amalgamation of the Unionist and South African parties.

General Smuts and family in 1921

Copyright, Akkersdyk, C.T.

until, in the first months of 1917, he left for France where, in due course, he was given the command of a battalion of Royal Scots Fusiliers.

Opposing ex-President Steyn's son Colin, a Nationalist, in Bloemfontein South at the general election of 1920, he gained the victory. It was a short-lived triumph, for he lost the seat at the stormy election of 1921. But the Prime Minister was determined to have Reitz in the House. He, therefore, used his tremendous influence at Port Elizabeth Central, a Unionist stronghold, and the young Boer was returned to Parliament as member for an essentially British constituency at a bye-election. So far so good. But when Smuts included in his Cabinet this young man whose parliamentary experience was negligible, there was much dissatisfaction. Yet Smuts had his way. Since that day Reitz has stood at his chief's side in fair weather and in foul, and no leader has had a stancher ally.

In order to make his alliance with the Unionists palatable for the Afrikaner element in his party, Smuts told these that it had been "the desire of General Botha to see the amalgamation of the South African and Unionist parties." But, if he had desired this, Botha had been careful not to say so. On the contrary, he had affected to be strongly opposed to such a union. "God help South Africa," he had said at Lichtenburg, "if the Unionists and the South African party unite. Should this happen, I foresee one thing only, that the Unionists will use the South African party as a rag with which to do their dirty work."

Nor was his prognostication belied by the event, for no sooner had the new Parliament been summoned than mine taxation was reduced to the extent of hundreds of thousands of pounds, the mines were granted exemption from provincial taxes, and the millionaire butcher, Sir David Graaf, acquired a virtual monopoly of the meat trade in South Africa. Yet in his election manifesto Smuts had said: "We are not the party of capital or great financial interests; those who go in for exploitation and excess profits must betake themselves to another party."

When once he was firmly established in power Smuts's dictatorial manner became more pronounced than it had ever been. Botha's restraining influence was there no longer to temper his arrogance, his overweening self-sufficiency, and his peculiar obstinacy. Opposition to his will served but to make him more stubborn and intractable. Even well-meant advice was distasteful to him. His colleagues discovered this very soon. They found that they were little more than clerks.

So self-centred did he become that it was impossible to collaborate with him. He had confidence only in Jan Smuts and chose to do everything himself. There were times when he went so far as to issue instructions to departmental chiefs not only without consulting the Ministers concerned, but often even without their knowledge. He went even further. He regarded Parliament as a source of obstruction and embarrassment. Frequently he was accused of adopting measures designed to curtail the freedom of debate, more particularly when a budget was being discussed in committee. On June 19, 1922, all the members of the Opposition walked out of the House as a protest against such methods. Men called him "the Dictator" and "the Oriental Despot." Unfortunately, Botha was no longer there to salve with tact the wounds dealt by Smuts in his ruthlessness.

By innuendo and direct attack the Opposition press sought to pillory him. Their efforts availed them little, for Smuts drove relentlessly on.

The senators whom he treated with little respect and scant courtesy resented his attitude, particularly since they knew that he regarded the Upper House as even more superfluous than the Lower one.

He became very unpopular, antagonizing people everywhere. Departmental chiefs and their subordinates stood in awe of him. He rode roughshod over them. He lost patience with them when they lacked initiative, were slow in the uptake, and could not follow the swift working of his dynamic mind. He did not know how to suffer fools gladly.

Personal considerations weighed not at all with him when he wished to achieve any definite object. He would desert his associates without a qualm if a greater purpose was to be served. He used people and then cast them aside without pity should the need arise. Yet, for all his ruthlessness, many remained loyal to him, not for party purposes but because he captured their imagination. This was the case particularly in the Transvaal, where to this day there are those who say, "After Christ comes Smuts."

Smuts had a sovereign contempt for everything small. It was in him to overlook "non-essential details which lesser men stumble over." He would see his goal clearly and, with the characteristic impatience of the man of action, he would be inclined to skip the intervening spaces. In this way he outstripped others and became impatient when they lagged behind. In England he had been in contact with important matters which had required the brain of a statesman. Unimportant administrative difficulties in South Africa formed a poor contrast. He was interested only in big things. As an administrator, therefore, he was a failure.

Intellectually he towered above his associates and colleagues. And he knew it. In sheer intellect and self-confidence lay his strength; and in his astonishing political acumen and nimbleness; in his imperiousness and in his "ruthless tenacity in pursuing his objective." But in spite of his strong personality he lacked in those days that quality which is almost indispensable to leadership—personal magnetism.

Lawrence of Arabia had a magnetic power which drew men to him. "I could have followed him over the edge of the world," wrote the late Lord Tweedsmuir. No man could ever say that of Smuts. He lacked the human qualities which make for inspired and inspiring leadership. There was in him a constitutional inability to "establish contact" with men. During Botha's lifetime this had not been very noticeable for, as Smuts himself had remarked, "I deal with administration. Botha deals with people." But now he could no longer depend on his former chief to step into the breach. He had to handle men himself, and he found great difficulty in doing so. The thoughts and emotions of the ordinary common or garden folk that constituted the great majority of the electorate held no interest for him. Cold and aloof, he stood above them. And even on the rare occasions when he made contact, his intellectual arrogance would not forsake him, and it would be patent to all that he "reached down" to his inferiors.

He was a lonely man with very few friends, if a man with his mind and interests can be lonely. Perhaps "aloneness" describes his state more accurately.

Far from being socially inclined and certainly not the polished gentleman, his elemental ruggedness drove him out of the parlour and into the veld. He was not interested in people. They generally bored him. But he was almost fanatically interested in ideas and in things—the plants and flowers and grasses and trees of Africa; the nature of life; evolution; a commonwealth of nations; the universe. One day, for some reason or other, there was great excitement in the House. Messengers were hurriedly dispatched to look for Smuts. They found him on his knees in his room, sorting out grasses, and so intent on his work that he was oblivious to all else.

His ostensibly unnatural conversion to and laudation of the British imperial creed almost immediately after the Boer War and so soon after his classic denunciation of it in *A Century of Wrong* must be attributed partly to his holistic philosophy (about which more will be said later on); partly perhaps to that insidious opportunism which in a greater or lesser degree holds the vast majority of politicians and even statesmen in thraldom; partly to an undoubted conviction that the welfare and safety of South Africa were inalienably bound up in Empire membership; partly to his abnormal interest in ideas and things as opposed to human beings; and partly to his lack of race consciousness. It is necessary at this stage to examine the last three factors only.

Smuts eschewed the unpractical romanticism of an era that had had its day—a romanticism which made a fetish of extreme Nationalism, unmindful of the dangers in it, and subordinated the practical advantages connected with membership of the British Empire to national heroics.

Moreover, the racial needs and political aspirations of human beings in the southernmost corner of Africa were as nothing compared to the magnificent idea of a great empire washed by the seven seas. Men were born only to die, and their desires and needs died with them—they were transient. But the things of Africa were "eternal," and so was the great, dark, brooding continent—immeasurably more important than the few mortals with national aspirations crawling about on its base. The big thing for Africa was Pan-Africanism under the aegis of the Empire, or membership of the Empire. Smuts's goal shone lustrously before his eyes. Impatient, as ever, of delays, he skipped the intervening steps, taking Botha with him. It was a sudden conversion. It was hardly decent, for the grass was not yet green on the graves of the Boer martyrs. But Smuts was not interested in people and their feelings, nor, for that matter, did he understand them.

His lack of race consciousness is a natural corollary. Nationality meant little to him. Take the case of Smuts and the Jews. He was supposed to be a great lover of Israel. Nothing was further removed from the truth. He helped the Jews and they helped him. Both were interested in capitalism and imperialism, albeit in different ways. Indeed, they had much more in common than had Smuts and certain sections of his own people. But Smuts was not more pro-Jewish than he was pro-English or pro-Commonwealth Afrikaner. To him it made no difference what a man's language was or his extraction, provided that he carried the image of the Commonwealth in his heart. He could co-operate much more readily and happily with holistically inclined Jews, Germans, Englishmen, and others than with Nationalists of his own race. He is essentially a holist.

Smuts is and will be pro-Jewish only as long as the Jews work in the interests of the Empire. Should they ever turn against it, he will turn against them and, if necessary, suppress them with cold calculation. But as yet all is well. And we find that Smuts and J. H. Hofmeyr between them open more synagogues than does the chief rabbi himself.

51

EVEN as Prime Minister with a substantial majority Smuts found that his life was fraught with much anxiety. To South Africa, after the war, came the selfsame social and industrial disturbances that had manifested themselves with great potency in Europe. Much unemployment and misery had resulted from the serious postwar depression. The financial situation was grave. Deficit after deficit necessitated drastic retrenchment in all directions. Men who had been loyal to Smuts were fast becoming his enemies.

"Smuts," said Hertzog, blaming his enemy largely for matters beyond human control, "Smuts has brought South Africa to the verge of ruin." And to the side of the Nationalist leader there rallied many men who had formerly despised him.

A Free Stater, Charlie Fichardt, was the Opposition's chief critic on financial matters. He could hardly speak his own mother tongue, but employed the King's English faultlessly whenever he made a speech. He had been educated in England. His untimely end—resultant upon the tragic death of a beautiful and talented daughter—brought a small measure of respite to the toilworn and harassed Minister of Finance, Henry Burton.

Smuts's difficult position was considerably aggravated by the constitutional weakness of his party. Many of his followers were aware of this defect. One of them analyzed the situation rather well in September 1922. The truth of the matter, he said, was that the basis on which the party had been established was both inadequate and defective. A large number of people could never be united by a leader's merely holding up to them a secession bogey. The new party was largely lacking in the element that appealed to the emotions. In the Nationalist party, on the contrary, that element was much in evidence, even if its appeal was directed at a patriotism which was narrow and bigoted: it stirred the hearts of the people. It was a cogent summing up of the position.

Since his party was composed of two separate groups holding briefs for what were virtually two separate ideologies, it was almost impossible for the Prime Minister to follow any fixed line of action at any time without clashing with one of the sections. "If he pleases the one lot," complained a disgruntled member of the party, "he offends the other, the result being that he can rarely speak his mind but has to resort to commonplaces more often than not."

On account of the incompatible elements in its party it was impossible for the Government to take vigorous action in connection with any pressing question. The party caucus and even the Cabinet itself were strongly divided on the question of protection as opposed to free trade; hence industrial development was almost impossible. In the course of time Mr. J. W. Jagger resigned from the Cabinet, "a martyr to free trade." Conflicting opinions on the native problem and on territorial segregation for non-Europeans forced Smuts to push these urgent questions into the background. In fact, the Government was able to preserve its unity only by avoiding all fundamental problems. It was solely the political genius of Smuts that prevented the incongruous elements in his party from falling asunder.

With almost uncanny elusiveness he artfully dodged searching inquiries as to the Government's attitude on any ticklish problem. He never seemed to disagree with any particular faction on any point of policy. Whereas in a predominantly British constituency he would declare himself as being unalterably opposed to segregation of the natives, for example, in the country districts, on the other hand, he would succeed in creating the impression that he was a strong advocate of such isolation. It was a game full of risks; but Smuts's life had been spent in sailing close to the wind, and he rode the storm with fortitude and not a small measure of success. The bolstering up, however, of an emasculated party could only be a temporary thing.

The Government's difficult financial position, the resultant increase in taxation, and drastic retrenchments were as nectar of the gods to Hertzog and his henchmen. While, however, they continued with contumely to denounce imperialists in general and Smuts in particular as the greatest of them all, these anti-imperial fulminations were delivered in the rural districts alone. In the urban areas the Nationalists found fault with the Government for imposing a heavy burden of taxation, and for its alleged ignorance and impotence in regard to financial matters, and accused Smuts of being directly responsible for the serious economic malaise with which the country was afflicted. These were the first signs of a rapprochement between the Nationalist party and Labour. It was inspired by Tielman Roos, the Transvaal Nationalist leader. Its object was primarily to unseat Smuts.

At the election of 1921 three-cornered contests had contributed greatly to Smuts's success. Roos and his confreres, desiring to have nothing of the sort in future, endeavoured to secure a "working agreement" with the Labour leaders. Whereas Smuts had attempted in vain to arrive at such an arrangement between the Labour and South African parties, the Nationalists' efforts were to be crowned with success. But as the majority of the Labourites were British who abjured secession, it was necessary to push the republican issue into the background and concentrate on economic ills—a process which was not unwelcome to the Hertzogites.

To accuse the Government of being responsible for all the inevitable hardships resultant upon the world-wide slump was a most efficacious mode of attack, at which the Nationalists and Labourites excelled. As the weeks passed by co-operation between them grew closer and closer. Smuts's party began to shrink perceptibly.

His constant struggle against the grim spectre of defeat left its mark on Smuts. He became exceedingly moody. His nerves were on edge. He often had bouts of malaria which he had contracted during the East African campaign. He was advised to take a long rest. He refused to do so. He fought the disease with drugs. By sheer force of will he carried on. Ever since 1914 he had been working at high pressure. He had been a glutton for work. But his imperious will was driving his magnificent constitution to death. So, at least, it seemed.

His irritability and offhandedness annoyed deputations. In Parliament he became disagreeable to both friend and foe. The former he drove along with the lash of party discipline; the latter with the sjambok of unyielding obstinacy.

A series of events which culminated in a bloody revolution on the Rand were to hasten the Prime Minister's downfall.

52

IN 1919 there were native strikes in Johannesburg, Pretoria, and Bloemfontein. In 1920 over seventy thousand natives working in the mines on the Witwatersrand went on strike, demanding more pay. They were driven back ruthlessly to their labours at Smuts's behest.

Not long after there was a student riot at the native college at Fort Hare.

In 1920 the president of the newly established Native Labour Union at Port Elizabeth strongly encouraged the members of the Union to go on strike and demand higher wages in view of the increased cost of living. He was jailed although no warrant had been issued for his arrest. Hundreds of natives soon congregated before the prison in which he had been lodged. They were armed with *kieries* (knobbed sticks). A great crowd of interested spectators flocked to the scene. Suddenly strong jets of water were directed at the mob of demonstrators. They immediately hurled stones at their assailants. In the subsequent tumult a shot was fired which threw the crowd into a panic. Then the police opened fire on them. There were six European casualties and sixty-eight native. The country was scandalized. In Parliament Smuts was called upon to shoulder the responsibility.

It has been said of him that he has an idea that Liberalism is an export article not applicable to South Africa. His attitude towards natives has certainly never been a liberal one. It has always been like that of his forebears in whose eyes the white man was the master and the native his servant. For many years he advocated native segregation, but afterwards he repudiated it in order to link up with his Unionist brethren and, incidentally, to garner such votes as could be swayed by such a reversal of policy. But there was no change of heart in Smuts. Towards the coloured races in South Africa his attitude to this day remains hard, uncompromising, and devoid of sentiment.

An event more disastrous in its outcome than any of the previous disturbances was to take place in 1921. Natives were concerned once more. Religious fanaticism was at the root of the trouble.

A native from the Union had visited America some years before and had become a "bishop" of what was known as the "Church of God and Saints of Christ." A flatulent spellbinder, he soon acquired a considerable following on his return to South Africa. His religious tenets were most acceptable to his flock, since he insisted that both Saturday and Sunday were Sabbaths and that even the Jewish Passover should be observed. To many natives who had seldom eaten their fill of substantial victuals the periodic feasts were indeed a gift from Heaven.

When the high priest was eventually gathered to the bosom of Abraham, a native named Enoch succeeded him and became known as the Prophet. The sect having acquired some land at Bulhoek near Queenstown in the Eastern Province, it became customary annually for Enoch to summon his followers to this spot to celebrate the Jewish Passover. Here they camped, chiefly on Crown land, and proved themselves a general nuisance, but they always departed at the end of the celebrations.

In 1920, however, they outstayed their time, paying no attention whatsoever to public servants sent to reason with them. They were waiting, they said, "for the coming of the Lord."

When the year drew to a close they were still there.

Meanwhile from all sides came complaints, but chiefly from farmers in the neighbourhood, who stated that the Israelites, as the followers of the Prophet were called, were stealing their cattle.

At length the Government decided to step in. A force of police arrived. The Prophet threatened them. They left in a hurry.

The fat was in the fire. Having successfully defied the Government, the natives appeared more determined than ever to defend what they genuinely believed to be their sacrosanct rights. God was their only master. His prophet, Enoch, had bidden them remain at Bulhoek. And there they would abide. No meddling from outside was tolerated. Tax collectors and health inspectors were prevented from entering the camp. Only the law of Jehovah was recognized.

Had the Government asserted its authority in time, the subsequent tragedy might have been averted; but its hesitant attitude added fuel to the fire, for the Israelites were now, if anything, more convinced than ever that they were God's Chosen People and that they could flout the laws of man with impunity.

In the meantime the parliamentary election of 1921 was held. After it, the Government suddenly decided that matters should be brought to a head. A strong force of police commanded by Colonel Truter was sent against the Israelites, who, brandishing assagais (spears), charged down on their foes fanatically, inspired by the Prophet's cry of "the hour of the black man is at hand!" At thirty yards' range the police mowed them down. There were close on three hundred casualties among the natives.

In Parliament the Government's dilatory attitude was stigmatized by the Hertzogites, who averred that the Premier's inaction had been the cause of the deaths of scores of misguided human beings and that it had been dictated by political necessity, since, in order to catch the native vote, he had refrained from taking action until after the election. Hertzog himself attacked Smuts violently. Actually the Nationalists cared very little for the lives of the natives. Their scandalized protests, directed mainly at the person of Smuts (whom they invariably blamed for everything), were inspired entirely by a desire to bring the Government into disrepute. There was fresh defection from the ranks of the South African party.

Busily engaged in making political propaganda out of the Bulhoek episode, the Opposition was still fulminating against Smuts when he sailed for England to attend an imperial conference in London.

It was a welcome change for the Premier. At home, in spite of his parliamentary majority, there was an atmosphere of uncertainty, unfriendliness, and carping criticism. In England, however, he was received with open arms. He spoke on matters relating to India, Japan, Russia, Palestine, and the League. He discussed foreign policy and empire defence. His speeches were listened to with great respect. He was feted. He was happy.

He went to Windsor Castle as the King's guest. Acting on Lloyd George's advice, His Majesty had agreed to visit Northern Ireland to open the new Ulster Parliament, since the "moral effect" of his presence was sorely needed in those difficult days. But in view of the recent disturbances in and around Dublin and the Irish people's deadly hatred of the British Black and Tan army of occupation, the forthcoming visit appeared to contain an element of risk, particularly as the rebellious south might regard such a gesture to the north as an open insult to itself. Smuts's genius, however, saw in this singular situation a "unique opportunity" to satisfy the Loyalists of Northern Ireland and to bring to the insurgents in the south a message of good will and of peace. At the King's suggestion Smuts drafted a speech which was delivered almost verbatim at Belfast by His Majesty after the South African Premier had been invited to discuss it with the British Cabinet. Its results were far-reaching. The British Government took their cue from it. The Irish rebels pricked up their ears.

Roger Casement's brother, Tom, whom Smuts had known in East Africa, visited the South African in London on behalf of the Irish leaders who wished to consult him, secretly, in Ireland. They begged him to come to them as they were in hiding and could not possibly visit him. Then came a letter from De Valera stating in detail his terms for a peaceful settlement. Sir Horace Plunkett wrote to Smuts: "From my pretty full knowledge of my countrymen at home and abroad I can truthfully say that no living statesman would be more acceptable to the majority of the Irish people as a political adviser than yourself. . . ."

Smuts consulted Lloyd George, who "was delighted," said Smuts. "He said it was the very thing to follow up the King's speech, and also, he said, I was the very man to do the job—no Englishman, an outsider, a Boer. He agreed that in this capacity I should go—not as an emissary of the British Government, but in my own capacity as an outsider and a Boer. And Lloyd George was to take no part in the business. Everything was to be left in my hands—I was to explore the position, see if peace could be brought about, say and do whatever I chose towards this end. No one else knew. Not another member of the Cabinet. Not the police. Nobody. We kept it an absolute secret."

Smuts left for Ireland as Mr. Smith.

The Irish rebels were on the quay at Kingstown when his boat arrived, asked for General Smuts, were told that there was nobody on board bearing that name, and departed, crestfallen.

Not long after, Smuts walked down the gangway, summoned a taxi driver, and told the man to take him to Dublin.

"It's dangerous to go there," said the driver.

"What! Dangerous to go seven miles?"

"Yes," replied the man. "They shoot!"

"That's just talk," said the general firmly. "You carry on."

Arriving at the Guildhall in Dublin, Smuts was told by the lord mayor, one of the rebel chiefs, that De Valera and the other leaders were in the city, awaiting his arrival. He was taken to them. Among others he met Erskine Childers and Arthur Griffith. He listened patiently to their complaints and their demands. Then he stated his case. He advised them to accept dominion status. Unmindful of the racial discord in the Union and the secession danger, he painted a wonderful picture of South Africa under dominion status—a country of happiness and promise. He had conveniently forgotten for the nonce the cry of the majority of the Dutch: "He has sold our right for a mess of pottage, shut the door in the face of our independence; we want to be relieved of the weight of England's troubles which we now have to bear; we are being sucked dry by the Empire."

Smuts argued and pleaded with the rebels for many hours but failed to make headway. Childers and De Valera were "most difficult to convince." Smuts suggested an armistice and a conference with the British Government. "They agreed," says Smuts, "before I left." Lloyd George fell in eagerly with the suggestion, but Winston Churchill and Lord Birkenhead were not enthusiastic.

Then came the armistice and a conference. But Smuts took no part in the discussions, for he had to hurry back to South Africa where serious trouble was brewing.

It transpired afterwards that Smuts's armistice had come in the nick of time, for a massacre was averted thereby. A large number of gunmen had been detailed to shoot down at an appointed time all the uniformed British agents in Dublin.

Meanwhile the Constitutional Conference which was to determine the true nature of dominion status or "higher status" for the Dominions had been postponed indefinitely. And with a purpose. Empire statesmen found it convenient to leave the conception of "dominion status" undefined and unsettled and to acquiesce in the existing anomalies and even absurdities in the constitutional position of the Dominions. Smuts could then, in accordance with the dictates of necessity, deny, in the case of South Africa, that most fundamental principle of freedom, the right of self-determination, and acknowledge its existence in the case of Ireland; and Lloyd George could, according as it suited him, admit that right as far as the Dominions were concerned and refuse to recognize it in the case of Ireland. And this, in point of fact, actually happened.

Lloyd George offered dominion status to Ireland. De Valera asked whether this included the right of self-determination. Lloyd George, fearing the consequences of a reply in the affirmative, said "No." Smuts, however, said "Yes," and in order to substantiate his interpretation of the matter he referred De Valera to the judgments given in the previous year by Messrs. Lloyd George and Bonar Law and by Lord Milner—pronouncements which formerly he had scouted and the majority of his party newspapers had exposed to derision. Smuts is an incorrigible opportunist.

From the fulsome laudation of Britain he returned to the disagreeable atmosphere of South African politics.

As he left his ship the unemployed booed him. In Parliament there was a measure of distrust and hostility. The Handy Man of the Empire, said the Opposition, had again risen to the occasion. As usual, he had concerned himself with the problems of the Empire, said the Opposition, and had neglected his duty to his own country. He had "brought South Africa to the verge of ruin," they said.

All kinds of deputations flocked round him clamouring for assistance. Railwaymen, taxpayers, miners, natives—all came with their grievances. These were the first rumblings of a mighty storm that was to convulse the great Rand—the industrial heart of the Union.

53

THE INDUSTRIAL UNREST which had manifested itself with so much persistence in the Transvaal in the years before the war and had given way temporarily to the exigencies of the Great Struggle, now suddenly burst forth on the Witwatersrand gold fields with unprecedented violence.

Impelled, no doubt, by a natural desire to reduce expenses to combat the impending slump, and actuated by a tremendous craving to break for all time the power of trade-unionism on the Rand, capitalism joined battle with labour in the fateful year of 1922. For Smuts it was a year fraught with destiny.

The trouble started over the abolition of the *status quo* agreement in terms of which on September 1, 1918, the mine magnates had undertaken not to replace whites by native labour and to preserve at an agreed ratio the numbers of white and native workers. Economic conditions, however, now appeared to justify a drastic revision of the agreement, a revision which threatened to take away from thousands of white labourers their sole means of livelihood.

The great trade-unions, having sponsored numerous successful strikes in the past, were sure of themselves. They now combined to form the Industrial Federation which was soon to measure its strength with the Chamber of Mines representing the interests of the landlords.

As a result of a five shillings' reduction of pay on January 1, 1922, the miners in the coal mines went on strike. When the mine magnates flatly refused to submit the matter to arbitration, the situation became serious.

And then a few days later, when the *status quo* agreement or conventional colour bar, and the statutory colour bar[1]—which was the direct outcome of the Mines and Works Act—were abrogated on the gold mines, 20,000 workers from these mines went on strike too. So did the engineers. Once again arbitration was refused bluntly. Thereupon began the great struggle between the millionaires and the proletariat.

Apart from making a few uninspired and abortive attempts to put an end to the deadlock, Smuts, who, it will be remembered, had been used most successfully by the British Government to settle strikes in Great Britain, refused to intervene. And yet it might have been possible for the Government at this stage to mediate between the parties and to effect a lasting settlement. Smuts pooh-poohed the idea of compulsory arbitration. He said that it had proved to be a complete failure in Australia and New Zealand. In point of fact, it had been an unqualified success in these Dominions.[2] But that is neither here nor there. Compulsory arbitration was not the point. Smuts's attitude was. His inexplicable inactivity contrasted strangely with the untiring efforts made by many a British premier in similar circumstances to bring about a settlement. Mr. Lloyd George is a case in point. "The British Premier's feverish activity during the great coal strike," Smuts's critics pointed out, "was phenomenal. He was on his legs night and day, now visiting one party, then the other.

[1] In 1921 the conventional colour bar protected 4,020 men in nineteen occupations, while the statutory bar protected 7,057 in thirty-two occupations.

[2] See *Commonwealth of Australia,* Wise.

Whenever an impasse was arrived at, he was at hand to act as mediator and to prevent a break in the negotiations." But Smuts said to the miners: "We shall draw a ring round you disputants and allow you to fight it out."

On January 26 800 men were dismissed from the coal mines for refusing to accept the terms of their masters. A disastrous crisis seemed imminent, and on all sides men demanded that a general strike be proclaimed. But the Industrial Federation declined to countenance such a suggestion. They had the situation well in hand, but as the days went by it became clear that a spirit of revolt was in the ascendant and that it was likely to culminate in activities subversive to peace. These needed but the passage of time for their fruition, and the dilatory attitude of the Government was destined to fulfil this need. To many it seemed that Smuts was intentionally waiting for the tortoise to stick out its head. He was called the "paid agent of the Chamber of Mines." He received anonymous letters from many who threatened to shoot him. Similar threats were made in public, and his farm was haunted by would-be assassins. To escape them he slept on the veld.

It was generally believed by the strikers that the Prime Minister and the capitalists were hand in glove, that they were avowedly bent on the destruction of organized labour, and that the overthrow of the Government was the *sine qua non* to future happiness. The overthrow of the Union's constitution was freely discussed and resolutions passed advocating the establishment of a republic.

Tielman Roos, the Nationalist Lion of the North, fanned this flame of unrest assiduously and with not a little malice. But Hertzog bided his time, waiting for Smuts to make mistakes. Nor did he wait in vain.

Meanwhile the strikers, by now organized into commandos, were patrolling the Reef and picketing the mines to prevent "scabs" from slinking back to work. There were repeated clashes with the police. On one occasion a policeman cuffed a woman demonstrator. A young man attempting to intervene received a bayonet in his side for his pains. Frequent arrests were made. Feeling ran high. And at this dangerous stage Smuts made one of the most fateful statements of his life in Parliament. He advised the strikers to return to work immediately. "On what terms?" asked a Labour member. "On the terms of the Chamber," was the reply. It almost seemed that General Smuts was acting on the assumption that mine owners had the indisputable right to dictate terms.

This momentous declaration was a devastating counterblast to the hopes of those who had expected an amicable settlement. There were disturbances all over the Rand, and on February 27 there was an inci-

dent at Boksburg, serious in itself and exceedingly grave in its consequences.

The police attacked a number of strikers who had been guilty of no
offence. (This was afterwards admitted in court.) Some were injured
and others taken to jail. While several of their friends were serenading
them on the following evening, the police opened fire on these men, killing three. In the House of Assembly on March 1, Tielman Roos, desiring to exploit the situation in the interests of the Nationalist party, demanded an inquiry. The Prime Minister bluntly refused to allow this, in
spite of the fact that inquiries had been held after the 1914 Rebellion,
after Bulhoek, and after the native disturbances in Port Elizabeth. And
then he gave expression to a significant utterance: "I think," he said,
"we shall allow things to develop." To this day Smuts frequently has
these words flung in his face.

To aggravate the situation, he issued this statement: "The police have
instructions . . . to protect all miners who return to their employment.
. . . I call on the mineowners to restart the mines." The police were in-
structed to induce miners to become "scabs."

Basking in the sunshine of Smuts's favour and emboldened by his
wholehearted support, the Chamber of Mines became completely intransigent. In a contemptuously abusive letter published on March 4, in
reply to a request from the Industrial Federation for a round-table conference, it stated arrogantly that it would not "waste further time in en-
deavouring to convince persons of your mental calibre. . . . The members of the Chamber . . . see no reason why they should discuss their
business with the representatives of slaughtermen and tramwaymen."
This was the signal for battle.

Few other things are able to impair the morale and upset the mental
balance of human beings half as much as utter hopelessness. The under-
current of martial hysteria which had been prevailing for weeks was now
whipped up into a delirious fury, and the tempo of events became too
frenzied for the moderate leaders of the Industrial Federation who could
no longer control the strikers. The result was that the revolutionary junta
of five, called the Council of Action, assumed command. The die was
cast. A general strike was declared. The striker commandos were dis-
persed all over the Reef and took control of practically all the important
key positions. All along the Rand thousands swarmed through the
streets of the towns and murder and massacre marked their trail. Mine
officials and natives were either clubbed to death or shot in cold blood.
In a number of cases policemen and natives captured by strikers were
handed to the womenfolk to be castrated. The operations were crudely

performed, and the patients suffered agony. It was a reign of terror. It was the beginning of a revolution.

Quietly and almost dispassionately Smuts decided to act, and to act ruthlessly and swiftly. "There will be no Mexico here so long as I am in power," he said. "I will preserve order."

Thousands of police armed with rifles were rushed to the Rand. Defence Force units and burgher commandos were hurriedly summoned. Machine guns were distributed among them and instructions given to shoot. Martial law was proclaimed. While announcing to Parliament that martial law had been proclaimed on the Reef, Smuts said: "The Government was very reluctant to declare martial law, knowing the temper of the people and that in the end there would be serious bloodshed . . . the choice has been taken away from the Government. This morning from practically one side of the Reef to the other the commandos attacked, and fighting has been going on over a large part of the Rand, and is still going on, and there have been heavy casualties. . . . All essential services have been brought to a standstill, and the natives are from one end of the Reef to another in a state of wild turmoil. . . ."

Soon after he left secretly in a special train for Johannesburg, taking with him his trusted associate, Louis Esselen. Although even his wife was unaware of his departure, the secret leaked out, and the strikers blew up the railway eighty miles south of Johannesburg. Smuts was warned in time. He took a car and hurried on. The chauffeur's nerves were on edge. He drove timorously, with a pistol in one hand. Smuts took it away from him. He entered Johannesburg amid a hail of bullets. Staring straight ahead of him, he did not seem to notice them. A tire of his car was hit. Johnson, the chauffeur, said, "Must I drive on?" "You know your duty," was the quiet reply.

Smuts is entirely fearless. General Coen Brits once said that he was the bravest man he had ever met. And Brits spent all the years of his life among brave men.

The last stage of the journey was done on flat tires.

Arriving at the Johannesburg Drill Hall at midnight, Smuts was stopped by a sentry, who pointed a bayonet at him. He brushed the bayonet aside impatiently and walked in. Police officers flocked round him. He conducted a stern and searching inquiry. He found everything in a state of chaos. The police were powerless, scattered as they were along the Reef guarding the mine shafts. The rioters controlled practically the whole of the Rand. The population was panic-stricken. The Government troops had not made much headway.

A severe attack of gastric influenza had sapped Smuts's vitality so much that his doctors had ordered a complete rest. The advice had fallen on deaf ears. On leaving Cape Town for the north he had been a sick man. His journey had been arduous and nerve-racking. But it was a cool, calm, alert, and ostensibly healthy man who, after midnight, was given the latest reports on the desperate state of affairs obtaining on the Rand. He listened quietly and unconcernedly to the harassed officials. He took in the whole situation, swiftly issued orders, and then calmly watched for the dawn. And to not a few of those present it was manifest that he would soon have the situation well in hand and restore order out of chaos.

With the first light of day a shattering rifle fire broke from the vicinity of Jan Smuts Avenue and the insurgents were driven back from the hills near by. Smuts mounted the parapet at police headquarters, untroubled by the flying bullets, and seemingly unaware of them. A dauntless, grey figure in the light of the early dawn.

Fighting systematically along the Reef, Smuts drove the strikers relentlessly from their strongholds. Some of the fiercest battles were those fought in the Reef towns, Benoni, Boksburg, Brixton, and Langlaagte. All along the line snipers took a fairly heavy toll of the Government forces. But Smuts pushed steadily on. The strikers were given no rest. They made their last stand at Fordsburg, not far from the heart of the city. Ruthlessly Smuts decided to bombard them into submission. Airplanes were sent to drop pamphlets over the town advising "all persons well affected towards the Government" to leave Fordsburg between the hours of 6 and 11 A. M. On the stroke of eleven heavy artillery opened fire on the strikers' headquarters. At noon the white flag was hoisted. Meanwhile two of the communist extremists had committed suicide.

In the course of a few days Smuts had quelled what had threatened to develop into a full-blooded revolution. It was a *coup de main*. The Prime Minister's ultimate management of an ugly situation was nothing short of brilliant. But his conduct prior to the declaration of a general strike together with his subsequent application of the mailed fist proved to be an irreparable political blunder, for labour was driven into Hertzog's fold and Smuts later into the political wilderness, there to languish for almost a decade.

The strike cost the country almost twice as many lives as had the whole of the South West Africa campaign. Fifty policemen were killed. On the eve of the outbreak of hostilities many of them had conversed on very friendly terms with strikers who on the following day became their deadly enemies. Wiser undoubtedly were those who were jailed for refusing to take up arms against their compatriots.

No sooner had the last shots fallen than the millionaires who had scurried away to the safety of Pretoria in good time returned to their mansions in Mayfair. They had every reason to feel pleased with themselves. Their propaganda department had served them well. And so it could. They made their influence felt through 95 per cent of the English newspapers in the country as well as a substantial percentage of those printed in Afrikaans, and their funds were unlimited. Their overseas newspapers had convinced the British people that the Bolsheviks had been at the bottom of all the trouble; that, in fact, Smuts had smashed a Red revolution. A similar story had been blazoned forth by their propaganda machine in the Union, and many believed it. At length they had received what they had been after for over twenty years. They had broken the might of organized labour.

Although the mining industry had been depicted as moribund by the capitalist press before the strike, it suddenly became a flourishing concern a few months after the cessation of hostilities. The discovery of new gold fields containing unbelievable riches was announced and the expansion of the industry on an unprecedented scale foreshadowed.

The degree of prosperity obtaining in the industry a mere twelve months later is revealed by the tremendous dividends paid out by the companies in 1923. Here are some of them: City Deep mine—45 per cent; Van Rhyn Deep—58 per cent; Government Areas—60 per cent; Crown Mines—67½ per cent; Meyer and Charlton—100 per cent; New Modder—100 per cent; Modder B—110 per cent; Rand Mines—120 per cent; Modder Deep—140 per cent.

The Chamber of Mines took back such men as it required on its own terms, but thousands were thrown on to the streets.

To accuse Smuts of having been in league with the capitalists would be monstrous. He can, however, be validly charged with tendentiousness. But the gravamen of the charge against him is that he allowed things to develop when he could have averted trouble, that he allowed matters to develop so far that he lost all control over them, and that the result was a substantial loss of human life. He himself said in Parliament: "Well, the situation did develop. For a couple of days we did lose control, and during those days we saw a state of affairs on the Rand which I hope will prove an object lesson to the people of this country forever."

When the smoke of battle cleared, Smuts stood triumphant. But it was a triumph bought at much blood in a country where the spilling of blood is regarded as a mortal sin. It was a Pyrrhic victory. Smuts realized this.

He returned to Cape Town in chastened mood. This was temporarily dispelled by the vociferous welcome accorded him by the members of his party. He was hailed as the "hero of the hour," but Hertzog called him "the villain of the piece!" As he entered the Chamber on his return, all his party followers rose to their feet shouting loud applause. The Nationalists said vindictively afterwards that it had all been a prearranged affair and that the South African party members had intended singing "See the conquering hero comes," but that there had been a hitch somewhere.

Smuts's first act was to ask Parliament to indemnify the Government for declaring martial law. His request was met with shouts of derision from the Nationalists.

The revolution had been a very costly one: there had been wholesale destruction to houses and property; a great deal of damage had been done to the mines; casualties had been numerous; life on the Witwatersrand had been completely disarranged. Twenty thousand police and troops with cannon, machine guns, armoured cars, bombs, and airplanes had only with difficulty managed to quell the revolution.

The tremendous loss of life and money, said the Opposition, could have been avoided if Smuts had dealt tactfully and wisely with the strikers instead of wantonly displaying extreme partisanship. It was just like him to do as he pleased and then ask to be indemnified.

Hertzog opposed the motion, saying that Smuts himself was responsible for all the misery and bloodshed. He added that Smuts's career was drenched in blood. Drawing attention to the strikes of 1913 and 1914, the Passive Resistance Movement of the Indians, the Rebellion of 1914, the Great War, the native disturbances at Port Elizabeth, the trouble at Bulhoek, and the Rand Revolt, he ended on a high falsetto, shrieking, "The Prime Minister's footsteps drip with blood! His footsteps will go down to history in that manner!"

It was pointed out that within a period of less than ten years Smuts had proclaimed martial law three times, and on each of these occasions an indemnity bill had been introduced to secure the Government concerned against legal responsibility.

For three days Smuts spoke not a word. He sat staring before him, his steel-blue eyes apparently seeing nothing, his face impassive. But hot fires smouldered within him, fires of intense resentment. And yet he kept his peace while around him the battle raged between the opposing factions and fierce taunts were hurled to and fro across the floor. When he broke his silence at a congress of the South African party and alluded to the references made in regard to his allegedly bloody record, he little thought that blood would flow again so soon.

Overshadowed by the stirring occurrences on the Witwatersrand there took place in the mandated territory of South West Africa an event of no small importance early in 1922.

The Bondelswarts, a race of mixed Bantu and Hottentot blood, dwelling in the Warmbad district in the south of the colony, refused to pay an "unjustifiable dog tax," and then suddenly there was an outbreak of violence among them.

Airplanes were sent from the Union and after other persuasions had failed these uncivilized human beings were bombed into submission. A large number were killed in the process.

Not entirely without justification, serious charges were made against the authorities concerned, and subsequently the Permanent Mandates Commission of the League declined to accept the Administration's report upon the mandate, demanding an authoritative account of the operations against the Bondelswarts. In spite of reassurances and explanations by General Smuts, the affair left an unpleasant taste in the mouth.

In Parliament the unfortunate episode had its repercussions and, as was generally the case in such instances, the discussion resolved itself into a personal affair, an attack on Smuts:

Smuts: ". . . tonight the whole fire seems to have been concentrated on me. It leaves me cold."

A Labour Member: "Murder always does."

Smuts: ". . . Then take Bulhoek. I am posted in Moscow as the Butcher of Bulhoek. That is my reputation in Russia."

A Labour Member: "Yes, and not only in Russia."

When, a few years later, Smuts gave to the world his famous philosophic treatise on *Holism and Evolution,* the brilliant South African poet, Roy Campbell, unforgetful of the past, venomously ridiculed the soldier, philosopher, and statesman in his sparkling *Adamastor.*

Holism

The love of Nature burning in his heart,
Our new Saint Francis offers us his book—
The saint who fed the birds at Bondelswart
And fattened up the vultures at Bull Hoek.

A rather scathing indictment. But it would not be too much to say that all classes of the community were scandalized by the Bondelswart episode. The Nationalists, of course, were most vehement in their censure. Here was a splendid opportunity for scoring off Smuts. Such a man, they said, should be deprived of power. They prophesied his downfall. And with good reason, for at this stage of his affairs the general situation looked very black for Smuts.

54

ALTHOUGH HAUNTED by the spectre of defeat and—as he admitted to a friend—"down in body and spirit," Smuts was determined to go on fighting. He made a desperate attempt to draw British Rhodesia into the Union.

It would be dishonest to pretend—as his enemies did at the time—that Smuts's courtship of the British colony was actuated merely by political necessity. In fact, it would be extremely foolish to do so, for it must be obvious to all that a handful of Rhodesian votes could not have affected Smuts's position materially. The prospect of getting them furnished the Premier with what was, at the outside, a forlorn hope. Naturally he grasped at it, as any man in his position would have done. But it is not too much to say that this aspect of the matter was, so to speak, incidental. More compelling reasons urged Smuts to do his utmost to persuade Rhodesia to join the Union.

Expansion to the north, where lay the great Katanga copper belt and all the tremendous resources of the Dark Continent, would be achieved only through the territory which Rhodes had placed on the map. And it was the Union's manifest destiny to open up this vast hinterland. This Rhodes had realized; and for this he had laboured. It was a vision of greatness that had appealed mightily to Smuts since the days of his youth. Speaking of "a great African Federation of States," he had said, a few years before, "The day will surely come when we shall not think of the south of the Limpopo only, but when the British states in Africa will all become members of a great African dominion stretching unbroken throughout Africa . . . the term South Africa will surely one day be dropped from our national vocabulary and there will be a united British Africa, which will find the solution of our pressing problems an easy matter." Now, at long last, had come the opportune moment to incorporate Rhodesia in the Union. Smuts felt that so great a chance must not be missed.

The Chartered Company's control of Rhodesia was about to terminate, and the people of that territory were given the choice between self-government and incorporation in the Union of South Africa. It soon transpired that the great majority of Rhodesians desired the former alternative, but the pro-Union minority subsequently launched so effective a campaign against their opponents that the British Government suggested that a deputation be sent to consult Smuts. The hint was taken, much to the delight of the South African Premier, who suddenly saw a flickering ray of hope in the darkness which had threatened to engulf him, and felt that the first great step towards the realization of his Pan-African dreams was about to be taken.

He immediately declared himself prepared to allow Rhodesia to send representatives to the Union Parliament, and he proposed a basis of representation which was certainly liberal and, therefore, most attractive to the Rhodesians.

Several months later thirteen representatives from Rhodesia met him to discuss terms of incorporation. The immediate result was a declaration by Smuts in Parliament to the effect that negotiations would be conducted by the Government alone; that the terms of union would be disclosed when everything had been settled; and that a bill to give effect to their discussions would be introduced on the eve of amalgamation.

When, eventually, the Smuts-Malcolm agreement was published, the terms of incorporation were made known. They were generous. It appeared that the Union Government had agreed to pay the Chartered Company several millions of pounds for their property, exclusive of mineral rights. It is impossible at the moment to traverse the entire gamut of concessions granted to the Rhodesian settlers themselves, as apart from the people directly concerned with the Chartered Company. Suffice it to say that authoritative publications on finance in Britain stressed the magnanimity of the South African Premier's offer and even Lord Milner felt that Rhodesia could hardly expect to get better terms.

In the Union Tielman Roos said of the Prime Minister: "He has gone a-wooing. Miss Rhodesia is being wooed by General Smuts. And how does he do it? . . . He offers to buy her. . . ." Other political foes averred that the Prime Minister and his promises to the Rhodesians were strangely reminiscent of the Greeks bearing gifts.

From all sides pressure was brought to bear upon the Rhodesians to accept the generous terms. Even the British Ministry intervened, and Mr. Churchill is reported to have stated that the imperial Government would cancel Rhodesia's £2,000,000 war debt only on condition that she enter the Union.

Incidentally, the publication of the Smuts-Malcolm agreement immediately caused a mighty boom in Chartered Company shares.

Thinking that he might bring home to the people of Rhodesia the advantages of linking up with the Union, Smuts decided to put in a personal appearance on the scene of action.

Strong arguments could be advanced in favour of Rhodesia's entry into the Union: here lay its vital markets; South African railway officials ran the trains right up to Bulawayo; the Rhodesian legal system was cast in the same mould as that of the Union—in point of fact, Rhodesia found it convenient to avail itself of the Union's Appeal Court at Bloemfontein; amalgamation with its great neighbour in the south was patently Rhodesia's "traditional destiny."

On the other hand, there were numerous reasons which impelled the Rhodesians to fight shy of incorporation, such as the racial strife in the Union and the frequent industrial disturbances and the poor-white problem. These factors were temporarily pushed into the background by the urgent eloquence and compelling personality of Smuts, who begged the Rhodesians to adopt "the broader point of view, the future of the subcontinent." No sooner, however, had the Prime Minister returned to his country than the settlers began to entertain fresh doubts as to the advisability of incorporation and "all the old fears returned."

When the plebiscite was held, fifteen thousand people voted. Smuts's project was defeated by a majority of 2,785.

55

RESULTANT upon the revolt on the Rand there were several executions which proved to be highly deleterious to the interests of the Prime Minister and his Government. As in the instance of Jopie Fourie the Opposition did not fail to exploit these executions to the full. Especially was this the case in regard to the Hanekom brothers and one Stassen. The former had been shot out of hand for being caught red-handed while sniping. The latter was hanged for killing two natives. In his case, however—so it was alleged—there were extenuating circumstances.

For almost two months Stassen, a young man, twenty-seven years of age, faced death in the condemned cell pending execution. During that harrowing period his hair turned grey. Meanwhile very strong pressure was brought to bear upon the authorities on his behalf. Dozens of public meetings passed resolutions begging the Government to exercise mercy. Numerous deputations approached Smuts, and thousands of telegrams were sent with the same object. But on a cheerless, grey morning in October Stassen was led to the gallows.

From the ranks of the Nationalists a terrible outcry arose. Smuts was accused of having deliberately sacrificed Stassen on the altar of party politics. Having lost prestige, they said, with the natives and coloured people as a result of the shooting at Port Elizabeth, the Bondelswart episode, and the Bulhoek tragedy, Smuts was trying to reinstate himself in their effections by giving to them the dead body of Stassen as a sop. These charges against the Prime Minister were monstrous. Nevertheless, they served their purpose in stirring up a fresh storm of hatred and indignation against him.

Almost coincident with the execution, General Smuts started on a political tour of the Free State. Although his friends tried to dissuade him, the Prime Minister felt that it was his duty to make this tour. It proved to be exceedingly unpleasant. On entering Senekal Smuts found large placards in every street bearing inscriptions such as, "Where is Stassen?" and "Where are the Hanekoms?" At Dewetsdorp and in many other towns he met with equally disagreeable demonstrations. But in spite of the efforts of the Opposition to wreck it, the tour was a success.

Not only was Nationalism rampant in the Free State but there was dissatisfaction everywhere, and the Smuts administration was in bad odour in a greater or lesser degree in almost every corner of the Union. Both Nationalist and Labour politicians fanned the flames of discontent by making what capital they could out of Smuts's "bloody adventure" on the Witwatersrand. The target of their animosity was invariably Smuts. He was compared to Judas Iscariot, was denounced as "the tool of capitalism," and was called a "bloody butcher." At length things came to such a pass that Smuts's life was endangered, the result being that he was shadowed by police officers in plain clothes wherever he went. It was feared that he might be murdered by certain Communists who had passed sentence of death upon him.

Many of the charges against Smuts had little verisimilitude. Others, again, were true. But his enemies managed to distort everything to their own advantage.

In 1923 he attended an imperial conference in London. He was glad to get away from the poisonous atmosphere in South Africa and of the chance to address himself once more to the world.

When he was still on the high seas the leading newspapers of Britain began to proclaim his coming. He was described as the mightiest factor at imperial conferences and the virtual ruler of the Empire. It was incredible that such a man could be at death's door politically in his own country. Europe needed him. His work in Africa was done. His future belonged to the world.

His arrival in Britain coincided with the German failure to pay reparations and the French Government's declaration of its intention to send troops into the Ruhr, against the advice of the British Government. In Britain feeling was strong against France.

Smuts led the attack. He said that the occupation of the Ruhr was "illegal" and "a breach of the Treaty of Versailles." "France," he added, "has made impossible the conference on reparations, which I had proposed. . . .

"From the purely reparation point of view all the experts whom I have consulted are unanimously of opinion that, as long as the Ruhr occupation continues, there can be no reparation payments by the German Government. . . . Four or five years ago we were singing songs of victory; today we are all marching to certain and inevitable defeat— victor and vanquished alike. The economic and industrial structure of Europe is cracking in all directions. . . . The time has come for the convocation of a great conference of the Powers who are mainly interested in the reparation question. . . ."

The speech created a tremendous sensation throughout the world. The French were incensed. They assailed Smuts virulently in their newspapers. Elsewhere the South African Premier was variously hailed as "the Modern Moses" who stood between the living and the dead and reviled as an "ignorant interloper." In New York the cable pages of great newspapers were splashed with huge headlines giving the gist of the speech. The League of World Fellowship telegraphed to Smuts: "God aid you. It is the lead which England and the world have been waiting for." The contrast between this "daring and well-thought-out" speech and Premier Baldwin's "hackneyed platitudes" was duly emphasized. Thus to many was Smuts "the man of the hour."

But in the Dominions the speech caused considerable surprise and a fair amount of consternation. "This is plunging into the foreign policy of Europe with a vengeance," wrote a dominion editor. The Nationalist press in South Africa roundly accused Smuts of being the mouthpiece and tool of the British Cabinet on whose behalf he had castigated the French. Baldwin, it said, had not dared to do so himself since the British electorate were divided on the question of intervention between Germany and France. "We cannot believe," stated a Canadian newspaper, "that a man in his [Smuts's] position would make so bold a contribution to the very delicate discussion of European affairs without the permission of the British ministers."

"The Handy Man of the Empire has played his part once more," said the enemies of Smuts, and feverishly they plotted to bring about his eclipse.

Soon their common desire to hasten the downfall of Smuts actuated the Nationalist and Labour parties to draw more closely together, and the practicability of a "working alliance" between them was mooted. Then steadily they moved towards the consummation of their plans —secession from the British Commonwealth was prudently shelved for the time being by the Hertzogites, while Labour asseverated that the "democratic and socialist commonwealth" was nothing more than an "ultimate objective." Thus they made themselves wholly acceptable one to the other. Moreover, they made a bold and determined effort to win over those townsmen who, while having lost faith in the Smuts government, nevertheless feared that Hertzog, given the chance, would "cut the painter." They made public "an explicit understanding" that, in the event of Hertzog's becoming Prime Minister, "no Nationalist Member of Parliament will use his vote to upset the existing constitutional relation of South Africa to the British Crown."

Thus the "pact" between the two opposition parties came into being, much to Smuts's mortification. He called it an "unholy alliance." He declared that its component parts were incompatible with each other.

But the pact was a more natural structure than Smuts chose to admit. The parties composing it vied with each other as regards their hatred of the Prime Minister, who had shot down "rural rebels and urban revolutionaries" in the troublous past; they were united by a common aversion for the Unionists, since the Nationalists loathed the imperialism and the Labourites the capitalism with which they identified these gentlemen.

Their chief political aims, too, were very similar: both were determined to look after the interests of a "white South Africa"; both desired "a regulated economy which should exclude external competition"; both had decided to take drastic action in regard to internal competition; and, last but not least, the great majority of miners on the Rand were by now Afrikaners who depended on the Labour party to see to their economic interests but looked to the Nationalist leaders for guidance on "constitutional matters."

The decks were cleared for action. The battle was about to commence. It is doubtful whether the man in the street realized to what extent circumstances were advantageous to the pact. The ghosts of the revolution on the Rand were still stalking through the land. The farming population were suffering acute distress as the result of a prolonged drought and a widespread plague of locusts. The first of the slumps that succeeded the postwar boom had in South Africa reached its zenith. Smuts's former majority of twenty-four had been reduced to eight—the result of bye-elections. The Government was tottering on its feet. A series of unsuccessful financial enterprises undertaken by the Administration deprived Smuts of the support of a large number of adherents. The grain-elevator scandal at Durban was a case in point. An elevator had been built at the Natal port with extreme prodigality, and construction defects were subsequently charged. The resultant waste amounted to over £200,000. A multiplicity of such unfortunate ventures aroused so much resentment that it became all too manifest early in 1924 that Smuts *cum suis* had outstayed their welcome, in spite of the fact that the Government's terms of office had another two years to run.

Then suddenly a bye-election at Wakkerstroom, a rural constituency in the Eastern Transvaal, sealed the fate of Smuts. The Government did everything in its power to secure a victory. It was a seat that Smuts's party had held at three successive general elections since 1915. In order to ensure its retention, the Prime Minister prevailed upon Mr. A. G. Robertson, the Administrator of the Transvaal, to accept nomination for the South African party. Mr. Robertson was well liked by all sections of the community and had much influence in the Wakkerstroom division, where he was a progressive farmer. His Nationalist opponent was A. S. Naude, an almost unknown man, crippled for life by wounds received in the Anglo-Boer War. The cripple won at the polls. The South African party suffered a tremendous shock. But little did the rank and file realize that they had heard the knell of the South African party government. Even Smuts's colleagues were unaware of the fact. Only Smuts knew.

Stung by the taunts of his opponents, nettled by the perplexing problems that beset him, and harassed by the clouds which were fast gathering round him, Smuts's temperamental impatience overrode all considerations. The world had acclaimed him. He was universally recognized as one of the few great statesmen on the face of the earth. But this tiny people, hidden away in the southernmost part of Africa, neither valued his talents nor appreciated his qualities. He bitterly resented their attitude. Let them throw him out if they dared!

After the intolerable strain of many months of uncertainty, irritation, and overwork, his nerves were frayed and his health was poor. Frequent bouts of malaria had played havoc with his system. In a sense he had come to the end of his tether, but his spirit was undaunted. He was arrogant. He was defiant. He gave the country an opportunity to decide whether it wanted a change or not.

Without consulting his Cabinet and without sounding the caucus of his party, he decided to resign and test the feeling of the country in a general election. A few hours after the bye-election result became known, he entered the House of Assembly and bluntly announced his decision. The House was electrified, and there was wild excitement as the news became known. There was also fierce resentment within his party for his highhanded conduct.

Some of Smuts's followers were furious. His conduct, they said, had not only been autocratic but his resignation had been premature and unnecessary, for he still commanded a working majority. Their plaintive protests, however, made no impression on the Prime Minister. Having made his angry decision, he was too proud to look back. Parliament was dissolved.

The election was chiefly notable for the bitterness of the attacks upon Smuts. He was depicted as the incarnation of evil. He was the target of the Opposition's venom and the butt of their caustic wit. In the Bezuidenhout Valley a number of Labourites entered a hall bearing a standard adorned with the device: "No More Smuts—Use Pact Soap!"

Smuts was overextravagant in connection with his election promises, undertaking in many instances to bring about certain changes to which he had been strongly opposed for many years. These engagements evoked particularly acidulated attacks from Hertzog, who said that it was characteristic of Smuts to make promises without ever considering their fulfilment. He drew the attention of the electors to the election of 1921.

But Hertzog and his brethren were needlessly fighting so hard. The country was tired of Smuts's making fine speeches on world issues and on matters of empire interest while the people suffered, albeit in consequence of drought and the postwar depression. If Hertzog would fill their bellies, his plain bread-and-butter politics suited them down to the ground. When Smuts dined with kings and princes, they said, they received not even the crumbs that fell from the table. Smuts's head was in the clouds. They could not comprehend him. Give them plain Hertzog, who spoke a language they understood, the language of food and clothing and shelter. *He* was not concerned with Empire needs and with world problems. He was concerned with South Africa alone—with them and with their children. Give them Hertzog, they said.

On June 17, 1924, the people flocked to the polls after a bitter campaign during which many of Smuts's own meetings were broken up. The Government party was badly beaten. Even Smuts lost his seat at Pretoria

West to George Hay, an obscure Labourite. A safe seat was found for him at Standerton, in the eastern Transvaal.

Thus, while in the plenitude of his powers, Smuts fell. It was the end of an era.

The fall of Smuts marked the end (at least temporarily) of British predominance in South Africa and the beginning of Afrikaner emancipation, chiefly in the economic sphere. It marked the end of the importing period and ushered in South African industrialism. The story of Smuts since the early days of this century has been the story of South Africa. His ups and downs have been distinct periods in South African history. He is the epitome of forces and development in his country in this century.

A gradual but nonetheless distinct transformation in the nation's mental attitude preceded the South African party's defeat and its leader's eclipse. Smuts was aware of its coming and uneasily conscious of its threatening aspect. He stood helpless before its advent. He could no longer compromise as he had done so successfully in the past.

A mere twelve years, then, after he had been driven, an outcast, into the political wilderness, Hertzog became Premier of the Union of South Africa. Almost an unknown man, he had started from scratch, pitted himself against the most powerful party in the land, established Hertzogism, "a new political faith," which ridiculed everything that Smuts and Botha stood for, formed his own party, went from strength to strength, and became at length South Africa's political leader. His success, it must be admitted, was due, in a sense, to his limitations. Unlike Smuts, he was completely satisfied with a limited political future in an exclusively South African environment. Nevertheless, had he tried, he could not have approximated to Smuts's world stature. He, as the apostle of Afrikanerdom, extolled that narrow nationalism which was the vogue in those days and had always been very dear to the heart of the Afrikaner. In this way he came to be a fetish to Afrikanerdom, and cut away the ground from under Smuts's feet.

So in the winter of 1924 Smuts was overthrown—primarily in consequence of what he and his followers regarded as Hertzog's "defect of political narrowness." For more than fourteen years Hertzog remained Prime Minister of the Union of South Africa—nearly a world record among premiers of the democratic countries.

SECTION VII

56

No MEMBERS of the Pact Cabinet except Hertzog had held a portfolio in any ministry before. Even prior to his defeat Smuts had predicted that the formation of a pact government would bring about the hurried withdrawal of overseas capital from the Union, and that its advent would usher in a catastrophic period in South African history. Such a government, however, he had added, could not last for long. Now, after the new Cabinet had taken office, Smuts said scornfully that he would not be able to go overseas, as matters would speedily come to such a pass as to necessitate his taking over the reins of government. General Hertzog was unfit to be Prime Minister of South Africa; the Nationalist party consisted of amateurs and fanatics. "We'll have lots of fun in the House," Smuts told the members of his party.

But Smuts had underestimated his opponents, who proved to be both powerful in debate and effective in administration. Moreover, good fortune smiled upon them, for no sooner had they taken over the administration than the rains came, the clouds of depression lifted, and prosperity returned gradually to the country. Rich fields of platinum were discovered in various parts of the Transvaal. Money poured into the Union.

Hertzog's ministry lasted for almost nine years. The first five were very prosperous ones. They drew to a close with the coming of the Great Depression in the first months of 1930.

Not the least factor contributing to the success of the Hertzog administration's record was the financial acumen of N. C. Havenga, a young country attorney, who, as a boy of seventeen, had joined the Boer forces, had been severely wounded, had served as Hertzog's private secretary in the field and had, in the course of time, become his chief's protégé and very close friend. He became Minister of Finance in

Hertzog's Cabinet, much to the amusement of Smuts and his cronies. What a mess he would make of things, they said. But their amusement was short-lived. For Havenga achieved what no other Union Minister of Finance had ever done: every budget of his showed a surplus and his surpluses increased as the years sped by. To be sure, everything was in his favour.

The prophecies of Smuts were not fulfilled. And he was not slow to perceive that Hertzog had come to stay. The realization of this was most galling to him. He felt humiliated—a prophet without honour in his own country. Resentment flared up in him only to die down again and leave him with a feeling of flatness and impotence. There were moments when his thirst for power filled him with an unspeakable unrest. After years of constant labour comparative idleness irked him. He shunned his fellow men and was seldom seen in public.

But the healing hand of Time dealt kindly with him. He learned in due course that man must expect no permanence from anything. He took himself in hand and schooled himself to patience. He made a great effort to be more human. He resumed a normal life.

In Parliament his attitude surprised both friend and foe alike. Haughty and emotional despite his impassive exterior, he disciplined himself to bear in silence the taunts and insults showered upon him by his victorious foes. It was a pride mingled with contempt. Let the mongrels yap at him. He could bide his time. He made no attempt to defend himself. Nor, had he done so, would his defence have been of much account, for Smuts, for all his brilliance of intellect, is incredibly inept at repartee. Instead he stared fixedly at the ceiling or with chin in hand sat gazing into space, motionless, ostensibly seeing nothing, hearing nothing, feeling nothing. But underneath that cold veneer there smouldered fires of resentment that would occasionally flicker up when he was touched on the raw, and then his cheeks would become crimson and his steel-blue eyes would glint dangerously, as he stared straight at the offending speaker.

In the beginning he found it difficult to accustom himself to his new and inferior role as leader of the Opposition. Having called the tune in Parliament for close on a quarter of a century, he got annoyed when members of the new Ministry caught the speaker's eye before him. His all-too-obvious irritation induced Dr. D. F. Malan to draw a parallel at Malmesbury in the Cape between Smuts and the cock which had kept on jumping about after his head had been chopped off, and of which an Irishman standing by had said jokingly: "The blighter is dead but doesn't know it!"

With the passage of the years the leader of the Opposition became accustomed to a milieu where J. C. Smuts was not the dominating factor, and, chastened by disillusion, he schooled himself to swallow insults impassively.

Opposite to him sat Hertzog. As Prime Minister, only he had a bench to himself on which he used to lie at full length with his eyes shut, or sit with his head resting on a book on the desk in front of him.

From this attitude of feigned somnolence he would periodically leap to his feet and, with characteristic violence, heap virulent abuse on Smuts's head. Once he harangued Smuts and his party for more than an hour. Journalists in the press gallery counted twenty-five different adjectives with which he coupled Smuts's name. Nearly all were libellous. It was a stupendous effort to which Mrs. Hertzog and Mrs. Smuts sitting side by side in one of the galleries listened quietly. Meanwhile Smuts, without a trace of concern, sat admiringly by. And no sooner had Hertzog resumed his seat than he crossed the floor, sat down beside the Prime Minister, and commenced chatting amicably. In this way he disarmed many a would-be detractor and sometimes cajoled him into silence.

His patience and self-control in adversity—the result of rigorous self-discipline—excited the envy of many of his greatest enemies. The living stillness of the man under torrents of abuse was an inspiring spectacle of stoicism, particularly to those who realized that the flaming spirit was unquenched. He was waiting for Opportunity to come his way. He could well afford to wait. Into thirty years of intense and hard living, wrote a commentator, he had crammed the experiences of a hundred lives—the hopes and fears, the triumphs and disasters, the exertions and aspirations of a hundred human beings—but he was, as yet, in the fullness of his powers, and in him there burned the fierce fires of ambition, unquenched and unquenchable. As strong and healthy as he had been twenty years before, he was still more strenuously active than many a man of thirty. He had every confidence of being able "to bend events to his will." But he could hardly have foreseen that in the Crucible of Time there were being shaped events transcending all that he had ever witnessed, and that Jan Smuts was destined once again to play a leading part in world affairs.

Unlike Hertzog, he never allowed differences of opinion, political or otherwise, to affect his personal relationship with people. He was always on speaking terms with every member of the House. In striking contrast to the Prime Minister, who was only too prone to lose his temper and become vicious, particularly in debate, he always remained calm. "When I cannot control my temper," he said once, "I walk away." Hertzog was frequently pulled up by Mr. Speaker. This never happened to Smuts.

There are only one or two recorded instances of Smuts's losing his temper. Once Botha was being vilified and accused of being traitor to his country, when Smuts leaped up in a rage and said with great heat: "You remind me of a lot of yelping curs snarling round the grave of a dead lion."

Apart from never making a personal attack on his opponents, Smuts never attacked a newspaper. But then the vast majority of newspapers were on his side; so much so, indeed, that reporters regarded whatever he did as "news," the result being that many of his common or garden acts were glossed over and his failures turned into successes.

On a certain occasion he addressed a meeting at Stellenbosch, which is a hotbed of Nationalism. He soon sensed that the large body of students were against him and adroitly turned from politics to "mountain fires." He spoke on this subject for one-and-a-half hours. On the following day he was reported to have made a "fighting speech."

Smuts is no orator. His delivery is of middling quality. The pitch of his voice is rather high. It has been aptly said that he gives voice to rugged thoughts brought out jerkily without polish. His Malmesbury burr is so pronounced that it grates upon the English ear and is commented on even by Afrikaner audiences to whom the sound is a familiar one. It is characteristic of the man who has so frequently addressed most distinguished assemblies in the English-speaking world that he has never attempted to rid himself of that disturbing idiosyncrasy.

The majority of his speeches are mediocre, particularly when they are concerned with South African politics and are made for home consumption: Smuts cannot be bothered with trivialities nor will he cast his pearls before people whose mentality he despises. But when he broadcasts to the world on world problems or addresses a distinguished gathering of international scientists or statesmen, when, in short, it is worth his while, he rises to flights of eloquence unsurpassed. The big thing again!

He is better "in broad assertion than in close argument." He seldom essays a riposte when lunged at in Parliament or on the platform but is inclined to ignore awkward sallies made at his expense.

Should the occasion demand it, few men in South Africa can sway an audience with greater effect than Smuts, in spite of his not being an orator in the accepted sense of the word. At the same time, no man can on occasion say so little with a multiplicity of words and yet convey the impression of having said so much. Frequently he uses language to conceal rather than to reveal his actual standpoint. This he does with remarkable skill and in such a way as to leave his hearers none the wiser.

Smuts is an adept at creating a strong impression without making a definite statement in so many words. Often the impression he creates is favourable to conflicting factions. At the "coalition" election of 1932 he addressed a large concourse at Calvinia in the Cape Province. After the meeting many of the supporters of both candidates believed that Smuts had given his support to their own particular man.

Of all the leading politicians' speeches in South Africa Smuts's are least referred to by his opponents, as quotations from them can rarely be used against the speaker, since Smuts can, if he wishes, create a concrete impression with an unsurpassable vagueness of words. On a well-known occasion a South African politician affirmed in all sincerity that Smuts had made a certain statement in regard to imperial relations, in a broadcast speech. His assertion was supported by everyone who had listened to the speech, but when he was challenged to read the speech he could not find the alleged statement in so many words anywhere in it.

Smuts's artfulness in dealing with an audience is not necessarily confined to his speeches. Once, before an election, he held a meeting at Piquetberg, in the southern Cape. He was forewarned by his supporters that one of the enemy was going to question him about his religious tenets. Now church-going among the narrow Calvinistic Dutch is so intensely serious a matter that politicians in South Africa, whether religiously inclined or otherwise, frequently make a practice of attending church services in their constituencies. Smuts, however, does not subscribe to this practice: in fact, he is reported to be a freethinker. Thus the situation at Piquetberg was, to say the least, somewhat embarrassing. But Smuts was equal to the occasion. When the meeting was about to commence, he walked to the edge of the platform and said solemnly: "Brothers, in view of the serious times in which we are living, let us open this meeting with prayer!" And, bowing his head, led a solemn invocation. This created a wonderful impression. No questions were asked about his religious convictions.

The natives of the North Eastern Cape inhabit a region which is often ravaged by drought. They call Smuts *Ra Tjalapi* (Father of the Eels; i.e., rain maker). During his first premiership Smuts had occasion to visit their territory once or twice. He chose his times well. Experts from the meteorological department advised him as soon as weather conditions over the North Eastern Cape were favourable for rain. At the opportune time he would then pay a visit to the native territories and say to the assembled Bantu: "I notice that you are suffering much from drought. But be of good cheer, for I have brought you rain." And invariably the rains came.

Although somewhat chastened by his defeat and more human than the despot who had ruled with the mailed fist, Smuts, after 1924, nevertheless remained an autocrat at heart, cold and impassive, showing little consideration for his colleagues.

His attitude in the House was little different then from what it is today. He is friendly and aloof at the same time. New members are invariably drawn to him in the beginning on account of his friendliness. He makes a practice of approaching any newly elected member, irrespective of what party he belongs to, and congratulating him on his success at the polls. He then enters into conversation with the highly flattered newcomer and immediately puts him at ease. While, on the one hand, there is this superficial friendliness about Smuts, on the other he is detached and secretive and no one knows what is going on at the back of his mind. He makes almost all his decisions without consulting his colleagues. The latter frequently complain of his mental and spiritual inaccessibility and his highhandedness.

His general demeanour in the House is best described as suave; the more heated the attack and the greater the difficulty in which he finds himself, the blander he becomes.

His statements and the actual facts of the matter in dispute are not always compatible with one another; but the more pronounced the difference the more inclined he is to have recourse to the highest moral pleas, and the greater is his astonishment at any want of accuracy on the part of his opponents. All this he does with the most astounding *sang-froid* and show of gravity. "The graver he becomes, the more inclined we are to suspect him," the Nationalists say.

Often, with most convincing solemnity, he avoids the issue by completely disregarding his opponents' chief arguments and focusing attention on the most insignificant points raised, more often than not even suggesting that those trifles are of the utmost importance.

His skilful disregard of and dexterous divergence from facts, whenever it suits his purpose, in dealing with a subject, have long since ceased to annoy his opponents. Rather does his dialectical skill and amazing parliamentary strategy fill them today with emotions, not unlike the ones that overwhelmed the gaping rustics as they stared at Goldsmith's Village Schoolmaster.

57

THE TRIUMPH OF Hertzogism, as was to be expected, brought about a tremendous change in South African politics.

Smuts's idea of a great United States of South Africa was no longer regarded as practical politics, for Hertzog's rejection of British overlord-ship and his anti-imperial utterances antagonized Rhodesia and scared off the native protectorates, which have always had a predilection for British Negrophilism.

During Smuts's tenure of office honours had been showered in ever-increasing numbers on influential political friends of the Government. Anti-imperial sentiment as well as other considerations induced Hertzog to abolish titles in the first year of his premiership. The Nationalists were jubilant. All those ribbons and orders and stars, they said, belonged to a bygone age; even in Europe they had lost all meaning; as a rule they were nothing but a medium of exchange wherewith unscrupulous gov-ernments increased their party funds or bought supporters. They were incompatible with the whole spirit of democracy; they no longer had anything in common with true aristocracy but were the symbol of plutoc-racy and the most effective manure for the soil in which snobbery flourished.

The disappointment among the members of Smuts's party was acute when honours were finally done away with, for they had been led to believe that the forthcoming visit of the Prince of Wales to the Union would be followed by the customary "generous distribution of titles."

To add to their mortification Hertzog decided to dispose largely of the preferential tariff assigned to British goods; stressed South Africa's "in-dividuality as a national state"; brought about the recognition of Afri-kaans as one of the Union's official languages, and made arrangements for the compilation of a standard Afrikaans dictionary; threatened to do away with the Union Jack; and stimulated "economic Nationalism" by assisting primary producers and by promoting the growth of secondary industries—to the detriment of the interests of British importers—by means of a protective tariff in certain cases as well as dumping duties.

Accusations of "anti-British prejudices and race hatred" were levelled against the Premier. In those parts of the country where the British element predominated, there was acute dissatisfaction with and much criticism of the Government. At every turn it was attacked by the Opposition, with Smuts in the vanguard, fighting valiantly in the interests of the Empire.

With such determination did the ex-Premier set himself against the erection of a state-controlled iron and steel works at Pretoria that Hertzog was forced to resort to the expedient of a joint sitting of both Houses to pass a bill to make provision for the setting up of the industry. Today the success of Smuts's war effort is largely due to the Iron and Steel Corporation.

The controversy over the Union Jack was a more serious matter. For many months feeling in the Union was at fever pitch in consequence of it. Smuts said afterwards: "Public opinion was worked up until the pot almost boiled over. The state of feeling in this country was such as I have not seen since the Boer War."

At the head of the opposing factions were General Smuts and Dr. D. F. Malan, Minister of the Interior in Hertzog's Cabinet. In 1925 the Government expressed its desire to substitute a national flag, "the outward symbol of our independent nationhood, and our accepted national status," for the Union Jack, anathematized by most Afrikaners as the symbol of oppression. British sentiment, however, was taken into consideration to some considerable extent, in that it was laid down that the Union Jack would be flown along with the Union flag on certain occasions.

When it became known that the Nationalists demanded a flag "having no association with the past" and, therefore, no trace of either the Union Jack or the republican flags in its make-up, the British people in the Union clamoured loudly and with tremendous insistence.

The various British patriotic associations led by Smuts organized a great campaign to defeat the enemy. The leader of the Opposition undertook a tour of the country, addressing meetings in many centres, and condemning everywhere the Government's attitude in regard to the flag question. He was received in the rural areas with catcalls and shouts of derision. Hostile men and youths wrecked his meetings. Once a band of young Nationalists entered a hall where he was to explain his standpoint. They drove off the police. They smashed up the furniture. They ended up by tearing to pieces a large Union Jack which had been draped over a table. The minds of men were dangerously inflamed throughout the country. Especially was this the case in the British province of Natal, which threatened to break away from the Union. A miasma of hatred lay over the land. Matters were working up to a grave climax.

Although Hertzog had weakened perceptibly after a successful visit to

England, Dr. Malan, who was in charge of the bill, remained inexorable. It seemed as if nothing could prevent his project from being carried into effect. He was sure to have his way at a joint sitting of the two Houses.

But at the eleventh hour the party leaders compromised, after "powerful influences" had come into play and the Governor General, the Earl of Athlone, had used his personal influence to bring Hertzog and Smuts together. It was agreed that there would be two flags: the Union Jack, to be flown at certain times, at certain points, and the Union flag comprising the orange, white, and blue of the Dutch House of Orange with a panel in the middle containing in miniature the old republican flags and the Union Jack.

It is only reasonable to assume that the British Government's opportune and indisputable recognition of the Union's equality of status with Great Britain was a factor which expedited greatly the settlement of the flag dispute. This timely acknowledgment of complete autonomy was made at an imperial conference held while the Battle of the Flags was raging furiously.

On the eve of his departure for Britain to attend this conference, Hertzog had declared that he would request of the British Government "a clear declaration of the free and independent status of the Union." It was a startling announcement. The imperialists, at any rate, found it so. Hertzog's mission was denounced by the British South African newspapers as being directed at the dissolution of the Empire. Smuts, speaking in Johannesburg, said that "a declaration such as General Hertzog has adumbrated means the breakup of the British Empire." It was felt that Hertzog's mission was doomed to failure.

The Prime Minister, however, was phenomenally successful at the conference, and sailed for South Africa with the Balfour Declaration which proclaimed the Dominions and Great Britain to be "autonomous communities within the British Empire, equal in status, in no way subordinate one to another in any respect of their domestic or external affairs. . . ." Certain surviving anomalies, it is true, tended to obfuscate the "mutual constitutional relations" of the members of the Commonwealth. These irregularities, however, it could be reasonably expected, would be cleared away in time.

Now, far from setting in motion the dissolution of the British Empire, as Smuts had feared and the British South African newspapers had predicted, the Balfour Declaration drew into the imperial fold men like Hertzog, Tielman Roos, and Dr. Malan. They stated openly that South Africa had at last achieved sovereign independence, albeit in the Commonwealth, and that the republican issue was dead. It would seem that by a long and devious route they had reached at length the house in which Smuts dwelt.

58

WHEN Hertzog became Prime Minister Smuts had to leave Groote Schuur. Nor did he do so regretfully, for he had felt out of place amid the luxury of the great house and was, in a sense, relieved to get back to the discomfort of the farm, Doornkloof, near Irene, where the open veld came right up to the very steps of his simple homestead.

The house had been an old military clubhouse for officers at Middelburg in the Transvaal during the Boer War. Smuts had bought it for three hundred pounds and made of it his home. Mrs. Smuts called it a *blikhuis* (tin shanty) but preferred it to all the most luxurious homes she had ever visited. So did Smuts. They were very happy there.

One entered the building, a spacious one, through a narrow hall, the walls of which were closely packed with the heads of almost every species of African buck. On a long, low table lay a few pistols which Smuts had used in wartime and above them hung a flag. Everywhere there were books—in bookcases, on chairs, on benches, and on tables—large numbers of them strewn about in every room and passage of the house. The library was so closely crowded with them that one moved around with difficulty. Two of the windows had been closed up to make room for more books. In addition to the poets, works on philosophy, travel, economics, biography, world politics, education, and law adorned the shelves. Smuts read (and still reads) every important new book on philosophy, science, and world affairs appearing in English, Dutch, German, and French. It was necessary for one to visit the old wood-and-iron house at Irene and to spend some time in the library if one desired to get the atmosphere of Smuts.

The drawing room was the only part of the house subscribing to ordinary, conventional European ideas. Numerous small tables stood about packed with autographed photographs of famous people, such as the Earl of Athlone (then Governor General of the Union of South Africa) and his wife, Princess Alice, the Prince of Wales, and Admiral of the Fleet Lord Jellicoe, who had written these words above his signature, "To a great man from a friend."

Smuts enjoyed being back at Irene. Since his tastes were severely simple—almost harshly so—and he could not bear pampering himself or being pampered (he never smoked and only on rare occasions did he indulge himself to the extent of having a glass of beer or some wine), he slept on the stoep on a very uncomfortable, hard bed next to which stood an old kitchen chair. On this there was barely room for his lamp, a cup of coffee, and a book. Sometimes he would make his own bed, when there was a bad mood on him. This was always a sign for his family to leave him severely alone.

Rising at about seven o'clock in the morning, he would slip into an old khaki shirt and an ancient pair of baggy trousers and go to attend to his great collection of plants. His chief interest, of course, lay in grasses. It was an interest he shared with Hertzog and one which has contributed not a little to the tremendous progress made in South Africa in recent years in the scientific study of grasses, which may in time to come solve many of our problems of pasturage.

Botany was Smuts's favourite hobby and the long tramps he undertook in search of botanical specimens his fondest form of recreation and of exercise. To him the veld was an entrancing, inexhaustible "treasure house of nature," and often he was to be found striding along, a picture of health and energy, enthusiastically pointing out rare specimens of African flora to companions (occasionally punctuating his remarks with a staccato, "Don't pick it! Don't pick it!"), or eagerly searching for something new. His grass press always went along with him. Dr. Marloth, world-famous botanist, was one of his firmest friends. He had a very high opinion of Smuts as a botanist. They went on many a botanizing expedition together. Dr. Pole-Evans was another close friend. Smuts originally brought him out to South Africa from Kew Gardens to improve the grasses of the Union in particular and the flora in general.

In spite of his passion for botany, Smuts did not care for gardens. Mrs. Smuts once had a beautiful flower garden round the house but gave it up to please her husband, who much preferred to have trees around him and the open veld.

Animals, on the whole, did not appeal overmuch to him, although he was fond of horses and greatly interested in his pedigreed cattle. These he would inspect after breakfast sometimes, before disappearing into the veld on horseback or on foot. No one was allowed to shoot wild animals on his farm at Irene or on either of his other two farms for that matter. He loved watching them sometimes, but his interest in them went no further.

Like all true South Africans, he loved the land. Apart from owning land he desired to possess nothing, for his wants were few. Most of his

General Smuts and General J. B. M. Hertzog (then Premier), joint leaders of the United South African National party from 1933 to September 4, 1939.

General Smuts in his library at Irene.

money went into his farms, without spectacular results, so that frequently the size of his overdraft at the bank alarmed Mrs. Smuts to the extent of inducing her to take severe measures to reduce it. He was generally quite unaware of the state of his personal financial position, nor did he take any notice of any reference made to it by his bank manager or his wife. Much money was expended on bulls imported to improve the strain of his cattle. Modern electrical machinery and refrigerators flanked the old blikhuis. Money was no object. It did not interest Smuts. But the land—that was different! It was part and parcel of his make-up.

Of his farms he loved Doornkloof at Irene best, for there was to be found the very heart of peace. But he was fond also of visiting his other farms, particularly the one in the Bushveld, where he would camp enthusiastically and live even closer to nature than he could at Irene. Here in the wilds he would occasionally entertain friends. Once such a party included the Governor General and his wife, who, knowing Smuts, evinced no surprise when they realized that the only bedroom on the farm was a large barn—a stone building—cold as charity. In it the women slept in a row against one wall and the men on the opposite side with wagons, carts, and harness in between. The sleeping problem never worried Smuts. It made no difference to him whether he slept on his uncomfortable bed at home or on the hard African earth. Sometimes a young private secretary found it embarrassing to share a double bed with him in the spare room of a remote and humble farmhouse and was surprised to perceive that his chief found nothing unusual in the situation.

Near to his farm at Irene there was a splendid golf course, but Smuts showed no interest in it. Even now when, as leader of the Opposition, his cares were fewer, he had neither the time nor the inclination for any of the usual forms of sport. Walking was good enough for him. Motoring did not appeal to him, but ever since the day he found his first motorcar —presented to him by some admirers—standing at his front door, he preferred driving himself to being driven. When at the wheel he was inclined to take risks. He loved speed. Nevertheless, he found riding preferable to driving. This had been evident in the East African campaign when he frequently rode as many as three sturdy horses in one day, tiring them out one after another.

If he could walk anywhere he refused to ride. During week ends one generally found him on foot in the veld walking briskly with long, easy strides towards the great Rietvlei Dam some miles from Irene or, when the House was in session, scrambling youthfully up the steep sides of Table Mountain. While visiting some friends in Cape Town in 1926,

Winifred Holtby walked one day on the slopes of this mountain. It happened to be the time when Parliament was sitting. "We had no reason," she wrote to a friend afterwards, "to connect this fact with the appearance of a man in shirt sleeves who suddenly strode down the path, followed by a yelping mongrel. His eyes were like the Pied Piper's, green and blue like a candle flame when salt is sprinkled on it. He walked with the ease of a countryman, so we guessed that he was a Boer farmer; also that he was interested in botany because he stopped to examine a flower." Attending a luncheon a day or two later to meet General Smuts, leader of the Opposition, she came face to face again with the Pied Piper of the mountain. He was Smuts.

Not from the companionship of the great or the acclamation of the multitude, but from the peace of Irene, from the loneliness of the open veld, and the eloquent stillness of the billowing hills and the rugged mountains—from the great heart of Africa come the qualities of strength that are in Smuts's make-up.

His physical well-being in the trying years he spent as leader of the Opposition was largely due to the veld and the mountains, but perhaps, in a small measure, also to his lack of faith in doctors. He had no confidence whatsoever in ordinary licensed medical practitioners. But near Irene there was an herb doctor, a quack. In him Smuts had a firm trust, and so had Mrs. Smuts.

It must remain to Mrs. Smuts's lasting credit that in the early, difficult days of his eclipse, she ministered to her husband's needs with an admirable, almost saintlike devotion. It was a trying time, for Smuts was frequently petulant and moody. But Mrs. Smuts was eminently suited to the task.

A motherly, kindhearted soul, cultured and well-bred but absolutely unspoiled, it was the essence of her philosophy to take the bitter with the sweet.

In between knitting, supervising in the kitchen, doing menial labour and attending to her husband's business affairs, she would read extensively in English, Afrikaans, and one or two foreign languages.

She had never possessed any such thing as a personal maid and was most unconventional in her attire, frequently walking about on the farm in a loose cretonne overall and simple veld shoes. Often she would receive distinguished guests, clad in a simply made, shapeless cotton frock, her bare feet thrust into slippers or old canvas shoes. A hat seldom adorned her short, curly hair even when she attended a garden party or accompanied Smuts on an official visit.

Sometimes on the farm, when the sun was too hot, she would put on a man's Panama hat, nor, much to the surprise of strangers, did she on occasion think of removing it when visitors turned up.

Often the Smuts family partook of a meal on a table unadorned by tablecloth, and helped themselves to canned foods from the original cans and to salt from an eggcup. Smuts, the philosopher, never even noticed that anything was wrong until horrified relatives asked him to remonstrate with his wife. Then, shrugging his shoulders, he said dispassionately: "Leave Isie alone: she is a child of nature."

One day while Mrs. Smuts was knitting in the sun on the stoep at Groote Schuur, wearing, as usual, an odd assortment of garments, a party of American tourists came up and asked whether they would be allowed to look over the historic old building.

"Well," said Mrs. Smuts, "visitors are not permitted while the Prime Minister is in residence, but I'll ask the steward if he will make a concession." And she walked off to consult Mr. Bennington.

"He will allow you a quarter of an hour," she said, returning.

As the party was on the point of leaving some time later, the leader turned to Mrs. Smuts, who was still enjoying the sun, took some money from his pocket, intending apparently to give it to her as a tip. Then, suddenly, he seemed to think better of it, lifted his hat, and walked off.

"I do believe he took you for the housekeeper and was going to offer you a tip," a friend who had witnessed the scene said indignantly.

"Yes," came the reply, "and I'd have taken it like a shot."

One of Mrs. Smuts's main tasks in life was (and still is) to keep press cuttings of all her husband's speeches. She took a very keen interest in his career, frequently assisting his party on the political platform. Her whole life was centred in him. People said that she was clever, but one never noticed it—she had sunk her whole personality and individuality in her husband's. More than anyone else she was his guide and comforter and friend. From the depths of despair she would draw him forth, inspirit him, and stir him up to new efforts, and he would be a man revived. Not a little of Smuts's success in life has been due to her self-effacing devotion.

Perhaps the children owed her even more, for she was both father and mother to them, Smuts being away from home more often than not. She trained them well—a good and an unselfish mother.

Almost as simple in their tastes and in their needs as Smuts himself, his family lived a happy, carefree life at Irene. Their home language was Afrikaans. This in itself was not surprising, despite Smuts's pro-British proclivities. But it smacked of rank heresy that English should so frequently be spoken in the home of Hertzog, the High Priest of Afrikaner-dom.

Like his wife, everyone around Smuts lived for the Oubaas (the old chief). He was Oubaas to all the members of his family, but his children regarded him with awe. "My children," he once remarked, "treat me as a distinguished stranger." They did not know him very well. And, like all South Africans, they were puzzled by his brilliant personality and some-what embarrassed by it. Mentally he was always a number of steps ahead of everyone, the result being that all around him—his wife, his children, and his subordinates—had an inferiority complex. At the end of 1925 his private secretary, a highly intelligent young man, told Smuts that he was leaving him.

"Why are you going?" asked the Oubaas.

"If I stay with you," came the reply, "I'll lose what little personality I possess. That, and that alone, is my reason for leaving you."

Often the whole family would sit through a meal without speaking a word when it was quite obvious that the Oubaas was up in the clouds. And they would say to one another afterwards: "He has again been busy with higher things." On such occasions Smuts became aloof, but not through vanity. He would forget that there were people around him, and his mind would travel far and fast. At such times not even Mrs. Smuts had the courage to bring him back to earth.

When strangers visited Irene or friends stayed with him, Smuts took pains to be sociable. In the dining room stood two trestle tables. At meal-times the children would sit down at one which had no cloth on it, while at the other, over half of which a starched white tablecloth had been thrown, would sit the guests with Smuts and his wife to partake of solid Boer food from inexpensive thick white kitchen dishes.

In this simple way the Smutses entertained people of high birth and plain country folk. Even in the case of the aristocratic Lord Milner and his wife no distinction was made when they stayed at Doornkloof. And, what is more, they enjoyed the simple life and homely fare.

Most welcome on the farm were the Gillets of Oxford, "Uncle Ar-thur" and "Aunt Margaret" (as Smuts called them), friends of his student days in England. Of Smuts's very small circle of friends they were closest to him.

59

IN THE NERVE-RACKING DAYS of his premiership Smuts had often spoken with keen anticipation of the time of his retirement, when he would be able to stay at Irene for good and do to his heart's content the things he liked, such as farming, walking, and reading. Yet now, when he had leisure for these things, he soon became surfeited. He was surprised to find that his heart was not in farming, for all his love of the land. He longed to be back in power. Leading the Opposition was too tame and too sterile. He wanted to be up and doing. He wanted to be planning, achieving, directing. He lusted for power. But there was no immediate prospect of his ousting Hertzog.

With a tremendous effort he curbed his impatience and bided his time. But he could not rest. He was never idle. He laboured incessantly. Mrs. Smuts, a Jeanette MacDonald enthusiast, was fond of going to the cinema, but she could rarely prevail on him to accompany her. He could not bear wasting time. He had no leisure hours besides those he devoted to walking and climbing. His private secretary never had office hours. Work started at about 8.30 A.M. and might finish at midnight. The young man could make no engagements. He had to be at his chief's disposal at all hours of the day, every day of the week. Once he arrived at a dance at twelve o'clock to meet an irate partner. Smuts had simply overlooked the fact that he was dressed for a dance and had kept him working. When the House was in session the secretary often slept on a sofa in Smuts's office. On these occasions the Oubaas would do likewise.

His world-wide correspondence took up a great deal of their time. Letters were sent to and received from famous scientists, philosophers, and statesmen all over the world. There was nothing more important to him than this correspondence. When, later, he became Minister of Justice he could hardly be bothered with the work of this department, and the men in it had frequently more work to do in connection with overseas correspondence than with Justice.

Smuts's famous book, *Holism and Evolution,* was written at this time. During one of the rests he was taking while devoting himself to his holistic philosophy, Smuts wanted something to read. His secretary got him a book by Eddington on relativity, a standard work on Einstein. Returning it a few days later, Smuts said,

"You may take the book back to the library."

"What do you think of it?" asked the secretary.

"Einstein," came the reply, "hasn't gone far enough. After all, Newton's laws of gravity were simple and to the point; Einstein is still groping about and has reached no finality."

Smuts then foreshadowed what was a later development and simplification of the theory of relativity by two American professors of mathematics.

Smuts's amazing brain was constantly overwhelming those around him. It could absorb anything—unlike Hertzog's one-track mind. It was constantly assimilating and cataloguing a multitude of facts. And in the light of his great knowledge Smuts sometimes knew and sometimes shrewdly guessed correctly what was to come. His prescience became a byword.

In 1925 a fruit control bill was being handled in the House of Assembly. It was introduced by the Hertzog Government. It was decided to make a non-political issue of the matter. A conference was held between Smuts and Hertzog, who were accompanied by secretaries. One Minister was present. The draft bill was discussed in detail, Smuts being very helpful and even gentle in his criticisms. In the end he said to Hertzog: "Barry, next year you will bring in amending legislation to this bill." He predicted that it would have quite an unexpected reaction. Hertzog replied heatedly: "God! You're just being perverse again."

Hertzog's secretary said afterwards: "Smuts was trying to show off." But, in just over a year, what Smuts had forecast took place: the bill had to be amended.

Meanwhile Smuts completed his *Holism and Evolution,* and to his secretary was assigned the task of typing from cover to cover the manuscript written in the author's appalling handwriting.

It did not disturb Smuts in the least that the young man had to work for twenty-four hours during the last day, typing through the night, to get the manuscript off in the morning. He made no comment. He merely sat down and worked all night too. Next day he said to a very tired young man: "Take my car and go to the Bushveld and enjoy yourself." He was almost shy of showing appreciation.

At the end of a particularly trying session, subsequently, he gave his private secretary a week's leave without thanking him specially for his assistance during the past months. But when the latter got off the train at Irene station on his return, the Oubaas was there in person to meet him.

Holism and Evolution was pondered on amid the storms and stress of the author's first months as leader of the Opposition when his world, so it seemed in the bitterness of his defeat, lay in ruins and the great structures he had helped to create and endeavoured to perpetuate appeared to be crumbling. The triumph of Hertzogism and the Locarno Treaty were a menace to the solidarity of the Empire, and before the eyes of men the League of Nations was disintegrating. He had sought to combine smaller parts into great unions—into wholes—but these were being broken down again. It was, however, patent that in the universe there was a constant striving towards wholeness, everything desiring to be one: "Matter and spirit, the temporal and the eternal, the finite with the infinite, the particular with the universal. . . ." He decided to crystallize and develop his ideas on this natural impulse towards wholeness that is immanent in and permeates the entire system of nature. Ever since his student days at Cambridge, when he had completed with much labour a manuscript entitled *Walt Whitman, A Study in the Evolution of Personality,* he had been engrossed in the idea of Wholeness in the universe. It became "the companion of his life." It constituted his philosophy of life. At Vereeniging it suggested to him tremendous possibilities of development for the South African states within the mighty "whole" of the imperium. Since then it has not only fascinated him in the field of biology but has been the great driving force behind all his political endeavour. In 1926 its elaboration into a philosophical treatise afforded him a welcome escape from the galling frustration of his irremediable eclipse and acted as a sublimating channel for his restless energy. Within six months, amid the hurly-burly of intense South African politics, without receiving any assistance, he produced a book, in style redolent of the poets and in content indicative of exhaustive scientific study, a profound knowledge of the philosophers and a dynamic and original mind.

The word "holism" was derived by Smuts from the Greek *holos,* whole. According to him evolution was "a rising series of wholes from the simplest material patterns to the more advanced." The universe, therefore, consisted of wholes which were constantly combining with one another to form larger, more complicated, and better wholes. "This," wrote Smuts, "is a whole-making universe; it is the fundamental character of the universe to be active in the production of wholes, of ever more complete and advanced wholes. The evolution of the universe, organic and inorganic, is nothing but the record of this whole-making activity in its progressive development," human personality being the consummation of this forward movement. The tiny atom of oxygen, for example, was a whole. It combined with two atoms of hydrogen (two separate wholes) to form another whole, an entirely new substance, a molecule of water. Carbon atoms again combined in their turn with water to give man the important carbohydrates, his principal food. So with ever-increasing complexity and ever more perplexingly entangled intricacy of pattern evolution progressed, always forming greater, more involved, and more important wholes "until the range of human life is reached."

When Smuts's political career is examined in the light of his holistic philosophy of life, its ostensible inconsistencies take on a logical disposition. Already feeling, in the twenty-third year of his life, that "the greatest work that can be done in this world is the harmonization, in accordance with the law of freedom, of the unit with the whole," it was not until after the Treaty of Vereeniging that he abjured the narrow national aspirations of the Afrikaner people and embraced holistic British imperialism. His subsequent efforts to bring about a union instead of a federation; his zealous imperialism as evidenced, for instance, by his frequent repudiation of South Africa's right of neutrality and self-determination and his accentuation of the indivisibility of the Crown; his suppression of the 1914 Rebellion which imperilled the organism of empire; his strenuous exertions on behalf of a league of nations; his Pan-African idea; his amalgamation with the Unionists in 1920 in an effort to smother the strong spirit of Nationalism that had been rekindled in the hearts of his people—a spirit which thereafter he sought to extirpate by resisting the introduction of a South African flag and a South African national anthem to supersede the Union Jack and the "King" respectively —all these were manifestations of holism in the political sphere. In pursuance of this aspect of his philosophy he was to embark, before many years had passed, on a great experiment of fusion of the races in his country. But it was foredoomed to failure, since it did not take into account the fact that heterogeneous elements frequently could not form a homogeneous whole.

In many respects Smuts's political outlook belies his holistic philosophy. He has never been able completely to fuse the two. Here are one or two cases in point.

Conveniently regarding the Marxian doctrine as outmoded, he has always anathematized socialism and in doing so has failed to face up to one of the greatest holistic concepts of all time.

His native policy, too, if such it can be called, has ever given the lie to his holistic professions. In an overzealous attempt to preserve white predominance in Africa and in order, incidentally, to safeguard his own political existence in a land where the European vote is paramount, he has at various times either connived at or partaken in the establishment of the vast black proletariat of Southern Africa in a position of degradation and virtual serfdom. There is all too often, in practice if not in theory, a law for the white man and a law for the black—a different type of justice in either case. Restrictive legislation in educational, political, and other spheres has deprived the black man in his aboriginal home of privileges that the Europeans have come to regard as their special prerogative. The native problem is probably the most important issue in South Africa. It vitally concerns the vast majority of the body politic in the subcontinent. Thus it is almost inconceivable that a man with Smuts's background and his vision should, like the veriest "die-hard of the Backveld," dismiss the matter with vague suggestions for and against segregation on the one hand, and, on the other, advocate labouring for white masters as a solution. Political necessity has pushed holistic ideals into the background, and the greatest ethnological whole in Southern Africa must needs waste away mentally, physically, and otherwise, instead of being allowed to fulfil its destiny in the creation of greater and better wholes. It is the negation of holism.

60

THE HALCYON DAYS that marked the first few years of Hertzogism in power drew gradually to a close, and the shadows slowly lengthened over Hertzog's grizzly head. Many convinced republicans, while temporarily acquiescing in the new sovereign independence within the Commonwealth, certainly did not share the sentiments of the Prime Minister, who was pleased to regard that status as the realization of their dreams. Soon dissatisfaction grew within the Nationalist party. It was aggravated by a mounting conviction that an intimate association between conservative landowning Nationalists and Socialist Labourites was bound to cause friction in the end—a presentiment which was ultimately realized when the Labour wing of the pact split into "two warring factions."

Meanwhile alleged favouring of Afrikaners in the making of appointments and the conclusion of a trade treaty with Germany further inflamed the local British, who had already been greatly incensed by the flag quarrel, the disposal of the preferential tariff formerly given to British goods, and sundry other "pinpricks." Moreover, government restrictions on diamond production were the cause of much dissatisfaction on the alluvial diggings. At the Provincial Council elections it seemed that the tide was turning against Hertzog.

Soon the general election of 1929 was at hand.

Smuts and his party had high hopes of being returned to power.

Prompted by the artful Tielman Roos, Hertzog, although he had prepared a strong programme, hardly availed himself of it at the election, but he exploited the native question, making caustic references to the obstructive tactics employed by the South African party in connection with his native bills. His master stroke was levelled at the person of Smuts. In a speech made at Ermelo in January, the latter, speaking in the Rhodes tradition, had foreshadowed a vast African federation of states. The speech in itself was nothing more than one of Smuts's customary holistic Pan-African utterances, but it inspired a devastating Nationalist manifesto in which Smuts was denounced as a "man who puts himself forward as the apostle of a black Kaffir State, of which South Africa is to form so subordinate a constituent part that she will know her own name no more," and who desired to secure "equal political rights for all— Kaffirs and white men everywhere on an equal footing. . . ." The continued existence or the downfall of the white man and his civilization in South Africa was at stake.

The charge was obviously false and plainly inconsistent with sense and reason. Smuts's record served to show its falsity. Nevertheless, it swept through the South African towns and villages, which were all too sensitive on the question of colour, and it penetrated to the remotest farms. And everywhere the cry was heard that Smuts was the "Apostle of a Kaffir State."

Among people abroad the impression was created that Hertzog and his henchmen, in direct contrast to Smuts *cum suis,* were incorrigible protagonists of a policy of "little South Africanism." And so they were.

However, the Afrikaners voted solidly for the Premier, who was returned to power with a clear majority over all the other parties combined. Labour lost heavily.

Smuts, defeated and dispirited, saw Hertzog enter the land of promise once again, and then journeyed wearily homeward.

He was thoroughly disgusted with politics. He felt the need of a change. He decided to accept an invitation from Oxford to be the Rhodes Memorial Lecturer for 1929. His lectures were a source of keen disappointment to the Negrophils. He spent the Michaelmas term at Oxford, received an honorary D.C.L., stayed with the King at Sandringham, visited Scotland, where he addressed large audiences on David Livingstone, and was everywhere received with great deference and tokens of affection.

At Cambridge he was asked to address the South African students in residence. He commended their sagacity for not having a separate South

African club, saying that it was wise of them to get into very close contact with students of all creeds and races, thus to extend their vision and shake off their prejudices. A week later he spoke to the South African students at Oxford. At both universities he was listened to with pride by his countrymen, who never ceased to marvel at an Afrikaner's being held in such high honour in Great Britain. Wherever they went, they were questioned about Smuts, and they heard men singing the praises of the great holist.

After his term at Oxford Smuts sailed for New York, there to attend the tenth anniversary celebration of the League. Touring Canada and the United States, he addressed great assemblies, received honorary degrees at famous universities, and was accorded everywhere every mark of esteem and respect. At Johns Hopkins one of the alumni said: "What we students are here for is to see a man without money get an honorary degree." At the White House he was received by President Hoover, and while the Senate was in session, he was allowed in the Chamber—an exceptional honour—and shook hands with the senators who filed past him.

Even the American Negroes warmed to him until he said compassionately, but somewhat tactlessly, that black men were "the most patient of all creatures next to the ass."

As ever the champion of the Jews, he told the American Jews that Palestine belonged to them to go to if they desired. "One of the greatest vows in history" had established it as such and the hand of Great Britain had confirmed it. He made no mention of Britain's promise to T. E. Lawrence and the Arabs.

No sooner had he set foot again in South Africa than he discovered that a bill to restrict further immigration of Jews from eastern Europe was under discussion in Parliament. Dr. Malan was handling it. The whole of Smuts's South African party with the exception of the five Jewish M.P.s and two other members (representing divisions with a very powerful Jewish vote) had supported the second reading. Smuts was scandalized. He hurled himself into the fight. He reasoned. He expostulated. He threatened. . . . A day or two later the South African party, with Smuts in the lead, opposed the bill to a man. Such was the influence and power of Smuts.

While the battle of the Quota Bill was being waged and he was being taunted, in Parliament and out, with being the greatest of all Jews and the King of the Jews, Smuts received an invitation from the British Association for the Advancement of Science to preside over the Centenary Meeting of the association to be held in London in September 1931. It was a signal honour. "Nothing in my chequered life," wrote Smuts, "has ever happened of which I am prouder than this presidency." In a letter to him Professor J. B. S. Haldane wrote: "No president in recent (or, indeed, former) times has had anything like the same knowledge of philosophy, as well as science, as you have." *Holism and Evolution* had brought Smuts fame as a philosopher-scientist. He had found admirers in men like Professor Arnold Toynbee and the eminent psychoanalyst, Dr. Alfred Adler, and a galaxy of other scientists and philosophers.

Five thousand of the world's foremost scientists attended the Centenary Meeting of the British Association. When Smuts delivered his presidential address, entitled "The Scientific World Picture of Today," the hall in which he spoke was overcrowded, while hundreds of people had to be turned away.

Thereafter he delivered many addresses on all manner of subjects, presided at numerous meetings of the association, attended scores of banquets, at many of which he had to speak, and was the recipient of a large number of honours. He had never been happier in his life.

In addition to taking part in the great Festival of Science, he had other fish to fry in those busy days. He chose to regard that period as one eminently suited to allocutory admonition. He lectured politicians and others on the problems of Europe and their solution, on the vexed question of world peace, and on Empire interests. Those who differed openly with him on any topic were frowned upon by the general public. The Empire builders made much of him; the scientists made much of him; the great newspapers made much of him; the man in the street made much of him. Once again he was the man of the moment in Britain. He returned home with his reputation enhanced.

61

MEANWHILE in South Africa Hertzog was riding for a fall.

Towards the close of 1929 the whole of the civilized world had entered upon a period of economic instability which soon culminated in one of the gravest intervals of depression in human memory. The bottom dropped out of Wall Street, and there was a serious run on the Bank of England, resultant upon similar ominous events on the Continent. Before long South Africa, too, was involved in the toils of a grave depression.

There was a slump in the diamond market; wool prices declined rapidly; so did the prices of maize and many other agricultural products. The farmers became desperate, and, to add to their misery, a drought without precedent in their time was ravaging the land.

Soon the prestige of the Government was declining and Havenga, the "Minister of Surpluses," was no longer a financial conjurer. Salary cuts and increased taxation bred a measure of disloyalty, while internal dissension had a debilitating effect upon both Government and party.

When, towards the end of 1931, an emergency national government took office at Westminster, Britain went off gold. The world was startled. Many nations linked up with sterling. This happened at the time of the Centenary Meeting. Smuts, having consulted leading economists, urged the South African Government repeatedly by cable to abandon the gold standard. All he got for his pains was ridicule. If "slim" Jannie tells us to link up with sterling, said his enemies, it is obvious that we must do nothing of the kind. "South Africa is on the gold basis," said Havenga, "and will remain on the gold basis." Hertzog swore that his cabinet would resign rather than go off gold. And backing up the Government was their whole party and, for that matter, Smuts's own followers. Almost everybody thought that it would be calamitous to link up with sterling. Indeed, only a few understood what all the pother was about. Among these were the spokesmen of the gold-mining industry, Mr. John Martin and Sir Robert Kotze. Their intervention served but to confirm the Government in its attitude of inflexibility. Smuts and the capitalists! A precious assortment of rascals, it was said, to give advice!

Meanwhile Smuts was conducting a vigorous campaign against the Government's policy in the country and in Parliament, and before many weeks had passed men flocked to his side to back him up. This enraged Hertzog, who repeatedly attacked the leader of the Opposition with characteristic virulence. Speedily the question of the gold standard became a party issue.

In the meantime the results of the Government's intransigence had been nothing short of catastrophic. South Africa was drifting dangerously near to the maelstrom of economic collapse. The exchange rate was levelled directly against her. Export trade dropped alarmingly and was soon almost at a standstill. Everywhere there were bankruptcies. The Orange Free State Administration became insolvent. Farms became unsalable. The Reserve Bank was faced with ruin. The party enthusiasm which had been so manifest a characteristic of Nationalist zealots was on the wane. So, too, was party discipline. In fact, things came to such a pass that the Government won a bye-election at Colesberg, a pact stronghold, by a very narrow majority after straining every effort to hold the seat. To hasten what appeared to be an impending rout, Smuts, realizing that the people were turning against Hertzog rather than towards him (Smuts), appealed to Labour and other interests to co-operate with him with a view to securing industrial and social reforms, and succeeded in winning over some of the Labour leaders.

There was a bye-election at Germiston in December 1932. It had been a strong Labour seat. The South African party candidate was J. G. N. Strauss, former private secretary to Smuts. The result of the poll was declared—a sensational victory for Strauss. As Wakkerstroom had sounded the knell of Smuts, so now it seemed that Germiston foreboded Hertzog's doom.

But the Government refused to give way. Smuts said that the Union was being "crucified on the cross of gold." He begged the Government to listen to reason. But Hertzog and Havenga were adamant. A serious deadlock had been reached. Nor did it seem likely that anyone would be able to cut the Gordian knot and deliver the country from a calamitous financial impasse.

In this fateful hour there reappeared on the stage of South African political history no less a man than Tielman Roos.

Tielman Roos had been for many years one of the leading men in the South African political world.

Having embraced Hertzogism in its infancy, he did much to further its cause in the Transvaal in spite of the powerful influence of Botha and Smuts. His efforts did not go unrewarded: he became Deputy Prime Minister of the Union under Hertzog. He was popularly known as the "Lion of the North." But anything less like a lion it would be difficult to visualize, for he was short and stout and jovial.

Smuts's downfall and Hertzog's meteoric rise to power were due in no small measure to Roos's personality and political acumen. He knew what the people wanted and he gave it to them. Roos surpassed even Hertzog as a protagonist of Nationalism. Always he strove to outdo his chief. When the latter railed at Botha's "one-stream" policy, he outdid him, advocating secession from the Empire; when Hertzog came forward with the slogan of "South Africa first," Roos excelled him with the cry of "South Africa alone"; when Hertzog referred to the Union Jack as a "rag," even Roos could not go one better, but he promptly reinstated himself in the affections of the Nationalists as champion slanderer of the British by referring to the influenza epidemic of 1918 as the "khaki pest." "When he settles down to the task," wrote a political commentator, "the Lion of the North is not easily outroared."

"I regard politics as a game," he once said in Parliament, adding hurriedly, "a serious game." It was a game he could play well. He was a splendid mixer, very popular with the man in the street. "My King, sir," said a poor white to a magistrate one day, "my King is Tielman Roos." It was a popularity sedulously cultivated by a peripatetic politician more often to be seen and heard in country towns and villages than in Parliament, gathering Afrikaners and others into the Nationalist fold and constantly exposing to ridicule the person of Smuts. He was a friendly soul, but for some reason or other he detested Dr. D. F. Malan and General Smuts.

He could manage a rowdy and ill-disposed crowd with greater ease than any other South African politician. Unlike Hertzog and Smuts, he was never refused a hearing.

Realizing in 1921 that the downfall of Smuts could not be achieved speedily by a mere racial appeal resting upon republican agitation and its concomitants, his agile brain began to cogitate on new ways and means. He watered down the secession issue, which to Labour was anathema, all but quenched the racial fires which he had fanned so assiduously himself, and engineered a "working alliance" between the Labour party and the Nationalists. Somebody called it a "masterpiece of political ingenuity," and so it was.

He became Minister of Justice in Hertzog's first ministry.

In his new capacity his kindheartedness was exploited by all and sundry. He was stopped in the streets and on trains by women begging him to set their erring husbands free. He released large numbers of transgressors from jail. It was said that he was vying in this connection with "Ma" Ferguson, the woman governor of Texas.

Despite his benevolence, Hertzog found him an uneasy bedfellow. He precipitated crisis upon crisis in the Cabinet and finally resigned on account of bad health to become an appeal judge. But his heart was not in his new occupation. He wished to get back into politics and into the Cabinet. To that end he sounded the Prime Minister through Malan and through Piet Grobler, another of Hertzog's ministers. But Hertzog's heart had hardened against Roos. His reply to Grobler was: "I shall not give my consent. I shall not take him back into the Cabinet. I thank God that he is out of it."

Deeply incensed at being dealt with so summarily, Roos remained on the bench and bided his time.

Just before Christmas of 1932 he resigned from the bench and heaved his Pickwickian portliness back into politics. And he roared—he, the Lion of the North—as he had never roared before. The sound was heard in all the four provinces of the Union. The effect was dramatic, its tenor being "off gold."

As if it had never heard that cry before South Africa responded as a clarion. South Africans flocked round Roos. Like a Roman general celebrating a triumph, he made his entry into towns and into cities. Tremendous audiences listened to him with rapt attention and applauded him with glowing enthusiasm. At long last the country was firmly persuaded that the gold standard was untenable. And, in anticipation of the inevitable, investors sent large sums of money to Britain where the value of the South African sovereign approximated to one pound eight shillings and sixpence. What, at the start, had been a lazy trickle of money leaving the country now became a sweeping flood. The flight from the South African pound assumed alarming proportions. The commercial banks informed Havenga that the situation was fast becoming desperate. On December 28 the Government that had said that it would rather perish than go off gold, having no alternative, linked up with sterling—but it did not perish. It remained in office.

Thus within a week Roos became the saviour of South Africa, merely by echoing the cry which Smuts had been sending up for well-nigh fifteen months. But the success of Roos was not haphazard. He had chosen the opportune moment; his personality was unique; his charm, generous nature, and irresistible bonhomie had given him with all sections of the community a peculiar popularity possessed by no other political leader; and, above all, unlike Smuts, he had the power to enforce his will, for in the House of Assembly there were eleven Nationalists who had sworn allegiance to him, and, in doing so, had placed in the hollow of his hand the balance of power in Parliament.

While Tielman, a rotund and frolicsome Jove, having stolen Smuts's thunder, was blithely hurling thunderbolts, Smuts, wholly unaware of the political crisis, was happily botanizing in the Northern Transvaal. Hurriedly cars were sent rushing all over the veld in search of him. When at last he was run to earth, a scandalized reporter found him more interested in a rare specimen of plant life which he had just discovered than in the great crisis. Nor was this a pose, as many a man who has gone with him into wild places, at some critical phase or other of South African history, can testify. For when the noise and the bustle of the city and the madding crowd have been left behind, Smuts identifies himself with the veld at will, and with the stones and the plants and the mountains on the mighty bosom of Africa, switching off completely and forgetting the political exigencies of the moment.

The effect on South Africa of linking up with sterling was amazing. Not in their wildest dreams had the followers of Roos expected anything like it. The price of gold rose from four to seven pounds an ounce. On the stock exchange there was a boom without precedent in South African history. Gold shares rose in many instances as much as 600 per cent. Low-grade and formerly unprofitable mines now yielded excellent returns. It seemed that the prospects of gold mining in South Africa were limitless, since tremendous tracts of land all over the Transvaal and in the northern Free State were known to be auriferous. It was nothing for established brokers to make as much as two thousand pounds a day in brokerage alone. Many new gold companies were floated. Within the space of two years Johannesburg, a boom town, changed its shape entirely and became a new city. The Government reaped tremendous profit from mine taxation and from the mines it leased. There was work for everyone—and money—in the mines, on the railways, in the building trades, everywhere. The country that had languished in the Slough of Despond was now proudly riding on the Wave of Prosperity. Had it given ear to Smuts fifteen months before, it would have saved itself much misery and fifty million pounds.

62

WHEN Roos had set the Union agog with the cry of "Off gold" he had added to it another: "Off racialism." It was, he said, his sworn purpose to heal the breach which had long been separating the races. He begged all parties to unite under his leadership. It was, he proclaimed, his intention that his own followers on the Government benches should assist Smuts to bring about the overthrow of Hertzog in the House, and that after a general election he, Roos, should become Prime Minister with Smuts in his Cabinet as well as one Labourite, four Nationalists, and four Smutsites. The leader of the South African party, in reply to an invitation, expressed his willingness to negotiate for the formation of a Coalition government, but not on Roos's terms. Although thirty of his followers in Parliament were willing to sacrifice Smuts, among others the veteran F. S. Malan, the majority refused to serve under Roos. Negotiations were broken off. Roos himself refused to play second fiddle to any man. As for his followers on the Government benches, the mere thought of exchanging Hertzog for Smuts, "the lifelong archenemy of the Nationalist party," made them squirm.

Meanwhile the Nationalist Cabinet was greatly bewildered at the turn of events and not a little embarrassed by the presence of the enemy in their midst. It was impossible to estimate to what extent their ranks had been undermined by Roosism. Pirow favoured a *rapprochement* with Smuts, while Dr. Malan strongly urged his chief to go to the country.

Such, then, was the state of affairs when Parliament assembled in Cape Town early in 1933. Just prior to its assembly negotiations were reopened with Roos, who conceded a majority to Smuts in his shadow Cabinet but insisted on becoming Prime Minister himself. Had Smuts accepted this latest offer, Hertzog's government would have fallen within a few days. But all attempts at final settlement hung fire, pending discussions within the South African party caucus.

No sooner had the parliamentary session commenced than Smuts moved a resolution to effect the resignation of the Hertzog ministry and to accomplish the formation of a national government. The whole country, he said, desired fervently to see the end of party strife and demanded that a "constructive effort" be made to place the politics of the Union on a new basis. He strongly emphasized the need for Coalition in order to bring about material unity, race collaboration, and economic stability. A division on this resolution resulted in its being defeated by fourteen votes.

But despite their apparent victory the Government's position was desperate. Hertzog writhed with mortification at the knowledge that he owed his position to Roos, whose followers had voted against the Smuts motion at the direction of their leader. It was an open secret that Tielman was determined to have the Government overthrown as soon as he and Smuts had come to an agreement. The latter, secure in the knowledge that Hertzog must come to heel or perish, did not close the door to Roos . . . but waited patiently.

Torn by conflicting emotions, the Prime Minister raved and ranted. His ministers, Pirow and Havenga, tried to persuade him to accept the hand of Smuts, pointing to the possibility of his being able to weather an election and reminding him of the fact that Smuts was willing to serve under him.

Barely a month after Louw Steytler, an outstanding Cape Nationalist, had been evicted from the Nationalist party caucus for supporting Coalition, and a mere week or two after the Smuts motion had been railed at by the Prime Minister and defeated in Parliament, Hertzog threw a bombshell into the midst of his party caucus. He gave them the choice between accepting Coalition and losing him as a leader. Thus in a trice he split from top to bottom the party he had so laboriously built up. Forty-one members of his caucus voted with him; the rest abstained.

Meanwhile, in order to preserve the solidarity of his party in the event of the fruition of his coalition plans, Smuts had taken measures to shelve *sine die* any questions, such as the native and provincial problems, on which the various sections of his following had strong differences of opinion at the time. His wise precautionary measures kept his South African party intact. In his party caucus the feasibility of union with Roos as opposed to coalition with Hertzog was freely discussed. Many objected to Hertzog on personal grounds. They recalled with heat the abuse he had heaped upon their leader's head for more than two decades. After listening patiently for two days to his followers, Smuts broke his silence. Roos must be rejected; Hertzog accepted. He had his way. Without a dissenting vote his party empowered him to arrange a coalition with Hertzog. This was finally accomplished soon after. And on February 28 the Prime Minister announced formally in the House that a Coalition Ministry would be established and that he would go to the country.

63

COALITION had become an accomplished fact. The seemingly impossible had been achieved. The bitter feud between Smuts and Hertzog which had torn South Africa in two for close on twenty years was ended. The breach was healed.

Tielman Roos had thrown the generals into each other's arms and, in doing so, had brought disaster on himself. Had the Hertzog government been able to remain on gold, Roos might have secured Smuts's co-operation on his own terms. But Finance Minister Havenga's all-too-prompt acceptance of sterling upset his applecart. No sooner was the gold issue a thing of the past than Roos discovered that his personal magnetism had died with it. His former friends of the Rand golf fields, having no more use for him, cast him aside without a qualm. Of course Hertzog refused to have him in his Coalition Cabinet.

Two years later, at the age of fifty-six, Roos died, a poor man. A fund, raised on behalf of his widow and children, realized six thousand pounds, which was less than mere agency work procured for first-class brokers in

the course of a single week during the boom period. A contribution of
two hundred and fifty pounds was sent by one of the Rand's greatest
mining houses, a concern which Roos's intervention had saved from utter
ruin and furnished with unbelievable prosperity in the shape of profits
amounting to millions of pounds.

In the new Cabinet of twelve, containing six Nationalists and six
members of the South African party with Hertzog as Prime Minister and
Smuts as his deputy, Dr. Malan declined to take office. Later, when
Coalition ripened into the fusion of the Nationalist and South African
parties, Dr. Malan and his die-hard followers hived off as the Purified
Nationalist party.

Working unobtrusively behind the scenes—as was his wont—during
the nerve-racking days immediately preceding Coalition was Louis Esselen, organizing secretary of the South African party and for many
years a powerful force in the politics of the Union. Having seen service
during the Boer War with Botha and Smuts, he relinquished a good position in the Land Bank to become secretary of their party and their
right-hand man. A wise and trusted counsellor, he was the intimate associate and confidant of Smuts for almost forty years, until, at the close of
1940, he became a railway commissioner. Young Cabinet Ministers constantly looked to him for guidance and counsel. To no man does Smuts
owe more. During the long years of their association Esselen only too
frequently was the pilot who carefully guided through treacherous shoals
and mortal storms the great ship sailing under Smuts's command.

Despite the magnanimous motives of race collaboration, national
unity, and the achievement of economic stability attributed to the generals by the powerful press supporting them in the accomplishment of
Coalition, it was, in point of fact, to a large extent a marriage of con-
venience and not a joining of hearts. Despite the allied parties' crushing
victory at the election, Coalition did not altogether come from the heart
of the people. It was patent from the start that a great proportion of the
Afrikaner element, particularly in the Cape, was indifferent, if not antipathetic. Several factors, however, contributed to their acquiescing silently in the new settlement. Among these not the least important were
Hertzog's tremendous personal influence as undisputed champion of
Afrikanerdom and a so-called "coupon" arrangement which guaranteed
to sitting members their re-election.

While in regard to the Coalition and to the subsequent fusion of parties one cannot discount the motivating influence of Smuts's holistic aspirations as affecting the Union *per se,* his efforts to establish an alliance
of parties and his ready acceptance of Hertzog's leadership as the *sine*

qua non thereof had a more personal and a wider significance. A party victory two years later would, according to Smuts, have been both "barren and dangerous." Hitler's rise to power; the collapse of credit in the United States; Japan's threatened withdrawal from the League—all these were clouds upon the world horizon. He could not ignore the signs—he who had predicted the storm. In the interest of the Empire's solidarity it was necessary to break the neutrality party which, in the event of war, might prove recalcitrant. By effecting Coalition Smuts produced a crack in the fabric of Nationalism; with Fusion it burst asunder.

For a man with Smuts's mental attitude it was not hard, in the circumstances, to serve under Hertzog. Honour and position were not of paramount importance in his life. Power was. The honour of holding the premiership was as nothing compared to the power he would wield in the Cabinet by virtue of the preponderance of his followers in the Coalition phalanx and, after the fusion of parties, in the United party. It was a predominance which was barely perceptible in the beginning but which steadily increased, until with the hiving off of the Malanites it became manifest to all. Smuts was thus able to persuade Hertzog gently but firmly to carry out his pro-Empire policy with greater effect than he himself could have done without Hertzog's support. Thus by sacrificing the position of honour he was enabled to achieve his great holistic design, the consolidation of the Empire.

The wielding of power in the interests of the reinforcement of imperialism—which so far had been the acme of holism translated into practical politics—gave Smuts a spiritual satisfaction which a sense of security and a position of honour could never bestow. He was quite satisfied not to sit in the coach resplendent in frock coat and top hat—the man at whom all the onlookers stared. Much rather would he be the person who held the reins, who drove the coach, with the man and the frock coat and the silk hat, wherever he pleased.

Co-operation between Hertzog and Smuts was facilitated by the latter's inimitable ability to compromise. It did not matter to him whether there was all the world of difference of opinion between him and the Premier on matters of exceptional importance to South Africa provided that he could use the Nationalist leader to further the cause of Empire.

No sooner had he taken office under Hertzog than he made it his object to wean him and his satellites from Nationalism and gradually to educate them up to holistic British imperialism.

As an instructor Smuts was eminently suited to his task. As disciples many of the Nationalists proved only too eager to learn.

Under the tactful effacement of Smuts, who readily allowed his for-

mer enemy to have all the limelight, Hertzog himself proved to be surprisingly docile. Smuts's task with him was greatly simplified by a chain
of favourable circumstances. At the epochal Imperial Conference of
1926, British diplomacy, by means of exceptional concessions in the Balfour Declaration flattering to his vanity and by subtle blandishment, had
done much to detach Hertzog from his anti-British prejudices. So much
so that on his return he had expressed his willingness to lead a Coalition
government and had been prevented from doing so only by the stubborn
inalienability of his powerful lieutenant, Dr. D. F. Malan. The Statute
of Westminister, which gave legal form to the Balfour Declaration, and
the pro-British leanings of his intimate associate, Havenga, whose friendship had been systematically courted by the Opposition and who had
been designedly lauded by the Empire press as the great man of the Ottawa Conference—these factors had, in a sense, given the *coup de grâce*
to Hertzog's deeply rooted aversion to anything British.

The success of Smuts's efforts to instruct his Hertzogite colleagues in
the art of thinking imperially was soon obvious to all, for these men were
obliged to vindicate standpoints that they would never have defended as
members of the old Nationalist party and to take steps at which formerly
they would have shied. Examples of their change of front were legion:
the watering down of the language policy of the old Nationalist party
which protected the *pro rata* rights of Afrikaans; their guarding of the
interests of the capitalistic mine industry to the extent of agreeing to a
very moderate taxing of its enormous excess profits; Hertzog's own description of his former neutrality policy as a "folly of the past"; General
Kemp's renunciation of his former republican aspirations; Pirow's flirt-
ing with schemes of imperial defence; the efforts of the entire Hertzogite
faction in Parliament to shipwreck the Malanites' persistent attempts to
put a stop to Jewish immigration; their unanimous rejection of proposals
to abolish the appeal to the Privy Council; various speeches of Hertzogites in defence of the retention in South Africa of the British national anthem, which they had formerly anathematized; Hertzog's suddenly discovered feeling of friendship for his "friends" in Johannesburg and Durban (formerly execrated as "capitalists" and "jingoes" respectively)
whom he begged to forget his sins of the past—all these and many other
proofs there were of a wholesale conversion from Nationalism to Smuts-
ism.

64

AFTER the brief post-election session of 1933 a large number of resolutions came from branches of the two parties, begging Hertzog and Smuts to carry into effect a fusion of the parties. It was a step that had been implicit in the Coalition idea. While the great majority of Nationalists in the Transvaal favoured it, those of the Cape Province as well as many others for whom Coalition had held little attraction now became restive. Soon, under the leadership of Malan, they broke away completely from Hertzog. Their parliamentary representatives became the official Opposition in the House.

Here, with an unfortunate display of petulance, Hertzog now refused to greet his former associates, the Malanites. "I do not want to know these people," he said. "It is best that I should not know them and that they should not know me." But Smuts was his own suave self, treating alike political friend and foe, friendly, but not too friendly, and mostly wrapped up in his cloak of detachment. But often, perforce, his aloofness would fall away from him, and he would stand revealed a very human human being.

On one occasion, when he was introducing a bill, the Speaker, following the customary procedure, bade him lay a copy of it on the table of the House. He rummaged about in his desk but failed to find a copy. Smuts was equal to the occasion. Picking up a piece of blotting paper, he walked up to the table and solemnly handed it to the clerk who, with equally quick wit, as solemnly read the title of the "bill" in the two official languages. The House's "Standing Orders" had been duly complied with. The incident amused members on both sides of the House, and an equally amused parliamentary newsman watching from the press gallery recorded that "General Smuts secured the First Reading of a piece of slightly soiled blotting paper!"

As befitted an Empire builder and world statesman, Smuts was, as always, impatient of matters of detail, arrogantly contemptuous of what he regarded as the non-essential niceties of parliamentary procedure. It was still the Olympian contempt of former days for democratic institutions like Parliament which hampered a man of vision in the attainment of his goal. He would gladly have brushed aside the silly debates and the interminable and, often, awkward questions—which were a waste of time—and have got on with the job. Who were they, at any rate—these small men in Parliament—to question his doings? He would dispose of them by any means. Not the means, but the end—yes, only the end mattered. Thus, in an effort to avoid what to him was useless wrangling and so to speed up matters and jump the intervening spaces that kept him from the objects of his vision and ambition, he resorted in Parliament to all manner of subterfuges.

He was noted for the tactful and cunning way in which he sailed through the intricacies of his departmental estimates and avoided the pitfalls set for him by the Opposition. With an unexampled deftness he managed to give to his thinnest arguments at least the semblance of importance—an effect which was curiously enhanced by the sober earnestness of his expression and tone. He was able with a straight face lightly to glide over ticklish points and knotty problems raised by the Opposition, and he was famous for his skill at giving evasive yet seemingly effective replies to questions. Every member's particular difficulty was treated with great earnestness and promised thorough investigation. This courteous and encouraging treatment, interspersed here and there with a good-natured little joke, generally tended either to keep his critics in a good mood or to disarm them completely.

Once he was dealing with the estimates in connection with his own particular department. He was bombarded with questions on policy and representations in connection with a multitude of matters in various districts. It was customary for the secretary and other officials of the department concerned to sit near by and every now and then to send notes to their Minister containing information, guidance, and counterarguments from which he would draft his replies to members. Ministers generally were only too eager to make use of this assistance, but Smuts could not be bothered with these details. They were of no importance. What did it matter whether the small fry there in front of him were kept in ignorance? After all, they were only trying to hamper him. On this particular occasion the barrage of questions and criticism was particularly heavy. Note after note reached Smuts from the officials of his department. After a while he became impatient, walked hurriedly over to the bench where his industrious subordinates were sitting, and said curtly: "Don't send me any more little notes! They just cramp my style." At first the men were dumbfounded. Then subdued laughter came from their quarters. Afterwards they recalled the classic joke of Smuts and the "remounts scandal."

After the campaign in South West Africa a member of the Opposition had asked Smuts, then Minister of Defence, an awkward question in Parliament as to the amount of money that had been spent on remounts. At that time there was a so-called "scandal" about this matter. On making inquiries at Defence headquarters, Smuts was told that a large number of clerks would require several weeks to work out the figures. When, however, he was again questioned on the matter in the House a day or two later, he rose quite unconcernedly and said in all innocence and sincerity: The sum spent on remounts was exactly nine hundred and seventy three thousand four hundred and fifty-two pounds ten shillings and ninepence. Then he sat down. Afterwards, when the departmental secretary asked him anxiously where he had got the figures, he said: "Man, if it will take you and your clerks, with an easy access to all the records, several weeks to find out what the amount was, it will take the Opposition the rest of their life to find out that I dug those figures from my imagination!"

65

THE 1934 SESSION of Parliament was notable chiefly for the passing of the status bills, which were introduced in order so to amend the South African constitution as to bring it into conformity with the new constitutional position resulting from the adoption of the Statute of Westminster, which gave the Dominion equal partnership with Great Britain and full autonomy in their external as well as their internal affairs. It was hoped by means of a foolproof act to settle for all time the vexed question of "status."

When, finally, the bills were passed it was claimed by Hertzog, Smuts, and the majority of legislators that South Africa's position as a sovereign independent state within the Empire had been ratified. In this act Smuts saw both the realization of the ideals of English-speaking South Africans who were determined to retain the ties linking them to Britain and, in effect, the fulfilment of the dreams of the republicans.

While to the vast majority of Smuts's followers the bills had been made acceptable by the spirit of good will and conciliation engendered by the Coalition, by their leader's cogent arguments, and by the very fact of his personal acceptance of and enthusiasm for them, there were those who had wavered from the start. And with the final accomplishment of the Status Act they became irreconcilable, for they believed that it had weakened the bonds of Empire. They were a small minority of three. Their leader was Colonel Stallard. Soon they hived off to become the Dominion party.

The Status Act, and the hearty welcome accorded to it by Britishers in the Union prepared the way for a speedy "transition from Coalition to Fusion." As at Vereeniging, at the Union Convention, and on many historic occasions thereafter, it was again the voice of Smuts and his peculiar genius for compromise that won the day. He settled doubts. He smoothed out difficulties. He effected concessions. Night and day he laboured.

Towards the close of 1934 Fusion became an accomplished fact. Of all Smuts's experiments in holism it was by far the most amazing, this attempt at fusing a number of heterogeneous groups into a single whole. It was an almost incomprehensible and certainly unprecedented endeavour to blend together dissimilar and divergent elements: Smuts and Hertzog; Imperialist and Nationalist; Britisher and Boer; mineowner and labourer; and even, in a measure, Capitalist and Communist.

If Coalition and Fusion are regarded as two phases in the development of Smuts's British holistic ideas as applied to South Africa, it is clear that their elaboration as part of an evolutionary holistic process broke down on account of one or two fundamental defects in their structure.

It was impossible suddenly to produce a united nation by an arbitrary amalgamation of two great parties. Genuine fusion went deeper. At the very least it presupposed a mutual urgency which in this case was almost wholly lacking between two sections whose ideals and interests were poles apart. Numerous resolutions were sent in after Coalition by party branches clamouring for Fusion, some inspired by material considerations and by the branch leaders' personal influence and others instigated largely by grateful members who had been returned to Parliament without a struggle on a Coalition "coupon." It was a mistake to assume that a homogeneous whole would result from a combination of heterogeneous elements. It would, however, be presumptuous to suppose that Smuts was unaware of the defects inherent in his holistic experiment, as affecting South Africa itself. The fact of the matter was that the holistic aspect was merely incidental to the amalgamation of parties.

The Fusion Ministry, with Hertzog at its head and Smuts still second in command, took office at a time when South Africa, by virtue of the golden harvest from her mines, her thriving secondary industry and general prosperity, was flourishing and happy despite disquieting news from abroad.

Thus with more or less everything in its favour the Government set to work with a will. After effecting important social and financial legislation it tackled the native problem, the solution of which—in accordance with Hertzog's ideas—was part of the price Smuts—or, more correctly, his party—was to pay for Fusion.

But before the native bills (making provision for far-reaching social changes) were introduced, Smuts proceeded to Britain, there to be installed as rector of the University of St. Andrews.

As his rectorial address Smuts delivered his never-to-be-forgotten speech on "Freedom" that echoed throughout the world.

"Aristotle and Pliny," said Professor Blyth Webster, "taught the world always to expect something new from Africa. This is the first rector that Africa has given to a Scottish university. . . ."

An honorary degree was conferred on Hertzog *in absentia* in recognition of his new complaisance.

Returning to London, Smuts broadcast a speech on foreign affairs. It was received with boundless enthusiasm. The *Times,* in response to numerous requests, decided to publish it in pamphlet form. As usual Smuts was lionized here, there, and everywhere. At a reception given by the Lord Mayor of London, the great company of famous people rose to a man at his entrance and applauded him vociferously as he walked across the hall to a platform at the far end.

He left for home in a blaze of glory to face and acquiesce in the somewhat inglorious native bills, which made provision for the disenfranchisement of natives and the general curtailment of rights hitherto enjoyed by them. Negrophilists indignantly inquired whether this Smuts who was supporting the bill was the same man who had so eloquently espoused the cause of freedom at St. Andrews.

Fusion alone made the passage of the Representation of Natives Bills possible and gave to Hertzog on his seventieth birthday the satisfaction of witnessing the fulfilment of what he had striven for in regard to the problem of native representation for more than a decade.

While ostensibly unanimous on the score of native legislation, the component parts of the United party (as the Fusion party was called) had not the same measure of agreement in respect of the Indian, Jewish, and coloured problems. Proposed restrictive legislation in regard to Indians and the unchecked mass immigration of Jews from Central Europe after the sanguinary advent of Adolf Hitler set in motion strange crosscurrents in the party and stirred up animosity between Hertzog's die-hard Conservatives and Smuts's cosmopolitan Liberals. The coloured question was, if anything, an even more sensitive subject of dispute between the two wings of the party, since the Hertzogites could not but sympathize with their former brethren, the Malanites, who, first, were pressing for legislation to impose a ban on mixed marriages and to arrange for complete segregation between Europeans and half-breeds in respect of residential quarters and, second, were advocating economic and industrial segregation. It was expected to prevent further wholesale miscegenation with the former; with the latter, it was hoped to achieve an easy solution of the disturbing "poor-white" problem.

It was an uneasy collaboration which Smuts endeavoured to hold intact by smoothing over differences of opinion on matters of policy with honeyed words and with diplomatic utterances designed to placate factions in the United party. Filled with anxiety by the trend of events in Europe and desiring on that account to avoid a break with Hertzog at all costs, he diligently oiled the unwilling cogs of the unwieldy machine of his part creation. And he waited—somewhat like Fabius Maximus. To the world outside it seemed, at first, that all was well.

When, gradually, the enthusiasm for Fusion faded, men with discriminating minds discerned a rift in the lute. Apart from the antipathetic Liberal and Conservative elements in Cabinet and party, there were personal rivalries in the highest circles, strained relations between town and country, and dissatisfaction about the assignment of portfolios to a few "politically necessary incompetents." It was patent that a large number of Smuts's adherents would have been more at home with the Stallard imperialist group, while many of Hertzog's following were manifestly Malanite isolationists at heart. Even the leaders themselves disagreed on matters of fundamental importance, such as the right of secession, the divisibility of the Crown, and the question of neutrality.

Somewhat unseasonably under the circumstances, for a British newspaper, but with a rude pertinence, the Natal *Witness* inquired of what use unity was between leaders and groups that were compelled to maintain it by means of an agreement to differ from each other on almost every problem. And of what value to the nation's welfare, if, for the sake of unity, fundamental principles were subordinated to superficial compromises.

Indeed by the very nature of its composition and that of its motley following, the Government was constitutionally incapable of facing up to some of the country's most pressing problems.

But, for all the friction inseparable from a party so constituted, the United party, held together by Smuts's genius for compromise, did much to merit the approval of the public. It was, therefore, with almost unabated confidence that they faced a general election in May 1938. The

Austrian *Anschluss* and Hitler's almost simultaneous pronouncement laying claim to all the former German colonies did much to rally to the Government the bulk of the electorate.

The Fusionists' sanguine expectations were surpassed by the event. Although the Malanites gained much in strength, the Government retained one hundred and eleven of their one hundred and seventeen seats. It was a trifling loss. But the ratio between Smutsites and Hertzogites in Parliament had been considerably altered in favour of the former. This displeased Hertzog and his satellites. They were resentful. What rankled was the realization that the victory of the United party was in reality a victory for Smuts. To their resentment many have attributed the fact that the period between the election and the outbreak of war was one teeming with crises in the Cabinet and with "incidents."

On Union Day, less than a fortnight after the election, "Die Stem," an Afrikaner anthem, was played at military parades in large towns throughout the country, and "the King" was omitted. A storm of British indignation swept the land, since it was believed that Pirow, Minister of Defence, had deliberately engineered this slight and that the Prime Minister had been a party to the deed. Bristling with indignation, Stuttaford, Minister of the Interior, resigned. For a short while it seemed that Fusion was in grave danger. But Smuts poured oil on troubled waters and saved the situation. And Stuttaford returned to the Ministry.

Hardly had this crisis passed than the Cabinet was badly shaken by the resignation of two prominent ministers. It was a protest against Hertzog's wayward behaviour in giving a seat in the Senate, vacated by one of the representatives of the natives, to a friend (notoriously lacking in any of those qualifications which the South Africa Act required of native representatives), and thereafter assigning to him a portfolio specially set aside to accommodate him.

The ominous clouds fast gathering on the European horizon and a recrudescence of extreme Nationalism in the Union—resultant upon a symbolical ox-wagon trek during the centenary celebrations of the Great Trek in the latter half of 1938—were common dangers which brought about a temporary reconciliation between the two United party factions. Smuts could breathe freely again.

The Czechoslovakian crisis found the Government divided on the question of neutrality. But the intense feeling of Nationalism, begotten of the Great Trek celebration, and the general conviction that the Sudeten Germans "had a case" were factors which argued strongly for the maintenance of neutrality. At all events Smuts, apparently without the knowledge of his colleagues of the old South African party, was afterwards said to have agreed to support an attitude of neutrality if England should become involved in war over Sudetenland.

The Munich Agreement brought relief to many anxious hearts. Smuts said, "We are grateful to the four leaders of Europe. . . . A great champion [Chamberlain] has appeared in the lists." He believed that England had recovered the "moral leadership" of Europe and that the dove of peace was on the wing. Again he pointed to the League as the obvious panacea. It was an illusion swiftly dispelled by Germany's sudden demand for the restoration of Tanganyika and by the rape of Bohemia and Moravia. And now Smuts referred to the British Navy (not to the League) as "the greatest force for peace in the world."

In April 1939, just before Hitler's birthday, Smuts sent strong police reinforcements with machine guns to Windhuk in South West Africa, explaining afterwards that the trained Hitler Youth and Nazi organizations in the Mandate had been on the point of effecting a *coup d'état.* "Austria and other small states," said he, "have been invaded on the plea that they could not keep internal order, but the Union will never lay itself open to invasion on that ground."

The Opposition swore that the step had been an act of provocation, perpetrated by the man who had drawn the Union into war in 1914 and was trying to do so again, and Dr. Malan said that the whole business was strongly reminiscent of the deceit practised in connection with the Nakob incident in 1914. On that occasion Smuts is alleged to have fabricated evidence relating to a German sortie into the Union in order to get the Members of Parliament to vote for war. For all the Opposition's protestations, however, the sending of police reinforcements was justified right up to the hilt, as the event proved. Strong Nazi organizations in the Union and South West Africa were subsequently discovered.

Meanwhile the Italians pounced upon Albania, and the full blast of Goebbels' propaganda machine was directed against Poland. Men said that the storm was about to break.

In South Africa the question of neutrality became a burning issue. At the time of Fusion, Smuts and Hertzog had spoken of it as an "academic" question, but it could no longer be regarded as such. Britishers in the Cabinet openly affirmed that South Africa could not remain neutral if England went to war. Smuts supported them as a rule, but in the rural districts, where Afrikaners preponderated, he wisely said that time would show them what to do and that Parliament would decide. Hertzog refused to make any statement on the issue. Glaring headlines in the Malanite press drew the people's attention to what it termed the advisability of the Union's keeping out of a war which did not concern it.

"Why," it demanded, "should we fight for Britain, the only country which has ever attacked us? At this rate, no matter where, when and why Britain chooses to fight, we shall *ipso facto* be embroiled too." Hertzog remained silent. Smuts remained watchful, and so the Union moved rapidly towards the ineluctable end.

On September 1, in the early dawn, Hitler's mighty army swept into Poland. Two days after, France and Great Britain declared war on Nazi Germany.

Just before Hitler's act of aggression, members of the South African Parliament had been hurriedly summoned to Cape Town to extend for a month or two the life of the Upper House, which was about to reach the limit of its allotted span under the Constitution. Now the outbreak of hostilities demanded that Parliament decide between neutrality and active participation in the war. Actually it had no mandate from the people to come to any such decision as the question of neutrality (on which Smuts and Hertzog had agreed to differ), had never become a point in dispute, and people's minds had been set at rest by the so-called "academic" nature of the question. Legally Parliament had the right to declare war or otherwise.

At a Cabinet meeting held on September 3 Hertzog advocated a "qualified" neutrality, Pirow, Havenga, and three other ministers siding with him. On the other hand, Smuts plumped for war and carried with him six of his colleagues in the Cabinet. The Opposition had previously promised the Premier their full support in respect of a maintenance of neutrality.

On September 4 a hushed House, its galleries filled to capacity, was told that the Government, disagreeing on the neutrality issue, had irreconcilably split in two.

In an impassioned tirade Hertzog counselled the acceptance of a qualified neutrality. Then, rising quickly, Smuts addressed the Assembly. Hitler, he said, was out for world domination. He would demand South West Africa after Danzig, and then the security of the Union would be of little value. It would be suicidal for the Union, "poor as it is in defence, rich as it is in resources, to dissociate itself directly or indirectly from its associates in the Commonwealth."

When the vote was taken the Prime Minister's resolution was defeated by eighty votes to sixty-seven. Supplemented by a number of Hertzog's former supporters, Smuts's own followers had massed behind their leader in a solid phalanx.

Hertzog resigned. He requested the Governor General to dissolve Parliament. The petition was refused. Smuts was called upon to form a ministry and included Colonel Stallard and Mr. Walter Madeley, the leader of the depleted Labour party, in his cabinet.

War was forthwith declared on Germany.

Thus in his seventieth year Smuts plucked the fruit of years of planning, concession, and compromise: the subversion of neutrality at the eleventh hour, the resultant preservation of the Commonwealth's solidarity and, incidentally, the premiership. It was a masterpiece of strategy. It was a triumph of diplomacy.

SECTION VIII

66

Thus in the seventieth year of his life Jan Smuts was back in power after many years of waiting. In his old age he was called upon by the Governor General to lead South Africa, as Prime Minister and commander in chief of the nation's forces, in a titanic struggle which was to convulse the world.

The leaders of the English-speaking peoples of the Empire said fervently: "Thank God for Smuts!" For only *slim* Jannie had the power to overthrow "the great personal authority of General Hertzog," Prime Minister of the Union without a break since 1924; only he could have brought South Africa into the war; only he could have closed the ranks of the Commonwealth of Nations.

A prowar majority in Parliament could have been secured only with a substantial measure of Afrikaner support, and the greater part of the Afrikaner element which backed Smuts on the war issue would have backed no other man. At least 80 per cent of his Afrikaner followers in the United party of today are concerned not at all with party principles but with Smuts, their leader, whom they will follow blindly at all times and under all circumstances. Indeed, it has been an Afrikaner characteristic since the early days "to follow men rather than abstract principles," so that in the towns and villages of the Union and on the veld Afrikaners have called themselves Botha-men and Smuts-men or Hertzogites and Malanites, as the case may be, for several decades. Mainly for this reason it is difficult to imagine how the United party of today could exist without Smuts. His presence in it is altogether indispensable. He is irreplaceable. According to a well-known South African politician, "He is more than the leader of the party—he is the very soul of it; he has become more of a tradition than he is a human being. What General

251

Smuts has succeeded in doing in this country nobody else could get away with."

Hurriedly Smuts formed a cabinet. The majority of its members were chosen from the United party or what remained of it after Hertzog's defection, while to the Labour and Dominion parties, which had stood by him on the war issue, Smuts also gave representation. The veteran Labour leader, Walter Madeley, who, having fallen foul of Hertzog, had been ejected from the Pact Cabinet a dozen years before, became Minister of Labour and Social Welfare, while Colonel C. F. Stallard, leader of the Dominionites, received the portfolio of Mines. His ultraloyalty had caused him, a few years before, to break away from Smuts, whose liaison with Hertzog had filled him with doubt and mistrust. Smuts's determination, however, to stand by Britain had dispelled his suspicions. "I was addressing a meeting at Albert Falls in Natal," he said to an audience in Johannesburg soon after his elevation to cabinet rank. "In my speech I said there was one man who could lead the country on the right lines, and that was General Smuts. I pledged myself and the Dominion party to support a government formed by General Smuts if the Governor General sent for him.

"About half an hour after my speech I was called to the telephone at the local hotel. Someone wanted to speak to me. I picked up the receiver and to my astonishment I heard the voice of General Smuts speaking from Cape Town.

"He said: 'I am forming a new government and I want you to come and join me.'

"I immediately replied that I would be happy to do so, and left for Cape Town."

Smuts was working fast. By Tuesday, September 5, his Cabinet was complete. It contained, among others, sons of two ex-presidents of the Free State, one of whom, Deneys Reitz, had once said: "I rode behind General Smuts as a boy with a rifle on my shoulder and I have followed him since for forty years." But, after Smuts, by far the most important member of the new Cabinet was that brilliant young classicist, Jan Hendrik Hofmeyr, familiarly known as Klein (small) Jannie.

A few months after being expelled from Hertzog's Fusion Cabinet and ejected from the caucus of his party for having the courage to disagree on matters of principle with the intolerant and autocratic old Premier, J. H. Hofmeyr became Smuts's Minister of Finance and right-hand man.

In a ministry containing, among others, a few inexperienced men Hofmeyr was indispensable. It was generally felt, in the beginning, that the brunt of the more difficult administrative work would devolve upon his shoulders.

It was remembered that, from time to time, he had taken over half-a-dozen portfolios in the Hertzog Cabinet in the absence of other Ministers, and that he had, on these occasions, assimilated the essential details of administration in the departments concerned with amazing industry and lightning rapidity.

As an orator he has few equals in the English-speaking world. In the political arena he is regarded as the logical successor to Smuts.

Nephew of the famous Jan Hendrik Hofmeyr, by whom Smuts was sent to Kimberley to eulogize Mr. Rhodes before the Jameson Raid, he was an infant prodigy, matriculating brilliantly at twelve and taking separate degrees in literature and science with high honours when he was barely sixteen. A Rhodes scholarship took him to Balliol, where he was strikingly successful. Then followed successive professorships in classics at the Universities of Cape Town and the Witwatersrand, while he was still in his early twenties. Soon he became principal of the latter university. But, although he found an academic career highly satisfying, he forsook it before he had reached the age of thirty and became Administrator of the Transvaal at Smuts's invitation. Early in 1930 he entered Parliament as a member of Smuts's African party and became a power in the land.

Hofmeyr is the most successful public man of all Rhodes scholars the world over. He and Smuts are the most brilliant South Africans of their respective generations.

A lay preacher in the Baptist Church, he is deeply religious and transparently honest. He is handicapped somewhat as a politician by his high principles and religious scruples.

In the Union Cabinet he and Smuts are whales among minnows.

Not satisfied with the mere premiership, which, in truth, would have been sufficiently onerous in itself for any leader, particularly in those trying times, Smuts also shouldered the portfolios of External Affairs and of Defence.

No sooner had the essential groundwork been completed down at the Cape than he hurried north to Pretoria by plane to "test the loyalty of officers" at Defence Headquarters.

Throughout his long and arduous public life Smuts has, as a rule, taken gracefully the bitter with the sweet. Honours have been showered upon him in great profusion, and his name has been extolled throughout the English-speaking world. Among many of his fellow Afrikaners, however, he has been an object of hatred and derision for almost thirty years. Amid his victories and defeats, amid the hosannas of his friends and the execration of his enemies, he has had about him almost always that peculiar air of detachment which takes little account of either triumph or disaster, and he has proceeded with quiet dignity along his predetermined holistic path, unafraid. After his assumption of office under the novel circumstances obtaining in September 1939, he was seemingly unaffected both by the blandishments of the Natal jingoes, in whose eyes he had suddenly become *persona gratissima* because of his war policy, and by the bitter denunciation of the hostile Nationalists.

From the first he was called upon to face the combined strength of the Hertzog and Malan factions. All their bitter fury was concentrated upon his person while little attention was paid to his British colleagues and associates. For his enemies he epitomized at once all that was most evil in what remained of the United party. And his Afrikaner followers were regarded as being almost as bad. They were contemptuously dubbed the "loyal Dutch," despicable disciples of that "Arch-jingo," Jan Smuts, who, his detractors remembered with wicked glee, had been called the "greatest imperialist of the century" by the British press itself. "If there is one thing," said a young hothead, "of which the Afrikaner is more tired than of General Smuts, it is democracy." And Dr. Malan, speaking of his former Sunday-school teacher, said, "We are old enough, and we have experienced enough, to know a jackal when we see one." Referring to the German South West campaign of 1914, Colonel Jacob Wilkens, a Nationalist stalwart, said in the House that he and his brothers had gone to fight after having been deceived by Generals Botha and Smuts into believing that the Germans had attacked the Union. One of his brothers had been killed during the campaign. "General Smuts," he shouted finally, "is my brother's murderer!"

Thus in Parliament, in the press, and on public platforms was Smuts assailed and taunted by his enemies. But although he was strongly advised to muzzle the Opposition press and to take stern measures against his slanderers, he refused to do so. Unconcernedly he followed his star. "The dogs may bark," he once said, quoting an Eastern proverb, "but the caravan moves on."

What rankled particularly with the Malanites and the Hertzogites in the beginning was the ease with which Smuts had accomplished his coup on September 4, despite the strength of their opposition. Hertzog shrieked that Smuts's act had split the United party from top to bottom and had also debased the freedom of the nation to a nullity, and Dr. Malan maintained with his customary vigour that Smuts had not the right to rule since his accession to power had been tantamount to usurpation. Parliamentary usage demanded that the Government should go to the country if any change in its composition involved a fundamental change in the party itself. This had happened in 1921 with the amalgamation of the South African and Unionist parties, and again, in 1933, when there was a radical change in the political situation. Smuts held no mandate from the people. He was a usurper.

The Governor General's action in refusing to dissolve Parliament, when requested to do so by Hertzog, was severely criticized in the House, a particularly strong case being put up by Mr. J. H. Viljoen, a Nationalist member. The King, he averred, had never, in human memory, refused to dissolve Parliament. By what right had the Governor General done so? Indeed, at the Empire Conference of 1926 it had been decided to place the appointment of governors general in the hands of the Dominion cabinets, so that His Excellency was supposed to act exclusively on the advice of the Prime Minister. According to constitutional practice it had been incumbent on him to accept Hertzog's recommendation in regard to dissolving Parliament.

Towards the close of 1939 the *Cape Times* affirmed that the only strong sentiment common to the Hertzogites and the Malanites at the time was undoubtedly dislike of General Smuts. Be that as it may, a mere three months after war was declared the two factions were fraternizing, although it was manifest that the bitter antagonism which had divided them for six and a half years had not been completely dissipated. It could not be in the nature of things. Forcibly as Mr. Eric Louw, a Nationalist M.P., asserted that Smuts and his personal Afrikaner followers were the "imperialists, jingoes, and renegades," the Hertzogites could not help remembering that a few short months before they themselves had frequently been referred to by Mr. Louw's henchmen as "renegade Afrikaners." Nor could Dr. Malan *cum suis* forget General Hertzog's numerous scornful references to the Nationalist Opposition: indeed a mere six months before the irascible old general had spoken bitingly of "the leader of an Opposition of the smallest and pettiest party there has ever been in this country." However, in an effort to establish a United Afrikaner front with which to fight Smuts, the factions sank their differences and the Reunited National or People's party came into being with the septuagenarian Hertzog at its head. While agreeing with his deputy, Dr. Malan, that republicanism "is best suited to the traditions and aspirations of the South African people and is the only effective guarantee that South Africa will not again be drawn into the wars of Great Britain," Hertzog, nevertheless, endeavoured to exert a restraining influence upon that element in the new party which, thoroughly incensed by South

Africa's participation in the war, was determined to act drastically, if the need should arise, in the interests of Afrikanerdom's emancipation. The conviction that Hertzog would yield again to the British element and acute resentment at his fiery, autocratic ways were gradually to set the younger Nationalist leaders against the veteran. And in time he was to be ousted from the party. But before that took place much was to happen.

The immediate result, then, of Smuts's declaration of war was the formation of a racial bloc, determined, as a Stellenbosch professor said, "not to jump to attention when the British bugle blows" and equally determined to secede from the Empire as soon as possible. At Smithfield Hertzog told a large audience that by his participation in the war General Smuts had contributed more to the severance of all bonds with Britain than any other person since the days of Lord North. . . . By his destruction of the great United party Smuts had brought about a reestablished National Afrikanerdom.

Soon in every part of the country great demonstrations were held by excited Afrikaners hungrily clamouring for a republic. In July 1940 seventy thousand would-be republicans assembled at the Women's Memorial at Bloemfontein, which commemorates the deaths of Afrikaner women and children during the Anglo-Boer War, to demand that the Union secede from the British Empire. It was stated that plans had been made to establish a British republic in Africa in the event of the Allies' losing the war. It would comprise the majority of the British states on that continent. General Smuts would be the first President. Such wild talk was being indulged in freely throughout the Union.

Numerous demands for a republic reached the Prime Minister, who quietly ignored them at first. At length, however, he made a public declaration at Potchefstroom to the effect that it would be "dishonourable to accept a republic from Hitler." Whereupon much abuse was showered down upon his silvery head. One newspaper stated that when General Smuts spoke of its being dishonourable to accept a republic from Hitler, he was forgetting his own past. He was adopting the same attitude towards Germany that he had adopted towards Britain in the South African War. During the war, General Smuts had written to President Kruger condemning the atrocities of the British, yet later he had avowed his loyalty to the Union Jack. General Smuts was now condemning the German barbarity, but if Germany won the war, there would be nothing to prevent him from avowing his loyalty to the swastika. . . . His holistic philosophy always drove him to choose the side of the greatest and mightiest. By means of half-truths and poisonous innuendoes unscrupulous men among his opponents sought to undermine the Prime Minister's authority. But in spite of their most strenuous efforts he continued to dominate the South African scene.

Together with the demands for a republic came urgent appeals for a separate peace which were renewed with great importunacy whenever the Allies suffered a setback. This was particularly the case after the fall of France. A deputation of nine thousand women marched in procession to the Union Buildings in Pretoria to beg the Government to come to terms with Adolf Hitler. For all these clamorous voices Smuts had but one reply: to conclude peace with Germany would be a dishonourable act. Thereupon in Parliament Dr. Malan referred scathingly to Smuts's efforts at peacemaking during the Anglo-Boer War. "This," he cried, "is the man who prates of dishonour in respect of the Opposition and who talks of the French Government's peace overtures as an act of betrayal. There sits the Pétain of the Second Boer War of Independence!"

Meanwhile feeling ran high throughout the land: there were many serious clashes between civilians and soldiers; in point of fact, there were more casualties among soldiers in the streets of Johannesburg in the first week end of February 1941 than there had been among the South African troops shortly before at El Yibo in East Africa. Bomb outrages began to be common occurrences; there were frequent cases of sabotage. Meetings became wild and disorderly affairs, and at one of them the Minister for the Interior, Mr. Harry Lawrence, was severely manhandled and seriously injured. "Subversive elements" accused of plotting against the Government were removed from the police force—one day three hundred were taken into custody on the Rand.

Much of this unrest was attributed by Britishers to the machinations of an influential Afrikaner organization known as the Ossewa Brandwag (Sentinels of the Ox Wagon). In consequence of the symbolic Great Trek by ox wagon in 1938, the Federation of Afrikaner Cultural Societies had received a tremendous fillip. And at the same time the Ossewa Brandwag had come into being ostensibly with cultural aims, but, in actual fact, as a political organization, first and foremost. Gradually it developed into the most powerful Afrikaner organization that the Union has ever known. Its avowed purpose was to "set South Africa free" and to abolish the "democracy of the jingo-imperialist-Jew creation." Its political outlook was essentially National-Socialist. It clearly wanted Germany to win the war, for only in that event could it set up a republic in South Africa. At the beginning of the war it was hand in glove with the Reunited National or People's party, as Malan's party was now known. Indeed, tens of thousands of Afrikaners belonged to both organizations. But during the second half of 1941 all ardent Sentinels of the Ox Wagon broke away from the Reuniteds. By this time the United Afrikaner front of which Dr. Malan and General Hertzog had spoken so proudly a bare eighteen months before was non-existent: Hertzog had retired from politics in high dudgeon, and a handful of his closest friends had hived off to form the Afrikaner party; tens of thousands of Dr. Malan's followers were resigning from the People's party in order to give their full allegiance to the Ossewa Brandwag and its leader, Dr. J. H. van Rensburg. Mr. Pirow and a number of his totalitarian-minded friends in Parliament were showing signs of unrest in the People's party; subsequently, early in 1942, they swarmed off as Pirow's "New Order" Group to await hopefully the coming of *Der Tag*.

When asked in August of 1941 why he was so gentle in his treatment of these people, Smuts said with a smile: "Why should I hang them when they are cutting one another's throats?" He had never believed that a United Afrikaner front could last for any length of time, for he had known that the leaders would soon be quarrelling with one another as Afrikaner leaders had done for more than two hundred years.

67

"The most powerful Opposition South Africa has ever had has begun its offensive. In the first assault smashing blows have fallen upon the only strong fort in the imperialist lines, General Smuts. . . ." This was the general drift of leading articles in the Opposition newspapers a day or two after the opening of Parliament in January 1940.

At the time, it is true, no one doubted the potential strength of the Opposition, particularly in comparison with the relative weakness of the phalanx of largely inexperienced politicians arrayed on either side of Smuts and behind him. For that matter, even the Government press admitted that the first war session opened in an atmosphere of "great political uncertainty." But lack of harmony between the factions comprising the Opposition, rivalry between leaders of one and the same faction— as, for example, between General Kemp and Mr. Pirow—and the peevish intolerance of General Hertzog were factors which were seriously to impair the Opposition's striking power. And then—more important than all these factors put together—there was the inspired, fearless, and almost diabolically clever leadership of Smuts, the man who alone in South

Africa could "meet and beat the challenge of danger" to the Common-wealth of Nations. Not for nothing did Britishers the world over thank God for Smuts; not for nothing did Sir Charles Smith refer to him as "the only South African who could have survived such an impasse as that of last September"; not for nothing did Mr. Churchill pay a glowing tribute to "the great General Smuts of South Africa—that wonderful man with his immense and profound mind, his eye watching from a distance the whole panorama of European affairs."

No sooner had he, in the words of Mr. Peter Fraser, Prime Minister of New Zealand, "saved South Africa for the British Commonwealth" and closed the left flank of the Empire against the enemy, than he faced in the House an irate and potentially dangerous Opposition, snarling like a pack of wolves. After fifteen years he was back in the Prime Minister's bench—an old man with a grey beard and thin silvery hair, but with a healthy, ruddy face, pale, grey-blue, piercing eyes, and a superabundance of vitality. A lonely figure he looked there in that bench all by himself. But not a man to be pitied, despite the menacing attitude of the Oppo-sition. For Jan Smuts was the dominating personality in the House, and never throughout that first trying session and thereafter did he cease to be such.

With truth it has been said of him that "as a dialectician, as a con-jurer, building up a tremendous case on the flimsiest of premises, General Smuts has no rival in South Africa, or, for that matter, in the whole of the Anglo-Saxon world." This valuable gift he exploited with great effect, particularly during the early days of the war when the Opposition, bid-ding fair to become a devastating entity, was striving to encompass his downfall, when the political situation was still obscure and out of hand, and he was playing urgently for time. Calmly ignoring the main argu-ments of his enemies, he would seize upon unimportant weaknesses in their speeches and cleverly twist them into a seemingly strong case for himself. Such and other dialectical devices he could use with great effect, to the undisguised disgust of members of the Opposition and the secret envy of friend and foe alike.

With the passage of time the situation eased somewhat and the big guns of the Opposition fired with less certainty. Smuts even managed to spike some of them. Mr. Pirow was one of these.

A fine athlete, a first-rate orator, and the possessor of a strong per-sonality, Oswald Pirow was Minister of Defence in Hertzog's Fusion Cabinet and regarded by Smuts before the war as one of the "coming leaders of the country." 'As an administrator," said the London *Sunday Times* in October 1938, "he probably has no superior in the British Empire." At the time, in fact, Britishers in South Africa regarded him as "the blue-eyed boy of the Cabinet." There was no gainsaying his ability. There was no doubting the power he wielded. Even those members of the United party who were not enamoured of him nevertheless respected him. His popularity and influence with the Fusionists was considerable.

When, however, at the time of the civil war in Spain he visited Franco's headquarters instead of calling on the Republican Government, thereafter gave expression to the opinion that "Germany should be a colonial power in Africa," and interviewed Hitler without subsequently divulging to the world what had transpired at the meeting—when, in short, he began to show manifest signs of totalitarian bias, his British friends began to look askance at him. And when at the outbreak of the war he sided with Hertzog on the neutrality issue, they became openly hostile towards him, chiefly because they feared him, and they began to speak scornfully of him as the "little Hitler of South Africa" and the "Pocket Führer." And because he had been Minister of Defence, and the outbreak of hostilities found South Africa wholly unprepared for war, Smuts's followers turned fiercely upon the former "blue-eyed boy," blamed him alone for the state of the Union's defences, and started a whispering campaign against him, alleging that "he had intended to lead a rebellion in the country with the support of the Defence Force."

At the beginning of the war, it is true, South Africa's army and air force were in a deplorable state, although large sums had been voted by Parliament for defence. But Mr. Pirow's former colleagues should have known all about the state of affairs obtaining in the Defence Department from 1933 to September 1939. If they did not, it was most reprehensible. One would think that General Smuts, at any rate, concerned as he was about the war clouds fast gathering in the north, would have made it his business to be in possession of all the facts. Perhaps he was. Perhaps it was only Hertzog's touchiness on the neutrality issue which had prevented him from insisting on drastic defence measures in the trying and uncertain days of the Fusion Cabinet.

In the circumstances, however, it was imperative to make a scapegoat of Mr. Pirow. The man was dangerous. He had to be killed politically. And so Smuts encouraged the attacks on him and studiously ignored his demands for a select committee to institute a thorough investigation. "I ask Mr. Pirow," said one of Smuts's followers, "is it true or not that secretly when he was Minister of Defence he sabotaged our defence by pressing a policy of neutrality? If that is so, it is not a case for a select committee, but we should ask the House to impeach him for his neglect of duty." For days the storm raged round Pirow's head. Smuts attacked nobody else. At length the pugnacious and, ordinarily, eloquent Mr. Pirow was helpless with rage. He could not fight against this avalanche of criticism which was overwhelming him. He remained silent.

Thus by taking the offensive against Pirow in connection with the all-important matter of defence and wearing him down, Smuts deprived him of the confidence of most of the electorate and stripped him of his reputation for thoroughness and administrative ability. He was rendered innocuous. But this successful attack achieved more: it made men realize afresh the genius of Smuts as a parliamentary strategist; it gave confidence to his followers both inside the House and out; it upset the Opposition's applecart temporarily and threw them out of their stride; and it enabled Smuts to take the offensive elsewhere.

Using the weakness of the Union's defences and the country's serious lack of ordinary war material as pretext, Smuts now ordered all rifles and ammunition in the possession of private individuals to be handed in at magistrates' offices throughout the country. Obviously these weapons could not be used by the Army because of the great variety of pattern. The true reason for the step taken was to be found in the state of unrest prevailing in the country. The Government was anxious to prevent dangerous subversive activity on the part of disgruntled Afrikaners. There was, to be sure, a great outcry against this commandeering of rifles, particularly on the part of farmers in outlying districts where wild animals and natives were often sources of danger. But the trouble soon blew over. And Smuts, it was generally admitted, having disarmed the burghers, had strengthened his position substantially.

When the Nazis became masters of Norway there were severe repercussions in the Union. "Loyalists" demanded more internments and stricter measures generally against fifth columnists. Feeling ran high. There was much hysteria. There was also much irresponsible talk. "Only General Smuts," it was observed, "remained silent while these things were going on. He remained silent but watchful. Always planning to outwit his enemies. Always ready to grasp an opportunity to disarm the Opposition of criticism and power."

The opportune moment for emergency regulations presented itself. He seized it and a heated debate followed. In his bench the Grey Cardinal sat listening to the voices of his enemies raised in heated condemnation of the measure. He was unmoved by the venomous attacks made upon his person. Calmly he contemplated the scene as he bided his time. Then, suddenly, the moment arrived for which he had been waiting. The Opposition had spent itself. Mr. Pirow was in the House. Smuts caught the speaker's eye and rose to reply to his critics. He drew the members'

attention to much more drastic regulations which had been formulated
by Mr. Pirow, as Minister of Defence, for just such an emergency. . . .
Mr. Pirow's regulations were, in reality, martial-law regulations—a
vigorous control of the press, the usurpation of power, the taking over of
broadcasting, the banning of listening to foreign broadcasts and of foreign
news—regulations that looked perilously like the methods of the Gestapo.
Yet the man who proposed them, Mr. Pirow, was still allowed by the
present Government a freedom of speech unknown to any order of government save a democracy.

Almost all along the line Smuts proved too subtle and crafty for his
opponents. He managed skilfully to disarm them at very nearly every turn.
The War Measures Bill was introduced at a time when the Opposition
was becoming formidable in consequence of a *rapprochement* between
the Malan and Hertzog factions. When they were about to launch a carefully prepared, violent onslaught on the bill, Smuts wisely deleted from
it the specially vulnerable plenary-powers clause, much to the disgust of
his enemies, whose plan of attack had been built up round that particular
clause. Their chagrin was all the greater when they realized that the
Prime Minister could well afford to drop the plenary-powers clause since
future emergency regulations, promulgated when required, could furnish
him with almost any powers he desired.

The strongest man in the Opposition and Smuts's most relentless politi-
cal enemy and devastating critic is the friend of his boyhood days, Dr.
D. F. Malan. He and Smuts are the chancellors respectively of the
Universities of Stellenbosch and Cape Town. The former institution is
overwhelmingly pro-Nationalist Afrikaner, and the latter strongly pro-
British.

68

More so even than in the 1919–24 period, Smuts is today not only the
Prime Minister of South Africa but the whole Government. He wields
more power by far than he did during his first premiership by virtue of
the solid phalanx supporting him in Parliament on the war issue and of
the scores of emergency-war regulations which have made him the virtual
dictator of South Africa. Everything in the Union revolves around the
dynamic personality of Jan Smuts. His hand is upon every pulse. He controls everything and everybody. His spirit broods over the land.

No sooner had Parliament assembled in 1940 and Smuts taken his seat on the Prime Minister's bench than the House became aware of the fact that he was determined to exercise almost absolute power. The old Smuts, who had always regarded Parliament as a nuisance, was back in the saddle again. He felt convinced that he could rule the country best without the "interference" of the two Houses, particularly in wartime. Forthwith he set limits to the debate on the all-important War Measures Bill by employing the "guillotine"; never, during his most autocratic moods in former days, had he made such abundant use of the Closure of Debate; and in order to bring the session to an end before the middle of May, he compelled the House to sit in the mornings, in the afternoons, and at night, even before it had passed the Estimates, and he determined to rush through Parliament during the last ten days of the session a great deal of work relating, *inter alia,* to the Electoral Laws Amendment Bill, the Advertising and Ribbon Amendment Bill, the Industrial Development Bill, the Unemployment Benefit Amendment Bill, the War Pensions Bill, the Income Tax Bill, and the Rents Amendment Bill. "How General Smuts," said a Nationalist member, "expects to press all this work into so short a space of time, without forcing a tired and rushed House to pass ill-considered legislation, is beyond all understanding. One wonders what would happen in Great Britain if the Premier should decide to ride rough-shod over his Opposition, force the British Parliament to pass important legislation in a haphazard way, and then send Parliament home for seven months." Even a strongly pro-Government paper, *The Forum,* referred regretfully, on May 11, 1940, to Smuts's "steam-roller methods applied during the past few weeks." To the question, asked repeatedly, as to why he was so anxious to bring the session to a close, the Prime Minister vouchsafed no reply.

The session was a stormy one and probably one of the most tiring and unpleasant ones in Smuts's experience. The following one was of a similar nature, but it furnished the Prime Minister with one of the most pleasing —if rather amazing—incidents in his life. One afternoon he was sitting back in his bench gazing thoughtfully at the floor when all of a sudden he heard Dr. Malan say: "I wish to pay a compliment to the Prime Minister. The Prime Minister does not often receive compliments from me, but I intend paying him one this afternoon." And he went on to thank Smuts on behalf of the Opposition for his "conciliatory attitude over the question of summoning Parliament." The Prime Minister's face lit up with pleasure. It was a novel experience indeed for him to receive a compliment from Dr. Malan. "Thank you," he said quietly.

Because he frequently reacts to a situation quite differently from the way one would expect a man to react and because of his autocratic ways, some of the ministers—the younger ones in particular—are afraid of Smuts, much in the same way as schoolboys are afraid of the headmaster. Therefore, when they wish to obtain a few days' leave, more often than not they avoid facing him by asking one of his secretaries to get permission for them. Even the Prime Minister's wife and children stand in awe of him to this day, and Mrs. Smuts sometimes finds it necessary to approach him through his chief private secretary. But at times, when Smuts is in a bad temper, no one but his personal stenographer, Mrs. du Toit, will dare to enter his room. She invariably gets a good reception. "My child," Smuts said to her one day, "I am always glad to see you."

Although he has mellowed a great deal, Smuts is still a hard taskmaster. He demands the highest degree of efficiency from his subordinates, but he has ceased to take things for granted as he did twenty years ago. He is more human and frequently shows appreciation for services rendered. He is both considerate and kind to competent civil servants in his departments.

Mrs. du Toit is a very efficient stenographer. She has served Smuts since her seventeenth year. "He's been a wonderful chief," she says. In 1937 she resigned to get married. Smuts asked her to stay on until after the elections.

"But, General," she said, "I can't put off my marriage any longer."

"I don't want you to do that," replied Smuts. "But I want you to stay on for a while."

Thirteen months after her marriage her husband had a stroke, since when he has not spoken again and has always required a trained nurse in attendance. On being told of the tragic occurrence, Smuts immediately tore up Mrs. du Toit's letter of resignation, sent in three months before, and said: "You will remain in the service, and your salary increments will continue as though you had never resigned." Ordinarily a female civil servant who resigns in order to get married must begin at the bottom of the ladder on resumption of service.

Whenever the Government moves the one thousand miles from the executive to the legislative capital, Smuts's stenographer is provided with a free ticket for her husband. Even at the beginning of 1941, when he was extraordinarily busy with affairs of state, Smuts remembered to say to one of his secretaries: "See that Mrs. du Toit gets a ticket for her husband."

The stenographer tells another very human story about the Prime Minister. "I had cashed my monthly salary check some time in 1937," she says, "and put the money in my bag. I then happened to go out for two minutes, and on my return found that the money had been stolen. I did not tell the general about this, although I was terribly upset. But Mr. Louis Esselen happened to come into the room, heard of my predicament, and insisted on telling the general. Soon after the latter rang for me and said smilingly, 'My child, we'll have to send a hat round for you.' A little while later he rang for me again to take out some letters, and when I looked through them, there was a letter for me containing a check covering my salary—a personal gift from General Smuts."

In spite of the "air of lofty reserve and cold indifference" which ordinarily clings to him like a garment, Smuts unbends from time to time. Just before Christmas, 1939, a senior man in the Prime Minister's department came up to one of Smuts's private secretaries and said that in past years the staff had always managed to persuade General Hertzog to go along on Christmas Eve to a little "beer drink." He wondered whether Smuts would join in. On being asked whether he would, the latter said, "Yes, with great pleasure." At the function he made a neat speech, mentioning sharp cleavages in politics and saying that he did not mind what the politics of members of his staff was. All he asked of them was efficiency and loyalty.

When Christmas Eve, 1940, was drawing near, the Prime Minister received another invitation. But he said in his brisk, staccato manner, "No, no. It will be altogether wrong." When he was asked whether the staff had offended him, he replied, "No, no. But last time I was with you. Now I must give the party." He invited everybody, including the messengers, and a most enjoyable party was held at Libertas, the Prime Minister's new official residence in Pretoria. After one of the men had made a speech to thank Smuts, he reciprocated. He thanked his guests for coming and for the work they had done during the past year, and reminded them of what he had said at the previous party, adding that he was aware of the fact that some members of his staff held political opinions differing from his own but that their work had not been affected. He created an excellent impression.

Libertas was named by the Prime Minister himself after a historic farm a few hundred yards away from Mrs. Smuts's birthplace at Stellenbosch. It is a sumptuous residence, which has housed many distinguished guests since the outbreak of the war, the Greek royal family among others. The room which the King of Greece occupied is now known as the "King's room." In it hangs Kazdy Kovac's "Autumn Landscape." A dressing room, a bathroom, and a private balcony leading from it make it one of the most desirable bedrooms in the house. There are, however, also several other luxurious bedrooms. It is typical of the simplicity of Smuts and his dislike of luxury that he chose for himself the smallest and least convenient room in the building. It was originally intended to be a sewing room. It contains a single bed and a modest teak suite.

The Smuts family rarely stay at Libertas. They much prefer the homeliness of their wood-and-iron home at Doornkloof. Mrs. Smuts was delighted when the Prime Minister flatly refused to move into the new official residence.

Smuts's kindness to subordinates and his delightful simplicity often go hand in hand. His chauffeur has dined with him on numerous occasions. Moreover, when the man drives the Prime Minister about, he frequently takes his wife and children with him on the front seat of the big Cadillac. He is treated like a member of the family by both General and Mrs. Smuts. The latter even calls him by his Christian name. This ultra-democratic facet of Smuts's complex character has astonished many people and delighted not a few.

In October 1940 he had to go to a village called Settlers to receive three thousand pounds collected for the South African Spitfire Fund. He was accompanied by his chief private secretary and the latter's wife.

On their way to Settlers they stopped at Doornkloof for lunch. A reporter who had been detailed to "cover" the function drove along with Smuts's bodyguard of detectives in a police car, which arrived at the farm immediately after the Prime Minister's. As he was escorting his guests to the house, Smuts turned to his chauffeur.

"Have you had lunch yet?" he asked.

"No sir," replied the man.

"Well, come on," said Smuts. And then he noticed the reporter, O'Connor, hovering sheepishly in the background, and he called out pleasantly, "Come on! What are you standing there for? Come and have lunch!" And all of them sat down at the same table—Prime Minister, reporter, chauffeur, and the others.

To General Hertzog, who has slandered and vilified him times without number, Smuts has shown much consideration in recent years. One of the first things he did when he came into power in September 1939 was to place at the ex-Premier's disposal one of those special railway coaches to which, normally, only ministers are entitled. Some months later, on the occasion of his opponent's birthday in 1940, he crossed the floor of the House, shook Hertzog heartily by the hand, sat down beside him, and conversed with him for some time in a very friendly manner. When, subsequently, Hertzog resigned his seat in Parliament and went into retirement, Smuts secured for him a pension of two thousand pounds per annum.

69

OF ALL the leading statesmen in the world, young and old, none is more active mentally than Smuts is today in his seventy-third year and few are as active physically. Never has the South African Premier worked harder than he has since September 4, 1939. Never has he lived more strenuously. Yet he appears to thrive on it all.

In June 1940 Air Chief Marshal Sir Robert Brooke-Popham visited the Union to discuss with Smuts an important air-training project. He said afterwards: "The more difficult the outlook becomes, the younger, the more active, the more alert General Smuts seems to be. I was immensely struck by his recuperative powers. After a very hard week he went out to his farm at Irene.

"I saw him one Sunday spending the whole of the morning walking round his farm. Here he was, young and active, playing with one of his grandchildren, talking about the land and the cows, and ready for a fortnight's really strenuous action.

"There on the land, in touch with Africa, he seemed to throw off every other care and be absorbed by his farm and his grandchild. We went for a walk in the garden, and in a moment he was discussing with lively interest and acute insight the affairs of Europe."

A few weeks after, wild rumours were circulating in regard to Smuts's health. The Prime Minister has suffered a stroke. . . . General Smuts is on the point of a nervous breakdown. . . . He has collapsed in his office. . . . The rumours were malicious ones. They gained widespread credence, mainly because of wishful thinking on the part of the Prime Minister's enemies.

In actual fact Smuts was enjoying his usual rude health at the time and going for regular twelve-mile walks across the countryside at Irene, clad in an ancient pair of trousers, thick boots, a shapeless hat, and an old khaki shirt with buttonless sleeves flapping untidily in the breeze.

The false reports about his health reached his ears. "So?" he said, looking quizzically at his informant. "Now please return these two books. They are most interesting." And he passed on *The Negro's Struggle for Survival* by Holmes and another book called *The Culture of the Organs*. As he turned to his work again he looked up suddenly. "How many doctors do they say are attending me?" And, without waiting for a reply, he added, "But some people do imagine ridiculous things." And a second or two later he was hard at work again.

Both at Groote Schuur and at Irene Smuts rises well before seven o'clock, takes a stroll, and reads the pro- and anti-Government morning papers. He generally skims through the evening papers while driving home for dinner. When Parliament is in session in Cape Town he arrives at his offices punctually at 9 A.M., works steadily up to 12.45 or 12.55 P.M., and then walks across Parliament Street to have lunch at the House. At 2.15 P.M. Parliament assembles. Smuts attends debates punctiliously, rarely absenting himself from any of them. When the House adjourns at 6 P.M. he drives out to Groote Schuur to dine, but is back again at eight o'clock to attend to his duties, and leaves for home only when the day's work is done. On his return to Groote Schuur he reads for a while or works, and then goes to bed. He used to sleep outside; but now, for security, he sleeps indoors.

There are always detectives about him. He was quite unreasonable in the beginning when the commissioner of police sent men to guard him. On one occasion at Irene he shooed off a detective quite angrily, and it was only after the police chief had had a heart-to-heart talk with him that he yielded to persuasion.

In Pretoria Smuts works even harder than in Cape Town. His office hours are certainly much longer. One of his private secretaries tells of an instance where he left his office at twelve-fifty to have lunch on his farm at Irene. "He must," says the secretary, "have arrived there at the earliest at one-ten, have had lunch, and have left at the latest at one fifty-five, as he was back at the office at two-fifteen, and he brought back to me seven letters to post!"

Even Smuts's week ends are strenuous. On Saturday afternoons he generally has to attend functions, such as fetes, bazaars, and garden parties. He finds all these affairs very boring, as he is not yet by any means socially inclined. He much prefers to walk his ten to twelve miles on a Saturday afternoon at a very brisk pace. As a rule he attends to his personal correspondence on Sunday mornings. He does not make as much use of stenographers as he should. He writes out all his personal correspondence, which is tremendous, since even today he corresponds with philosophers, botanists, statesmen, and others in many parts of the world as well as with his cronies in the Union. Hertzog used to keep open house on Sunday afternoons at Groote Schuur. This tradition has been carried on by Smuts, and, as a rule, crowds of people gather on the broad stoep of the great house or in the spacious reception rooms. But the Prime Minister does not enjoy these gatherings.

Apart from his parliamentary labours and the ordinary routine work connected with his departments, Smuts is called upon to fulfil many other duties. He often speaks in public and on the radio; he addresses troops going north or sailors on board British warships that call at South African ports. He is in constant touch with the imperial Government in an advisory capacity; he has frequent consultations with important visitors from overseas—he held weighty discussions some months ago with the Greek and Jugoslav governments, and before that with General Wavell, who flew down from Egypt to see him. Day after day he has to perform a multiplicity of duties. Yet amid all the toil, trouble and responsibility, inseparable in these critical days from his high position, he has not lost interest in the ordinary things of life. Not very long ago an American newspaper informed its readers that, when Hiram B. D. Blauvelt of Oradell, New Jersey, special correspondent for the New York *Herald Tribune,* returned from South Africa, he had brought with him a collection of seeds of various African grasses, a gift from Prime Minister J. C. Smuts to President Roosevelt. One of the types, star grass, had runners fifty-three feet long at three months; a teaspoonful of the seed would plant eleven acres. General Smuts had thought the grass might be useful in the drought areas.

Smuts's ability to shed care and responsibility at will makes it possible for him at his age to live an abnormally active life and do what he does. "I have seen him working under unbearable pressure," says his chief private secretary, "from 9 A.M. to 12.55 P.M., then we'd go over with a few people to lunch at the House. General Smuts would switch off completely and talk about things not remotely connected with his work. His conversation would depend on the people present. If erudite, he might discourse on philosophy and kindred subjects. On the other hand, again, should his guests be farmers or veterans of the Boer War, his conversation would comprise tales of that harrowing period, or he would talk about agricultural problems. At two o'clock he would be working at full speed once more."

Smuts's amazing physical fitness at the age of seventy-three, despite his strenuous way of living, is due to numerous factors. Among the most important of these are undoubtedly his ascetic habits and his love of vigorous exercise in the open. It is characteristic of him that, while scores of men half his age get to the summit of Table Mountain by means of the cableway to attend the South African Mountain Club's annual memorial service to members who fell in World War I, General Smuts, who regularly attends this service, invariably climbs the three thousand feet to the mountain's flat top and then walks briskly to the rendezvous at Maclear's

Beacon. "I have never been up the cableway," he says with a twinkle in his eye. "I've always been too nervous to do so."

70

WHEN SMUTS TOOK OVER the reins of Government important tasks awaited him. Greatest of all was the establishment of an effective war machine to protect South Africa's shores and to guard her northern boundaries.

After taking prompt measures against internal subversive elements by locking up dangerous Union Nationals as well as aliens in hastily established internment camps, setting guards over all key positions and essential services, and promulgating the first batch of emergency regulations, Smuts began to consider the task of building up a war machine.

He was compelled to start from scratch, as there were no army and air force to speak of. Though the man in the street had fondly believed that the Union possessed a national reserve consisting of one hundred thousand men, such a reserve was, in fact, non-existent. There were only thirty-nine thousand "reasonably trained men" in the Army. There were hardly any instructors. In the air force there were a fair number of well-trained pilots, but except for two high-speed bombers they had no modern equipment with which to face the enemy. Two armoured trains, two obsolescent armoured cars, and two obsolete tanks were the sum total of South Africa's *panzer* units. There was a staggering shortage of artillery. While Cape Town and Durban were reasonably equipped with coastal guns, East London and Port Elizabeth were wholly unprotected. Such, then, was the state of affairs in respect of the Union's defence equipment when Smuts assumed the premiership. It is said that Hitler laughed when he was told that South Africa had declared war on Germany.

Smuts's first task was to create a seaward defence force to carry out anti-submarine duties, sweep enemy mines from South African waters, and establish regular coastal patrols.

Then he tackled the problems confronting him in regard to the building up of an army and an air force, "designed specifically to protect the northern frontiers of Kenya and Uganda." "For the protection of our country," said Smuts, "the protection of those territories to the north of us against any attack is a vital and an essential condition to the safety of the Union itself."

He became commander in chief of the Union's forces with Sir Pierre van Ryneveld as his chief of staff. He appointed General J. J. Collyer his military secretary, and Colonel C. H. Blaine became the new Secretary for Defence.

There was a great response to Smuts's appeal for volunteers. Men flocked to the colours by the thousands. Instructors-to-be were speedily trained in the methods of modern warfare and then drafted to the various training camps which had been hurriedly established all over the Union. Before long the new army was rapidly taking shape.

Meanwhile equipment had to be obtained for the soldiers. At the outbreak of war the only armament factory in the Union was a very small one at the Royal Mint. It manufactured .303 ammunition in very limited quantities. A great armament industry had to be created, new factories erected and old ones reorganized to supply the new army with the majority of its requirements. Smuts appointed Dr. H. J. van der Byl, the very efficient managing director of the South African Iron and Steel Corporation, as his Director General of War Supplies.

Soon the War Supplies Organization was in its stride. Dr. van der Byl was given what was tantamount to "authoritarian powers over industry." His organizing ability proved to be without precedent in South African industrial life. Before long scores of factories were working at top speed producing uniforms, blankets, helmets, boots, socks, sleeping bags, buttons, shirts, badges, and food. And from great armament works poured an ever-growing stream of howitzers, shells, bombs, hand grenades, portable airplane hangars, girders for bridge building, armoured vehicles of various kinds (of which certain parts came from America and Canada), and dozens of other essentials.

From Great Britain also and from the United States came much war material of the kind that could not be manufactured in the Union. A large number of bomber and fighter planes were landed at South African ports and Smuts's air force grew into a formidable fighting machine.

A year later General Wavell stated that the "Springbok army was the best equipped of all his forces in the north."

And the Union became known as the "great repair shop of the Middle East," for, in addition to producing large quantities of war material, South African factories renovated and repaired large numbers of engines of war that had been damaged in the north.

On June 10, 1940, as night was falling, Mussolini brought Italy into the war. Gesticulating fiercely, he shouted: "Italy has done all she possibly can to arrest this terrible war. Today we have decided to confront the risks and sacrifices of war. . . . This is the hour of irrevocable decisions."

Early next day the South African Air Force launched an attack from bases in Kenya on military objectives in his Abyssinian empire and wrought much damage. After this first assault Yavello, Bardera, Kismayo, Mogadishu, Neghelli, and many other Italian bases were continually bombed with telling effect. Sir Archibald Sinclair said subsequently: "When the Italians come to draw up a list of the factors that caused them to lose their East African Empire, they will place the South African Air Force somewhat near the top of that list."

Men like Jackson, Kershaw, Theron, Quirk, Driver, Pare, and Frost battered Mussolini's much-vaunted *Regia Aeronautica* to pieces over Abyssinia, Italian Somaliland, and Eritrea, and then proceeded to try conclusions with the Luftwaffe over the Western Desert.

Meanwhile Smuts's new army had come north to Kenya to pit themselves together with their British comrades against the Italian legions in Abyssinia. The army comprised Afrikaans- and English-speaking South Africans in the strange proportion of 70 to 30. The general officer commanding in East Africa was General D. P. Dickinson, who was afterwards superseded by General Cunningham.

All the world knows the splendid record of the Union forces in Abyssinia, their later triumphs in the Western Desert at Sollum, Bardia and Halfaya Pass, and their epic stand at Sidi Rezegh.

The South African Army and Air Force more than justified themselves. Their achievements constituted a personal triumph for their commander in chief, Field Marshal Smuts.

It was on his seventy-first birthday that the King honoured Smuts by creating him a field marshal. Many years previously both he and Botha had declined to become peers of the Realm. "Baron Botha of Rusthof" and "Lord Smuts of Doornkloof" were titles that would have sounded strange to Afrikaner ears. After this refusal Smuts had been the recipient of many honours, but the field marshalship was, perhaps, to him the crowning honour of his life.

On September 30, 1941, he received from the governor general of the Union his field marshal's baton. At the same time he was handed a letter from His Majesty:

MY DEAR FIELD MARSHAL,

I was hoping to present your field marshal's baton to you personally in England, but I well understand the reasons why you do not want to be away from South Africa for so long at the present time.

I am, therefore, asking the Governor General as my personal representative to hand it to you on my behalf.

I would like you to know how proud my field marshals are to count you among their number.

With all good wishes believe me, yours very sincerely,

GEORGE R. I.

"He [Smuts] is a great rock in a weary land," said Sir Patrick Duncan as he made the presentation.

71

ALTHOUGH he could hardly afford to leave the Union—where his presence has been the chief guarantee against serious trouble since the beginning of the war—Smuts flew north to East Africa and Egypt on several occasions in 1940 and 1941 and again in 1942 to visit the South African troops and hold consultations with the British Ministers of State and military leaders in the Middle East.

Arriving at Doornkloof late one afternoon, early in November 1940, he said to Mrs. Smuts, "I may pay a visit to our boys up north."

"Good," was the reply; "but don't rush about too much! What you need is a holiday."

A couple of days later at sunrise Smuts, accompanied by Sir Pierre van Ryneveld, flew north in a fast American bomber piloted by his personal pilot, Colonel Pieter Nel, a stockily built veteran airman with more flying experience than any other South African, having flown more than one and a half million miles with a record of over eleven thousand hours.

In Kenya Smuts was joined by Sir Alan Cunningham, the new commander in chief of the forces in East Africa. Together they visited the front and inspected the various outposts by plane, closely protected by a number of South African Air Force fighters against a possible attack from *Regia Aeronautica*. At one of the numerous encampments near the Abyssinian border Smuts visited his second son, Second Lieutenant Jan Smuts, who received from him several packages sent by Mrs. Smuts.

While in Kenya Smuts attended functions, made speeches, walked long distances through the bush, inspected troops in the field and hospitals at the bases, and held lengthy consultations with army chiefs—all in the space of a couple of days. Almost everyone remarked on his cheerfulness and astounding energy.

Having completed his tasks in East Africa, he headed north again to meet Mr. Anthony Eden at Khartoum for discussions. Mr. Eden found him "amazingly vigorous and looking twenty-five years younger than his actual age." While their talks were in progress the temperature was 118 degrees in the shade. It is said to "have affected Mr. Eden more than it did General Smuts."

The British Minister was much impressed by the South African Premier and said afterwards: "It was of the greatest value to me to be able to take counsel at Khartoum with a statesman of these rare qualities of vision, wisdom, and courage."

Four months later, in March 1941, Smuts flew north again. After a forced landing at Dodoma in Tanganyika, on the afternoon of the first day, the party headed for Nairobi. On the way they saw the majestic "Monarch of Africa"—as Smuts calls it—Mount Kilimanjaro, one hundred miles away. For years it had been Smuts's ambition to climb to the snow-clad top of the great mountain and look into its enormous crater, but the opportunity had never come his way and his years were mounting fast. At his request Colonel Nel now directed the airplane towards the mountain.

They circled round it higher and higher, said Smuts afterwards, until they passed low over the top at an altitude of about one thousand feet. Seldom had it been seen to such advantage, with the white glaciers gleaming clear in the morning sun, far above sparse, fleecy clouds. With his cine-kodak—given him as a birthday present by fellow members of Parliament—Smuts took a number of films which he hoped might not be quite unworthy of this grandest sight in Africa. . . .

Passing over the top of that mountain without any physical effort, and with nothing worse than a slight feeling of giddiness, proved one of his greatest experiences. He could—he added with a smile—now talk on level terms with his son, whose name was in the tin receptacle at the top of Kaiser Wilhelm Spitse with a few other names of successful conquerors of Kilimanjaro.

After spending a day at Nairobi the party flew north to Khartoum and then proceeded to Cairo.

On this occasion Sir Pierre van Ryneveld, chief of the South African General Staff, was again one of Smuts's companions. As the plane flew speedily across the vast continent Van Ryneveld's thoughts must have travelled back to those eventful days in 1920 when he and Sir Quentin Brand astounded the world by flying from the ancient land of Egypt to the Cape of Good Hope, and were knighted for their prowess.

In Cairo Smuts was welcomed by a number of important people. Among those present were Sir Miles Lampson, the British Ambassador in Egypt; Sir John Dill, chief of the Imperial General Staff; Sir Archibald Wavell, commander in chief of the Army in the Middle East; Sir Andrew Cunningham, commander in chief of the Mediterranean Fleet; Sir Arthur Longmore, commander in chief of the Air Forces in the Middle East; and the British Foreign Secretary, Mr. Anthony Eden.

At subsequent conferences "the whole Middle East position," says Smuts, "was passed in review."

Ten days after leaving for the north, Smuts entered the Houses of Parliament in Cape Town and took his seat unobtrusively, looking the picture of health.

In August 1941 the South African Premier travelled north again, accompanied on this occasion by Mrs. Smuts. The plane in which they travelled was an American Lockheed Lodestar machine, piloted by Colonel Pieter Nel and Major Len Inggs.

Once again a distinguished party welcomed the South African Premier on his arrival at Cairo. Among others there were General Sir Claude Auchinleck, the new commander in chief, Middle East; Air Marshal A. W. Tedder, air officer commanding Royal Air Force, Middle East; Lieutenant General Sir Thomas Blamey, commander in chief of the Australian forces and second in command in the Middle East; Admiral Sir Andrew Cunningham; and Captain Oliver Lyttelton, temporarily British Minister of State in the Middle East.

During their three days' stay in Egypt General and Mrs. Smuts were the guests of Sir Miles and Lady Lampson at the British Embassy. In between important conferences with the "war chiefs" Smuts inspected hospitals, the South African base camp, and the troops near Cairo, and also flew out to the Western Desert to visit the South African Air Force and the first and second South African divisions. He was met with "miles of cheers."

Addressing the soldiers from the Union, he said that he felt that the war in the Middle East was only beginning. The war would come to the Middle East in a far more serious way. After Russia, the Middle East and the Mediterranean might become the historic battlefields of humanity. "Here in the Middle East," he said, "will be the testing place—here the Armageddon."

The entry of Japan into the war seemed to confirm Smuts's belief that the greatest and decisive battles of this greatest of all wars would be decided in the Middle East, the Cradle of the Human Race.

72

THE EIGHTH ARMY or Desert Army (comprising companies and divisions from almost every part of the Empire) suffered a sudden and disastrous setback in North Africa in May, June, and July of 1942. Generals Auchinleck and Ritchie were hurled back swiftly by the intrepid Rommel, commander of the Afrika Korps.

Tobruk fell. Thousands of Smuts's finest soldiers were taken prisoner. South Africa was plunged into gloom. Smuts himself was utterly dejected.

The victorious Axis forces, after pushing the Desert Army back four hundred miles, depriving it of 80,000 men, and capturing tremendous quantities of transport, supplies, and munitions, were soon battering at the "Gates of Egypt." The position was a critical one.

It was only with tremendous difficulty that Rommel was halted at El Alamein by the heroic efforts of a thin line of Auchinleck's men entrenched behind fortified positions which the foresight of General Sir James Marshall-Cornwall had established in that desert waste.

From Russia, too, came disquieting news. In many sectors of the vast front the Soviet armies were crumbling before the devastating hammer blows of Hitler's powerful armies. From Stalin's suffering millions came insistent demands for a second front.

Towards the end of July Mr. Churchill decided to visit the Middle East and fly thence to Russia to have heart-to-heart conversations with Premier Stalin himself.

"The spirit of the troops [in the Middle East] was admirable," said Mr. Churchill subsequently, "but it was clear to me that drastic changes were required in the High Command and that the Army must have a new start under new leaders. I was fortified in these conclusions by the advice of the chief of the Imperial General Staff, who accompanied me, and also by the massive judgment of Field Marshal Smuts, who flew from Cape Town to Cairo to meet me and also, of course, to see the South African divisions which he had sent into the line."

As a result of the discussions in Cairo, Generals Alexander and Montgomery succeeded Generals Auchinleck and Ritchie.

Speaking of Smuts at a press conference in the Egyptian capital, Churchill said: "He is a wonderful man. . . . He flies at great heights without oxygen, and jumps out of his plane—almost leaping out of his skin with energy."

On August 10 Smuts was back in the Union. "The talks in Egypt," he said, "and the consequent conferences in Moscow are likely to have a far-reaching effect upon the conduct of the war generally."

Addressing the annual congress of the South African Gifts and Comforts National Organization at Pretoria on September 8, the South African Premier said: "The most vital theatre of this war is the Mediterranean base, and we cannot win this war without clearing this base." This had been the leitmotiv of his speeches for many months. He was the first to regard the Mediterranean "not only as a sea that is vital to the maintenance of British maritime security and imperial communications, but as a base . . . for offensive operation against the enemy, not on the African continent only, but also on the European mainland." To dominate the Mediterranean and, if necessary, strike at Germany through southeastern Europe where, economically, strategically, and politically, serious injury could most effectively be inflicted on her—that was the essence of the Smutsian vision.

In 1942 the Allied leaders were faced with two alternatives in respect of a second front. Smuts favoured a "pincer movement beginning on both sides of the Mediterranean"; others desired an offensive on the Western Front. The fact that it was decided to carry the former plan into execution was due, in no small measure, to Smuts's persuasive tongue and tremendous influence.

It was felt in England that Smuts's rare ability to view the war objectively and as a whole was lacking in practically all the other Allied leaders. After the Smuts-Churchill conversations in Cairo the South African Premier's all-embracing, holistic attitude to the war appears to have been adopted without reserve by Mr. Churchill who, heretofore, had shown a singular inability to visualize Allied strategy in terms of one strategic impulse co-ordinating the various campaigns into a single whole, and to direct it accordingly.

Smuts's plans for a tremendous offensive in North Africa were very soon to be carried into effect. The launching of large-scale attacks by American and British armies was to synchronize with the South African Premier's first visit to England for several years.

73

SMUTS DECIDED in August 1942 to go to England. His object was "the acceleration of the plans of high strategy in the general conduct of the war."

Heretofore he had declined many urgent invitations from Mr. Churchill to visit London for consultations, as he had been unable to venture abroad for any length of time because important matters required his personal attention at home.

Leaving Pretoria on October 8, he flew to Cairo in a Lockheed Ventura. He was accompanied by his son, Captain Japie Smuts, who acted as his aide-de-camp. A long-range bomber took them from Cairo to London, which they reached on October 13. A few minutes after his arrival Smuts drove off with Mr. Churchill to No. 10 Downing Street to attend a meeting of the War Cabinet.

In a statement published in the press next day he emphasized the importance of Africa in the war. "From the moment Germany launched her attack," he said, "we (the Union Government) appreciated its world-wide effects and that in that world struggle South Africa would occupy a key position.

"When Japan entered the war our concern for South Africa and the vital Cape route was extended to our communications in the Indian Ocean. We did not want a repetition of the Indo-China incident which finally resulted in the loss of Malaya and Singapore and the almost total collapse of the Allied position in the Far East.

"Our participation in the East African, the Middle East, and the Madagascar campaigns has been the result and, considering our slender resources, our contribution has had its value.

"More and more Africa is emerging as a dominant feature in our war strategy, on which the future outcome of the war will largely depend.

"I have, therefore, continued to emphasize to the best of my ability the importance of the African theatres of war. The central and vital position they occupy in our world-wide strategy is becoming plainer every day. . . ."

Smuts also declared that he felt convinced that with the resources the Allies then commanded victory should be theirs if they followed the right strategy with the utmost energy. . . .

For two years the British Commonwealth had stood alone, but there-after it had had the support of the heroic and truly colossal effort of Russia.

"And now with the grand American effort coming into full swing, we enter upon a new phase where the defensive can be replaced by the offensive and the war can be prevented from dragging on endlessly to the destruction of all the material apparatus of our civilization."

Smuts arrived in England at a "stern and sombre moment"—to quote Mr. Churchill's words.

"There has never," said an observer at the time, "been real despondency in this country about the war, but a certain grimness has entered into the English mentality in the last few months."

It was a grimness which the coming of Smuts did much to dispel. From Africa had come the man whose opportune arrival in 1917 had brought hope to the hearts of Englishmen. Then he had been hailed as "the destroyer of German power in Africa." Now he was lauded as the man who, in no small measure, had been responsible for Allied victories in Abyssinia and North Africa. He radiated vigour and energy. He inspired confidence. Here he was, boldly predicting "a new phase" of the war "where the defensive could be replaced by the offensive," at a time when the war situation appeared, at best, to be rather bleak.

"What a comfort he is," said a member of the British Government. "What a comfort he has been, and in the darkest days."

It had just recently become apparent to the observant that a new phase of the war was indeed about to begin: American troops had landed in the republic of Liberia on the west coast of Africa; the Italians and Germans were known to have removed the bulk of their troops from Chios, Lesbos, and Samos in the Aegean Sea to strengthen Rommel; and the Luftwaffe's furious attacks on Malta during the previous week were indicative of German and Italian fears about a new Allied offensive in North Africa.

The fact that Smuts's arrival synchronized with these signs was a significant one. It was freely commented upon in the press and elsewhere.

"General Smuts's first visit to London since the war began," said a diplomat, "is of the utmost significance since he has always been consulted on any major questions of strategy. . . . General Smuts's flying visits to Cairo invariably presaged important decisions which were sooner or later reflected in the field of battle."

The *Times* was enthusiastic in its welcome of Smuts. It said that often in the darkest hours through which the Empire had passed, often when purposes had seemed divided and the grand strategy uncertain, the thoughts of men had turned towards the great imperial figure of keen intellect, high courage, and wide experience of government and war. . . . His presence in London meant that one of the Empire's best judges had recognized the imminence of a great and, possibly, the greatest turning point in the war. . . . No other statesman still active in the leadership of the United Nations spoke with the authority of his great experience.

"Big things are brewing," wrote Mr. J. L. Garvin. "No ordinary call has brought him [Smuts] here. His arrival now is a conspicuous sign that the Allies mean business in a new sense. The sequel of his action cannot appear tomorrow. Neither can it be long retarded."

To England in a fateful hour had come "the father of African strategy," who emphasized that Africa was emerging more and more as a dominant feature in the Allies' war strategy. The man, it seemed, was there; and the hour was at hand. A tremendous Allied offensive in North Africa seemed about to be launched. Gault MacGowan of the New York *Sun* stated that the large crowds which had greeted General Smuts suggested that that straight, keen-eyed soldier was the man the public wanted to direct central strategy on the African front.

In the meantime, while Smuts's dramatic arrival in London was being widely discussed in the British Isles and across the seas, the South African Premier was experiencing one of the busiest periods of his life. He attended meetings of the War Cabinet (twice daily), the Defence Committee, the Privy Council, and the Pacific War Council, frequently returning to his hotel well after midnight; he had long talks at the War Office with the chief of the Imperial General Staff and the service chiefs; with the Allied governments' Foreign Ministers he discussed problems affecting their countries and the commonweal; Mr. Churchill and he addressed "the largest gathering of coal workers ever assembled under one roof, and one of the most dramatic and moving in the history of mining in Britain"; he spoke to "the biggest press conference yet held in London during wartime"; he made dozens of other speeches; in a striking address he suggested the formation of a "supreme anti-U-boat staff"; he broadcast in Dutch to the peoples of Belgium and Holland; he discussed financial and economic matters with experts, the "future of the League of Nations," and postwar reconstruction; he inspected all the most important centres of war production; he was received several times in audience by the King; he had talks with the kings of Yugoslavia and Greece and other royal personages, and with the Polish and Belgium

Prime Ministers, the United States Ambassador, the service chiefs, and High Commissioners of the Dominions, and scores of other men in high places; he rose early in the morning and, more often than not, retired late at night.

His energy was phenomenal; his stamina amazing. He was so busy that he was unable to go to Aberdeen to receive the freedom of that city. It was duly conferred on him by the Lord Provost, who came down especially to London for that purpose.

Here in the capital Smuts saw his grandsons, Richard and Jan Clark, for the first time. Aged four and seven respectively, they had come to London from Somersetshire with their parents, Mr. and Mrs. Bancroft Clark, to visit the general. He liked to have the boys with him whenever this was possible. Frequently, in his hotel, they would accompany him as he entered a room to meet "important visitors." On one such occasion Smuts said smilingly, "I get on splendidly with these young rascals, who seem to have appointed me an unofficial referee to settle their childish disputes."

Smuts's moments of leisure were few, but he found time to call on Mr. Lloyd George at Churt, to visit his old college at Cambridge, and to meet informally at South Africa House South Africans serving overseas. He was particularly pleased to have a few words with Squadron Leader John Nettleton, V. C., and the air ace, Wing Commander P. Hugo.

He also found great pleasure in renewing acquaintance with Mrs. Roosevelt, whose visit to England coincided with his. At the time he was being urged by Mr. Malcolm MacDonald, Mr. Averell Harriman, Mr. John Winant, and others to visit America. And there was much speculation as to whether he would avail himself of the President's invitation (issued several months previously) to visit the States.

"Are you perhaps bringing an invitation from the President to General Smuts to visit America?" a reporter asked Mrs. Roosevelt soon after she had come to London.

"But indeed," she replied, "General Smuts needs no invitation. He is more than welcome at any time. My husband is very fond of him, and we have great respect for him in America."

On October 15 Mr. Churchill informed the House of Commons that General Smuts "would address members of both Houses of Parliament soon."

Mr. Churchill: "We were sure that Parliament would like to have an opportunity of meeting this illustrious statesman and soldier while he is in this country. (Tremendous applause.) He has kindly consented to address members of both Houses on an early occasion."

Sir Percy Harris: "Will the press be admitted, and is it proposed to broadcast the speech?"

Mr. Churchill: "The idea is that Field Marshal Smuts will be able to speak not only to us but to the world."

On October 22, at 4.30 P.M., General Smuts entered the hall where one thousand people (members of the two Houses and other distinguished guests) had gathered to listen to the speech which had been widely publicized and which all the Allied nations were eagerly awaiting. The first Dominion Prime Minister to be accorded the honour of addressing members of the two Houses of the British Parliament, Smuts walked towards the platform behind the speaker, Captain Fitzroy, Mr. Lloyd George, Mr. Churchill, and Lord Simon, the Lord Chancellor.

Mr. Lloyd George (who presided) described Smuts as "one of the foremost statesmen of his generation." "No one," he said, "in calmness or discernment exceeds him in this age."

Smuts's speech, delivered in a calm, clear tone, was magnificent.[1] With that rare eloquence which characterizes only his important speeches, Smuts sketched masterfully the whole course of the war, giving cause and effect. He was confident about the outcome. He spoke feelingly about peace.

Significantly the South African Premier said: "Once the time has come to take the offensive, and to strike while the iron is hot, it would be folly to delay, to overprepare, and perhaps miss our opportunities. Nor are we likely to do so; of that I feel satisfied."

Proposing a vote of thanks, Mr. Churchill referred to the "comfort and inspiration of General Smuts's presence."

The speech was heard in all parts of the world. Extracts were translated into all the languages of Europe as well as dozens of others and broadcast.

Far away on the farm at Irene Mrs. Smuts listened in pridefully to the Oubaas, but Louis Weyers, a grandson, twelve years of age, soon became impatient and left the room. "Grandpapa's talking too much," he said, as he departed. "He's already talked for half an hour. Won't he ever finish?"

The Allied Nations received the speech with acclamation.

In the New York *Post* Dorothy Thompson stated that the speech "must be regarded as one of the great political documents of the. war.

[1]Full text in Appendix.

The philosopher on Table Mountain.

Courtesy, British Combine

Smuts addressing the two Houses of the British Parliament in London in October 1942. Seated, on his left, are Mr. Lloyd George, British Premier in World War I, Mr. Winston Churchill, and Lord Simon (the Lord Chancellor).

. . . In unequivocal words the South African leader announced the offensive."

Practically every newspaper in Great Britain was enthusiastic about Smuts's address.

From Washington came this report: "The speech was front-page news for most of the New York morning newspapers. American commentators say the speech justifies the conclusion that the United Nations are ready to take the offensive."

And so the United Nations were.

74

On friday, October 23, 1942, the British Eighth Army in Egypt, under the inspiring leadership of General Montgomery, struck unexpectedly and heavily at Rommel and drove him back relentlessly from the approaches to Alexandria and the Nile delta.

It was a tremendous assault (a "great thunderbolt of assault," as Mr. Churchill called it). In the forefront of the attacking army was Smuts's First Division, led by Dan Pienaar, most brilliant South African officer of the World War II and best beloved of all generals in the Middle East.

By November 10 the victorious Eighth Army was at Sollum and Sidi Barrani. Thousands of prisoners had been captured and much booty taken. Rommel was being driven forward mercilessly in headlong flight. By November 12 the Axis forces had suffered 59,000 casualties. On November 13 Tobruk was retaken by the Eighth Army, the South African armoured cars being the first to enter it.

To Danie Pienaar General Smuts cabled, "My hearty congratulations to you, General Pienaar, and our gallant South Africans on the reoccupation of Tobruk, which at last is properly avenged."

Retreating swiftly to the west, Rommel was given no respite. By January 23 the Axis forces had been hounded out of Libya, Tripoli had been taken, and Tripolitania was being cleared. On February 5 Eighth Army patrols had reached the Tunisian border.

Meanwhile, in almost complete secrecy, the "largest armada in history" had brought to North Africa a great American army, complete with stores and equipment.

On November 8 it was reported that landings had been effected "at various points on the Atlantic and Mediterranean coasts of French North Africa." At Oran and near Casablanca units of the Vichy French Fleet resisted stubbornly. On November 9 British troops landed at Algiers.

Meanwhile Admiral Darlan had assumed command of the French forces in North Africa. The "cease fire!" order came from him on November 11, after General Henri Giraud had arrived from France "to rally the French forces in North Africa on the side of the Allies." No sooner had resistance to the invading army subsided than the American Lieutenant General Dwight Eisenhower, commander in chief of the Allied army in French North Africa, pushed on towards Tunisia. Early in February only the "eastern coastal strip" of Tunisia was still in German hands.

Five months after Smuts and Churchill had met in Cairo to discuss the grave war situation, the fortunes of battle had changed completely: the great pincer movement in North Africa had been crowned with amazing success; the Russians, having destroyed a great Axis army of 330,000 men at Stalingrad, were tearing the enemy to pieces all along the vast Soviet front; in the Pacific zone the Americans were on top; Madagascar had fallen; the secret meeting of Mr. Churchill and President Roosevelt at Casablanca and the British Premier's subsequent conferences in Turkey with Marshal Cakmak and President Inönü presaged great events and were causing no little uneasiness in Axis circles.

Smuts was satisfied. The tide had turned at last.

75

RETURNING from England by air after the middle of November, General Smuts touched at Gibraltar. Here he discussed the North African campaign with Admiral Sir Andrew Cunningham, commander of the Allied naval forces in the Mediterranean, and General Eisenhower.

Having inspected the South African First Division and the South African Air Force in North Africa, he flew south to Pretoria, where he landed on the twenty-sixth, looking remarkably fit as he stepped briskly from his plane. With him he had a German helmet, which the South African Major General Frank Theron had sent along from the Middle East as a gift for Mrs. Smuts. A note attached to the helmet bore the legend *Rommel se stertvere* (Rommel's tail-feathers).

During Smuts's absence his sometime associate and life-long rival, General Hertzog, had died in Pretoria. Smuts expressed regret at not having been able to attend the funeral. "General Hertzog," he said, "maintained a standard of manliness, patriotism, and honesty which I hope will always be maintained in South Africa."

Speaking at a reception held in his honour in Johannesburg, Smuts referred to the war situation. "We have still hard knocks," said he, "and much hard work ahead, but victory is assured, and the end may come sooner than we expect. It will come suddenly, smashingly, and victory will be there like the dawn, almost before we know it is there."

On December 6 he broadcast a message to the British people. Having said that he was satisfied with the "planning and direction" of the war and having eulogized the British Empire and its "war machine," he paid a special tribute to Mr. Churchill: "In all practical matters," said Smuts, "I have found open-mindedness and single-mindedness in the Prime Minister, and fanatical inflexibility only in his objective of winning the war.

"May I conclude with one more word about him? To him, above all, the success—whatever it may be—of my visit has been due, and my deepest thanks are also due to him, my old enemy, and later comrade of a lifetime.

"Forty-three years ago I had to sit in judgment on him in the Boer War and condemn him to internment as a combatant passing under the guise of a press correspondent.

"I was right then; and ever since he has continued as a fighter, a combatant, in spite of the aliases of politics and literature. What else can one expect from a member of the tribe of Malbrouk?"

The day after his arrival from England, Smuts was hard at work in his office in the Union Buildings on the slopes of Meintjieskop in Pretoria. For days thereafter he laboured at his desk in order to bring his work up to date and presided at numerous Cabinet meetings where political and social problems were discussed and an agenda was drawn up for the approaching parliamentary session.

"The Prime Minister," said one of his Cabinet colleagues, "is in even better form than he was a year ago, and then he was amazingly vigorous."

On January 16, 1943, the South African Parliament went into session. It was obvious from the first that Smuts's position was even sounder politically than it had been in 1942. For that matter his position was practically unassailable. Never before in all the years of his political career had it been more secure. Thousands of those who were against him at the outbreak of the war were for him now. The Nazi juggernaut's ruthless invasion of Belgium and Holland; the Luftwaffe's savage destruction of Rotterdam and Belgrade; the wretched thraldom of the peoples of occupied Europe; the perilous position of small neutral countries in almost every part of the world; the Yellow Peril striking treacherously in the East and, at one time, threatening the strategically important harbours of South Africa—all these manifestations of evil and danger had struck cold fear into the hearts of large numbers of isolationists and had set them thinking along holistic lines. There were also other factors that contributed to Smuts's growing power: division in the ranks of the New Order and Afrikaner parties; the steady deterioration of the once-powerful Ossewa Brandwag; the fact that the exigencies of war had deprived the Nationalists of the strongest planks in their political platform; and the phenomenal successes of the Allies in many of the theatres of war.

On September 4, 1939, Smuts had defeated Hertzog and brought South Africa into the war by 80 votes to 67. It was a perilously narrow majority, but through bye-elections and resignations from the anti-war groups Smuts's working majority in Parliament increased to about 20 in a House numbering 150 elected members. Smuts's supporters claimed throughout that even this workable and fairly safe majority did not represent the true balance of sentiment in the country. The anti-war Oppositionists, on their side, claimed that the Government's majority in Parliament was fortuitous as no election had been held on the war issue. When the 1943 session of the Union Parliament drew to its close, Smuts decided to challenge the strength of their claim. The existing Parliament had run its allotted span of five years. Smuts could have extended its life by legislation, as had been done in the case of the British Parliament. He decided, instead, on a general election—and the result surprised even the most sanguine expectations of his confident supporters. The country returned 107 prowar candidates and 43 anti-war Nationalists, giving Smuts a clear majority of 64—a big step-up from the thirteen majority of September 4, 1939! Smuts's United Party alone secured a clear over-all majority of 28.

July 7, 1943, the date of the general election, gave Smuts the greatest triumph of his long and eventful life. As ever, he dominates South Africa and Parliament by the sheer force of his personality. He has a healthier look about him than all his colleagues in Parliament—this septuagenarian.

Recently a representative of *Time* remarked that his face looked like fine Cordovan leather.

76

WHILE HIS THOUGHTS are almost wholly intent on the great problem of winning the war, Smuts is, nevertheless, devoting much attention to the question of the New Order which he is determined that an Allied victory shall bring. He prescribes, as a panacea for the ills of the world, a new great League of Nations.

"The failure of the League," he says, "was chiefly due to the fact that it had no central authority. . . . The central organization must possess the necessary authority and power to look after the common interests of mankind. The traffic and relations between the nations shall be free in commerce; and trade, economic relations, and monetary matters shall be freed of obstructive restrictions as between nations. Between individual human beings there will be social fairness and justice; among the races right will prevail and there will be no coercion or violence.

"Freedom will be upheld. In such an international society there will be no room for self-appointed leaders and führers. He who wishes to be the master will have to be the servant. Our aim and motto will be:

> *"A nation of free men and women;*
> *An international society of free nations."*

There is, as Oliver Baldwin has said, "a mixture of cunning and mysticism in Smuts's eyes." Many people have seen this mixture. In these dark and dreadful days the mystic quality seems to predominate, and also through his eyes there shines a strange serenity of spirit.

A victory for the Allies will bring to the council chambers, not of Europe, this time, but of the world, a great triumvirate from the democratic countries. It will comprise Winston Churchill, Franklin Delano Roosevelt, and Jan Smuts, the man of many facets—complex and contradictory, but, for all that, the epitome of holism.

As a scientist of repute, a world-famed political philosopher, a great soldier in three wars, and an illustrious statesman it is to be doubted whether, from the holistic standpoint, Smuts has an equal among great men in the world today. In him one finds embodied uniquely a multiplicity of outstanding qualities that have given to history the man who, for close on half a century, has dominated the South African scene and for twenty-five years has been among the foremost figures on the world stage.

THE OFFENSIVE PHASE[1]

The historic speech delivered by General Smuts to members of the two Houses of Parliament in London on Wednesday, October 21, 1942.

I am very sensible of the great honour you have done me today. I appreciate this vast audience and the affectionate welcome you have given me, but more, I appreciate today the presence of the chairmanship of my old leader "L. G."

Words fail me to express my feelings on an occasion like this, but I am here today to address you on the war. The Prime Minister has led me to this; he brought me here, he created this occasion. I feel now like a sacrificial lamb being led to the slaughter, but I rely on your sympathy and support to see me through.

This is a great occasion for me, and I am deeply conscious of the exceptional honour you are doing me. In my experience it is a unique occasion. It is no small thing to be called upon to address the members of this Sovereign Parliament of the United Kingdom, this Mother of Parliaments and free democratic institutions, this Senate of Kings, to use the phrase once applied to the Roman Senate.

I appreciate this honour, which I have not deserved, and which but expresses your good will and interest in me and in the country and young nation I am privileged to represent.

I know you have singled me out for this distinction largely because I happen to be the last surviving member, still active in high office, of the War Cabinet of the last war. I was the youngest and the least of that notable band, and no doubt for these good and sufficient reasons I have been spared, perhaps overlooked, by the subsequent storms and the years.

And now that I reappear on this scene after many years you are interested in this somewhat mythical figure and curiosity from the past.

I know the subject of war cabinets is a minor matter of controversy

[1] Reprinted from *The Daily Telegraph and Morning Post.*

among you, and I shall therefore avoid invidious comparisons between then and now. But you will at least allow me to refer to the two leaders in the two supreme crises of our sorely tried generation.

I am very proud to be honoured by the presence here today of my old leader, Mr. Lloyd George, but for whom who knows what might have happened in the mortal crisis of twenty-five years ago. Today, in this greater crisis, we gratefully remember his imperishable service and thank God for the gift and saving grace of his great historic leadership. He stands out as the supreme architect of victory in the last war.

No less have we been blessed with distinguished leadership in this vaster struggle of today. I sometimes wonder whether people in this country sufficiently realize what Winston Churchill has meant and continues to mean, not only to them but also to the Allied peoples, the United Nations, and to brave men and women everywhere in the world.

His words and foresight, his courage and energy have been an unfailing inspiration to all of us. He remains the embodiment of the spirit of eternal youth and resilience, the spirit of a great undying nation in one of the greatest moments of history. Let us recognize with gratitude that we have been nobly blessed with wonderful leadership, both in the last war and in this.

I have spoken of the two great actors, the two greatest actors, in the drama, the continuing drama of our age. I call this a continuing drama because I view this war as a continuation of the last war, and the whole as perhaps another Thirty Years' War, which began in 1914, was interrupted by an armistice in 1919, improperly called a peace, was resumed with greater ferocity in 1939, and may continue (who knows?) till 1944. The intervening armistice was a period of feverish rest or unrest and dreams and illusions.

I have referred to two great actors in this drama of our age. There is a third and greater actor to be mentioned. I refer to the British people and the spirit that animates them and the young nations around them in the British Commonwealth of Nations.

One occasionally hears idle words about the decay of this country, about the approaching break-up of the great world group we form. What folly and ignorance, what misreading of the real signs of the times! In some quarters what wishful thinking!

It is true that this greatest human experiment in political organization, this proudest political structure of time, this precedent and anticipation of what one hopes may be in store for human society in the years to come, this Commonwealth, is being tested as never before in its history.

But is it not standing the test? Is not this free and voluntary association, is not this world-wide human co-operation today holding together more successfully than ever before under the most searching test?

Knowing the dangers and temptations we have had to face, the stresses and strains imposed on us, nothing has been more remarkable to me than the cohesion of this vast structure under the hardest hammer blows of fate. We have suffered, we are poorer, we shall be poorer still. We have had heavy setbacks and an exceptional run of bad luck.

Is it a wonder that in the fourth year of this war there may sometimes come moments of disappointment, of fatigue, and occasionally even a sense of frustration? But still this great Commonwealth remains the heart of the defence against the most terrible onslaught ever made on human rights and liberties. It stands unshaken by the storms and setbacks.

The people of this island are the real heroes of this epic world-wide drama, and I pay my small tribute to their unbending, unbreakable spirit. I have been absent from this country for almost ten years, and coming back now I can see for myself the vast change which the trials and sufferings and exertions of the war period have wrought.

I remember this smiling land, recovered and rebuilt after the last war, where a happy people dwelt securely, busy with the tasks and thoughts of peace. And now I have come back to a country over which the fury of war has swept, a country whose people have had to face in their grimmest mood the most terrible onslaught in its history.

Many of its ancient monuments are damaged or gone forever. The blitz has passed over cities, ports, churches, temples, humble homes and palaces, Houses of Parliament, and law courts. Irreplaceable treasures of one thousand years of almost uninterrupted progress and culture and peaceful civilization have disappeared forever.

War, the horror people still call war, but in its modern scientific form something very different from what passed under that name before, war has come to this favoured land and attempted its worst. Much has gone which is lost forever.

But one thing is not lost—one thing, the most precious of all, remains and has rather increased. For what will it profit a nation if it wins the world and loses its soul? The soul remains. Glory has not departed from this land.

I speak not of outward glory, of what your Gallic neighbours called "la Gloire" in their past revolutionary fervor. I speak rather of that inward glory, that splendour of the spirit, which has shone over this land from the soul of its people, and has been a beacon light to the oppressed and downtrodden peoples in this new martyrdom of man.

Let the enemy say "Gott strafe England." "God bless England" has been the response from the victims of this most fiendish onslaught in history.

But for this country—the stand it made from 1939 onward, its immeasurable exertions since and up to now, its toil and sweat, its blood and tears—this world of ours might have been lost for one thousand years, and another dark age might have settled down on the spirit of man.

This is its glory—to have stood in the breach and to have kept the way open to man's vast future. And when, after a long absence, I see today this flame of the spirit above the flame of the blitz, I feel that I have come to a greater, prouder, more glorious home of the free than I ever learned to know in its palmiest days.

This is the glory of the spirit, which sees and knows no defeat or loss, but increasingly nerves, nourishes, and sustains the will to final victory.

I have singled out for emphasis the spirit and service of this country because they have been the most important, indeed the crucial factors hitherto for our Allied cause. But the spirit of resolution and endurance and sacrifice is not confined to Britain.

Other Allied nations, each in its own degree, share in this spirit. When we survey the world heaving today in its agony we see everywhere the same spirit lighting up the sombre scene.

Think of China and its five years of suffering at the hands of the Japanese war lords, busy with their so-called "co-prosperity sphere" in Asia. Think of Russia and its unbroken spirit amid the hardest blows and most cruel sacrifices of this war.

Look at the wonderful resurgence of the brave little nations of Western Europe, whom no adversity, no defeat, dangers, or chains can hold down. Think of the heroic guerrillas of Serbia and other small nations. Look at the new glory of Greece which has so effectively dimmed the tinsel grandeur of Mussolini's Rome—truly a new Hellas has arisen to fulfil the poets' great vision.

And looking further afield, watch the young nations of the British Commonwealth at the job. Last and greatest of all, see America in her invincible might under one of the greatest of leaders, marching to the flaming ramparts of the world in East and West.

And shall we forget France, not dead, but, like Lazarus, only sleeping, and waiting for the dawn to shake off the torpor which has temporarily overcome her historic genius?

No, the spirit of man is neither dead nor decadent. It will never bend the knee before the new slavery.

The light of freedom which has guided our slow and faltering advance through the ages still shines in the night which has overtaken us. The glory is still with us, and we shall follow it with all our strength and devotion to the new dawn which surely awaits our race.

But a rough and terrible passage lies before us, and it will call for all our combined resources, all our concentrated will and effort, all our highest leadership to carry us to our goal. There is no place for complacency or wishful thinking.

The mortal struggle is on, and it will become more cruel and desperate as the end draws nearer. For it is indeed a struggle of life and death between the contending systems and ideologies which now divide mankind.

I, therefore, pass on to the war situation. For the first three years of the war our role had necessarily to be a defensive one.

That role was imposed on us by the intensive secret preparations of the enemy for six years before the war, by the false sense of security he had sedulously fostered among us, and by the mood of appeasement which had thus been created.

That advantage no premature offensive could possibly have overcome. We could barely maintain our self-defence against the terrible odds.

In those cases where we were in honour bound to take the offensive in support of other small peoples we have suffered reverses which still further weakened us. Let us, however, never regret the help we did our best to bring Norway, Holland, and Greece in their hour of need.

In these common sufferings which we shared with them the United Nations were born. But these efforts were indeed beyond our resources at that time, and we suffered discouraging reverses. Only in Africa could we successfully assume the offensive, but modesty prevents me from dwelling on that theme.

Then came the most deadly catastrophe of all when France fell. It was an awful moment in history. The sudden fall of a great nation and world power is a phenomenon almost unknown in history, and this particular blow was as unexpected as it was deadly.

The enemy looked upon it as also for us the end, and this infatuation of his providentially saved us. Instead of immediately turning on London he persevered on his planned course to Paris, and gave us the opportunity to recover our breath and prepare for the blitz against London. And what a defence it was!

Surely never in history did the future hang on so slender a thread, nor was the outcome so painfully and prayerfully watched by so many millions over the whole world! Providence saved us there, and let us admit that the devil helped him. Such is always the ultimate function of evil in this world.

The defeat of the Luftwaffe in that supreme crisis saved not only London and Britain but, I firmly believe, the whole Allied cause and the future of the world.

The fall of France was followed by two other events, both of the greatest importance for the subsequent course of the war. The first was another fatal mistake of Hitler.

Baulked in his air attack on London, he saw that it was unsafe to attempt an invasion of Britain before first clearing his rear in Russia. The magnitude and duration of Russian resistance have surprised not only Hitler but probably everybody else.

Probably no such losses on both sides have ever been suffered in the history of war. If the Russian losses must be terrible it is equally true that the German Army is bleeding to death in Russia.

The appalling bloodletting which is necessary for Hitler's ultimate defeat is being administered by the Russians, and they alone can do it. In spite of their losses in men and material and territory, the Russians show not the least sign of giving in, and the bitter defence will go on to the bitter end.

This impression is confirmed by all the best inside information. Hitler has done his best to avoid Napoleon's example, but history may yet record that the course he actually adopted was even more fatal than was Napoleon's retreat from Moscow.

The course for the Allies to follow is clear. Whatever help in whatever form we can give to Russia to sustain her in her colossal effort should be given in the fullest measure and with the utmost speed. She is bearing more than her share of the common burden.

The second result of the fall of France was the almost total loss of the entire Allied positions in the Far East. Vichy opened the door to Japan in Indo-China, and through that unexpected opening the flood poured into Siam, Malaya, and Burma.

Indo-China was the back door to Singapore, a back door which we never dreamed would be opened by our ally against us—an event for which the defences of Singapore made no adequate provision and which made its fall inevitable.

And when Singapore fell the whole Dutch Indies and the other island groups in the Far East were doomed, and it has only been possible to stop the flood at the very shores of Australia and New Zealand.

People who have not followed or understood the inevitable, the terrible logic of events have blamed the Allies for these tremendous setbacks, and the ill-disposed have taken the loss of Singapore as a proof of decadence, and a sign of the approaching downfall of the Commonwealth.

As a matter of fact it was merely a consequence of the downfall of France, and no more.

We mourn these our losses; we mourn especially the temporary loss to Holland of her great empire in the Far East, which has been a model of colonial government; we deplore our diminished opportunities at the moment of helping China in her stout defence.

But these things will pass. For Japan just as surely as for Hitler's Germany the writing is on the wall. All that will remain of this spectacular Japanese success will be "Japan for the Japanese."

For Japan has infallibly sealed her own doom. Pearl Harbour was at once a challenge to America, to Western civilization, and to the principles of good faith on which it is basically founded. In the long run Japan will not be good enough as an associate even for Germany. There are degrees in infamy.

Not that I deplore Pearl Harbour! From our point of view it was a heavy price, but well worth paying for the immense gains that have accrued. It was what the chemists call a catalyzer.

It suddenly crystallized, precipitated, and solidified American opinion as nothing else in the world could have done. At one sudden leap America was in the war.

These are the steps that have marked our climb out of the abyss into which the fall of France had all but plunged us:

First, the defeat of the German Luftwaffe over London.

Second, the treacherous attack of Germany on Russia, in spite of the peace treaty between them.

Third, Pearl Harbour and its sudden and timely effect in carrying America 100 per cent. into the war while Admiral Nomura and Mr. Cordell Hull were talking peace at the conference table.

We have much to be thankful for, but not least for the colossal mistakes of our enemies. Will a fourth blunder be committed? Will Japan, in spite of her peace treaty with Russia, launch a treacherous attack against her also in Siberia? Time alone will show.

We have now reached the fourth year of this war, and the defence phase has now ended. The stage is set for the last, the offensive phase. Let me set your minds at rest at once; I am not going to discuss the future offensive strategy of the war.

The amateur strategists can do that with greater freedom and less responsibility in the press. I only wish to emphasize that one phase has ended and another must now begin.

The final alignments both of the Allies and our enemies have been made. Resources have been developed and mobilized on a very large scale, ours still on the increase, those of the enemy on the decline.

Our man power is still growing, that of the enemy is getting depleted, while he makes ever-heavier drafts on his suffering vassal peoples. The spectre of want, hunger, and starvation is beginning to stalk through the subject countries, the spirit of unrest is heaving and rising.

The explosive limits of endurance are nearing. We are approaching the point when both on the war fronts and on the home fronts in enemy countries the situation is ripening for far-reaching developments.

So far, time has been in our favour, and has, on the whole, been kind to us. In spite of heavy setbacks and many disappointments, we have had the necessary time to prepare to parry deadly blows, and to assemble and consolidate the forces and resources on which we rely for the Allied victory.

Once the time has come to take the offensive and to strike while the iron is hot it would be folly to delay, to overprepare, and perhaps miss our opportunity. Nor are we likely to do so—of that I feel satisfied.

On this point it would be unwise for me to say more and thus to set going unnecessary and perhaps harmful speculations.

I would only point out to you that today is Trafalgar Day. It reminds us of that dark hour, the darkest in the Napoleonic War, when your great national hero, the embodiment of the heroic offensive spirit of this people, sought out the superior naval forces of the enemy and dealt them that fatal blow which not only saved England from invasion, but turned the whole tide of the war, and finally saved Europe from being overwhelmed by the insensate domination of one man.

This anniversary is not only a reminder, but an inspiration to us to go forward and do likewise. I am sure it will not be lost on us and our gallant Allies. For us, too, the great offensive moment is ripening.

I now pass on to another point and wish to emphasize the deeper significance of the struggle on which we are engaged. It is no ordinary political issues that are at stake, and the outcome of this war will not be immaterial to the future character and trend of our civilization. In spite of the specious promises of a New Order and the alluring appeals to the idealism of youth, actual events have in the last three years revealed the true nature of the Nazi ideology. We know beyond all doubt what Hitler's New Order means.

Persecution, domination, suppression, enslavement of the free spirit of man, aye, extermination—those are the dominant features of the new creed as practiced in the occupied countries. It is written in the blood and tears and nameless suffering of vast numbers of innocent men and women of all ages and conditions.

It is in contrast to this that I have emphasized the heroic spirit of the suffering Allied peoples now under Hitler's heel, because I feel that this is the heart of the matter. This, at bottom, is a war of the spirit, of man's soul.

Hitler has tried to kill this spirit and to substitute for it some ersatz thing, something which is really its negation. He has instilled into German youth a new racial fanaticism.

He has sought strength in the ancient discarded forest gods of the Teuton. His faith is a reversion to the pagan past and a denial of the spiritual forces which have carried us forward in the Christian advance which constitutes the essence of European civilization.

He has trampled under foot the great faith which has nourished the West and proved the greatest dynamic of all human history and made Western civilization the proudest achievement of man.

He has trampled on the Cross and substituted for it the Crooked Cross, fit symbol for the new devil worship which he has tried to impose on his country and the world. Nietzsche's Superman is substituted for the Man of Nazareth as the new leader of the human race and the human advance.

He has stamped on the human virtues which we had learned to cultivate under the symbol of the Cross. Decency, sympathy, mercy, are not words found in his new code.

He has trampled on the spirit of liberty which has become the accepted political creed of the modern world. He has started a new era of martyrdom for the human spirit, an era of persecution such as mankind has not known since its emergence from the Dark Ages.

The suffering he has inflicted on Jews and Christians alike, the tide of horrors launched under his Gestapo regime over the fair West, constitute the darkest page of modern history. He has outraged and insulted and challenged the very spirit of humanity and tried to found a new barbarism.

After what has happened since 1939 in the Occupied Countries and elsewhere, both in peace and war, there is no more doubt about the meaning of it all. The real issue has now been made clear. There is a challenge to all we have learned to value, and to prize even above life itself.

Behind all the issues of this war lies the deeper question now posed to the world: which do you choose—the free spirit of man and the moral idealism which has shaped the values and ideas of our civilization, or this horrid substitute, this foul obsession now resuscitated from the underworld of the past?

This in the last analysis is what this war is about. At bottom, therefore, this war is a new crusade, a new fight to the death for man's rights and liberties, and for the personal ideals of man's ethical and spiritual life.

To the Nazi fanaticism we oppose this crusading spirit, which will not sheath the sword till Nazidom and all its works have been purged from this fair world. And in that spirit the United Nations will march forward to victory and to the world which will follow that victory.

I therefore come to the question: What is the sort of world which we envisage as our objective after the war? What sort of social and international order are we aiming at? These are very important questions, deserving of our most careful attention, if we mean not only to win the war but also the peace.

Our ideas on these matters twenty-two years ago were much too vague and crude, and at the same time much too ambitious, with the result that when they came to be tested by hard experience they proved wanting, and their failure helped to contribute to the present conflict. With that experience before us we ought this time to hammer out something more clear, definite, and practical.

A great deal of thought is no doubt already being given to these matters, and one may hope that we shall approach the peace much better informed and equipped than we were last time.

Certain points of great importance have already emerged. Thus we have accepted the name of "the United Nations." This is a new conception much in advance of the old concept of a league of nations.

We do not want a mere League, but something more definite and organic, even if to begin with more limited and less ambitious than the League. "The United Nations" is itself a fruitful conception, and on the basis of that conception practical machinery for the functioning of an international order could be explored.

Then, again, we have the Atlantic Charter, in which certain large principles of international policy in the social and economic sphere have been accepted. That, too, marks a great step forward which only requires more careful definition and elaboration to become a real Magna Carta of the nations.

Again, we have agreed on certain large principles of social policy, involving social security for the citizen in matters which have lain at the roots of much social unrest and suffering in the past.

We cannot hope to establish a new heaven and a new earth in the bleak world which will follow after this most destructive conflict of history. But certain patent social and economic evils could be tackled on modest practical lines on an international scale almost at once.

Then, again, we have accepted the principle of international help underlying the Mutual Aid Agreement. The helping hand in international life is thus already a matter of practical politics, and could be suitably extended after the war. This, too, is a far-reaching innovation, pointing the way to fruitful developments in future.

All these are already indications of considerable advances to a better world and a richer life for mankind. To these we may add much of the social and economic work of the League of Nations, which remains of permanent value.

Much of the League organization could thus continue to function for the future well-being of mankind. In sober resolution, in modest hope, and strong faith, we move forward to the unknown future.

There is no reason why we should not hopefully and sincerely attempt to carry out for the world the task which now confronts us as never before in the history of our race. An American statesman has called this the century of the plain man, the common people.

I feel that in this vast suffering through which our race is passing we are being carried to a deeper sense of social realities. We are passing beyond the ordinary politics and political shibboleths.

It is no longer a case of socialism or communism or any of the other isms of the market place, but of achieving common justice and fair play for all. People are searching their own souls for the causes which have brought us to this pass.

May it be our privilege to see that this suffering, this travail and search of man's spirit shall not be in vain.

Without feeding on illusions, without nursing the impossible, there is yet much in the common life of the people which can be remedied, much unnecessary inequality and privilege to be levelled away, much common-sense opportunity to be erected as the common birthright and public atmosphere for all to enjoy as of right.

Health, housing, education, decent social amenities, provision against avoidable insecurities—all these simple goods and much more can be provided for all, and thus a common higher level of life be achieved for all.

As between the nations, a new spirit of human solidarity can be cultivated, and economic conditions can be built up which will strike at the root causes of war, and thus lay deeper foundations for world peace.

With honesty and sincerity on our part it is possible to make basic reforms both for national and international life which will give mankind a new chance of survival and of progress.

Let this programme, by no means too ambitious, be our task, and let us now already, even in the midst of war, begin to prepare for it.

And may Heaven's blessing rest on our work in war and in peace.

BIBLIOGRAPHY

Addison, C., Politics from Within. London. H. Jenkins, Ltd., 1924.
Alport, C. J. M., Kingdoms in Partnership. London. L. Dickson, Ltd., 1937.
Alston, Leonard. The White Man's Work in Africa and Asia. London and N. Y. Longmans, Green & Co., 1907.
Amery, L. S., The Times History of the War in South Africa. London. S. Low, Marston & Co., Ltd., 1900–09 (7 vols.).
Armstrong, H. C., Grey Steel, London. A. Barker, Ltd., 1937.
Armstrong, H. C., and others, Great Contemporaries. London. Cassell & Co., Ltd., 1935.
Arthur, Sir G., Not Worth Reading. London. Longmans, Green & Co., 1938.
Arthur, Sir G., Lord Haig.
Ashmead-Bartlett, E., The Riddle of Russia. London. Cassell & Co., Ltd., 1929.
Ashmead-Bartlett, E., The Tragedy of Central Europe.
Asquith, H., Moments of Memory. London. Hutchinson & Co., Ltd., 1937.
Badenhorst, General C. C. J., Uit den Boeren Oorlog.
Baker, Herbert, Cecil Rhodes. London. Oxford University Press, 1934.
Baker, R. S., Woodrow Wilson and World Settlement. N. Y. Doubleday, Page & Co., 1922.
Baker, R. S., Woodrow Wilson. Life and Letters. N. Y. Doubleday, Page & Co., 1927–39.
Baldwin, Oliver, The Questing Beast. London. Grayson & Grayson, 1932.
Barnes, Rt. Hon. G. N., From Workshop to War Cabinet. London. H. Jenkins, Ltd., 1924.
Barnes, Leonard, The New Boer War. London. L. & V. Woolf, 1932.
Baruch, Bernard, The Making of the Reparation and Economic Sections of the Treaty. N. Y. and London. Harper & Bros., 1920.
Beak, G. B., The Aftermath of War. London. E. Arnold, 1906.
Beer, G. L., African Questions at the Paris Peace Conference. N. Y. The Macmillan Co., 1923.
Blackwell, Leslie, African Occasions.
Blunt, W. S., My Diaries. London. M. Secher. 1919–20.
Bodenstein, Dr. H. D. J., Was General Botha in 1900 een Verraader? Amsterdam. J. H. de Bussy, 1916.
Boissevain, Charles, The Struggle of the Dutch Republics. Amsterdam. Handelsblach Office, 1900.

Bolitho, H., James Lyle Mackay, First Lord of Inchcape. London. J. Murray, 1936.
Brand, Hon. R. H., The Union of South Africa. Oxford. The Clarendon Press, 1909.
Brandt, van Warmelo, Johanna, Het Concentratie-Kamp van Irene.
Bryce, Brooks, Carnegie, etc., Briton and Boer. N. Y. and London. Harper & Bros., 1900.
Brookes, E. H., History of Native Policy in South Africa from 1830 to the Present Day. Pretoria. J. S. van Schaik, Ltd., 1927.
Burger, A. J. V., Worsteljare.
Butler, Sir W., From Naboth's Vineyard.
Buxton, Earl, General Botha. London. J. Murray, 1924.
Callwell, Maj. Gen. Sir C. E., Field Marshal Sir Henry Wilson, His Life and Diaries. London. Cassell & Co., Ltd., 1927.
Calpin, G. H. There Are No South Africans.
Cambridge History of the British Empire. N. Y. The Macmillan Co. Cambridge. University Press, 1929–40.
Campbell, C., General Smuts, a Great Afrikander (ex. "The African World Annual," Dec. 30, 1916).
Cana, Frank R., South Africa from the Great Trek to Union.
Chamberlain, Sir A., Politics from Inside. London. Cassell & Co., Ltd., 1936.
Charteris, Brig. Gen. J., Field Marshal Earl Haig. London. Cassell & Co., Ltd., 1936.
Chilvers, Hedley A., Out of the Crucible. London. Cassell & Co., Ltd., 1929.
Chilvers, Hedley A., Seven Wonders of Southern Africa. Johannesburg. Authority of the Administration of the South African Railways and Harbours, 1929.
Chirol, Sir V., India. Old and New. London. Macmillan & Co., Ltd., 1921.
Churchill, Winston S., The World Crisis, 1911–18. London. T. Butterworth, Ltd., 1931.
Collyer, Brig. Gen., The South Africans with General Smuts in German East Africa. Pretoria. Government Printer, 1939.
Colvin, Ian. The Life of Jameson. London. E. Arnold & Co., 1922.
Cooper, Duff, Haig. London. Faber & Faber, Ltd., 1935–36. Doubleday, Doran & Co., 1936.
Courtney, W. L. and J. E., Pillars of Empire.
Crowe, Brig. Gen. J. H. V., General Smuts' Campaign in East Africa.
Dane, Edmund, British Campaign in Africa and the Pacific.
Dawson, R. M., Development of Dominion Status. London & N. Y. Oxford University Press, 1937.
Dawson, W. H., South Africa.
Davitt, Michael, The Boer Fight for Freedom. N. Y. Funk & Wagnalls Co., 1902.
de Villiers, O. T., Met de Wet en Steyn in het Veld.
Devitt, N., More Memories of a Magistrate. London. H. F. & G. Witherby, Ltd., 1936.
de Wet, C. R., Three Years War. N. Y. C. Scribner's Sons, 1902.
de Wet, J. M., Die Filosofie van Smuts en Boodin.
de Wet, J. M., Jopie Fourie.
Dodds, E., Liberalism in Action. London. G. Allen & Unwin, Ltd., 1922.
Dolbey, R. V., Sketches of the East African Campaign. London. J. Murray, 1918.
Downes, W. D., With the Nigerians in German East Africa. London. Methuen & Co., Ltd., 1919.
Doyle, A. Conan, The Great Boer War. N. Y. McClure, Phillips & Co., 1900.

du Bois, W. E. B., Article on Smuts and Native Police (ex. "Foreign Affairs," April 1925).

Dugdale, Blanche E. C., Arthur James Balfour, 1st Earl of Balfour. London. Hutchinson & Co., Ltd., 1936.

Elibank, Viscount, A Man's Life. London. Hutchinson & Co., Ltd., 1934.

Emden, Paul H., Randlords. London. Hodder & Stoughton, 1935.

Engelenburg, Dr. F. V., General Louis Botha, Pretoria. J. L. van Schaik, 1938.

Enock, A. G., The Problem of Armaments. N. Y. The Macmillan Co., 1923.

Erskine, Mrs. Steuart, King Feisal of Iraq. London. Hutchinson & Co., Ltd., 1933.

Esher, Viscount, Journals and Letters of Reginald, Viscount Esher. London. I. Nicholson & Watson, Ltd., 1934-38.

Evatt, H. V., The King and His Dominion Governors. London. Oxford University Press, 1936.

Farrelly, M. J., The Settlement after the War in South Africa.

Fitzpatrick, J. P., The Transvaal from Within.

FitzRoy, Sir Almeric, Memoirs. London. Hutchinson & Co., 1925.

Fort, G. Seymour, Alfred Beit. London. J. Nicholson & Watson, 1932.

Fort, G. Seymour, Dr. Jameson. London. Hurst and Blackett, Ltd., 1918.

Foster, H. A., Making of Modern Iraq. Norman, Okla. University of Oklahoma Press.

French of Ypres, Field Marshal Viscount, 1914. Boston. Houghton Mifflin Co., 1919.

Fry, A. Ruth, Emily Hobhouse. London. J. Cape, 1929.

Gardiner, A. G., Certain People of Importance. London. J. Cape, 1927.

Garrett, F. E., The Story of an African Crisis. N. Y. New Amsterdam Book Co., 1897.

Garvin, J. L., The Life of Joseph Chamberlain. London. Macmillan & Co., Ltd., 1931-32.

Gie, Prof. Dr. S. F. N., Geskiedenis van Suid-Afrika. Pub. in Union of South Africa, 1920-28.

Godley, Lt. Col. R. S. Khaki and Blue. London. L. Dickson & Thompson, Ltd., 1935.

Gooch, G. P., Before the War. London. Longmans, Green & Co., 1936.

Goold-Adams, South Africa Today and Tomorrow. London. J. Murray, 1936.

Graumann, Sir Harry, Rand Riches and South Africa. Cape Town. Juta & Co., Ltd., 1935.

Guitry, Sacha, If Memory Serves. N. Y. Doubleday, Doran & Co., Inc., 1935.

Gwynn, D., De Valera. London. Jarrolds, 1933.

Haarhoff, T. J., Creative Wholism (ex. The Stranger at the Gate). The Stranger at the Gate. London and N. Y. Longmans, Green & Co., 1938.

Haig, Countess, The Man I Knew. Edinburgh. The Moray Press, 1936.

Hammond, J. L., C. P. Scott of the Manchester Guardian. London. G. Bell & Sons, Ltd., 1934.

Harris, Col. Sir David Harris, Pioneer, Soldier, and Politician. London. S. Low, Marston & Co., Ltd., 1930.

Herrman, Louis, The History of the Jews in South Africa from the Earliest Times to 1895. London. V. Gollancz, Ltd., 1930.

Hiley and Hassell, The Mobile Boer. N. Y. Grafton Press, 1902.

Hillegas, Howard C., The Boers in War. D. Appleton & Co. N. Y., 1900.

Hobhouse, Emily, The Brunt of the War. Die Smarte van die oorlog. Published in Union of South Africa, 1923.

Hobson, J. A., The Proconsulate of Milner.

Hobson, J. A., The Psychology of Jingoism. London. G. Richards, 1901.

Hofmeyr, J. H., Het Leven van J. H. Hofmeyr.

Hofmeyr, J. H., South Africa. London. E. Benn, Ltd., 1931.

Hofmeyr, N., Zes Maanden by de Commando's.

House and Seymour, What Really Happened at Paris. N. Y. Scribner's Sons, 1921.

Jordaan, G., Hoe Zij Stierven. Burgersdorp. A. Coetsee, 1904.

Juta, Marjorie, The Pace of the Ox. London. Constable & Co., Ltd., 1937.

Keith, A. B., The Constitution, Administration, and Laws of the Empire, London. W. Collins Sons & Co., Ltd., 1924.

Keith, A. B., Responsible Government in the Dominions. Oxford. Clarendon Press, 1912.

Kemp, Gen. J. C. G., Vir Vryheid en vir Reg.

Kestell, Dr. J. D., Christiaan de Wet. Kaapstad. Nasionale Pers, 1920.

Kestell, J. D., and Van Velden, D. E. The Peace Negotiations Between Boer and Briton in South Africa.

Kestell, Dr. J. D., Through Shot and Flame.

Keynes, J. M., A Revision of the Treaty. N. Y. Harcourt Brace & Co., 1922.

Keynes, J. M., The Economic Consequences of the Peace. N. Y. Harcourt Brace & Howe, 1920.

King, Marina, Sunrise to Evening Star. London. G. G. Harrap & Co., Ltd., 1935.

King-Hall, Stephen, Our Families.

Kolbe, Monsignor, A Catholic View of Holism. N. Y. The Macmillan Co., 1928.

Kritzinger and McDonald, In the Shadow of Death. 1904.

Kruger, Paul, The Memoirs of Paul Kruger. N. Y. Century Co., 1902.

Lansing, R., The Big Four and Others at the Peace Conference. Boston & N. Y. Houghton Mifflin Co., 1921.

Laurence, Sir Perceval, The Life of John Xavier Merriman. London. Constable & Co., Ltd., 1930.

Lennard, W., Alfred Milner. Fortnightly Review vol. 78 (n.s.v. 72) pp. 52–65.

Levi, N., Jan Smuts. London. Longmans, Green & Co., 1917.

Livingston, Brig. Gen. G., Hot Air in Cold Blood. London. Selwyn & Blount, Ltd., 1933.

Lloyd George, D., War Memoirs of David Lloyd George. London. I. Nicholson & Watson, 1933–36.

Lucas, Sir Charles P., The Empire at War. London. H. Milford, 1921–26.

Lyon, L., Pomp of Power. London. Hutchinson & Co., 1923.

McCartney, M. H. H., Five Years of European Chaos. N. Y. E. P. Dutton & Co., 1923.

Macaulay, N., Mandates. London. Methuen & Co., Ltd., 1937.

Macdonald, J. Ramsay, What I Saw in South Africa. London. "The Echo," 1902.

Mackenzie and Stead, South Africa, Its History, Heroes, and Wars. Chicago, Philadelphia. Monarch Book Co., 1899.

Macmillan, W. M., Banty, Boer, and Briton. London. Faber & Gwyer, Ltd., 1928.

Marcosson, J. F., Jan Smuts (ex. "Saturday Evening Post," January 8, 1921).

Margalith, A. M., International Mandates. Baltimore. Johns Hopkins Press, London. H. Mulford, Oxford University Press, 1930.

Maritz, Manie, My Lewe en Strewe.

Marriott, Sir John, This Realm of England. London & Glasgow. Blackie & Son, Ltd., 1938.

Marriott, Sir John, The Evolution of the British Empire, etc. London. Nicholson, 1939.

Marriott, Sir John A. R., Queen Victoria and Her Ministers. London. J. Murray, 1933.

Maurois, A., King Edward and His Times. London. Cassell & Co., Ltd., 1933.

McDonald, Ds. R. D., In die Skadu van die Dood. Kritzinger, Gen. P. H. & McDonald, R. D. Kaapstad Nasionale Pers Bpk, 1939.

Meech, T. C., This Generation. London. Chatto & Windus, 1927–28.

Methuen, A. M. S., Peace or War in South Africa. London. Methuen & Co., 1901.

Miller, D. H., The Drafting of the Covenant. N. Y., London. G. P. Putnam's Sons, 1928.

Millin, S. G., The South Africans. London. Constable & Co., Ltd., 1926.

Millin, S. G., General Smuts. London. Faber & Faber, Ltd., 1936.

Molteno, Sir James Tennant, The Dominion of Afrikanerdom. London. Methuen & Co., Ltd., 1923.

Molteno, Sir James Tennant, South African Recollections.

Molteno, Sir James Tennant, Further South African Recollections. London. Methuen & Co., Ltd., 1926.

Moon, P. T., Imperialism and World Politics. N. Y. The Macmillan Co., 1930 (1939).

Moore-Ritchie, With Botha in the Field. London. Longmans, Green & Co., 1915.

Morley, F., Society of Nations. Washington. The Brookings Institution, 1932.

Mostert, Dirk, Slegtkamp van Spioenkop. Kaapstad. Nasionale Pers, 1935.

Muir, R., Brief History of Modern Times. N. Y. Longmans, Green & Co., 1935.

Muller, Gen. Chris H., Oorlogsherinneringe. Kaapstad. 1936.

Nathan, Manfred, South Africa from Within. London. J. Murray, 1926.

Nathan, Manfred, Paul Kruger.

National Review, Smuts and the Protectorates.

Naude, J. F., Vechten en Vluchten van Beyers en Kemp bokant de Wet.

Neame, L. E., General Hertzog. London. Hurst & Blackett, Ltd., 1930.

Neame, L. E., Some South African Politicians. Cape Town. M. Miller, Ltd., 1929.

Neethling, E., Mag ons Vergeet? Kaapstad, 1938.

Nevinson, H. W., Changes and Chances. N. Y. Harcourt Brace & Co., 1923.

Nicolson, H., Peacemaking, 1919.

Noble, G. B., Politics and Opinions at Paris, 1919. N. Y. The Macmillan Co., 1935.

Nowak, K. F., Versailles. Berlin. Verlag für Kulturpolitik, 1927.

Ogden, H. J., The War against the Dutch Republics in South Africa. Manchester. Taylor, Garnett, Evans & Co., 1901.

Oliver, F. S., and Oliver, W. E., Anvil of War. London. Macmillan & Co., Ltd., 1936.

Oxford and Asquith, Earl of, Letters to a Friend. London. Geoffrey Bless, Ltd., 1933–34.

Parmoor, Lord, A Retrospect. London. W. Heinemann, Ltd., 1936.

Perham and Curtis, The Protectorates of South Africa. London. Oxford University Press, 1935.

Pickard, A. B. de Villiers, Kan ons Versoen? Is't ons Ernst?

Pieterse, H. J. C., Oorlogsavonture van General Wynand Malan. Kaapstad. Nasionalepers, berperk, 1941.

Phillips, Lionel, Some Reminiscences. London. Hutchinson & Co., 1924.

Playne, Caroline E., Britain Holds On, 1917–1918. London. G. Allen & Unwin, Ltd., 1933.

Pollock, Sir F., The League of Nations. Oxford University Press. London & N. Y. H. Milford, 1918.

Preller, Dr. Gustav S., Ons Parool. Kaapstad, 1938.

Preller, Dr. Gustav S., Scheepers se Dagboek. Kaapstad, 1938.

Priem, G. H., De Oorlog in Zuid Afrika. Amsterdam. N. J. Boon, 1900.

Raymond, E. T., Uncensored Celebrities. London. T. F. Unwin, Ltd., 1918.

Raymond, E. T., Mr. Lloyd George, a Biography. London. W. Collins Sons & Co., Ltd., 1922.

Raymond, E. T., Portraits of a New Century. N. Y. Doubleday, Doran & Co., Inc., 1928.

Reed, Douglas, Disgrace Abounding. London. J. Cape, 1939.

Repington, Col., The First World War, 1914–1918. London. Constable & Co., Ltd., 1920.

Riddell, Lord, More Things That Matter. London. Hodder & Stoughton, Ltd., 1925.

Riddell, Lord, Lord Riddell's War Diary. London. J. Nicholson & Watson, 1933.

Riddell, Lord, Lord Riddell's Intimate Diary of the Peace Conference and After. London. V. Gollancz, Ltd., 1933.

Robertson, Field Marshal Sir William, Soldiers and Statesmen. London. Cassell & Co., Ltd., 1926.

Rose, E. B., The Truth about the Transvaal.

Sauer, Dr. Hans, Ex Africa. London. Geoffrey Bless, 1937.

Schoeman, Johan H., The Other Side of the Rebellion.

Schreiner, Olive, An English South African's View of the Situation.

Schreiner, Olive, Thoughts on South Africa. London. T. F. Unwin, Ltd., 1923.

Seely, Maj. Gen. the Rt. Hon. J. E. B., Adventure. London. Heinemann, 1930.

Seymour, Charles, The Intimate Papers of Col. House. Boston & N. Y. Houghton Mifflin Co., 1926–28.

Sforza, Count C., Europe and Europeans. Indianapolis & N. Y. The Bobbs-Merrill Co., 1936.

Simpson, J. S. M., South Africa Fights. London. Hodder & Stoughton, Ltd., 1941.

Slocombe, G., Mirror to Geneva. London. J. Cape, 1937.

Smith, J. A., Brit en Boer.

Smuts, J. C., A Century of Wrong.

Smuts, J. C. and others, Our Changing World View. Johannesburg. University of Witwatersrand Press, 1932.

Smuts, J. C., Greater South Africa (Speeches).

Smuts, J. C., Holism and Evolution. N. Y. The Macmillan Co., 1926.

Snowden, Viscount, Autobiography. London. I. Nicholson & Watson, Ltd., 1934.

Spender, Harold, General Botha, the Career and the Man. Boston & N. Y. Houghton Mifflin Co., 1916.

Spender, J. A., Short History of Our Times. London. Cassell & Co., Ltd., 1934.

Stamperius, J., Met Generaal de Wet in 't Veld.

Stead, W. T., The Best or Worst of Empires—Which?

Stead, W. T., The Review of Reviews (Jan.-Dec., 1901; Jan.-June, 1902). London.

Steed, H. W., Through Thirty Years, 1892–1922. N. Y. Doubleday, Page & Co., 1924.

Stockenström, Eric, Geskiedenis van Suid-Afrika, 1700–1914.

Stoker, Dr. H. G., Enkele Gedagtes oor Gen. Smuts se Kreatiewe Ewolusie.

Temperley, Maj. Gen. A. C., The Whispering Gallery of Europe. London. Collins, 1938.

Temperley, H. W. V., History of the Peace Conference of Paris, Vol. VI.

Theron, Miemie-Louw, 'n Wiel Binne 'n Wiel.

Thomas, Rt. Hon. J. H., My Story. London. Hutchinson & Co., Ltd., 1937.

Tilby, A. Wyatt, South Africa, 1486–1913. Boston. Houghton Mifflin, 1914.

Tiltman, H. H., James Ramsay Macdonald. London. Jarrolds, 1929.

Toynbee, A. J., Study of History. London. Oxford University Press, 1934–39.

Tresling, T. P., De Generaals Botha, de Wet en de la Rey.

Trew, Lt. Col. H. F., Botha Treks. London. Blackie and Son, 1936.

van Bruggen, J. R. L., Bitterinders.

van der Merwe, Dr. N. J. Marthinus Theunis Steyn. Kaapstad, 1924.

van Hoek, K., Gesprekke met Dr. W. J. Leyds. Pretoria, 1939.

van Oordt, J. F., Paul Kruger. Amsterdam & Kaapstad. Jacques Duisseau, 1898.

Verschaeve, Curiel, Voortrekkers-Pad. Brugge, 1938.

Viljoen, B. J., Mijne Herinneringen uit den Anglo-Boeren Oorlog. Amsterdam, 1902.

von Lettow-Vorbeck, Reminiscences of East Africa.

Vulliamy, C. E., Outlanders (A Study of Imperial Expansion in South Africa, 1877–1902). London. J. Cape, 1938.

Walker, Eric, W. P. Schreiner, a South African. London. Oxford University Press, 1937.

Walker, Eric A., A History of South Africa. London. Longmans, Green & Co., Ltd., 1928.

Walton, Sir Edgar, The Inner History of the National Convention.

Webb, H. S., The Causes of the Rebellion.

Wells, H. G., Outline of History, N. Y. The Macmillan Co., 1920.

What the World Thinks of the British Dominions, Vol. I, No. 13.

Whittall, Lt. Commander, With Botha and Smuts in Africa. London, N. Y. Cassell & Co., Ltd., 1917.

Wilmot, W. A., The History of Our Own Times in South Africa.

Wilson, Mrs. Woodrow, My Memoir. Indianapolis & N. Y. Bobbs-Merrill Co., 1939.

Worsfold, W. B., Lord Milner's Work in South Africa. New York. Dutton, 1906.

Wrench, John Evelyn, Struggle, 1914–1920. London. I. Nicholson & Watson, Ltd., 1935.

Young, Brett F., Marching on Tanga. London. W. Collins Sons & Co., Ltd., 1918.

Herewith I wish to acknowledge my great indebtedness to the editors of all the leading South African newspapers and to the authors of the books named above. From these I have quoted extensively where necessary, have used their substance and their sequence, and have even employed their phrases. With the kind permission of one editor I have used some extracts from his paper without inserting quotation marks.

Quotations have been freely employed in regard to the Versailles section—a device which, although somewhat irritating at times, has, I trust, imparted complete authenticity to this portion.

F. S. C.

INDEX

Kaiser Wilhelm, flies to sanctuary in Holland, 136

Kant, Immanuel, his *Critique of Pure Reason* in Smuts's saddlebag, 41

Karl, Emperor of Austria, rumours of his desire for peace, 135

Károlyi, Count Michael, deposed by Béla Kun in Hungarian revolution, 155

Katanga copper belt, in Rhodesia, 199

Keats, John, cited, 10

Kemp, Jan Cristoffel Greyling, Boer guerrilla, 39–40; attacks Smuts in article, "Jan Smuts and John Bull," 47; 95, 240, 258

Kerr, Philip (later Lord Lothian), at the Peace Conference, 148–49; 57

Kershaw, 272

Kestell, Dr. J. D., 53–54

Keynes, John Maynard, British economist, on the Peace Conference, 145, 150; writes *The Economic Consequences of the Peace*, 152

Kilimanjaro, "Monarch of Africa," Smuts flies over top, 274

Kimberley, discovery of diamonds, 15; siege relieved by British in Boer War, 36; 178

King of Greece, 265

Kipling, Rudyard, 80

Kitchener of Khartoum, Lord, sent to South Africa in Boer War, 36; succeeds Roberts, 38; begins drive in Free State, 42; proclaims martial law in the Cape, 46; peace negotiations with Boers, 51–53; signs Treaty of Vereeniging, 54; 48, 58

Kotze, Sir John Gilbert, chief justice of Boer Republic, 23

Kotze, Robert, advises South Africa go off gold standard, 231

Kovac, Kazdy, his painting "Autumn Landscape," 265

Kraaipan, first shot fired in second Boer War, 35

Kriel, Pastor, prays at shooting of Boer traitor, 49

Krige, Christman Joel, brother-in-law of Smuts, 49

Krige, Sibella Margaretha (Isie), 10, 12; marries Jan Smuts, 21–22

Kruger, Stephanus Johannes Paulus (Oom Paul), President of Transvaal Republic, 16–17, 19, 21; conflict with judiciary, 22; opinion of Smuts, 27–28;

at Bloemfontein Conference, 30–32; his peace note rejected, 33; telegram from Rhodes's associates, 34; moves his government to Machadsdorp, 37; taken to Europe and dies in exile, 39; 26–27, 40, 47, 54, 56–57, 63, 66, 69, 72, 125, 167, 256

Kun, Béla, deposes Count Károlyi in Hungarian revolution, 155; 156–59

Kurtze, Ludwig, *see* Von Veltheim

Kuyper, Baron Abraham, Dutch Prime Minister, offers mediation between Boers and Great Britain, 51

"Laager" fortress, 3

Labour, wins victory in general election in Transvaal, 94; gets 12 seats in 1920 election, 171; loses in new election, 176; coalition with the Nationalists, 184–85, 204; split in party, and heavy loss in 1929 general election, 227–28

Labuschagne, mine striker, killed by soldiers, 91, 107

Ladies' Home Journal, 121

Ladysmith, siege of, 35; relieved, 36

Laing, John, 60

Lampson, Sir Miles Wedderburn, British Ambassador to Egypt, and Lady Lampson, 275

Landdrosts, abolished, 2

"Land of My Fathers," anthem sung by Welsh coal-mine strikers, ends strike, 130

Lane, Italian aide-de-camp, 156

Language rights in South Africa, 1, 77–78, 81, 85; Afrikaans recognized as official, and a standard dictionary compiled, 214

Lansdowne, Henry Charles Keith Petty Fitzmaurice, Lord, 51

Lansing, Robert, U.S. Secretary of State, 146–47

Lategan, leader of a Boer commando, 48

Law, Andrew Bonar, 121, 125, 133; on South Africa's right of secession, 174, 190

Lawrence, Harry, 257

Lawrence (of Arabia), Thomas Edward, his magnetic power, 181; 229

Lazarus cited, 291

League of Nations, Smuts's plan published, 140; accepted by President Wilson, 142, 147; mandatory system, 147–49; reparations, 150; Smuts believes it

Nomura, Kichisaburo, 294
North, Frederick, Lord, cited, 256
Northcliffe, Alfred Charles William
Harmsworth, 121, 126
Northern Neutral Committee, 128
Northey, Gen. Edward, 114
Norway, occupied by the Nazis, 261; 292
Nowak, Karl Friedrich, observation on
"mandatory," 147

Oates, Francis, 60
O'Connor, a reporter, 266
"Offensive Phase, The," speech delivered
by Smuts before British Houses of
Parliament, 288 *et seq.*
Old Adam, Hottentot shepherd, friend of
Smuts, 5, 7
Oliver, Frederick Scott, his *Alexander
Hamilton,* 72; comment on Smuts as
British Cabinet member, 125
Olivier, Sydney, Lord, on Milner's re-
sponsibility for hostilities, 32
Ons Land, newspaper, 13, 20
Oom Paul, *see* Kruger
Oordt, Joan Frederik van, his *Plato and
His Times* reviewed by Smuts, 13
Oran, landing of American forces at, 284
Orange Free State, established by Boers,
4; annexed by British on Queen's
birthday, 36; name changed to Orange
River Colony, 57; administration in-
solvent, 231
Orange River Colony, receives full self-
government, 63
Orangia Unie, political party in Free
State, 60; wins majority in elections,
63; merged in South African party, 82
Orlando, Vittorio Emanuele, Italian
Premier, 139; at Peace Conference,
143–44
Ossewa Brandwag (Sentinels of the Ox
Wagon), 257–58, 286
Ottawa Conference, 240
Oubaas (the old chief), a title applied to
Smuts by his family, 222–24, 282

Pact alliance, 204, 208, 227
Painlevé, Paul, President of France, 122
Pakeham, editor of the *Transvaal Leader,*
imprisoned, 29
Palestine, as a homeland for Jews, in
Balfour Declaration, promised also to
the Arabs, 134, 229
Pan-Africanism, 11, 16, 182, 200
Panzer units in South Africa, 270

Papegaaisberg (Hill of the Parrots), 9
Pare, 272
Passchendaele, 133
Passive resistance, weapon of Gandhi, 69
Peace Conference in Paris, 139, 142 *et
seq.;* 153, 165
Peace negotiations in Boer War, 52–53;
Treaty of Vereeniging signed, 54
Pearl Harbour, 294
Penn-Symons, Gen. William, defeated by
Boers, 35
Pensions, in demands on Germany, 151–
52, 154–55
Pétain, Henri Philippe, mutiny of his
men, 132; 257
Phillimore Commission, adopts Lord
Robert Cecil's plan for a league of
nations, 139
Philpotts, Owen Surtees, of the Consular
Service, 156
Pienaar, Gen. Dan, in attack on Rommel,
283
Pietermaritzburg, 4
Pirow, Oswald, favors "qualified" neu-
trality, 249; regarded by Smuts as
coming leader of the country, 259;
called "little Hitler of South Africa,"
260; 236, 240, 258, 261–62
Pitt, William, mentioned, 24
Platinum, discovered in Transvaal, 208
Pliny cited, 245
Plunkett, Sir Horace, Smuts as adviser
to Irish people, 188
Pogány, People's Commissar for War in
Hungarian revolution, 159
Poland, invaded by Hitler, 249
Pole-Evans, Dr., friend of Smuts, 218
Politis, Nicolas Socrate, 164
"Poor-white" problem in South Africa,
246
Post (N.Y.), 282
Pretoria, defended by Smuts, surrenders
to British, 37; peace negotiations be-
gin, 52; made capital of Union of
South Africa, 79
Pretoria Convention of 1881, 14
Prince of Wales, visits Union, 214, 217
Prometheus Unbound, 10
Purified Nationalist party, headed by Dr.
Malan, 238

Quirk, 272

Race equality in South Africa, 78
Ramat Jochanan Smuts, a memorial, 134